Pigeon River Country

Contributors

Sibley Hoobler
Ford Kellum
Harold D. Mahan
Gerald F. Myers
Eugene E. Ochsner
L. K. Titus

Pigeon River Country

A MICHIGAN FOREST

DALE CLARKE FRANZ

Revised Edition

The University of Michigan Press ❧ *Ann Arbor*

2010   2009   2008   2007   4   3   2   1

A CIP catalog record for this book is available from the British Library.

Library of Congress Cataloging-in-Publication Data

Franz, Dale Clarke, 1937–
    Pigeon River Country : a Michigan forest / Dale Clarke Franz. —
Rev. ed.
        p.   cm.
    Includes bibliographical references.
    ISBN-13: 978-0-472-03164-1 (pbk. : alk. paper)

    1. Pigeon River Region (Mich.)—History.   2. Pigeon River
Region (Mich.)— Description and travel.   3. Pigeon River Country
State Forest (Mich.)—History.   4. Pigeon River Country State Forest
(Mich.)— Description and travel.   5. Natural history—Michigan—
Pigeon River Region.   6. Natural history—Michigan—Pigeon River
Country State Forest.   I. Title.

F572.P53F73   2007
977.4'83—dc22   2007030973

The first edition of this book was made possible by a grant from the
Madge and Raymond Hoobler Foundation.

Maps by wildlife artist Rod Lawrence.

To FORD KELLUM
who expressed what was in all our hearts

Preface

Among changes addressed in this revised edition are a shift in the scientific community away from believing only humans think and have feelings and growing disappointment that formal agreement failed to stop hydrocarbon pressures arising to bedevil the forest. Potentially powerful threats emerged in mid-2007, too late for examination in our book: Oil and gas promoters now suggest that the Pigeon's off-limits resources be exploited to provide inexpensive energy for environmentally friendly technologies like solar panels, which take much energy to make. Even though it would override protections long in place, the idea appealed to some in a state facing one of the most severe money crunches in the nation. "Every generation has to fight anew to protect the Pigeon and places like it," Ken Glasser, chairman of the Otsego County Board of Commissioners, said.

There are two new chapters, "Ecology" and "Animals and People," plus an afterword, "Presence." We solve the mystery of the dam spill. We describe how global warming will likely affect this forest. A richer understanding of life forms gives us a new perspective on why places like the Pigeon River Country are so special. We give additional emphasis to threats from overuse and how many of its qualities can be enjoyed in other natural settings.

This is not a book to stuff into your pocket for a trip to the woods. It's one to curl up with on a winter evening by the fire. Of course, some forest surroundings can enhance any book. The first time I saw Lewis Thomas's *Lives of a Cell* in a shop near my Philadelphia apartment, I dismissed it for some forgotten intellectual reason. After moving to the north woods, a friend sent me a copy, and I remember a wonderful afternoon spent leaning against a pine stump in the Pigeon River Country waiting with my camera for deer to step into a clearing and reading that the giant clam, if he had a mind to, might be dismayed that he has incorporated so much of the plant world into his own complex clamhood while plant cells and algae might have tinges of conscience that it was they who had captured the clam on the most satisfying terms.

The forest is nearly a world apart from our normal experience. This book was first proposed as a guide to the Pigeon River Country but a more substantial concept soon emerged, reflecting a depth of affection for this forest impossible to ignore. The book is about Walter Babcock growing up in the Pigeon River Country and saying, "We took some schooling, missed a lot of it." It is about Sam Titus and a herd of elk listening to Bach on her car radio. It is about spruces pointing into the sky and winterberries nestled in the snow.

In one sense, this is a regional history, full of colloquialisms and peculiarities of this precise place. In another sense, this book is about forests everywhere and about people going into them. It is a book of the heart, an examination of how the Pigeon River Country is meaningful.

A visit to the forest would be enriched by the use of field guides such as those listed in the bibliographic notes at the end of this book. A map is essential.

In 1995, Joe Jarecki, the Pigeon River Country unit manager, noted there was concern on the advisory council about the aesthetics of putting boardwalks where established pathways passed through sensitive wetlands. He cautioned that such concern for wild settings should not slip into making the Pigeon River Country "inaccessible to people, because people control the PRC's destiny, and in our society, management strategies on public lands must ultimately be supported by the public, or they will eventually be overruled." The aim, he said, must be to encourage uses that have the least impact possible and, at the same time, promote "a love and understanding of wild areas so there will be support to continue to manage the PRC as a wild area." He said some access to wetlands, the most fragile places in the forest, is essential to providing people who are uncomfortable in wild areas the opportunity to experience them.

Inviting people to the remote forest has a certain irony since we run the risk of diminishing that which we would enjoy. We take the risk in the belief that what we encourage is a sensitivity that will, in turn, sustain and nurture our natural places.

Acknowledgments

This book is invitational, not exhaustive, as Sibley Hoobler put it. It suggests we tread lightly, leave few footprints, remain unnoticed. Many people who participated in the stories told here are not named. One of the Interlochen Arts Academy students who spent ten days camping in the snow near Pigeon Bridge campground in March 1972 was Kathy Bramer. Later, as a student in the master's program in environmental advocacy at the University of Michigan in 1976, Kathy worked as an intern for Roger Conner on the Pigeon River project. Like so many others, she devoted countless hours to the Pigeon River Country. Among them were Jim Welsch, Linda Myers, the early participants in the Pigeon River Country Association, and others too numerous to name. Among the many within the Department of Natural Resources who made their association with the forest more than an occupation are Bob Strong, Rita Rennie, and Doug Whitcomb.

Others, through their sensitivity and kindness, helped in the preparation of this book. We especially thank Rosemary Martek, William Granlund, Rick Packman, the family of Sandra Mosier, Doug Truax, and the staffs of the Otsego County Library, the Department of Natural Resources district office, and the Shell Oil Company production office. A special thanks to Mike Delp for his encouragement and to members of the Gaylord Area Council for the Arts writers workshop.

This project would not have received the long and careful attention that it has without the full-hearted and loving support of Sandra Myers Franz.

This is more than a book to those of us involved in the Pigeon River Country. It is people collecting photographs, saving scraps of paper, taping interviews, writing letters, caring. We dedicate the book to Ford Kellum because he spoke so clearly from the heart. Among many who have been inspirational in their devotion to the forest is Jerry Myers, who at 89 in 2007 continued to think and talk about the Pigeon River Country as one of our outdoor places deserving all the love we can give.

Joe Jarecki gave generously of his time and knowledge for the revised edition and provided invaluable electronic data files. Larry Leefers transferred minutes of all the Pigeon River Country Advisory Council meetings to electronic files. Richard Kropf also spent years attending advisory council meetings and putting material into electronic form. A whole cast of people has given much time to the forest since our first edition. They will remain mostly unsung heroes since this is an update, not a new book detailing all the many important issues of the last two decades.

Note: This book sometimes uses *north woods* and *northern Michigan* synonymously with *northern lower Michigan*. We hope anyone from the Upper Peninsula who feels territorial about the first two terms will forgive the generalization and perhaps be proud that those in a similar but southerly area identify themselves with northern concepts. Some names change over time. Fisherman's Trail is variously known as Fisherman Trail and now usually as Fisherman Road. Cornwell, as in the mill, became Cornwall Lake and Cornwall Creek Flooding.

Some of the science underpinning parts of the revised edition represents a personal journey of mine in trying to understand the most profound elements of a forest experience. My longtime friend Tom Stillings, who plays a rollicking beat on piano and banjo, applied his mathematical skills in tweaking scientific points, most of which did not survive in the text through my final editing.

I'm grateful for the generosity of several dear friends who worked their way through early drafts of new material. When John and Marge Compton, who could tackle any serious subject with ease, found some material dense, they were kind enough to say so, starting me on a path toward becoming more succinct. Our son, Dale Jr., was the first to read any of my manuscript and gave me great encouragement by not admitting any puzzlement and recounting afterward some of my most precious points. Our other son, Douglas, and daughters-in-law, Dawn and Ninette, in their attempts to fit early draft readings into their busy lives, provided a reminder that books need to be relevant and engaging. Ninette cast a keen eye on my efforts to summarize the revised edition. My wife, Sandy, demonstrated great strength by applying her considerable editing skills and urging me toward material not found in other books. As one points out in these pieces, any flaws remaining are entirely my own, for I sometimes did not follow good advice well.

Glen Sheppard, longtime editor of the *Northwoods Call* ("dedicated to the proposition that there is only one side to any issue involving natural resources . . . Nature's!"), got me interested in the Pigeon River Country shortly after I moved to northern Michigan in 1976. Glen wrote in a 2006 editorial that sprawl does more harm than global warming. We treat both of them as part of the same problem. John Hilton, editor of the *Ann Arbor Observer*, set aside time to read the ecology chapter and provided encouragement. Global warming will change our forests severely. In facing this most serious environmental issue, we need guidance. Possibly there's some in the Pigeon experience.

We have updated material where appropriate, but in many places we have left unchanged the phrasing from the first edition since in most respects it is still current. Forest conditions change minute by minute, so a lot of what we say about it can be considered historical, representative, or indicative rather than exactly matching anyone's moments spent there. Chapters written by contributors contain updates in brackets and italics. Harold D. Mahan said his chapter remains timely. Gerald F. Myers declined the invitation to update but supplied several leads for new material about the Pigeon. The other four contributors, Sibley Hoobler, Ford Kellum, Eugene E. Ochsner, and L. K. Titus, are no longer with us. They have been mourned by many. Notes from 1986, with a few corrections by Ford and Gene, showed up as I went through my old files one last time, as though they were still giving me a helping hand.

Members of the Pigeon River Country Association were among many enthusiasts for this revised edition. Some, who joined after 1985, have been unable to obtain a copy of the first edition. The forest headquarters over the years has continued to receive requests for the book, and Amazon.com, which was posting at high prices the few used copies available, specifically asked the association if the book could be made available again. George Barker of Trout Unlimited asked permission to quote from Doug Mummert's chapter for a public presentation. Such interest and support finally inspired me to prepare the revision I had long anticipated. For reasons enumerated in the text, the book is more relevant now than it was two decades ago.

Grateful acknowledgment is made to the following publishers for permission to quote excerpts from Lao Tsu, *Tao Te Ching*, translated by Gia-fu Feng and Jane English, © 1972 Gia-fu Feng and Jane English (New York:

Knopf, 1972); Aldo Leopold, "Obituary of P. S. Lovejoy," *Wildlife Society*, January 1943; Joseph Epes Brown, *The Spiritual Legacy of the American Indian* (New York: Crossroad, 1982); Howard A. Norman, *The Wishing Bone Cycle*, distributed by Santa Barbara Press, 1129 State St., Santa Barbara, CA, 19103; Mary Oliver, "Snowy Night" in *What Do We Know*, © 2002 Mary Oliver, reprinted by permission of Da Capo Press, a member of Perseus Books Group.

Recent photographs in the photo section and on the cover are by the author.

Contents

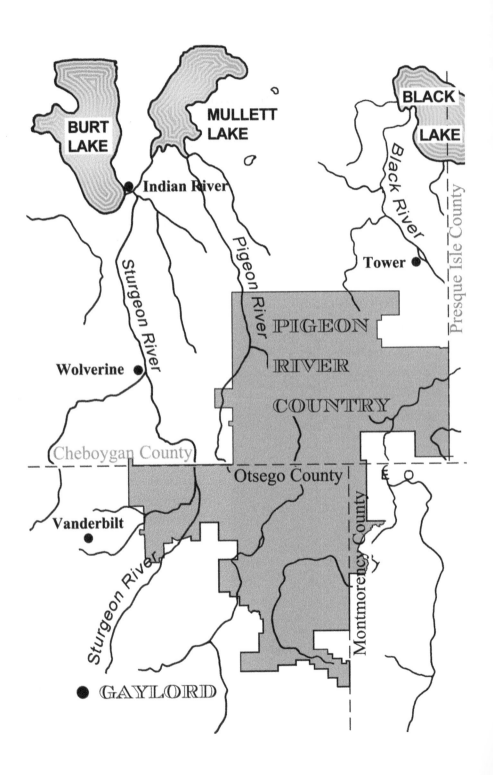

PIGEON RIVER COUNTRY

Tower

Presque Isle County

High Country Pathway

Osmun Rd.

Dog Lake Flooding

Wolverine

Webb Rd.

75

Clark Bridge Rd.

Cheboygan County

Pigeon River

Cornwall Creek Flooding

Pickerel Lake

Sturgeon River

Otsego County

Montmorency County

Headquarters

Blue Lakes

Lansing Club Pond

Tin Shanty Bridge Rd.

Black River

Pigeon River

Sparr Rd.

N

Part 1 ❧ Impressions

Introduction

We think we hold it within us, this place we call Pigeon River Country. But when we stand there again what is happening now does not translate to memories. And when this is over, the next time will be the only one. The moon, the birds, the air, the wind are never in the same place, providing the same songs, feeling just like this, moving quite this way. And the clouds move on.

Yet many things about the Pigeon River Country can be written down, remembered, related. This book is about what can be told and what can be evoked by this journey.

The easiest way to talk about the Lower Peninsula of Michigan is to show the palm of our right hand. There it is, thumb and all. The lower half is civilization as most Americans know it. The upper half consists of stretches of woodland, hills, and cool temperatures. Most people see only the edges of this world as they travel on highways from town to town or take a back road to some dwelling in a clearing. There are many clearings—and more every day. When we look for the forest, we are looking for places where there are few people or dwellings. As we gain familiarity with the woods, we think even the cabin is separate from the real forest.

Appreciation of these remote places is like a finely honed, double-edged sword. The more joy we find the more sadness lurks over the chance that somebody will ruin it. When my wife and I moved to northern Michigan, there were wild raspberries across the dirt road in a sunny patch about 50 feet long. Soon an enormous resort home was built on the property. The owners, who lived in southern Michigan, arrived to experience the woods and promptly uprooted every wild berry bush because, we were told, they harbor bugs. After half a dozen years and a dozen visits, they put

3

the house up for sale, then dispatched a crew of men to cut down most of the vegetation, including about one hundred trees, because the house was cold. On what I call my jogging path is an ancient stump that has been weathered into what looks like a cathedral. Sometimes I ignore that stump because I don't want to be disappointed if someone breaks it apart on a whim. What is so difficult about these things is that one edge of the sword brings enormous fulfillment, frees our spirit, helps us laugh, and makes us vulnerable to hurt from the other, mean-spirited side. It makes one philosophical as they say. For, if we watch these things and remain clear about them, what seems to be happening is that we grow and advance from these experiences to somewhat more admirable ground. That is part of what the Pigeon River story is about. It is tied up with oil and gas development, with logging, with the passenger pigeon. All of these parts of the story have an edge of poignancy. Yet as we tell them they add to our human experience, making us wiser in dealing with these difficult decisions of life.

North of Bay City on I-75, the traveler crosses the boundary between two major ecological zones that traverse North America, Europe, and Asia. The line runs east-west across Michigan just below the Thumb. To the south is the temperate zone, with largely agricultural soil, broad-leaved trees, and 75 percent of Michigan's population. To the north lie the conifer and northern hardwood forests.

On our right palm, the line runs along the base of the fingers. Ninety miles north, between the two knuckles of the middle finger, is the Pigeon River Country. It's about 12 miles wide and 20 miles long, half the size of New York City and one-third the size of Los Angeles. Yet it is the largest contiguous block of undeveloped state land in Michigan's Lower Peninsula. Until recently, it was the home of the only substantial wild elk herd east of the Mississippi.

What we see traveling north is not wilderness. There are wide stretches of scrubby jack pines. The other pines and the broad-leaved trees are thin and short compared with the forests of the East and West. Northern Michigan is cutover, burned-over land dotted with stumps that, even when hidden in 100 years of new growth, dwarf their surroundings with the idea of what the great forest was a century ago. Even the Pigeon River Country is not technically a wilderness but a managed forest in which logging, hunting, camping, trail skiing, and horseback riding occur.

Yet this forest is special in a state known for its natural resources. A handful of people inspired Michigan's longest, most visible environmental controversy there, involving half a dozen oil and gas corporations, all of the state's major environmental organizations, the state's largest hunting organization, the United Auto Workers, the Michigan court system, the state legislature, and the people who talked about the oil controversy at home, wrote letters to newspapers, and worried about how it would all turn out. In one sense, it turned out badly, the handful finally standing alone as all other parties to the dispute accommodated a compromise that allowed oil and gas drilling under apparently controlled conditions. In another sense, the game changed before it ended. It grew subtle, low key. Somehow the Pigeon River Country became central in the lingering environmental issues of the 1980s. The spill of detritus from behind a dam into the Pigeon River led the state into its first effective efforts to control how dams affect the quality of clear northern streams. Shell Oil Company, after quietly testing a new procedure in several states, chose to make public its new technology for reducing brine pollution in the Pigeon River Country. The forest's advisory council was the state's pioneering experiment in involving people of opposing points of view in the long-term management of its natural resources.

When the great visionary P. S. Lovejoy began Michigan's program to preserve land by using it wisely, he identified the vast acreage around the Pigeon River as the "Big Wild," a place where the forest and rivers would create their own environment. When the controversy over oil and gas development arose 50 years later, Michigan's natural resources routine was chaotic, with divisions of the Department of Conservation sometimes working at cross-purposes or in direct conflict. What emerged was the first sustained policy reflecting the public interest in preserving, as opposed to simply using, land. The state bureaucracy began to ask in a systematic way during the Pigeon River controversy what goals are foremost. And it began to listen in a systematic way to the public. Officials at the highest levels began to make resource decisions based on what they were learning from the Pigeon River situation. Other states looked to the Pigeon River experience for guidance in answering their own emerging questions about resource management.

When Joseph Sax, a University of Michigan (UM) environmental law professor, conducted a lecture tour in Japan during the height of the controversy, he found people there talking about the Pigeon River Country. "It is precisely the kind of litigation that people in other industrialized countries, facing very similar problems to ours, desperately need to get under way," he said.

As the controversy drew attention in the 1970s, more and more people visited this forest, the value of which, ironically, lies chiefly in its remoteness. It is inhabited by black bear and bobcat, as well as elk, simply because it is isolated enough for them to live there. Backpackers have told the Pigeon River forester that the 70-mile High Country Pathway, which passes through the forest, is the best hiking trail they have experienced in the Wisconsin, Minnesota, and Michigan area. It is the only Great Lakes hiking trail known to have three large wildlife species: bear, elk, and white-tailed deer. More than two hundred species of birds populate the forest, including the bald eagle, great blue heron, and pileated woodpecker.

Recreation facilities in a state forest, compared with a park, are purposefully simple and basic. In 2006, they included seven campgrounds and two group horse camps, 60 miles of pathways, 27 miles of horse trails, and several scenic attractions, including the Witness Tree, Inspiration Point, and the sinkhole lakes. It is a state objective that recreation opportunities in the forest be in keeping with the quiet, peaceful, and wild character of the area. Off-road vehicles (ORVs) are banned in the forest except on some county roads in Montmorency and Cheboygan counties, and there are no groomed snowmobile trails.

One way to get to the Pigeon River Country is to exit I-75 at Vanderbilt and follow Sturgeon Valley Road about 10 miles east to the forest. The lower half is in the northeastern corner of Otsego County and the upper half in southern Cheboygan County. Two thin strips on the eastern border extend into Montmorency County.

Another way to get there is to start from someplace else and maybe not physically get there at all. When we pause alone in the woods, any woods, what strikes us is that we have been going at too high a speed to participate in what is around us. It's not just seeing, smelling, and listening that we have to adjust but the way we feel. The Chesapeake and Ohio Canal runs along the Potomac from the north to Georgetown in Washington, DC. Joggers trot along the mule path next to the canal while, above, Washington rush hour hazes the joggers' air. Two fish splash out of the canal onto a spillway and disappear as the water runs on a slope down into the trees and undergrowth. Two joggers thump past across a footbridge over the spillway, not noticing. Off the trail, in the trees and undergrowth, the water plummets suddenly into a channel far below as though the brown canal water quickens in anticipation of its last few miles across a foul continent to the sea. It's something one may not notice without a Pigeon River experience.

Pigeon River Country is at the other end of water's cycle, only a few miles from the watershed of north-flowing and south-flowing rivers of northern lower Michigan. Water that recently was rain or snow begins its long journey from the three rivers that course through the Pigeon River Country north to the Great Lakes and eventually to the sea. They are the Sturgeon River to the west, the Pigeon River in the center, and the Black River to the east.

Northern lower Michigan is part of an ancient sea through which primeval organisms sank and compressed into hydrocarbons. The site of the Pigeon River Country later spent millions of years under glaciers that carved out the Great Lakes. After the latest glacial waters retreated, native people lived in the region for ten thousand years. They hunted along waterways like the Pigeon, Black, and Sturgeon, which flow down the Port Huron moraine to the bed of a glacial lake. When Europeans arrived from the densely populated and heavily timbered eastern hemisphere, the area was inhabited by Indians, wolves, bear, deer, bison, elk, moose, and caribou. The only ones to survive were deer, some bear, and a few Indians. The new people leveled all of Michigan's giant white and red pines and virgin hardwoods in little more than 50 years. The name Pigeon River comes from a creature believed to have been the most numerous of its kind on earth. What happened to it is a story of America, northern Michigan, and the vulnerability of natural things to certain human attitudes.

About the middle of May, 1850, while in the fur trade, I was camping on the head waters of the Manistee River in Michigan. One morning on leaving my wigwam, I was startled by hearing a gurgling, rumbling sound, as though an army of horses laden with sleigh bells was advancing through the deep forest. While I gazed in wonder and astonishment, I beheld moving toward me in an unbroken front millions of pigeons. They passed like a cloud through the branches of the high trees, through the underbrush and over the ground. Statue-like I stood, half-concealed by cedar boughs. They fluttered all about me lighting on my head and shoulders. (Chief Simon Pokagon, a Potawatomi and last chief of the Pokagon band in Michigan)

Surveyor William Burt passed that same year a little northeast on the same ridge, placing stakes to designate imaginary lines. The imaginary lines are still there, on maps and documents you might find anywhere; the pigeons are not.

When Europeans arrived to settle America, they observed flocks of a bird in such numbers they darkened the sun. The species was later estimated to have comprised one-fourth to nearly one-half of all the birds in North America. The bird was a wild pigeon, a type of turtle dove that looked like the mourning dove except it had twelve tail feathers instead of the mourning dove's 14 and was larger. Tribes of Algonquian linguistic stock, including those in what is now Michigan, generally called the bird variations of *O-mi-mi* (with the second *mi* pronounced abruptly), expressing a sound the bird made. Indians in Massachusetts called the bird *wuskowhan,* meaning wanderer. Scientists eventually agreed on a name, *Ectopistes migratorius;* both words indicate that the bird was a traveler. We call it the passenger pigeon, a name that reflects both its wandering nature and how it sounded: *passenger* is an ancient French and English word related to *passage* and meaning traveler; *pigeon* is of Norman origin from the Latin *pipio,* meaning a peeping, nestling bird.

The nesting area of the passenger pigeon ranged from New England west through the northern Lower Peninsula of Michigan to Wisconsin and southeast to Kentucky. The Pigeon River was named for the passenger pigeon, which used the area for nesting and feeding. George King, a guide and trapper, had "for many years lived in the section that formerly was the great pigeon nesting and feeding ground of Northern Michigan," W. B. Mershon wrote in his 1907 book *The Passenger Pigeon.* At the time, King was living in what is now the Blue Lakes area on the east side of the state forest.

When passenger pigeons came to northern Michigan, they generally nested along a stream, protected by valleys against the wind. They preferred cedar stands, common in the wetlands along the Sturgeon, Pigeon, and Black rivers, usually nesting near beech, which was one of the trees of the mature forest. The birds would nest in colonies up to two or three miles wide and perhaps 20 or even 40 miles long. Sometimes there were 90 nests in a single tree. Yet they would leave avenues one to five miles wide within their nesting range where there were no birds at all. They would remain in the nesting area for about 30 days, including three days building the nest and laying one egg for each pair of pigeons, 13 days incubation, and 14 days feeding the young.

For eight days after pecking out of its white egg, the young pigeon would be covered by a parent's body, then covered only during the ninth and tenth nights, then abandoned on the fourteenth day. The squab, a mass of fat, would sit crying in the nest for a day or two then flutter to the ground. Within three or four days, it could fly well enough to avoid capture, and within a week most of its fat would disappear.

When the Seneca took squabs, they said prayers and left gifts for the older pigeons, perhaps beads and jewelry in a brass kettle. The Hurons believed that the souls of the dead eventually changed into passenger pigeons and were reunited with the living when the birds were cooked and eaten.

According to Chief Simon Pokagon, "A pigeon nesting was always a great source of revenue to our people. Whole tribes would wigwam in the brooding places. They seldom killed the old birds, but made great preparation to secure their young, out of which [we] made squab butter and smoked and dried them by thousands for future use. Yet, under our manner of securing them, they continued to increase."

The manner in which Europeans settled the eastern United States did not increase the population of birds. John James Audubon described a visit to a roost on the Green River in Kentucky: "A great number of persons with horses and wagons, guns and ammunition had already established encampments. Suddenly there was a general cry of 'Here they come!' Thousands were soon knocked down by men with poles. The birds continued to pour in. Fires were lighted, and a magnificent and almost terrifying sight presented itself. The pigeons, arriving by thousands, alighted everywhere, one above another, until solid masses as large as hogsheads were formed on the branches. Here and there the perches gave way under the weight with a crash and, falling to the ground, destroyed hundreds of birds beneath."

At sunrise the next day, Audubon wrote, "the authors of all this devastation began their entry amongst the dead, the dying and the mangled. The pigeons were piled in heaps, until each had as many as he could possibly dispose of, when the hogs were let loose to feed on the remainder."

In about 1805, millions of squabs in a northeastern Pennsylvania nesting were collected for their fat, which was shipped in barrels down the Susquehanna River. Sometimes the oil was used as soap stock. Pigeon feathers were used for bedding. Sometimes the birds were killed for the feathers alone such as one incident on the shore of Lake Erie in New York in which one family in 1822 killed 4,000 pigeons with poles in one day and saved only the feathers.

The trade in passenger pigeons grew massive after railroads began to provide rapid transportation to city markets. In 1878, the following advertisement, typical of those in the trade journals of the time, appeared in the *Chicago Field.*

Wild Pigeons.—I leave for the Petoskey nesting, April 10th, and by the 15th, can fill all orders for birds.—E.T. Martin, 79 Clark St., Chicago.

The Petoskey nesting of 1878 stretched in a three- to 10-mile-wide band some 40 miles long through what is now Pigeon River Country. Birds from that great northern Michigan nesting were shipped by rail, by steamer from Petoskey, Cheboygan, Cross Village, and other lake ports, and by wagon. Martin said the official figures from Petoskey and Boyne Falls showed birds shipped dead or alive by express and boat to be 1.1 million that year. He assumed that an additional half a million died without being shipped. A million is an extremely large number, beyond comprehension in any real sense. At the rate of one bird per second, it would take 12 days without sleep to count one million of them and 31 years—without a second's pause—to count one billion. The passenger pigeon at the time North America was discovered numbered an estimated three to five billion birds.

Martin claimed that pigeons were so abundant during the 1876 and 1878 nestings in Michigan that the shipment of dead birds would not pay the cost of the barrels and ice because of the glut on the market. What kept the netters operating, he said, was the demand for live birds for trapshooting.

Live pigeons were placed in crates. Care was taken to keep them alive and in condition for shooting. Still, many died from the confinement or lack of water. One observer complained that these wild birds arrived with their feathers soiled with excrement and stuck together to such an extent that they could not fly.

Trapshooting began in the United States after 1825 and was widely popular by midcentury. Among the various devices used was a spring that propelled the pigeon into the air. If the bird could or would not fly, there were rules to govern the scoring. Some clubs used a mechanical cat to try to frighten the pigeon into flight. Those birds that managed to escape the trapshooters often fell to the guns of the men and boys who ringed the match area. Public sentiment against trapshooting grew, but the custom did not disappear until passenger pigeons were no longer obtainable. As late as 1891, there was an inquiry from Dayton, Ohio, looking for 2,000 wild pigeons for a tournament.

Although there is no way to determine precisely when the last wild pigeon was shot or seen, A.W. Schorger writes in *The Passenger Pigeon* (1955) that "the year 1900 may be considered as marking the end." At the time, no one knew for sure whether any pigeons still existed in the wild. A committee reporting on a game bill to the state legislature of Ohio in 1857 had declared, "The Passenger Pigeon needs no protection. Wonderfully prolific, having the vast forests of the North as its breeding grounds, travelling hundreds of miles in search of food, it is here to-day, and elsewhere to-morrow, and no ordinary destruction can lessen them or be missed from the myriads that are yearly produced." The American Ornithologists' Union, meeting in New York in 1909, made plans to search for passenger pigeons and to offer awards totaling $1,220 for the discovery of a nest or colony. None was ever found.

We treat our domestic chickens worse than trapshooters did the pigeon, for at least the pigeon was not caged its entire life nor forced to produce eggs continuously through the use of artificial light and chemicals. And the pigeon at least had a theoretical chance of escape. Nor have we ceased threatening to eliminate even well-known species from the planet. The Alaskan king crab, found only in seas along the south-end Aleutian coastlines, was once believed to be an inexhaustible, renewable resource. In 1983, the Alaska Department of Fish and Game ordered the first total shutdown of the two prime king crab fishing grounds off Kodiak Island in Bristol Bay because of a disastrous decline in the crab species that some experts said might be irreversible. One of the reasons given for the decline was that the year before more than one and a half million steel and mesh crab traps weighing 500 pounds each were dropped onto the seabed where crabs congregate, perhaps crushing tens of thousands of them. The fate of the passenger pigeon seems to be one story among many.

It is a particular irony that the Pigeon River Country derived its name from the passenger pigeon for the forest became the focus of efforts to protect fragile natural phenomena from the pressures of civilization, including fossil fuel exploitation. The great power of the Pigeon River Country lies in its inaccessibility to humans. In deep woods, we humans are mostly trail people. We can mosey along a path with some confidence; when it divides, unless the choices are clearly marked, a bit of uneasiness creeps in. When there is no trail at all, anxiety sets in born of centuries of inexperience in the woods.

One of the more instructive choices we make is to turn back before venturing far into the woods at night without light. No matter how comfortable or satisfying a woods may be to us by day or in the rain or even on snowshoes or skis by moonlight, there is a point in the dark when we come to terms with the limits of ourselves as human beings. There are things out there we cannot see; we turn back.

When people visit the woods from the city, they often want to know if there are any snakes in the area before they will head out onto a trail. The concern about harmful creatures is a sort of pleasant affirmation that there are, even in the nuclear age, fundamental strengths that reside outside the control of humans. At the same time, we have a deep sense of the lack of hostility in nature; what holds no particular malice toward us is nonetheless a source of fear to us.

One of the great values in large forests such as the Pigeon is that they stir deep questions within us. Such experiences affect us in ways we scarcely understand. They are surely central to the powerful attraction that outdoor activities hold for sportsmen. On the one hand, such purposeful activity in the wild activates ancient human abilities: to move gracefully, see and hear clearly, and respond quickly. On the other hand, the serious sportsman shares an intimacy with his or her prey that no customer of marketed meats can experience. It is heartening to observe that increasing numbers of people recognize these deep and powerful influences of natural areas and that many participate in them whether or not they are involved in game sport.

Northern lower Michigan is a place where you might look at a pond near the road on your way someplace and see a fawn, its muzzle in the water, eating young shoots just below the surface. Or you might observe a disjointed, snakelike creature with a large head that, as you get closer, turns out to be a duck and six ducklings walking in a row out of the tall grass onto the roadway. The fawn and ducks live their total existence outside the realm of human plans, controls, or even awareness. It gives pause to people who have to shop and make mortgage payments. It draws us into what might be called contemplative recreation, an activity that is not exactly hiking or skiing or tracking or photography, though it may involve doing those or similar things along with it. Frederick Law Olmsted said that most of our activities involve getting tasks done and natural scenery offers us the rare opportunity to engage instead in thoughts freed from duty and achievement, what he called invoking the contemplative faculty.

There is some awkwardness in our society about any activity that does not seem to have a purpose. We consider it lazy. Thus, terms like *nature lover* connote someone who is not quite connected to what we consider reality. It surely accounts for the fact that men seem to be more comfortable with being able to say they do something outdoors than they are with actually being out there. It is a curious situation that watching all manner of imaginary material on television is looked on as a more realistic pursuit than looking outdoors at plant and animal life interacting in all its complex forms.

Yet there is clearly an increasing interest in contemplative recreation not only among hikers, cross-country skiers, and mountain bikers. Among those known in our society as sportsmen, there seems to be an increasing emphasis on the value in simply being outdoors. People who have a refined sense of balance in nature and are hunters do not fit a stereotype any more than others do. They are often the people most sensitive to the way human beings have degraded the environment of the animal. Society's fear of wolves, for example, involves how all of us relate to natural things. Many who hunt in northern Michigan have a genuine concern for restoring the balance lost when wolves were no longer present to thin less healthy deer from the herd. Such people have no easy answers. They tend to respect the animals they kill, to know more about them than others do. They disdain hunters who drink, get lost, disturb the environment, and show insensitivity to the serious pursuit they undertake. Those who consider themselves quality hunters conduct themselves in a meat-eating society in the most honorable way they know. They are not necessarily proud of killing their prey, but they are proud of taking the animal on its own ground, of being mentally and physically able to pursue the animal in its own environment, and of the fact that they deal with the problem at close range, not from an academic distance.

The loss of species is of complex cause, involving the nature of what Western peoples have regarded as civilization. Western civilization defines freedom, in one sense, according to discrete objects known as personal property. You draw lines around these things and yourself; you are free to do what you want, within certain limits, inside the lines. When we plan and zone for commercial or residential development, the integrity of ecological systems is about the last thing we consider. Even natural areas are treated primarily as places to be used by humans not as places where various life forms depend on each other. The Pigeon River controversy raised an issue rarely considered by the public, the integrity of habitat for the whole range of indigenous flora and fauna. In the ordinary course of events, such things are almost never considered. Whoever owns the property has the right to chop down the trees. The concept baffled the Indian, who felt that we are all part of everything together.

In 1785 Congress imposed a grid system on the western lands, and by 1796 townships had been standardized into six-by-six-mile squares. Each of the 36 sections (square miles) in a township contains 640 acres.

A portion of the Pigeon River Country lies in what is known as Corwith Township. The first known settler in the township built a small house in 1873 southwest of what is now Vanderbilt, a dozen miles west of the Pigeon River. Most of the land in the area was granted by the U.S. government under homesteading provisions. Civil War veterans could get 160 acres, nonveterans 80 acres. Settlers had to live on their free land for five years (minus time in military service) and improve it. That usually meant clearing the virgin timber. The railroads received six sections for every mile of track built. Lewis Perry of Vanderbilt, who studied census records of the area, said, "The railroads were sacred cows. They had to have railroads; so they gave them anything. The railroads, in turn, would sell the timber rights."

Lumbermen came to the Pigeon River area in 1880. In 10 years, the white and red pine were gone. Over the next 25 years, the hardwoods were cut and shipped away by rail. Branches left behind dried into tinder. Fires consumed as much of Michigan's forest as the loggers cut. In 1911, it was so smoky during a fire that people around the Pigeon River Country could not see the sun for days. In those later years, lumber mills burned and were not replaced; there wasn't enough timber left to harvest. Logan, a thriving mill town of 350 when James G. Smith worked at Cornwell Mill on the Pigeon in 1909, disappeared. So did Bungtown and Trowbridge. There were no elk when James Smith worked in the logging camp. Elk in the eastern United States had disappeared in the previous century.

As Berdine Yuill, son of the Yuill lumbering family, describes the logging in Pigeon River Country, "In those days [1880] there was an abundance of wild animals . . . and a vast amount of timber. My family come, and they started in the logging business. . . . They hauled the logs to a mill in Logan. They cut the pine. Then the hardwood was shipped to Bay City," where it was made into flooring. "They . . . lumbered all these vast acreages. In time to come, the mill burned. After the land was lumbered, a big fire went through. It swept the country. I remember that. It got so smoky you couldn't see. After that, people commenced to farm this land. Then it grew up to second growth."

Farming on the sandy soils of the north woods proved to be an inappropriate use of the land, particularly in this short growing season. Farms failed; many properties changed hands 10 or 12 times. "People started leaving this area in the 1910s and it didn't start building up again until 1945," Lewis Perry said. During those years, the Pigeon River Country grew more isolated. The lumber industry pulled up its rails and ties and took them west. The massive fires were brought under control in the 1920s. The forest regenerated.

In April 1919 the state of Michigan designated 6,468 acres east of Vanderbilt in the northeast corner of Otsego County as the Pigeon River State Forest. The land had been abandoned by people who couldn't pay the taxes. The resident custodian lived in a farmhouse. In 1973, a network of adjacent state lands was merged into what is now the Pigeon River Country Management Unit. Some 65 percent of the property had been purchased with state hunting license money. About 10 percent of the land within the boundaries remains privately owned. At the end of 1982, some 6,440 acres of what had been a McLouth Steel Corporation private camp along the Sturgeon River, known as Green Timbers, was added to the forest, purchased with oil royalties. In 1990, the 2,608-acre Blue Lakes Ranch property along the east side of Meridian Road added three lakes and more Black River frontage to the forest via a $1.9 million purchase financed by oil royalties, which have been put into a Natural Resources Trust Fund for land purchase and conservation. Several smaller purchases have also occurred.

At 105,048 acres, or 164 square miles, including the in-holdings, the Pigeon River Country Management Unit is the largest, most solidly owned, single block of wild land in the Lower Peninsula, although it represents less than three percent of Michigan's state forest lands. Michigan has the largest state forest system in the country. It was administered as "state forests" until 1979, then "forest areas," and now "management units." From the southeast Michigan metropolitan area, it takes about four hours to drive to the Pigeon River Country.

Michigan has been selling leases for oil and mineral rights on state lands since 1921. Much of the land was never drilled, so the state reaped a profit with no appreciable loss. In 1968, the Department of Natural Resources (DNR) sold 10-year leases for some half a million acres, including the Pigeon River Country. The sale brought a million dollars into the general fund. By 1969, it was evident that a vast oil and gas reef, the Salina-Niagaran, ran for 200 miles in a northeasterly direction from Manistee on Lake Michigan to Rogers City on Lake Huron. The reef appeared to pass under the Pigeon River Country. Companies that held leases began to apply to the DNR for permits to drill. In June 1970, oil was discovered at the edge of the Black River Swamp in the heart of Pigeon River Country. Nineteen wells were drilled. Three oil pools were discovered in a cluster in a remote part of the southern forest. Five oil wells and a gas well were in operation by the time a temporary ban against further activity went into effect. It was to be a decade before major production resumed.

As a result of the controversy, an advisory council of citizens was established and given an official role in setting forest policy. Many people opposed to hydrocarbon development were appointed to the council. They were ultimately unable to prevent drilling but at least sat down with representatives of other points of view, including members of the hydrocarbon industry, in an effort to make the best decisions possible. It is an indication that the days of confrontation are giving way to a more complex pattern of interaction and cooperation.

A high percentage of visitors to the Pigeon River Country come from the Detroit metropolitan area of Wayne, Oakland, and Macomb counties, as many from each as from Otsego County, and more than from Cheboygan County, where the northern half of the forest is located. About half the visitors consider themselves to be there chiefly to hunt and fish. Other leading activities described by the visitors themselves are hiking, backpacking, mushrooming, camping, cross-country skiing, horseback riding, bicycling, and looking at scenery. Almost every activity described by visitors appears to involve contemplative recreation in which the quality of the forest as a place of solitude and scenic beauty is critical. Contemplative recreation also occurs in the activities mentioned by visitors in a 1982 survey: viewing wildlife, sightseeing, color tours, photography, studying winter ecology, picnicking, loafing, relaxing, enjoying the out-of-doors, walking, running, showshoeing, canoeing, biking, swimming, blueberry picking, and survival training.

More than 6,100 campers were registering yearly at the seven campgrounds. The $10 fee (raised to $15 in 2007) had been generating about $42,000 a year. Commercial timber sales for one recent year brought in more than 11 times that amount with the sale of more than 13,000 cords on more than 900 acres. Most of the forest is visible only on foot, and much of it is unmarked, thick with growth, and therefore inaccessible to most visitors. In such a place, people stick to trails.

A path in the woods has a certain tenacity. It's as if the bushes yield a place for people to pass through. For their part, people seem to appreciate a way through that does not require close attention to what you are stepping on and where you are going. A path has a roundness to it that is comforting, a U-shape that connects you ever so quietly with people who have passed through before you. An unused path flattens out, hides under occasional bracken fern and wild strawberry vines, inviting you to places where people have not participated in the forest's activities for a long while. Such a path fades away here and there, hinting that it may suddenly leave you where your ability to read is irrelevant and your experience as a social being useless.

When you walk in most forested areas of lower Michigan, the rustle and quiet are continually pierced by motors, tire drone, human sounds. Along much of the Black River the most prominent sound is the river and the wind. The mainstream of the Black runs thigh to waist deep from spring-fed creeks east of Gaylord through a pond at Saunders Dam; on through the remote Black River Swamp; past the Pinnacle, Old Vanderbilt Road, McKinnon's Bend, Tin Shanty Bridge, and Blue Lakes Ranch; and finally winding through private holdings such as the Black River Ranch. Then it slows and divides into impenetrable channels a few feet deep called The Spreads. It eventually deepens and reaches Black Lake half a dozen miles from Lake Huron. The Black River is joined along its route by Tubbs Creek, Hardwood Creek, and McMasters Creek from within the forest boundary and Canada Creek, Tomahawk Creek, and others outside the boundary, including Milligan Creek, which flows north from Duby Lake in the forest but reaches the Black some four miles north of the boundary.

The Pigeon River flows within two miles of the Black. Like the Black, it arises from wetlands between the rolling hills east of Gaylord and travels about 42 stream miles to Mullett Lake. There are an additional 38 miles of tributaries. The velocity of the current is moderate, and most of the main-stream is shallow enough for wading, though too cold for most bathers. More than a third of the Pigeon flows through state land and, with its des-ignation as a wild river, is protected from development by a vegetative cor-ridor up to 400 feet wide.

The Pigeon enters the southwestern forest through land that for many years belonged to Dr. Sibley Hoobler, who turned it over to the Nature Conservancy in the late 1970s and eventually deeded it to Michigan as part of the Pigeon River Country. The wetlands around the Pigeon in this sec-tion are a fen, or marsh, populated by century-old virgin cedar and swamp conifers. In the bog areas, leatherleaf, pitcher plants, and sedges grow in the acidic standing water. The Pigeon continues north through private land and again enters forest boundaries at Sturgeon Valley Road, where it flows under a bridge and past the Pigeon Bridge Campground.

Along the next dozen miles inside the forest boundaries, the Pigeon passes several facilities, including three more campgrounds, the headquar-ters complex, and a monument to P. S. Lovejoy. Like most cultural points of interest in the forest, the Lovejoy monument is so understated that it is scarcely visible from the road that passes right by it.

With the acquisition of the Green Timbers property in 1982, the forest boundaries came to include the third north-flowing river, the Sturgeon. The Sturgeon River is one of the fastest-running rivers in northern Michi-gan, faster than the famed mainstream Au Sable. Many portions of the Sturgeon are more than six feet deep. North of the forest, the Sturgeon contains rapids in at least two places.

The Sturgeon has been seen over the years by more travelers than either the Pigeon or the Black because it winds in and out near Wolverine next to the old U.S. 27 highway. U.S. 27 was the main north-south route through Michigan until the construction of the interstate highway, I-75, in the late 1950s. Old 27 is now a quiet, paved, two-lane alternative to expressway driving. The Sturgeon flows literally a few feet away, looking like a typical clear, northern stream. Actually, in the 1980s trout fishermen undertook a $30,000 project to clean excess sand out of the Sturgeon in order to restore the gravel bottom necessary for trout spawning. The sand eroded into the river from bridges and other land development. In cooperation with the Michigan Department of Natural Resources, which undertook measures to reduce erosion flowing into the river, the Michigan members of Trout Unlimited arranged to have large pits dug in the stream bed to slow down the water and capture the sand. At the height of the project, the pits had to be emptied every two weeks. The Michigan Youth Corps and the Soil Conservation District of Otsego County helped with the project, which is believed to have been the first such cooperative effort of its kind anywhere.

People who fish consider the Pigeon River Country's rivers to be among the finest northern streams. As a group, fly fishermen perhaps know more about rivers than anybody else. In a sense, fly fishing is an excuse to study and explore firsthand the relationship of water to the environment. David Smethurst, who never keeps or kills his catches, considers fly fishing the happiest discovery of his life. "It's an experience that never ends," he says. "When you use a planer or put together a mortar joint, you learn how to do something and from then on you repeat it. With fly fishing your knowledge is always growing."

A half-inch worm, for instance, builds the case it lives in from certain materials. When Dave Smethurst looks at the Black River, he notices whether those materials are there. "I know what happens on the top, the bottom, and the sides." When these worms hatch into insects, they float to the surface, remain for a matter of seconds, fly off into the woods for a day or two, return to the water, lay eggs, and die. Such a hatch occurs within a few days of the same date each year, depending on location and weather conditions. Fly fishermen record such information meticulously.

One insect, the trico, or white-winged black, hatches at, say, 6:30 a.m. and is back, dead on the water, by 9:00 a.m. "It's whole life is two and a half hours long," Smethurst marvels. Mayflies are insects of the order Ephemeroptera, as in *ephemeral,* from the Greek, meaning to exist for a day.

Good fishing for Dave is a matter of finding good sitting logs on which to watch the river. Some that jut out along the Pigeon and Black are 100 years old. One extends ten feet over the water and Dave found it at eight one evening, stretched full out on the log, and watched mayflies hatching in the black muck of a silt bed for three hours. "I never fished."

When he does fish, he bends the barb of the hook flat so it won't tear the trout's mouth. Unlike bait fishing in a lake, where a fish swallows the hook, fly-fishing hooks a trout in the lip. Dave slips the hook out with pliers, and the fish swims free without leaving the water or being touched by a hand.

The three orders of aquatic insects commonly recognized by northern fly fishermen, the stonefly, the caddis, and the mayfly, can be distinguished by the location of their wings. Looking at the insect nose to nose, the wings of a stonefly are flat across the top of the body, the caddis wings are slanted down like a pup tent, and the mayfly wings rise V-shaped from the body.

The insect most sensitive to pollution is the stonefly. In the 1930s, the Au Sable was fished with artificial stoneflies that blended with the live ones. By the end of the 1950s, when sewage was entering the famous stream near Grayling, stoneflies were gone from the Au Sable. Later the stoneflies were back, an indication that environmental laws of the 1960s are improving water quality. One way fishermen judge water quality on the Pigeon is by the variety of its hatches. All three orders of insect hatch there.

When Dave and his wife Sue passed through Gaylord after college on their way to a teaching interview in 1969, he neither hunted nor fished. They saw a want ad for resident manager of a wooded property on the Black River and within 12 hours became the resident managers of Blue Lakes Ranch just east of the Pigeon River Country. Dave Smethurst began to stop in at headquarters. Jerry Myers, a fisheries biologist who lived at the headquarters complex, talked to Dave about fishing. Walking through the woods one day, Jerry showed Dave a lion ant hill, built like a small volcano with a two-inch circumference hole on top. Jerry explained that when the lion ant's prey fell into the hole it could not scramble out because the sides were too sandy. He simulated the event by dropping a twig into the hole. A lion ant emerged. Dave got interested in trout fishing. His father occasionally fished lakes, which requires knowledge of lures, bait, and the location of fish beneath a vast surface. But Dave found the detailed work of stream fishing much to his liking, including the tying of artificial flies on a hook to resemble insects that reside, however briefly, on streams like the Pigeon.

Smethurst says his fly tying tends to be crude because he has more time to be at the water perfecting his cast and gaining knowledge of the stream. But he envies the perfection of flies tied by people who can fish the streams only half a dozen times a year. They relive those times while working on bits of thread and feathers at their fly-tying benches through the winter. In this sense, the Sturgeon, Pigeon, and Black exist as a state of mind separate from the actual continuous flow of water past the sweepers, fallen trees, undercut banks, and cedar roots.

I

North Woods

It lingers here yet: the smell of glaciers, mingled now with the sweetness of north country plants. Movement and change are the great forces of life. Elements like iron that were formed in the turbulence of stars now merge and shift in arrangements as complicated as human beings. One of our most deeply felt symbols of life force is a river system, particularly the clear-running rivers of the north.

Even the most peaceful forest is alive with the movement of water. In a scarcely understood arrangement between water and tree, water moves out of the ground and up the trunk just beneath the bark, bringing star stuff from the soil to feed the tree. Then the water departs through the leaves to continue its movement from air to earth and back again.

Put your hand in a stream and you touch the sky, the leaves, the tree, the roots, the earth. They say the water that dinosaurs drank is with us still, endlessly freezing, melting, and flowing. The bonding of two parts hydrogen with one part oxygen carries our past into our present.

If we stand by a river, it seems to come from some mechanical source, like a pump that is draining a reservoir—our long experience of getting water at a tap. If we stay by the river awhile, we get the sense of water on the move from all around. On a wooden footbridge over the Pigeon River after a night of rain, we see water over the banks, bending the grasses into long needles pointing the water on its way to the sea. It flows north to Mullett Lake, then into Lake Huron and on down the steps of the Great Lakes and the Saint Lawrence to the Atlantic.

In the collection of ancient Eastern writing called "The Way of Life," there is a thought about water translated as follows.

The softest thing in the universe
Overcomes the hardest thing in the universe.
That without substance can enter where there is no room

Not only is it the nature of water to shape without having a shape of its own. It takes on shapes that are infinite in their variety, those of snow crystals. Arctic natives are said to have 100 compound words to express different varieties and conditions of snow. Farley Mowat writes that "snow is crystalline dust . . . but on earth it is, in yet another guise, the Master Titan. Glaciers are born while the snow falls; fragile, soft and almost disembodied . . . but falling steadily without a thawing time. Years pass, decades, centuries and the snow falls." Michael Delp, a poet living in northern Michigan, writes in "Walking Over Black Ice":

First you are struck
by the very transparency of it,
the darkness,
the blackness of water below you.
Then, you notice the slightest apparition
of reflection

Its own weight depresses a glacier into black ice. The glaciers of the Pleistocene were two miles thick. They are not gone. Glaciers over Greenland toward the end of the twentieth century were two miles thick. Geologists say the Ice Age has just begun. Glaciers in North America have come and gone a dozen times, and there are about 50 more cycles to go. An average cycle lasts 100,000 years, meaning that we might have about 90,000 years to go before the snow again begins to accumulate summer and winter. A drop of 10 degrees Fahrenheit in the average north woods temperature would start a glacier, with snow packing down, recrystallizing, turning to ice. When the glacier gets big enough, it shears into horizontal bands and slides on itself, moving toward the equator. It can start in any place cold enough; those that over the last two million years reached New York City and nearly to Tennessee formed in many places and spread in all directions. It is not hard to imagine on a winter evening that a glacier might start in the neighborhood of the Pigeon River Country, perhaps within the city limits of Gaylord, which calls itself the Alpine Village because of its moderate elevation and not so moderate snowfall.

Glaciers are so frigid that they put enormous cold air masses into circulation, the kind that, on encountering humid air to the south, once turned Nevada into a string of lakes dotted with islands. The islands are now mountain ranges. When glaciers reach places that are warm enough, the melting equals the rate of movement. The glacier appears stationary at its edge even though it continues to move from the center. As a result, all the debris scrubbed from the earth drops or washes out, leaving hills of boulders, stones, pebbles, sand, silt, and clay.

Imagine ourselves very small, walking among piles of sand and twigs during the early spring melt in the north woods. The patterns of debris we find are much like the landscape itself. Walking up and down the hills of the Pigeon River Country, we rumble over an enormous spring thaw, kicking into pebbles, sliding through pieces of earth that were scraped up from far away, scrubbed, packed in ice, and brought here inch by inch to be left in enormous heaps. It's as if the glacier just left. Lakes freeze each season like residual glacial puddles, and men peer through holes cut in the ice looking into the dark water for fish.

And now the Michigan mitten rises, inch by inch, year by year, rebounding from the weight of the glaciers, rising, in fact, faster than mountains do. The last big glacier to crush Michigan melted away some 13,000 years ago into Saginaw Bay, leaving a series of moraines, including the base for Gaylord's Alpine Village. A birch, spruce, and fir forest grew in the warm interval that followed. Finally, another glacier, thinner than most, developed in the Superior basin, advanced across this forest—burying bison, mammoth, caribou, musk ox, and moose—flowed across the Upper Peninsula onto northern lower Michigan, and stopped at the Pigeon River Country against the old moraine where Gaylord now stands. It left iron-rich red drift where it passed, and when we in this century drink water from our wells in the north woods, we sip remnants of the 10,000-year-old Valders glacier and clean its stain from our wash basins.

When the Valders retreated 10,000 years ago, it left a high ridge that runs northwest to southeast through Otsego County. It is the highest elevation in the Lower Peninsula of Michigan. From the Otsego high ridge flow five river systems, the Sturgeon, Pigeon, and Black to the north and the Au Sable and Manistee to the south.

Most visitors arrive in the vicinity of the Pigeon River Country by way of I-75. It is about a four-hour drive north from Detroit. Along the way, they pass Saginaw Bay, out of sight to their right, the space between the mitten and the thumb. The immediate area around I-75 near the bay is flat, open farmland. It is a glacial lake plain that continues for 61 miles from milepost 130 to milepost 191. There I-75 begins to climb the Port Huron moraine and enter an ecological zone different from most of the United States. The moraine is part of the most prominent morainic system of all, stretching from Minnesota to New York, formed 13,000 years ago by the Saginaw ice lobe. It was against this moraine that the last advancing glacier, the Valders, stopped, forming the headwaters of the Pigeon.

As visitors drive out of the Saginaw glacial lake plain into the rolling hills, they enter a transition forest. This forest contains both the broad-leaved trees of the south and the evergreen conifers of the north. In the transition zone, beech and sugar maple from the southern forest grow side by side with spruce and balsam fir from the north. They grow alongside red pine, white pine, and stray remnants of hemlock—whose ranges are centered in this transition zone. The forest is unlike those found anywhere else. It is known as the north woods. Even at 70 miles per hour, the vista changes slowly. One notices fewer signs of human habitation, fewer hickories, sycamores, and dogwoods, more hemlocks, white pines, and jack pines. And when the driver finally stops, the fragrance and the sounds are unmistakably different.

Woods are an incredible experience for people accustomed to cities. You look out over ferns, bushes, trunks, and all that can be seen along the horizon are trees. We are accustomed to looking quickly, then moving on. It's easy to look quickly at the Pigeon River forest. All those thick, vertical lines standing quietly. As far away as you can see, there are trees and growing things. It's a look into infinity.

Trees creak. The sound of openness rustles all around. Only timidly does one listen without filtering the sound as we do in the city. We might say that birds touch us from far-off trees with notes in our hearing range below 20,000 vibrations per second. The liquor of plant secrets rushes in on every breath.

Changes in the forest may seem imperceptible to us. Such things depend on our sense of pacing. To our dogs and cats, we humans are eternal creatures who live four or five times longer than they do. A white pine is not considered mature until it is 300 years old. It is an act of incredible haste to cut one down in minutes. Yet even the virgin forests that remain in the north woods are young by earth's standards. The oldest villages in the Middle East are older than the virgin forests of the Great Lakes. Water is the most visible sign of youth here. The lakes and wetlands are signs of a young drainage system that in fact leaves much of the land undrained.

Some 20,000 of the 105,000 acres in the Pigeon River Country Management Unit are water or wetlands, where the groundwater table is at or near the surface all year. The United States in the 1970s was losing nearly half a million acres of wetlands each year; now it loses about 290,000 acres every year, or nearly 800 acres a day. The losses now are being offset, federal officials say, by people restoring and creating new wetlands. A federal inventory shows 108 million acres remaining, including coastal salt marshes. In the contiguous 48 states, we have half the wetlands we had 200 years ago. Wetlands sustain, acre for acre, many times the fish and wildlife of most other habitats. They are highly efficient filters that clean our groundwater.

It may be a fiction to say that there are four seasons; season watchers can detect changes every day. Yet there does seem to occur a flurry of activity in the transition time as one traditional season ends and another begins. As winter turns to spring, for instance, tree buds blossom almost overnight and leaves appear almost simultaneously. In fact, many leaves do appear simultaneously, one of the wonders of the incredible aspen. Almost universally known in the north woods as popple, after its scientific name *Populus,* the quaking aspen grows sprouts along its root system. The many stems are clones of one plant and identical genetically; they are the same color, the same shape, and they flower, grow their leaves, change to fall colors, and drop their leaves at exactly the same time all along the root system. Most clones in the north woods cover less than a fifth of an acre, but some older ones occupy up to four acres. Popple, which is denigrated locally because its wood is inappropriate for lumber or long-burning firewood, is actually quite a dashing figure among trees. It is a pioneer, what *A Sierra Club Naturalist's Guide* calls a specialist in catastrophe. Aspens spring up on the most infertile of soils after everything else has been swept away by people or natural phenomena. All they really need is some moisture and lots of direct sunlight. Aspen seedlings grow two feet tall (and clones about four feet) their first year, then up to three feet per year for the next ten years. In remote areas, aspen sometimes grow to a height of 80 feet and live up to 200 years. But most mature at 30 feet and live about 50 years. They are a one-generation forest, providing protection in their lifetime as the next generation of more enduring forest types emerges. Clones continue to pop up and quickly die out without full sun, yet the root system will live on for 100 years ready to spring forth after the next disaster. Aspen are the most common trees in the second-growth north woods, with most of them dating from the 1930s or later.

In this zone of change and diversity, the seasons of spring, summer, and fall have their own particular charms and attributes. but winter is the unmistakable edge against which humans can measure their place in the scheme of things. The southern part of Michigan gets, on average, 30 inches of snow in a season. In the Pigeon River Country, the average accumulation is more than 130 inches. When it begins to snow, often in October, it may snow for several days before stopping. Even in a mild winter, the warmest days of early spring may suddenly end with a snowstorm of several days' duration. And the warmest days of summer give way to cool nights in which sweaters or jackets may feel comfortable. The smell of glaciers lingers in the morning mists.

The coldest temperature in Michigan was recorded at Pigeon River Country headquarters on February 9, 1934, when the mercury registered 51 degrees below zero Fahrenheit. Temperatures in most winters reach 20 or 30 and sometimes 40 below. The thermometer is likely to fall below freezing in the Pigeon River Country twelve months out of the year. In one recent year, the only month without frost was September.

When people slip boots into bindings and move on snowshoes into Pigeon River hardwoods, they're likely to be walking through air that gathered in a mass over the coldest reaches of the globe and moved south, pushing warmer, wetter air out of the way. Air tends toward the same temperature and humidity over thousands of square miles in systems known as air masses. While the sun sends the air over the equator into a warm, rapid hum, areas such as northern Canada turn terribly cold in winter.

Air is a physical presence, a thin skin around the earth. It shifts and rolls like an ocean, heated unevenly by the sun and stirred by the spin of the globe and its trajectory through space. What we call air is actually swirling with clay, silt, sand, dust, smoke, ashes, salts, water, and other particles, most of them so small that if we could line a thousand of them up in a row the thickness of one human hair might hide it. These particles float in gases composed of 78 percent nitrogen, 21 percent oxygen, some carbon dioxide, and traces of several others with names like krypton and xenon.

The cleanest air is above the remotest parts of the oceans, the polar regions, and the upper reaches above the globe. In bright sunlight, this clean air looks blue and lends color to water. The sky looks blue because violet and blue waves, which are shortest among visible light waves, bounce around among the molecules of air while the longer light waves slip through, like short and tall soldiers marching through a field of boulders. The shorter soldiers, in blue uniforms, stumble and sprawl across the boulders while the taller soldiers, in red, march right over them.

Blue is a glimpse of the electromagnetic spectrum, which moves in waves. If you sit on the edge of Hardwood Lake, it looks like waves are moving ashore, which is an illusion. Actually, the wind moves across the water and the water heaves up and down in roughly the same place as the wind passes. The electromagnetic spectrum is as mysterious as the wind. Whatever it is, it makes waves. Some, like radio waves, can be as far apart as the width of Lake Michigan or even the distance between New York City and Detroit. Blue and the other colors we see make such small waves that we would have to cut the thickness of a dime into 1,000 slices to understand the dimensions. One of these dime slices, which is as thick as soap bubble film, is now sliced into 100 even thinner dimes. Hold 40 of these thinner dimes between your fingers and you have the wavelength of violet light. Add two more to the stack and you have the wavelength of blue light. A stack of 49 is green light, 57 yellow, 58 orange, and 64 red. Fewer than 40 or more than 71 are outside the range of what the human eye can see.

The shortest visible light waves careen through a glacier for the same reasons they color the sky. In one sense, these dimensions explain the blue color of glacial ice. Yet we take the measure of things in many ways. The hotter the springs in Yellowstone National Park the redder the algae. Blue is that more peaceful place, where activity slows down, turns silent like an evening snowfall. Ice may be clear, but deeper cold, silent cold, is blue. Blue lurks in a haze almost invisible behind the glare of sun on snow. It is the cold that creeps against your nose and through trousers along the front of your legs.

Cold is a memory of orange fire fading away, high-speed particles drifting off to leave an ache, a loneliness. Heat is information speeded up; cold is motion gone dead, toes aching to depart in silence from the body, while the edge of feeling, the hot edge where the foot is alive, radiates pain. Deep in the toe, the rapid pulse of life sends sharp messages that the surface is shutting down, the fire going out, the dance of energy slipping away.

As the earth has its thin skin of air, so do people. The body radiates a quarter-inch envelope of moist air along the skin, a 75-degree barrier against cold that at the same time releases excess heat. A sustained change of less than 10 degrees above or below the normal internal operating temperature will be fatal.

Cold and snow, like darkness and the lack of trails, tend to ease human pressure on the forest and leave it a relatively remote place that can support most of the flora and fauna existing in lower Michigan. The heavy snows of the north woods serve as insulation, protecting plants, animals, and the soil from the bitter cold. The climate is part of the equation that sustains the north woods since it is precipitation, on one hand, and evaporation and transpiration, on the other, that are largely responsible for where the north woods grow. Water passing through leaves into the air is called transpiration; it can add thousands of gallons of vapor to the air over an acre of forest in a single day. Heat and dry air can speed up transpiration and evaporation. In western Wisconsin and Minnesota, the southern border of the north woods angles northwest into Canada because there is not enough moisture to sustain the forest, even though the region is at the same latitude as the Pigeon River Country. Below the north woods are oak forest, savanna, and prairie.

Some of the best times to be in the forest are those times when other people stay home: on a gray, dreary day or during a rain. If we can find a bit of shelter so the sound of drops on our clothing doesn't distract us, if we can get away from generators and pumps and electric hums, then the rain will bring a musical sound that may remind us of some long forgotten day in our childhood. Rain runs to the tips of pine needles, swells into clear, fat drops, then falls to the forest floor. The coarse sand in the Pigeon River Country has large spaces between particles, so groundwater moves rapidly through it. A saturated sandy soil conducts water at about 15 feet per day, compared with about one inch per day through saturated clay. Every year roughly two tons of plant and animal material comes to rest on an acre of forest, where the soil creatures turn it under and break the complex material down into its simpler parts. Most soil animals, such as millipedes, mites, and springtails, can't digest fresh litter until it has been softened by microorganisms. But then they chew and grind it into smaller pieces. In turn, bacteria feed on the sugars and starches in leaf particles and, in the process, release carbon dioxide, which filters from the soil back into the atmosphere to be reused by green plants. Springtails can jump high into the air by gathering their tails under them and springing away. Certain springtails, known as snow fleas, appear in great numbers on the surface of melting snow in early spring.

Another tiny organism that comes up off the ground where humans can easily see it is lichen. Lichen is the green plant that grows like a scaly moss on tree trunks. It is one of the sturdiest plants in existence, growing in jungles and the coldest reaches of Antarctica on surfaces as inhospitable as bare rock. Yet lichen will not survive in the foul air of cities and is thus seldom seen in southern Michigan. Lichen is actually two and sometimes three life forms living together: algae from the Protista kingdom; and/or cyanobacteria (formerly called blue-green algae); and fungi, which grow in threads around the algae.

There are many experiences waiting in the rain and other quiet times. One of the easiest to describe is the reddish-orange of the wet trunk of a red pine, how it deepens and glistens, an unmistakable sign of something we can recognize, name, and thereby derive a certain comfort from. One of the hardest to describe is the fragrance of a forest in the rain. People sometimes say there is a certain scent in the woods that they don't smell anywhere else. One surefire way to re-create that smell is to crush a leaf from the sweet fern between your fingers. Although *Comptonia peregrina* grows throughout Michigan, except for the southernmost counties, this low shrub with saw-toothed leaves has an aroma that conjures up the north woods more easily than words or pictures ever could.

Part 2 ❧ Precedents

2

Forays

For in their interflowing aggregate, those grand freshwater seas of ours,—
Erie, and Ontario, and Huron, and Superior, and Michigan,—possess an
ocean-like expansiveness, with many of the ocean's noblest traits; with many
of its rimmed varieties of races and climes. . . . At intervals, they yield their
beaches to wild barbarians, whose red painted faces flash out from their pel-
try wigwams; for leagues and leagues are flanked by ancient and unentered
forests, where the gaunt pines stand like serried lines of kings in Gothic
geneologies; those same woods harboring wild Afric beasts of prey, and
silken creatures whose exported furs give robes to Tartar Emperors.

—Herman Melville, *Moby Dick*
(based on an 1840 Great Lakes voyage)

The beautiful old basswood tree . . . was planted there by the Great Spirit for
me to sport under, when I could scarcely bend my little bow. Ah, I watched
that tree from childhood to manhood, and it was the dearest spot to me in
this wide world . . . But alas, alas, the white man's ax has been there!

—Mack-E-Te-Be-Nessy (Chief A.J. Blackbird)
History of the Ottawa and Chippewa Indians of Michigan, 1887

If the 10,000 years since Michigan's last glacier could be compressed into an
hour-long movie, the last 60 seconds would show in a frenzy the native
peoples and animals disappearing, trees cut or burned to the ground, and
the population bursting into millions.

Yet the trees grow again, and what the Indians knew is just beginning
to be understood. The Pigeon River Country is a place set aside as an idea.
When P. S. Lovejoy said he didn't want any "parky fixings up" there, he at

once gave the past and present the gift of fulfillment. In the belief that what is created continues to participate in the present, we devote some portion of this book to finding out just where we are.

Europeans began exploring Michigan, about as early as any state in the union, in about 1620. They encountered a culture that had been developing for thousands of years even before the glaciers melted away. It is virtually certain that these early people inhabited what is now the Pigeon River Country. Paleo-Indian hunters followed the retreating glacial ice north along what is called the periglacial forest-tundra edge or spruce parkland where the capacity to support large game was high. Otsego County's high ridge was ice free for many centuries before the last glacier, the Valders, advanced to the ridge. The drainage system to the south remained in place even during the Valders glaciation. Meltwater from Valders eventually created a glacial lake at the top of lower Michigan as the glacier receded down through Pigeon River Country and on toward the Upper Peninsula. What are now Burt, Mullett, and Black Lakes—into which the Sturgeon, Pigeon, and Black rivers flow—were for a time part of an enormous strait of water between the Upper and Lower Peninsulas. The Pigeon River Country was virtually on the shore of the strait.

Details about Indian life in the region remain a matter of conjecture. But William Lovis, who has researched archaeological sites in the Burt and Mullett Lakes area, told this author that it is certain there was activity in Pigeon River Country even in the years just before Europeans arrived. The pattern of activity, according to this Michigan State University (MSU) archaeologist, involved small family groups that moved inland on snowshoes from the coast in winter, seeking food along creeks and rivers and relief from the fierce winter on the coast. John O'Shea, of the University of Michigan's archaeology department, concurred with Dr. Lovis, and other scholars since then have reported generally on hunting, fishing, and agriculture by natives in northern lower Michigan prior to European settlement. Although James E. Fitting, the state archaeologist for Michigan, cited reports that there were no direct accounts of Indians in lower Michigan at the beginning of European exploration, he apparently meant no European accounts. He acknowledged that there are numerous legends that Algonquin groups inhabited this area before 1650. Legends, handed down from generation to generation by specially designated persons, are the Indians' oral history.

The deep philosophic differences between Native Americans and Europeans are just beginning to be understood. The Indian concept of being human, for example, is not distinct from "the lower animal world," as *Webster's Third New International Unabridged Dictionary* defines the Western concept. Joseph Epes Brown writes that in Native American lore, myths, folktales, rites, ceremonies, art forms, music, and dances there is the understanding that animal beings are not lower, that is, inferior to humans, but rather, because they were here first in the order of creation, animal beings are looked to as guides and teachers of human beings.

The small Great Lakes societies that were forced to unite into what we call the Ojibwa (or Chippewa) tribe after the Europeans came, lived separately in little bands and usually identified themselves with the names of animals (Bear, Beaver, Catfish, Crane, Snapping Turtle, and so on).

"Beliefs concerning the nature, authority, and meaning of the animals in these traditions," Brown writes, "may perhaps be summed up in a general manner. In the people's intense and frequent contact with the powers and qualities of the animals . . . humankind is awakened to, and thus may realize, all that an individual potentially is as a human person. Human completion, wholeness, or religious awakening depends on this receptive opening up to the potentialities and sacred mysteries in the immediate natural environment."

A Zuni once asked an ethnologist who was meticulously transcribing each word of a traditional story, "When I tell these stories, do you *see* it, or do you just write it down?" According to Jamake Highwater, what the Zuni asked was if a European were capable of *entering* the story and having the story enter him. In one episode of the Don Juan stories, Carlos Castaneda's automobile disappears and reappears. The young apprentice asks his Indian teachers if such a mystical event had *really* occurred or if it was simply an illusion. The *brujos* laugh and tell Castaneda, "But everything really happens!" It is an idea outside the confines of Western thinking to suppose that dreams, hallucinations, and thoughts occur to us with as much validity as tripping over a rock.

Those of us raised in the Western tradition, while feeling more comfortable with scientific explanations of weather, nonetheless recognize that technicalities do not explain why some things seem to fit our moods or give us comfort. Weather in northern Michigan, like weather in other places, is not simply a matter of air masses but has a personal aspect. Even those who chiefly complain about the weather as inconvenient are aware that weather affects them, touches them, and may even from time to time recognize that they share with weather a link to certain mysteries involving the rhythms of life. In an ancient story, the people who inhabited this land for all but the scant last few years of human history speak freely of dreams, thoughts, and ideas as though they were as valid as stagnant anticyclones.

We Westerners understand things as component parts: stagnant anticyclones create temperature inversions that create concentrations of haze. We hardly know what to make of a *manitou*. Our science is rather skittish around concepts like fundamental life forces. The Indian, on the other hand, finds them all around yet is not particularly in awe of them. Their fundamental life forces seem as personable as, well, persons. We are accustomed to seeing Indians looking stern or sad, and we underestimate their fine sense of humor and their straightforward approach to things in life that give us pleasure.

This legend was collected by Mary Chamberlain for the *Michigan Pioneer and Historical Collections* many years ago.

High up in the heavens the Sun-god, he whose symbol is the white bird Wakohon, looked down upon the earth one day, smiling to see how well he had finished his labors of the year. Now the Sun-god is not the *One*—Ta-ren-ya-wa-go, Holder of the Heavens; no, he is only the Manito of the sun which, as we know, is the heart of the sky. He is fat and fair and lazy; then also he sometimes is very cross and out of temper, and at such times, sky, air, and water all feel his frown. Often, however, he is good humored; and then it is that all things rejoice in his smiles. But looking down this day and seeing all so well done—all the grain ripened and gathered . . . the Manito grew restive and bethought himself that he was much in need of a respite from such exceedingly good behavior. . . .

The better to help his meditations he filled and lighted his great calumet, his mighty peace-pipe, that should not have been smoked except in the council lodge, and so sat down to his musings. After a long time he hit upon a plan that filled him with glee.

"Aha!" he cried. "I will get me up and away into the far, frozen Northland where my brother Peboan (the winter) reigns, and I will help him strip these forests, still these rivers, and send the icy blasts sweeping over the great lakes and waters, drifting the powdery snow through the villages and piling it high about the wigwams. I'll nip the hunter's fingers and make the old men cover over the coals and the women and children wail in the storm. It will be rare sport to see my brother Seegway (the spring) work till he sweats to repair my mischief—the lazy fellow!"

After this, overcome by the labor of thinking out things for himself, to which he was not accustomed, and besides being still surfeited with the great feast of the Medway that was held but lately in the month of the Sturgeon when all the fruits and grains, the game and fish are most abundant and delicious, the lazy Sun-god failed to note the sly approach of Weeng, the Spirit of Sleep, who with his many hued pinions came fluttering softly in the air with a gentle, murmuring noise that in time stole away the senses of the Manito. . . . Then, as he thus slept, summer gaily tarried, flaunting her most vivid colors in the very face of the stupid Sun-god; the waters laughed softly, the winds murmured in gentle undertone, all things in nature conspiring together to laugh at and mock him, yet always so quietly as not to disturb his slumbers.

While he dreams the smoke from his great peace-pipe fills the air—you see it resting on the far hills and craggy uplands in a purple haze, there in the still valleys, there on the quiet waters and over all the landscape like a shimmering veil. And not till his mighty calumet is smoked out to its very latest spark will the fat and lazy Manito awake. This then is the Indian Summer.

❧   ❧   ❧

On March 28, 1836, certain members of the Ojibwa and Ottawa tribes, under duress, signed a treaty in Washington, DC, giving up Ojibwa and Ottawa possession of all the northern and northwestern portion of the Lower Peninsula of Michigan plus the eastern Upper Peninsula. Thirty-two years later the first European settlers entered Otsego County. Within a few years, the new people were settling in the northern portion of the county and beginning to cut the trees in what is now Pigeon River Country.

The first Europeans to pass through the area had come years before, entrepreneurs and traders who blazed trails or followed the old Indian routes. It is apparent that the Pigeon River itself was a route. When David Ward came north in 1854 to investigate cork pine land in Town 30 North of Range 3 West, east of Otsego Lake, he went by boat up the Great Lakes to the top of the Lower Peninsula then went south along the rivers that flow through the Pigeon River Country.

I left in September, 1854, with Umphrey Smith to assist me, taking the shorter route by Cheboygan River to examine and select said land. At Cheboygan we hired a small sail boat in which we sailed up through Mullett and to the south shore of Burt Lake, and there left our boat with half a bushel of good ripe potatoes raised on new cleared land. Then shouldering our packs we proceeded south through the woods and up the hills, following up the Pigeon Branch of the Cheboygan River which empties into Mullett Lake.

He observes that "after leaving Burt Lake we had continued warm, rainy weather, keeping the ground hemlock brush continuously wet for us to travel through. But we wasted no time in waiting for the rain to cease, disagreeable as it was, and were continuously soaked." He was in territory where enough exploration had occurred to give names to major landmarks, yet much of what he saw had been observed by few Europeans. Burt and Mullett lakes had been named for the men who surveyed the northern lands. Even today, Mullett is often confused with the fish, which is spelled mullet.

Ward grew chilled and feverish in the rain and wrote that the ague left him without an appetite. "However, we travelled on through the wet brush covered heavily with the summer leaves." The warm rain continued until the sixth of October, when it turned cold. The weather

soon covered the brush and ground hemlock with melting snow for us to return to Burt Lake through. We arrived there at our boat about the fifteenth of October. My appetite being poor I hankered after the potatoes we had left with our canoe. I soon washed clean a full peck and had them boiled, and Smith broiled the pork while I made the tea. Our banquet being ready at about two o'clock P.M., we sat down to it and I continued eating until I consumed the whole peck of potatoes, as Smith did not like potatoes. . . .

The following morning we launched our sail boat, the wind being fair from the southwest, and sailed rapidly through Burt and Mullett lakes to Cheboygan, and then took the steamer home to Port Huron. For nineteen successive days on this trip I was wet from head to foot continuously, only drying my clothes each night by our camp fire.

There is an even earlier account, one of the first official forays into the interior of the northern Lower Peninsula to survey the state military road from Saginaw to Mackinac in 1839. The party of 13 used four tents and carried flour, beans, pork, coffee, sugar, and dried apples plus some corn for the horses. They proceeded up the Tittabawassee River about 25 miles inland from Saginaw Bay, then into dense pine and fir woods to within 20 miles of the Au Sable River, which reaches Lake Huron at what is now Oscoda. Near the Au Sable, the surveyors were told by Indians and traders that they would find and have to cross within the first 100 miles going north "extensive shaking marshes that extended great distances east and west, with small tamarack in places, and where a man could shake the marsh a considerable distance around. The work was hazardous."

B. O. Williams ran the line. Each tree within three feet of the line was squared on three sides and the trees removed so the six packhorses could pass with their 200-pound packs. After considerable difficulties, entanglement in a cedar swamp, and near starvation, "it was agreed the survey of the road should be abandoned and that the only way to Mackinaw was in forced marches."

A raft was built and all the luggage placed thereon and shoved out into the river to float down and meet the ascending party. A north-westerly direction was taken mostly over high rolling land. A blind trail was found and within a week whortleberries of great size were seen. The trail was followed, increasing in size until it brought the party to an inland lake with wide beach. It was impossible to tell whether it was a bay or lake as neither end could be seen. . . . Food supplies were dangerously low. . . . Prints of a canoe on the white sand beach, a dog's paws and the footsteps of an Indian supplied a clue. Within a few miles, cornfields appeared and so did two aged, tall Indians. When Mr. Williams and associates told them they were from Saw-gee-nong (Saginaw), they unbent, shook hands, showed them where to camp and made liberal provision of potatoes, corn, fish, and pumpkins and corn fodder for the horses. It was ascertained that the body of water was a lake, called Mish-sco-to-waga-mish, literally fire water or rum lake, and that the stream that had been followed was called by the same name and that this was the most easterly of the great inland lakes, upon the Cheboygan river.

Viewed from high above Pigeon River Country, rivers and even trails show up as distinct thin marks without tree cover. The rivers look like natural routes through the vegetation. The Au Sable and Manistee rivers, which approach within walking distance of each other, have long been recognized as an ancient east-west route across Michigan. It is possible that the Pigeon River was part of a similar northerly route. Turtle Lake, the northernmost point on the Au Sable River, is only three miles from the southern headwaters of the Pigeon at Finnegan Lake. This three miles is on a ridge appropriate for portaging. On the same high ridge, about 10 miles to the east, is West Twin Lake, where 15 Indian burial mounds were found in the 1920s. The condition of the mounds indicated they were not just temporary burial grounds but a long-standing burial place.

When the Williams party surveyed in the north country in 1839, Williams told the State Pioneer Society many years later, the mosquitoes and gnats were intolerable; the animals suffered terribly, and the sole protection was dense smoke that presented other dangers. Mrs. Anna Jameson, wife of the attorney general of Upper Canada, in describing her 1837 journey by canoe from Mackinac Island to Sault Sainte Marie illustrates the range of experience a visit into the north country could engender.

> I cannot, I dare not, attempt to describe to you the strange sensation one has, thus thrown for a time beyond the bounds of civilized humanity; nor the wild yet solemn reveries which come over one in the midst of this wilderness of woods and waters. All was so solitary, so grand in its solitude, as if nature unviolated sufficed to herself.

On the other hand, she and her companions found "the whole region being one mass of tangled forest and swamp, infested with bears and mosquitos," which she describes as follows.

> They came upon us in swarms, in clouds, in myriads, entering our eyes, our noses, our mouths, stinging until the blood followed. . . . I had suffered from these plagues in Italy . . . but 'tis a jest, believe me, to encountering a forest full of them in these wild regions. I had heard much, and much was I forwarned, but never could have conceived the torture they can inflict, nor the impossibility of escape, defence, or endurance.

David Ward received a diploma in 1848 as a physician and surgeon, but he made his living before and after that as a "looker," a person who located and identified timber for lumbermen. He paid attention to what he saw of the land. Born in the Au Sable River Valley of Essex County, New York, in 1822, Ward came to Michigan in 1836. "The country about Detroit," as he observed it, "was flat, low, and undrained. In some places were open, hay marshes and timbered swamps, some of which were filled largely with a great growth of timber, mostly oak, elm, and black ash."

Ward estimated that "ninety-nine one-hundredths of the pine timber originally in Michigan was sap and Norway pine, but mostly sap, and the cork pine was generally in scattered patches, not large in extent, and usually located toward the headwaters of the various pine timber streams."

"Sapling" meant a tall and thrifty white pine with a good top, numerous branches, limbs extended downward. Such a tree was still growing and had not much heartwood; boards from it would contain many knots and would not be of high rank in the market. A sapling pine eventually grew to cork pine, a mature white pine with a small top, thin sap, and much heartwood, with lower limbs long gone. Cork pine wood was ripe and soft, good to work with saw and plane, and could be finished into good doors, sashes, blinds, and furniture.

Norway pine is now called red pine because of its orange-red bark. Its needles are grouped in pairs, stiff, and about four to six inches long. White pine needles are softer, shorter, and grouped five together.

Timber cruising led to settlement of Otsego County, first on the southern shore of Otsego Lake and then north into Corwith Township and the Pigeon River Country. Ward offers some of the earliest detailed glimpses of this virgin north country.

In the winter of 1854, another timber cruiser, John Mellen, told Ward that "in company with another man some years before he had travelled from Cheboygan through the unbroken forest to Saginaw some one hundred and sixty to seventy miles following a part of the way the north and south Town line between Ranges 3 and 4 west. In so doing he said he passed from one to one and a half miles west of Otsego and Bradford lakes, and that on travelling on a ridge west of these lakes he had passed through several miles of good cork pine."

Ward invested his own $3,000 and asked Dwight, Smith & Co. and William A. Howard, who were running a private bank in Detroit, to finance purchase of the pine if Ward could find it. He engaged three men to accompany him, two of them to return after delivering provisions to the site. They left Saginaw on March 16, 1854, carrying large packs for the walk north. John Bailey, chosen to explore the land with Ward, was "double-fisted, stout, hardy, willing, determined. . . . He carried his hundred pound pack with a rifle and ax in his hand from Saginaw to Bradford Lake without lessening the weight of his pack and without a murmur through the whole distance of one hundred and sixty-five miles."

They traveled on ice up the Tittabawassee River, up the Tobacco River Forks, through the forest to Houghton and Higgins lakes, and crossed the ice there. They continued north past the Au Sable River through snow that was three and a half feet deep on the level to their destination about 30 miles southwest of the Pigeon River Country. During the walk, the weather turned severely cold after a heavy thaw. The sky was clear and the wind continuously from the northeast, "the thermometer falling at times to thirty degrees below zero in the middle of the day. From the 20th to the 30th of March, the cold was so intense that all the way to Bradford Lake not one of us broke through the crust."

Ward's big toe froze in crossing Higgins Lake. Zene Cory, then 19 and later chairman of the Macomb County Board of Supervisors, "cried like a child from the intense cold after crossing Higgins Lake." The evening they reached Bradford Lake, a southern wind came up and gushed warm air so that by five the next afternoon, April 1, the snow level had dropped two feet.

Ward found the cork pine but had to race with timber cruisers from the St. Mary Ship Canal Co. and claimed his timber just hours ahead of his rivals. The acreage he claimed, just south and west of Otsego County, was as big as the whole Pigeon River Country. When Ward died in 1900, his estate had to be settled within 12 years. His executors ordered the tract of some 90,000 acres cleared within that period since Ward had never cut there. A site they called Deward became a town of 800 people overnight. It's now gone except for a few foundations, railroad rubble beneath the sand, and the stumps.

A. A. Dwight, who invested in the land with Ward, sent the first settlers into Otsego County in April 1868. Six men, a foreman, and one yoke of oxen came north from Almont in Lapeer County, hewing their way along a hunter's trail to the borders of what is now Lake Tecon. There they built cabins, a barn, and lean-tos. When winter approached, they left in disgust over the hardships. The following spring, Dwight sent Charles Brink and a crew of 14 men, who cleared 25 acres and planted crops that were mostly ruined by frost. By 1872, there was a village at the south end of a six-mile-long lake just east of Lake Tecon and lumbering was under way in Otsego County. At what Ward says was his suggestion, a railroad from southern Michigan to Mackinac was being laid through to Otsego County. One of the first women to arrive at the settlement on Otsego Lake was Mary Mead Smith, who remembers:

My husband, William H. Smith, in the spring of 1873, had just disposed of a grocery and commission business in Saginaw, and . . . accepted an invitation from a railroad man to take a trip . . . into the northern part of the lower peninsula on the Jackson, Lansing & Saginaw R.R., . . . which had just been pushed as far north as the foot of Otsego Lake. I well remember his enthusiasm [from a letter] in which he glowingly depicted the manifold charms of the beautiful Otsego Lake, and the grand old forests of magnificent beech and maple timber so abundant on all sides, and the lovely and balmy weather that prevailed at that time. . . . [He] camped out with a number of men who were also allured to this region and were about to locate homesteads. Robert Menzies, Sr., was numbered among these men.

To the best of my recollection a veteran of the Civil War was entitled to pre-empt on 160 acres of government land along the new railroad or between the railroad sections, and the time he served in the army would be applied to the time necessary to prove up on the claim. [The applicant described the land selected and asserted the purpose to be actual settlement and cultivation. Filing fee for 160 acres was $14.00. Land could also be purchased at $1.25 per acre.] . . .

[O]ne beautiful day in . . . August, 1873, we boarded the train at Bay City for northern Michigan and the wilds of Otsego County. My husband had advertised a piece of land that some one had previously located and for some reason had abandoned. It was near the head of the grade, as it was then called, and as the track was only laid as far as the foot of the lake, quite a number of other mossbacks, as they were then called, had reached the ground and were putting up temporary pole shanties along the lake front, we did likewise. My husband hired Robert Menzies to put up the body of a log house for us near his shanty. This was my first experience in pioneering, and it was really romantic to me then, having lived all my life in cities and towns. . . . We arrived late in the afternoon of August 29th, at Otsego Lake village and spent the first night in the log boarding house of the Smith, Kelly & Dwight Lumber Co.

Mr. and Mrs. F.M. Groat kept it, and made us welcome and very comfortable with my year old baby Bertha. There was but little there in the way of buildings . . . except the company's log store and boarding house. Mr. Charles S. Brink had his hotel partly built. I can recall walking down to the lake shore the next morning where I greatly admired the fine scenery untouched by the hand of man, and some lovely white pond lilies in the water at the foot of the lake. Then we entered a rough looking boat and started for our new home five miles up the lake. The row up the lake was highly enjoyed, as at that time the lake was surrounded by a dense forest of chiefly hard wood with some tall pines and hemlocks interspersed, raising their spires in some cases far above the maple, beech and birch trees. At that time our log cabin had no roof on it, so for a week boarded with a Henry Smith and wife in a log house with an addition of shakes, that stood a little north of our log house. Mr. Smith and wife did quite a business lodging and boarding anyone who came along. Mrs. Smith was a nice, sensible, hard working woman, and I liked her very much, but I think I never heard a man swear worse than Henry. This Henry Smith's chief occupation was to dispense vile whiskey to all comers, and he never seemed to open his mouth without letting out a string of villainous cuss words that would stop a mule and shock a saint.

About all the help Mrs. Smith had was what a delicate looking son of fifteen years could render her. I was obliged to go to bed in the only bedroom beside her own, and there was four beds in the room, but I made the best of what couldn't be helped. I took my baby and climbed the stairs and got to bed before dark. After dark I heard men coming up to bed, and in the morning I remained in bed until the men had gone down stairs. Mrs. Henry Smith was about forty years of age, and she had no conveniences and little bedding, having lost nearly everything in a shipwreck on Saginaw Bay, she told me. She worked very hard and would have been a good cook if she could have gotten the wherewith to cook with.

Mrs. Menzies lived in a nearby log cabin with her husband and her one child William. I shall never forget her first call on me in my log house. I had lost all track of time and so I supposed one bright morning it was Monday, and was busily engaged with the family washing when who should come in but Mrs. Menzies to pay a visit and make my acquaintance, and to my great astonishment she informed me it was Sunday instead of Monday, and I felt so ashamed as I tried to explain, but some how I always felt that I was in disgrace with her. I know my mother would have been shocked and would fear I had become quite heathenish.

Some of the houses had bark floors and a stove with an elevated oven in one corner and a bed made by driving poles into logs in another corner, a table and a few chairs or home-made benches to sit on. Not being able to get at that time what lumber was needed, Will, my husband, sent to Bay City for a thousand feet of rough lumber, which on arrival at Otsego Lake was towed up to the head of the lake on a big scow, an all day's job. By this means we had the first board floor put down in the county, but it was so rough and uneven that I kept little Bertha on the bed or carried her around so that she had no chance to learn to walk as soon as she might have done. With your conveniences now days you sure would have laughed could you have seen our kitchen. The room was so narrow we hardly had room for the stove and table, so Will decided to make it the whole length of the house, but there was a pine tree in the way which he didn't dare cut down for fear of its falling on the house. So he [went around it by] cutting a hole in the roof. Our first table was a few short boards fastened with cleats and hinged on one side of the house, so between meals we could let it down.

The older people will remember that there was a business panic in the year 1873, and the man to whom Mr. Smith sold his business in Saginaw was unable to pay for the stock, so Mr. Smith decided to bring some of the goods north to his new home and set up storekeeping for the accommodation of landlookers, parties of whom were coming in most every day. His shelves [were] stocked with staple articles in demand, such as tobacco and pipes, candles, lanterns, sugar, flour, pork, matches, crackers, candy, and a few notions.

[Later] Charley Osborn and family went up north onto their homestead, and so did Robert Menzies, but his wife went to the south part of the state to spend the winter.

That fall, 1873, a village was platted at the head of the grade by Hon. O.M. Barnes, of Lansing, then president of the Jackson, Lansing & Saginaw Railroad, and the place was first called Barnes, but was shortly renamed Gaylord in honor of an attorney residing in Saginaw, and head of the law firm of Gaylord & Hanchott.

That fall men began laying ties and putting down the rails for the extension of the road to the new village of Gaylord and late that fall trains began to run up from Bay City. At that time but one train a day each way was the rule, one baggage car and one passenger car and two or three freight cars, hauled by a small dinkey wood-burning engine that puffed and labored hard to make ten or twelve miles an hour. The smoke-stack was big at the top end and small at the bottom, and was protected on the top by a wire screen to keep the sparks from setting fires, which they frequently did, causing much unnecessary destruction of good timber, but which in those days was not regarded as much waste, because it was so plentiful.

The train would leave Gaylord at about 7 in the morning and pound along all day with many stops at woodpiles and watering places and scattered houses that have since become towns and would finally arrive at Bay City about 5 in the afternoon. It was a long, tedious and tiresome trip for there was nothing to be seen from the car window but dense woods and jack pine plains, for there was not much farming north of West Branch. The road was built to Cheboygan and Mackinaw in 1881–2. Gaylord increased from a half dozen families to a village of about 400.

In the summer of 1874 I was left alone in charge of the little store. I got along very well until snow came, then I was very lonely, for all my neighbors had moved away. Sometimes the railroad men would come in for tobacco, but they always treated me with respect. As the days grew shorter and it became dark earlier, I felt a little nervous, so I would hurry around with my work, put my baby to bed and turn the buttons on my door and put my light out. On several occasions when thus alone and along towards midnight I would hear the railroad men passing by and swearing and talking on their way to the Henry Smith boarding house or from "Mother" McCushe's camp at Buell's Landing but they never molested me.

I well remember hearing the loons' lone cry over the waters of the lake, and the incessant murmuring of the winds through the tops of the tall pines yet untouched by the woodman's axe, which at first sounded rather dismal, but after awhile came to be more musical.

I made up my mind to make my first visit to the new town of Gaylord to be. It was Sunday, and I rode up there on a bobsleigh drawn by a yoke of oxen, and I will never forget my first view of Gaylord. At that time there was I should judge about five acres of ground cleared on each side of the railroad track extending from the street south of the depot to what is now Main street just north of the station, and only a few rods wide. The rest was all primeval forest, just as nature made it. The little board depot, Bradford's hotel and our new log house was the extent of the town. I stood in front of the hotel and all I could see was snow and stumps, and everybody had to use snow water for all purposes as it was a big job to dig wells in those days.

I was alone a good deal of the time, and one day I heard that Mrs. Henry Smith was sick and I went over to see her. I found her in bed and she seemed quite worried about her sickness, there being neither doctors nor medicines to be obtained in the county. It was on a Thursday and her eighteen railroad men boarders had removed to a new camp about a half mile south of Gaylord. I could do but little to relieve her. The following Sunday late at night came a pounding at our door and a voice crying. There stood little Willie Smith telling us that his mother was dying. We did what we could to relieve her, but she grew delirious and soon breathed her last. My husband and some of the other men set to and made a coffin of rough pine boards and planing them, and it was lined with some white cotton cloth we had in the store. I had a pinking iron and tried to make it look a little better. Henry, the woman's husband, decided to take the body to Oakland county for burial. Her husband and little son had no suitable clothes to wear, so Charley Osborn and my husband loaned them shirts, hats, and even Will's best coat. Monday night they had plenty of "watchers" to sit up with the remains. The train came up from Otsego Lake and stopped opposite their home, and the rude casket was carried out and placed on the rear platform of the single passenger coach.

Mary Mead Smith says this was the first death of a settler in the county. Farther north, Robert Menzies built the first house in Corwith Township just southwest of what is now Vanderbilt, the closest town to the Pigeon River Country. He located his homestead in November 1872 and built a small log house in April 1873, then began clearing his land.

Frank Woodin, whose family was one of the Corwith pioneers, recalled later that much of the land was homesteaded by Civil War veterans. As people came up from the northern terminus of the railroad at Otsego Lake Village, "everyone was having trouble clearing the trail of fallen timbers and could only travel five or six miles a day." The first settlers had to pack their provisions from Otsego Lake, later from Gaylord, to their property. Seventy-five pounds was about the average load for a man.

A local historian asks us to "picture with me the country about here at that time. It was just a howling wilderness—wild animals about, with no roads constructed, merely trails cut through the woods." Frank Randolph, born in Ohio 36 years before, walked into the wilderness in August 1873 carrying 75 pounds of supplies on his back from Gaylord nine miles to his new property. He tried to eke out an existence from the soil and hauling settlers between 1873 and 1882. He moved one family back to Gaylord after only one week's stay, apparently despairing of the loneliness and hardship.

Corwith Township was organized in 1877. By the time of the first federal census there in 1880, some 250 people were living in Corwith, although there were no roads or schools and the railroad from Gaylord to Mackinaw City would not be constructed through Vanderbilt until the next year. Robert and Margaret Menzies listed their children in the census: William, ten; Charles, four; and Robert, two. Mr. Menzies's parents, Archibald and Jennie, homesteaded on the 80 acres next to his.

The 1880 census also counted three Yuill brothers, John, Thomas, and James, who were born in Scotland and arrived from Ontario, Canada, in 1879. John and Thomas homesteaded on the outskirts of what was to be Vanderbilt. James settled half a mile east and eventually began farming. Samuel, their younger brother, soon joined them and became an overseer of logging operations until his death in the late 1920s. John and Tom formed Yuill Brothers, a partnership that was to alter the face of the Pigeon River Country. Yuill Brothers at one time owned 230,000 acres of forest. They engaged in lumbering, shipping, the mercantile business, farming, real estate, and other businesses until the late 1930s.

All the pine taken from the Pigeon River Country and its environs was gone by 1891. The hardwoods came down over the next 25 years. In 1900, a large part of the forest was bare ground under cultivation.

Logging occurred mostly in winter, when logs could be moved by horse and sleigh across snow to shipping points. In 1905, the growing Yuill firm purchased the sawmill, logging railroad, standing timber, commissary, and housing facilities of the Rogers-Allison Lumber Company at what was then called Logan, two miles south of Vanderbilt. Logan was an active community for some 25 years; today it is farmland.

3
The Log House

When Lewis Perry was gathering history of the Vanderbilt area as a hobby, he clipped an article that read, "It is often what the unimportant do that really counts and determines the course of history. The greatest forces on earth are never spectacular, the summer rains are more effective than tornadoes but they get no publicity."

A log house that no longer exists would have been among the forgotten shards of history were it not for the affection of Mary Winters Clapp, who in 1977 wrote "The Log House, the Winters Family History," from which these passages are taken.

The log house west of Logan was a landmark . . . Grandfather Winters bought the forty acres and built the log house in 1879. He stayed with the Julius Denisons till he found the land he wanted for his farm. It was well wooded with hardwood which would furnish the logs . . . There was enough level ground to be cleared for the buildings, crops and pasture. The wooded hills would furnish fuel for cooking and heating for many lifetimes. Soon Grandmother came with the five children . . . Most of the material was on the spot, so with the help of friends and relatives they set about clearing the land. The first story was of large straight logs. I remember there were many maple logs. The second story and roof were of milled lumber and covered with shingles. With occasional repairs and additions it stood on the hillside for more than three quarters of a century.

Hiram Seeley Winters and his wife, Cynthia Ann Bickford, were friendly generous people. They had seven children of their own, but when-

49

ever new families arrived or there was a need, the latch string was always out at the log house.

Logan was a small settlement a half mile east by the Michigan Central RR tracks. There was a spur there that ran to the sawmill. The sawmill was a busy place and the reason for the cluster of tarpaper houses along the north side of the road. Mr. Roger Allison from Pennsylvania built the saw mill and the general store. There was also a shingle mill run by Mr. Lyle and a lathe mill run by Arthur Stevenson. Yuill Bros. bought up most of the property a few years later. It was just what they needed to work up their large tracts of lumber in the area.

Grandfather was always tall for his age and big boned. When the Civil War broke out, he was sure he looked old enough to join the Army. He tried several times to enlist and when he was 15 he was accepted in the Union Army. He was placed in the Cavalry as a chore boy. During his enlistment he caught the chicken pox and was very ill. His bed was a blanket under a wagon no matter the weather or season of the year. When the war was over he had rheumatism that plagued him the rest of his life. . . . His veteran's pension was twelve dollars monthly. It helped with the expenses and bought him some Edison phonograph records once in awhile. He led an active life for a few years, but spent many years on crutches. When the pain got too bad he would ask Leon to take him to Elmira with the horse and buggy. There he could take the train to the Soldier's home at Big Rapids. . . . [Then] he could walk with canes for awhile again.

Grandfather never talked to the younger ones much, but he would pass his little striped sack of peppermints around once. Grandmother had carried them home from the Logan store with her groceries . . . Grandfather always had an Edison phonograph and he usually played awhile for us. . . . He always played "The Vacant Chair" and "The Preacher and the Ba'r" and then we could ask for some.

Grandfather had a little black painted kitchen chair that he sat in under the tree when the weather was warm. Often people passing by would stop and visit awhile. He could look out across the valley and even see what was going on in Logan, on the highway or railroad. At mid morning Grandmother would bring out a pan of potatoes and a kettle of water. He would get out his knife and whetstone. When the blade was sharp enough to suit him, he would start peeling potatoes. He would make very thin peelings and see how long the peeling would get before it broke. He would hold it up and look at it with a pleased smile as it got longer and longer.

Grandmother was born in Branch or Farnham, Quebec Province,

Canada. That is southeast of Montreal. They moved to Michigan when the older children were quite young. Great Grandfather Bickford joined the Union Army. He was gone a long time and his family gave him up for lost. However he was in a southern prison camp and when he was able to make his way home he was very thin and feeble. He had ague and was told that the climate of Iowa would be better for him than Michigan.

I can remember Grandma telling me that her parents had brought her up to be a lady, however I never heard her complain and she did lead a hard life. She always loved to see any new things that we girls got and I can still hear the rasp of her gnarled fingers smoothing a new hair ribbon or feel her hand lovingly smoothing my hair. She always looked at the new babies fingers to see if they were going to grow long enough to reach an octave so they could play the organ when they grew up. When I was little she had a special place in the kitchen where I could get my Maryann cookies and often there were home baked sugar cookies with a big fat raisin in the center. I don't know how she found time to do any baking on top of the chores and gardening, but she always had bread and often biscuits to go with the chicken on Sunday. She kept enough cows and chickens so that she could keep the house going by selling cream, eggs and whatever else was in season.

The house was solidly built with large logs notched and fitted at the corners. The walls were finished by chinking mortar and sticks between the logs. It made a thick draft proof wall. There were two rooms on each floor. A roomy lean to . . . was added for a dining room–kitchen and a summer kitchen . . . built of milled lumber with tarpaper on the outside walls. The roof had tough roofing paper and the chimney for the kitchen range was stovepipe with an extension reaching well above the peak of the upright part of the house. The extension was well anchored with guy wires . . . on the roof. The extra pipe was needed for the stove to draw well and because of the danger of fire from sparks on the roofing and wood shingles. The house was a cosy friendly place and Grandfather always had time to visit. The only part of the house that was ever painted was the north door and the three window frames on the log part. They were painted a lovely sky blue.

Grandfather planted two sweet chestnut trees on the north line fence at the road. I think he brought the chestnut trees and silver maple from Ohio. Perhaps he brought some of the fruit trees, too. They had a fine orchard with early and late apples and pears. There were two mulberry trees and a blue plum outside the summer kitchen. The big strawberry apple tree was in the front yard. That was an early apple and very well flavored. Over in the corner behind the big garden was a big crab apple tree that bore bushels of apples every year. No matter how much jelly and spiced apples Grandma made there would still be a thick carpet of apples under the tree. As they got winey the bees would gather and then we all stayed far away. The russets were mellow and good in the middle of the winter and we always brought them up from the cellar with spies for eating on Sunday afternoon. The spies lasted well and were good to eat out of hand as well as for pies. The early pears were taken care of as soon as they were ripe. The sickle pears were picked late and buried in the hay mow to ripen. It was a real picnic to pick the sour cherries. The older girls got to climb the ladder and after we were done there was fresh cherry pie.

A long lane led back to the woods and pasture from the barnyard. On either side were fields used to raise corn, alfalfa, potatoes and other crops. In spite of the stoney ground the crops were good and made the farm quite self sustaining. They had the usual stock of cows, pigs, and a horse.

Grandma had great clumps of purple lilac bushes. In front of the house was a little flower garden with mostly perennials in it. There were red and pink peonies, cushiony little ivory daisies, roses and perennial sweet peas. Back by the summer kitchen were the tall golden glow, hollyhocks and ribbon grass. We picked the hollyhocks and took out the center and made doll hats. The big vegetable garden had certain perennials such as rhubarb, currants, horseradish and tame goose berries. Of course there were the usual annuals such as lettuce, radishes, carrots, beets, etc.

Logan was a half a mile away, but it was a part of the life of anyone living in the log house. Four times a day the whistle blew at the mill and it could be heard for miles. It blew at six in the morning, twelve noon, one o'clock and six at night. We lived our lives by it and I never heard any complaints of it being fast or slow. Those that had clocks reset them. People that had room took in boarders. The woodcutters would come up from the south to work out in the lumber camps. Sometimes when the job was finished they would get work at the mill. They might have their families with them or send for them when they were going to live in a town. They would live at the log house until another tar paper house could be put up. The little houses weren't very comfortable because they were just a shell. Often the people were from Kentucky and not used to the bitter cold. The summer weather wasn't much better because the sun beat down and the odor of the tarpaper permeated everything.

The Logan store was run by the owners of the sawmill. The Yuill Bros. had it the longest of anyone. It was a general store and carried a little of everything that wasn't perishable. The Company stores were a blessing or a necessary evil depending on the size of your bill. People working for the Company could get credit and it helped when the cupboard was bare or clothes or heat were needed. The other side of the coin was that the prices were a little higher and the store bill might be more than the winter's wages. It was hard to get ahead that way.

The one-room Logan School was on the south side of the road in Livingston Township. The road was the dividing line between Livingston and Corwith Townships so the mill children had to walk two and a half miles over to the Rush School.

Yuill Bros. had a large farm south of Logan. There was a tenant farmer and, usually, several hired hands. They raised stock and all the usual farm crops so it paid for itself by supplying food for the men and animals in the lumber camps.

Sunday afternoons and holidays always found us at the log house. The women did dishes in the kitchen while the men sat and talked away the afternoon in the dining room. When the Robert Galloways came, Uncle Rob always passed out cigars and the room would be blue with smoke as they talked of old times, present times and of people who had come and gone. I sat on my father's lap in the black cane rocker and drank it all in. The pity of it is that I don't remember it to tell. The talk was of lumbering, road building, farming, cars, and much more. Later the women would come in from the kitchen and the latest family news would be talked over.

The log house is gone now, and it is hard to believe all the lively times that were had there and, in later years, the quiet times. I'm glad I still have the old black rocker to remind me of those old days.

Uncle Robert Galloway, who married Effie Bell, the fourth child of Grandfather Hiram Seeley Winters and Grandmother Cynthia Ann Bickford, ran several lumber camps in Pigeon River Country. Effie's youngest brother, Roy, recalled Bob Galloway sending him into the Pigeon River Country with a team load of supplies. Roy had dinner at Yuill Brothers Camp 2. Then he drove through a snowstorm until eight that night without seeing a soul, coming out at last on a hill and seeing a light far off in a hollow. He found a road angling down to a wood hauler's camp. The wood hauler told Roy he was five miles from his destination and advised him to wait out the storm until daylight. He had to unharness the team to get them through the door of the low barn. "We had one of the best suppers I ever had—it was beans and soda biscuits," Roy told Mary Winters Clapp many years later. "I brought in a blanket off the sleighs and bedded down behind the stove. More beans and biscuits for breakfast. The wife and children were barefooted on the dirt floor. It was a very bare place but they shared what they had cheerfully."

The first settler child born in Otsego County was Vieva S. Parmater. In the summer of 1898, Vieva's former college classmate, Frank J. Shipp, came to Otsego County to assume the duties of superintendent of the Gaylord schools and to marry Vieva. It was only 30 years since the coming of the first settler. Mr. Shipp wrote:

There was little or no underbrush in the original white pine forest, only the straight trees, sometimes towering more than a hundred feet high, with a small tuft of branches at the top, from which fell enough pine needles to completely cover the ground. When the writer came to Gaylord in 1898 the pine forests had been cut little more than twenty years in the lands to the east of Otsego Lake. In the early days only the very best timber was taken. Logs with hollow hearts, even though the openings were small, were left on the ground to rot or burn. The top logs where the limbs were found were also left on the ground, as nothing but the clear logs were taken. Looking east from the east shore of Otsego Lake, you could see for miles, with only an occasional pine stump standing, and the ground strewn with top and defective logs where each spring a destructive fire raged, burning a little more of the logs each year, until finally extinguished by rain.

There were at one time four Hanson Lumber Camps in the Pigeon River Country. Louie Cahill was a Hanson camp cook in the late 1800s. Louie spent more than 20 years cooking in the northern Michigan camps. One of his favorite stories was about a group of loggers who were not wise in the ways of lumber camps. The first day one of the men asked what those things were hanging on the spruce and giant pines. The lumberjacks described the pinecones as a form of pineapple that, if stored where it was warm and dry, would ripen into edible fruit. Three of the newcomers harvested an enormous number of cones and carried them back to the bunkhouse.

4

Lumbering

Charles Blanchard remembered in the early lumbering days seeing flocks of passenger pigeons migrating north in the spring to breed. The millions of birds sounded like thunder as they approached in flocks that extended from east to west as far as he could see, so thick they obscured the sun. "It took as much as an hour for a flock to fly over," he said. "The men would snatch their guns and fire at them and get a lot of them."

He recalled lumbermen drinking, fighting, and carousing after paydays in Otsego Lake Village, the original settlement. He told about the shooting of Mr. Sartamour by a woman from one of the brothels. She was sitting outside cleaning a revolver as he passed by. Mr. Sartamour stopped, bent over, and said, "See if you can hit that." She fired, killed him, and received a three-year sentence.

While many moved north from Otsego Lake to the Vanderbilt area during the logging days, others followed trails east and then north into the Pigeon River Country. The Salling Hanson lumber camp just east of Otsego Lake operated in 1890. By the time Clarence Cross arrived a dozen years later, the settlement known as Salling was no longer a forest.

We landed in Salling on an Autumn day in 1901 or 1902. Even to a nine year old it was a sorry sight after just having left the lovely town of Rochester in Oakland County. The town consisted of a row of clapboard and tarpaper shacks strung along the railroad. The town was a sea of stumps. There was a good road to Gaylord with a bicycle path skirting it.

The town was peopled with the usual lumber town families with

English, Irish, Scots, Danish, Dutch, Polish and French Canadians. The English, Irish, Scots, and French Canadians had immigrated from Canada to Michigan and followed the lumber industry north from Saginaw as the mills moved farther north.

We youngsters had to find our recreation as our parents worked ten hours per day, six days each week. . . .There was plenty of open land . . . Turtle Lake at the time had a lovely white sand bottom with an old railroad bridge or pier running far out into the lake. The railway had been abandoned. . . . They used [the pier] as a loader for white pine logs which were hauled out on the ice in the winter time and left until the ice broke up. The flat cars would be run onto the pier and a derrick would load the logs onto them. When a train load was made up the logs would be taken to the saw mills at St. Helens and sawed into lumber. At that time the lumber mills were interested only in white pine and Norway pine. . . .

[We played] Indians in the spring and fall. We built teepees and hunted small game and birds. Many were the hornet's nest we broke up and I have many memories of being stung on all parts of my body. We found basements of old settlers cabins and usually were able to find snakes in them, which created excitement, especially when we would find a blow adder. In the summer we were mostly swimming or fishing with an occasional trip wild berry picking. When we would find a patch of wild raspberries we would put a guard on it until they were all picked. There was a boat house on Grubb Point (now Point Comfort) and we could earn a nickle or beg one. We headed for there as soda pop was sold there. We were never allowed there on Sundays or in the evening as Oney Grubb, the owner, operated a blind pig and sold home brew and bootleg liquor to the lumbermen.

The swamp north of the island at the north end of the lake had numbers of muskrat houses and we trapped muskrat and mink with steel traps. There were large numbers of turtles in the swamp and if you were lucky and caught a real large one (any turtle a foot across the back was a large one), we would meet the flyer, one of the two passenger trains that came through each day, and sell it to the cook in the dining car. An extra large one would give us as much as fifty cents, which was a lot of money in those days.

Sometimes the lake froze over before the snow came and we really enjoyed skating. I have skated to Otsego Lake Village and back with smooth ice there, the only danger being large cracks caused by the shrinking when extreme cold came. When the snow came we built toboggans out of barrel staves and used Grubbs Hill for our slide (that is the hill where

Ken Mar motel [and later Marsh Ridge resort] is now). We also made homemade skis and traveled quite some distance into the country. In February the ice crews came and cut in the bay between Point Sunset and Geiglers Resort. The railway company would build tracks right out on the ice and haul the ice away in coal cars. Large crews . . . would scrape the snow off with scrapers drawn to teams of horses, then gang plows set two feet apart would be drawn by teams which cut the ice to a depth of about eight inches. Then the men would spud the ice loose and endless chains would pull it out of the water into cars. When a place 100 by 200 would be harvested they would shift to a different location and do it all over again. When these ponds would freeze over we would have marvelous rinks.

There were a number of camps across the lake and the logs were hauled on big sleighs across the ice to the mill. Occasionally a load would go through the ice, team and all. I was on one of the loads when it happened. The teamster, a Mr. Elmer Marriot, cut the tugs with his knife, threw a chain around the horses necks and chocked them. They floated quickly and the two of us dragged the horses out on the ice where they got up and we led them into the stables at Salling. (Mr. Marriot got a calling down for spoiling good tugs.)

About 1902 or 1903 the "Y" branch was extended into Johannesburg where a sawmill and veneer plant had been erected and a town started. The Johannesburg Branch gave us kids more territory to play in. We could walk out the tracks to the swamps around New Toledo and as this country had not been timbered we found plenty of new kinds of plants, timber and animals to study. It was here I saw my first wild cat.

☙ ☙ ☙

New Toledo, also called Quick, was on the Pigeon River, downstream from Flannigan's Lake. When William H. Penfold was 71 years old, he told a local historian that he cooked in Flannigan's lumber camp as a flunky with Al Woods, who was the first cook. Al got $45 per month and Mr. Penfold $26. They cooked for 70 men and prepared a whole quarter of beef for a meal. Flannigan's and Quick are gone, but an account of life in Quick survives, written by a Mrs. Goodrich.

☙ ☙ ☙

The site of New Toledo . . . was quiet and lonely in the warm October sunshine. It lies . . . in a picturesque valley. The Old State Road winds through it, a road that once joined Alpena and Gaylord via Hillman and Atlanta. At Quick this road, rolling as it did through swamps and lowlands, became a wobbly corduroy, making travel at times difficult. . . . Even before the turn of the century, big companies [were] in operation thereabout—the Badger Lumber Co., Salling Hanson, Batchelor Lumber Co. of Saginaw. Frank Buell and Dirk Schreur [operated wood camps nearby]. The general store was built in 1900 by Quick Bros., Anson and Jim, who operated a similar store in Gaylord. It served lumberjacks, shingle weavers and rural folks for miles around.

Soon folks wanted a post office, which was established about 1895–1902. While our site was known originally as New Toledo, [there was] another New Toledo in Michigan, so the town was named Quick.

Across the road at the edge of the cedar swamp stood the shingle mill. A logging railroad was soon put into this mill. . . . My father Henry Lord operated this mill from 1902–1910 using cedar owned by Salling Hanson of Grayling. A work day was nine hours and required about 14 men to keep things going. They were a colorful lot, these shingle weavers, generous, lighthearted and gay. Some were fathers of families, lived in the shanties at Quick but they liked better the rough life in the bunkhouse.

Besides the store and mill, Quick had six or eight houses, a livery stable, a cook shanty, and a few tar paper shanties.

Lumbermen in the Pigeon River Country were called to meals either by a camp horn, about six feet long, or a railroad iron wired onto a tree limb that was struck by a hammer. They slept on double bunks piled with straw and covered with a blanket. They used their clothing for pillows. The men slept in their underwear and socks under blankets. A line of hay wire was strung all over the bunkhouse for drying clothes. A wood heater sat in the center of the bunkhouse. Benches were built on the side of the beds, and there were several washbasins and a boiler on the stove for hot water.

Log haulers used torches in winter so they could see to load logs on the sleighs before daylight. Some men danced or played jaw harps or harmonicas or fiddles. Many played cards or dice. Some whittled. No whiskey was allowed in camp.

Two sawyers usually worked together with a seven-foot crosscut saw. After felling a tree, they would trim it and cut it into 12- to 16-foot lengths. Swampers worked with the sawyers and cleared roads and skidways, where logs could be piled to be picked up by teamsters. The teamsters hauled the logs by sleigh to the banking ground near a railroad spur, where they were loaded onto flatcars and taken to the mills.

Even with the bustle of logging activity, the north woods were formidable, often dense and dangerous. Reverend Nield, who organized Congregational churches in Alba, Gaylord, and Vanderbilt, often walked more than 15 miles from Alba to Otsego Lake with only a compass to guide him through the dense forest. Once he lost his way and wandered through the woods for two days and nights without food or drink. When he found water, he waded into it and stood for some time before he drank any, realizing that in his feverish condition he was apt to drink too much. Another time he was caught in a severe electrical storm and took cover all night in a hollow log.

Winter storms could be fun. Herbert A. Hutchins, who gathered voluminous historical material, told his daughter that one of the favorite excursions of sleigh riders was the trip from Gaylord to Vanderbilt. They would call ahead to the Higgins Hotel and order oyster stew, then leave in early evening and not return until early morning, properly chaperoned, pulled by teams hired from livery barns in Gaylord. On one trip, a group left despite a snowstorm earlier in the day. On the way home, the riders were stranded in a blizzard. The storm piled up drifts too deep for the small team, which played out. The party walked to refuge at the Alex Campbell farm north of Gaylord. Alex built a roaring fire in his parlor stove to help thaw them out, then he and his hired hands went back to the stranded team and dug them out. The horses were brought to the barn for rest and shelter. At daylight, Alex hitched his team to a sleigh and returned the party to Gaylord.

On Christmas Day, 1903, the *Otsego County Herald* reported that "the weather was clear but the sky was darkened by smoke from forest fires." The balance of fire and new growth in the forest was, like so many other things in those years, out of control. Slash, the tops and branches left behind when logs were hauled away, turned into tinder. Fires burned for weeks. It is now estimated that fire took about as much virgin timber as loggers did, even though most big trees had survived previous fires.

James Smith, who spent 1908–9 in a Pigeon River lumber camp, said that "the first time I visited Cornwell the forest fires were raging and even the ends of the railroad ties were burning. My father sat on top of what we called the big hill, back of the mill at night and if the fire got too close to the mill or lumberyard he would blow the mill whistle and call out the crew to fight the fire. . . . That was the summer that the town of Metz burned. Dr. Campbell was the local doctor at Metz and in 1918 I was pretty badly burned. Dr. Campbell took care of me, so I profited by the experiences he gained by taking care of all the burns in Metz."

Metz, 30 miles east of the Black River, was destroyed by the fire. It had been an extensive sawmill town, with several general stores, a saloon, a hotel, two or three liveries, and a cigar factory. In October 1908, after there had been forest fires all summer, strong winds brought the flames to Metz and Posen. Metz residents boarded a logging train and tried to escape, but the rails melted and the train was derailed. Thirteen people on the train and two members of the crew perished. Other residents escaped to open fields and survived.

Written record of at least 17 lumber camps in Pigeon River Country survives; tangible evidence of any camps is virtually nonexistent. Perhaps the best clue is old railroad beds, which are usually higher than the surrounding terrain and more free of trees and tall bushes. In some places, such as the cedar wetlands along the headwaters of the Pigeon, the old narrow-gauge ties are still in place, leaving bumps at regular intervals along obscure foot trails.

Nearly all the land was cultivated soon after it was cleared and for a time was considered home by somebody. A row of stately maples, a lilac bush, or an old orchard stand as occasional evidence that people failed in the frosty north woods to get the forest soils to produce satisfactory crops. The most successful crop was the potato, which grows in barren soil.

Whatever inroads humans may make, nature quietly and persistently goes about its business of arranging living things to suit the environment, planting soil and seeds under shingles, expanding and contracting mortar until walls fall, reclaiming sidewalks and foundations with wildflowers. On a walk in the woods, one is likely to pass an enormous stump, charred and decaying but two or three times the diameter of the live trees, perhaps with a young tree growing up out of the remains.

Trees form dotted lines around their leaf stems and at the right combination of shorter days and cooler temperature cut their leaves loose to decompose into nutrients, which return to the tree. Among the things that appeal to us in the woods is the sensation that life is complicating and simplifying in a cyclical dance before our eyes.

5

Lovejoy

We abuse land because we regard it as a commodity belonging to us. When we see land as a community to which we belong, we may begin to use it with love and respect.

—Aldo Leopold
A Sand County Almanac, 1948

It was not for lack of trying that the idea of cultivating the wilderness died. In 1903, the *Otsego County Herald* ran two stories that, from our perspective, clearly show the desperation of an idea not working.

Settlers Wanted in Northern Michigan

Lansing, Dec. 17—Land Commissioner Wildey has disposed of 135,000 acres of state tax lands during the past year, and he is endeavoring to secure reduced rates from the railroad companies for actual settlers on state lands. . . . The railroads are desirous of inducing actual settlers to locate in northern Michigan.

Lansing, Dec. 18—Land Commissioner Wildey says that the receipts of his office for the present fiscal year are in excess of $200,000. This is the effect of the law which provides for the deeding to the state and the sale of lands that have been returned delinquent for taxes for five consecutive years or more and the recent restoration to market of agricultural college lands. The average price per acre during the period named was $1.37.

Aside from the proceeds of the sale of these lands, the state is a far greater gainer because the lands are now in the hands of private owners and are again on the tax rolls.

People not only failed to create a paradise out of the wilderness; they couldn't even pay taxes on the land, and it lay ravished and untended.

In 1903, a young Parish Storrs Lovejoy enrolled as one of the first students in the new School of Forestry at the University of Michigan. It had been only five years since Gifford Pinchot was appointed head of the Agriculture Department's new Forestry Division, which was to become the U.S. Forest Service, under legislation allowing the president to set aside land that would otherwise be destroyed by free enterprise.

In 1905, Lovejoy left the University of Michigan and entered the U.S. Forest Service. He was appointed supervisor of the Medicine Bow National Forest in Wyoming. In 1910, he transferred to the Olympic National Forest in Washington, and in 1912 he returned to Ann Arbor as an assistant professor of forestry at the university.

P. S. Lovejoy was one of the bright people of vision who, out of the desolation of the lumbering era, pioneered new concepts of land use management. He was an academic with mud on his shoes, an engineer who called himself "tec poobah." He is remembered with particular fondness in the Pigeon River Country because he was so instrumental in setting the area aside as the "Big Wild." The Pigeon was one of his favorite places, and when he died his ashes were placed near the river just downstream from the headquarters complex.

Lovejoy led the effort to enlarge the state's holdings around the forest. In 1919, 6,468 acres of tax-reverted lands were added. The Otsego Wildlife Refuge, some 13,320 acres east of Vanderbilt, was added in 1926, purchased primarily with hunting license money. The two areas were eventually combined. Altogether, some 65 percent of the forest before the addition of Green Timbers in 1982 was purchased with hunters' deer license revenues.

Lovejoy called the Pigeon the Wilderness Tract or the P.R. "The essence of our proper job on the P.R.," he wrote, was "to handle [it] to 10–25–50 years hence, [so] the then people (of the sort which count most) will not be cussing us; will mebbe be saying 'Good Eye.'" In 1916, Lovejoy began writing Paul Bunyan stories in the *American Lumberman,* out of Chicago, "in an effort to stimulate the old timers to supplement my collection." He wrote in a vernacular and in what he called the Bunyan code, "which is a peculiar but well defined minstrel-end-man thing, with the chief bard getting assistance from his end man for the (real or ostensible) benefit of a greenhorn." That means, he explained later, "Bumptullips Joe playing end-man to Freezeout Jake and the greenhorn listening in with his eyes bugged out." Such colorful language crept with increasing frequency into his public and private pronouncements, obviously an effort on his part to pry serious matters into consciousness through kidding.

His vision of the Pigeon River Country was "to handle so as to conserve (prevent bumming up of) the peculiar resources and facilities inherent in that sort of land and water," which he described as, first, permanent public ownership and, second, "Flavor and Feel of the Big Wild." He continued:

We should not at all try for (or permit?) such development or use as is already amply available . . . to the general public . . . because there is chance and occasion to provide something much wanted (needed) and *not otherwise readily available* to the public. . . .

Don't we all want, yen for, need, some considerable "getting away" from the crowds and the lawn-mowers and the tulips? (Or enough of us to make the fraction worth catering to?) Isn't that [the] yen for the Big Wild feel and flavor? I claim it is.

Therefore I claim that anything which jeopardizes the [Big Wild feel and flavor] of the Pigeon River et all (Refuges, State Forests etc.) *is all wrong—poison.* . . . [H]ighways and roads and trails . . . and parked-up camp-sites *are jeopardizing* the peculiar resources and facilities of our big wild-land tracts (of which the Pigeon River is biggest and best). . . .

I'd like to see the Pigeon opened up to insure really good fire protection and damn little more . . . so that it isn't too damn easy for the beer-belly gents and the nice old granmaws to get to, set on and leave their tin cans at. I figger that a whole lot of the side-road country should be left plenty bumpy and bushy . . . and some so you go in on foot—or don't go at all. I don't want *any* pansies planted around the stump.

In May 1923, Lovejoy told a friend that "without warning, the director of the state department of conservation has asked whether I would take over and swing the new 'Land-Economic Survey.' I helped invent the theory and technique . . . so I had to take it on." The survey asked local people, especially farmers, which lands were good for what purposes, classified it all on maps, then developed a plan for proper use of the land in the three major categories of agriculture, forests, and recreation. So the academician became an official Michigan technician, working for what later became the

Department of Natural Resources. He became the state's first Game Division chief in 1927 and later chief of the Land Planning Division.

Even as the departments grew up around him, P. S. Lovejoy continued to be his own man, complaining when public servants seemed blind to their obligations to inform and educate the rest of us. One story indicates where he must have gotten his skepticism of official channels. In his early years in the Forest Service out West, he and his contemporaries faced an undertaking of staggering proportions. "Here you are," President Theodore Roosevelt had said, in effect. "We are about to lose all our forests to our enemies, Fire and Greed. See what you can do to protect them for the present and perhaps for all posterity and also perhaps for nothing. There are and probably always will be, insufficient funds. To find out what we have and where it is and protect it as you go along, well, Giff, here they are," and he presented Gifford Pinchot with all the forest lands in the United States that still belonged to us.

During those lean years, foresters had to be resourceful. Adequate fire towers were too expensive. So three or four tall trees would be lashed together at the top, a platform installed, and a ladder of crosspieces nailed on. During the fire season, a man climbed to the top and kept watch during certain hours of the day. If there was smoke, he located it as best he could, climbed down, rode on horseback to the nearest telephone, and reported it to headquarters. P. S. desperately wanted a telephone wire to connect these towers directly to headquarters.

One day, while riding over the Crow Creek Military Reservation on an inspection trip, P. S. discovered the army breaking camp for the season. He observed that many miles of rolled telephone wire seemed to be abandoned on the outskirts of the camp. He asked the captain if he might have it to use on national forest lands. The captain seemed agreeable but asked him to wait until they were gone before taking the wire. Later P. S. and a ranger arrived to pick up the wire. It was still there, miles of it, but every bit had been cut into two-foot lengths.

P. S. suffered a stroke in 1931. To bring back the use of his hand and arm after paralysis and brain surgery, he carved duck decoys with a wood file all winter of 1931 and the spring of 1932. He made 48 decoys in great detail representing several species. He was almost totally preoccupied with his Pigeon River project during the early 1930s.

Aldo Leopold wrote P. S. Lovejoy's obituary for the *Journal of Wildlife Management*. Leopold, whose *Sand County Almanac* was compiled after his own death five years later, knew P. S. from their Forest Service days. Here is some of what Leopold wrote.

The parentage of ideas about egg-openers, iceboxes, and cigarette-lighters is recorded in the United States Patent Office. . . . The parentage of ideas about men and land is seldom recorded at all. By the time they appear in books they are usually step-children whose parentage has been forgotten.

I believe that P. S. Lovejoy sired more ideas about men and land than any contemporary in the conservation field. I here attempt to sketch some recent and unpublished chips from the Lovejoy block. Only a fraction of his output ever reached print. Much of it is recorded only in letters, and these are couched in a vernacular peculiar to him. In my office, and I fancy in many others, the arrival of a letter in Lovejoyeese was always heralded by titters from the mail room. My file of Lovejoyiana shows that his vernacular grew in extravagance and in wit as its contents deepened with advancing age. Why did he, a master of the Queen's English, insist on expressing even the most profound ideas in this jargon? It represents, I think, reaction against pretense, and a contempt for all pious solemnities.

No greater error could be made than to regard the Lovejoy vernacular as mere slang; it often carried figures of speech of poetical beauty. Two years ago, after he had recovered from an almost fatal illness, I remarked in reply to a brilliant satirical letter, that I was glad he had resumed his mental probings into the nature of things. He replied: "I've been living on borrowed time. It's fun now to work up wedge-stuff, and find season-checks to set 'em in, and keep splitting more and more slabs of savvy off the bug chunk." Slang, yes, but also a profound and dramatic definition of scholarship, rendered in the mental imagery of the lumberjack.

I once upbraided "P. S." for not publishing more papers. I told him he was like a squirrel who buried his mental garnerings in letters, instead of planting them in print where they could grow in many minds. He replied: "I've been watching those squirrels. They don't even try to remember where they put acorns. They just cache them all over the neighborhood, and then go and smell 'em up again, as wanted. The squirrel that plants an acorn is not always the one to smell it up. Meanwhile quite a lot of them have sprouted and grown into trees. Caching things in print is not always the best way to get things *growing*." In this homely parable is compressed his own picture of his service to society.

Lovejoy's early writings dealt with physical resource problems, and with land policy. The deflation of the lake states land boom, the recognition of forestry by the agricultural profession, and the realization that forest lands as well as farm lands may be submarginal are in no small degree

Lovejoy's personal handiwork. He also contributed largely to the recognition of wildlife as a land crop, and to the initiation of wildlife research.

In his later years, his thinking focused not on policy, but on people. He saw that the average citizen had given nothing but lip-service to either forestry or wildlife management, and he wanted to know why. Unlike most publicly employed conservationists, he did not mistake the growth of appropriations and the proliferation of bureaus for the accomplishment of the ends for which they were created. He became engrossed in analyzing the reasons for the failure of "conservation education."

His findings are expressed in "Ecological Engineering." I consider this one of the most important papers on conservation published during the current decade, but like other Lovejoy "acorns," it was cached at random in an obscure spot.

Conservation, Lovejoy says, is reason applied to environment. Reason, to the mass mind, is like oxygen to the animal body: a little is essential, but too much is toxic, and induces pain followed by defensive reactions. Tolerance for reason may be increased by education, but only by slow degrees. Agricultural extension has developed techniques which recognize the limits of public tolerance; it administers small doses of "science" heavily diluted with economic and social persuasion. Conservation must do the same.

Lovejoy's distinction between educator and extensionist is elaborated in a recent letter (3/8/39):

"The standard campus illusion is the *Homo* can and should be educated so that he will not much, if any, (or anyway not in public) behave like a mammal. All the while everybody knows he will.

"Skillful advertisers, politicians, and evangelists know in advance that most of the time people will react to stimuli and inhibitions which have little or nothing to do with the campus formula.

"The extensioner splits the difference. He does not expect his customers to be much or often rational. He uses fact-logic only when it seems to work. When it doesn't work, he contrives bait and drift-fences and banana-peel arrangements which do. His job is to bridge the gap between the latest Experiment Station dope and the specific action-program. When the educator has done his stuff, the customer is due to be intelligent, but the extensioner is content if he thereafter acts as if he were."

I add from "Ecological Engineering":

"It is an almost universal assumption that there is something pathological in politicians. This, assuredly, is a misconception. The politician has always been associated with civilization, and has a function corresponding to that of leucocytes in the blood. The splitting of differences of interest among the governed is a perennial job. Our ecological engineer may be glad to have someone tending the minor chores while he himself is computing another social modulus, or triangulating to place another banana-peel where it will do the most good. Our engineer will bear in mind that *Homo sapiens* is still considerably sap. The normal function of the politician is to take the public where he thinks it wants to go; the function of our engineer is to take the public where it will be glad to be when it gets there.

"Testing his materials in advance of construction, a proper engineer will discover that a very small quantity of clay impairs the strength of his concrete. He will therefore proceed to wash his gravel. He will not merely curse the clay. So, our ecological engineer will recognize the ubiquity of *Homo's* rationalizations, and that these are protective devices used to dilute facts to non-toxic concentrations."

. . . For those unfamiliar with Lovejoyeese, I present a few selected idioms and a few characteristic quotations:

pack-ratting: collecting reprints "in the standard campus manner"

terra-tinker: a land-use expert

barber shop biologist: a sportsman

mirabile dictuing: telling tall tales

rat-hole project: an ill-conceived official undertaking

sacred sawloggers: forestry propagandists

Novos, Demos, and Buros: researchers, politicians, and bureaucrats; novos nest in litters of old papers, from which, at irregular intervals, they hatch out monographic young

words with high muzzle-velocity: good writing

clubs: "There are three kinds of clubs. One kind peels all its birches, another only a few, another puts white paint on the scars of the old peelings."

research: "Hire a dozen techs. Turn 'em loose and they'll smell out, trail, and flush facts, fetch 'em home, and lay 'em on the hearth all-same cat and fieldmouse. When they lay another separate on the Altar of Research, they have done their stuff. It's up to somebody else to carry on from there."

appetite: "As a kid I often ate all the apples I could, but never as many as I wanted to."

. . . In conclusion, I venture the personal opinion that the professions of forestry and wildlife management, as now constituted, will one day be adjudged to have been deficient in critics. If I am right in this, then P.S. Lovejoy, as one of our best critics, will grow in stature with the years.

In any case, he did his valiant best to find new wedges, and season-checks to set them in, and to split new slabs of savvy off the bug chunk.— Aldo Leopold, Madison, Wis.

Pigeon River Country headquarters was often the scene of meetings of a group of Conservation Commission members such as Lovejoy, Harold ("Opie") Titus, and K. C. McMurray (a professor of geography at UM). These were men who helped establish Michigan's second-growth forests and manage wildlife and recreation. They called themselves the Northern Michigan Academy of Science and Letters. They met one week each spring and fall. Occasionally someone would fish or take a walk with a gun, but for the most part they would reminisce and talk about the future. K. C. McMurray would plan meals and cook. People would sleep only when they felt the need. They would generally grow beards and dress in old, wrinkled clothes. After each trip, they would return to their professions refreshed and stimulated. The group continued to meet long after P. S. died.

The director of the Michigan Department of Conservation, P. S. Hoffmaster, wrote in a footnote to the obituary by Aldo Leopold that Parish Storrs Lovejoy "was born at Princeton, Illinois, January 23, 1884 and died at Ann Arbor, Michigan, January 20, 1942. . . . On June 7, 1942 a bronze tablet commemorating his services to conservation was dedicated on Pigeon River State Forest, one of his favorite areas, and a monument in itself to his labors."

Speaking on behalf of the forest to senior officials from Lansing, Dave Smethurst suggested in 2000 that "when anything coming down the road doesn't match P. S. Lovejoy's dreams and words and vision [of a Big Wild], even if it makes sense under present day conditions, if it doesn't pass through the P. S. Lovejoy filter, we don't do it. That is the only way those values can be protected for the long term."

Jim McMillan, the DNR's Northern Lower Peninsula forest supervisor, replied that the Pigeon River Country "is the most inefficient unit in the state" because pressures and challenges are purposely being left by Lansing to be sorted out through the established, unstreamlined ways, including a separate manager and the advisory council. And George Burgoyne,

DNR Resource Management deputy director, added that what P. S. Lovejoy said can be used as a guide, but "isn't an absolute easy filter. If it were, every council vote would be eighteen to zero. . . . Each of us interprets the vision a little bit differently."

Lovejoy once noted that "if an invader's troops attempted to occupy and devastate say fifty million acres of our more fertile lands, we should be vastly excited. But some such acreage has recently been eroded into virtual barrens, we are assured, and we are yet hardly aware of it, or much concerned." He paraphrased the secretary of the interior in 1935 as saying, "A nation which has complacently chewed its gum while its forests were being devastated, is not easily diverted from the current divorce of a . . . movie queen."

P. S. concluded, "If there is any occasion to attempt the deliberate and sustained engineering of human affairs, surely the place to start will be . . . physical habitat." And so began a sustained human effort to deal with forest fires, water pollution, and the uncontrolled taking of whatever is above, on, or below the surface of the earth that someone felt could be turned to profit.

The year 1918 is remembered locally as a time when men began standing in the fields around Vanderbilt planting trees. They built fire lanes through the brush, stumps, and charred slash so that people could get to and contain the kind of fires that only seven years earlier had burned through the whole area, nearly wiping out the small game and deer. To people at the scene, the forest in 1918 looked dead, and they began to bring it back to life with seedlings spaced evenly in straight rows along the charred ground. Most of the Pigeon River Country has a more haphazard look, that casual balance of species finding their own appropriate conditions for regeneration. Ironically, even in those times of "ecological engineering," the forest recovered mostly by being left alone.

Some 15,000 acres were planted in Pigeon River Country, not all of them successfully. Beginning in 1920, horses and mules pulled plows to make furrows in which two-year-old red, white, and jack pine seedlings from a nursery at Higgins Lake were planted by hand. The Pigeon River area had been an official Michigan forest for one year.

6

State Forest

GERALD F. MYERS

Jerry Myers joined the Michigan Department of Conservation in 1940, renamed the Department of Natural Resources in 1968. Jerry worked at state fish hatcheries in Harrisville and Bay City. After military service in 1942–45, he worked with the Institute for Fisheries Research in Ann Arbor, then moved in 1949 to the Pigeon River Trout Research Station. He lived at headquarters until his retirement in 1975, then managed a private lodge in Crawford County for five years.

Michigan established its first state forest in 1903. It had thousands of acres of cutover, burned-over stump lands in the north it didn't know what to do with. So it set aside 34,000 acres in the vicinity of Houghton and Higgins lakes and called them a state "forest"—lands that more closely resembled a blackened, barren desert. That was the beginning of the Houghton Lake and Higgins Lake State Forests and likewise the beginning of the state forest system. Other forests were organized in this order: 1913, Fife Lake and Lake Superior; 1914, Ogemaw; 1915, Presque Isle; 1916, Alpena; 1919, Pigeon River; 1925, Hardwood; 1927, Black Lake; 1928, Mackinac and Au Sable; 1940, Allegan.

Between 1930 and 1940, most state forest land was acquired through tax abandonment. Pigeon River State Forest by 1940 reached 89,624 acres covering parts of several counties, including Otsego, Charlevoix, Cheboygan, Presque Isle, and Montmorency. State lands in northern lower Michigan were leased in 1968 for hydrocarbon exploration and development. The Michigan DNR, in an effort to protect the unique central area, reduced the boundary in 1973. The boundaries grew to 93,000 acres with the addition of the Green Timbers property in 1982 [and to 105,048 acres with the addition of the Blue Lakes Ranch in 1990, as well as other parcels, all purchased with revenues from oil and gas development].

The first headquarters was built in 1919 one mile downstream from the present headquarters, where a clearing now exists near the south end of Osmun Road. The house and building were frame, farmhouse-style, the standard type used at several state forest headquarters. The house was two stories with a dormer on the roof. Four bedrooms and a bath upstairs, wood cookstove, with running water from the creek—as long as there was plenty of water in the creek. Sometimes it went dry in the summer. There was a barn, garage, bunkhouse, a team of horses (no tractors), and a hay field across from the present headquarters. The hay field is now grown up into brush.

The five log buildings [on a site a mile upstream in the early 1980s] were constructed by laborers from the Civilian Conservation Corps (CCC) during the early 1930s. There were two CCC camps, one at the corner of Clark Bridge Road and Osmun Road and the other at Pickerel Lake.

The Civilian Conservation Corps was a Depression era program created to employ World War I veterans and young men from cities, villages, and farms. It was run like a military camp. The CCC began in Michigan at Higgins Lake on May 22, 1933. By its end in early October 1941, more than 500 bridges were built in the state, 221 buildings erected, 33 airplane landing strips constructed, 5,600 miles of road laid, some 140,000 man-days spent fighting fires, and 134,000 acres of trees planted in Michigan. The only evidence of where they stayed in Pigeon River Country is a band of sidewalks in the field approaching Inspiration Point on the west side of Osmun Road in the northern forest.

This new headquarters [along the Pigeon] was built to house the state's first conservation school, which was moved in the 1940s to Higgins Lake. The buildings were constructed from large pine logs salvaged from a fire in Crawford County. Foundations are concrete, 18 inches thick. Stonework above ground level was cut by CCC labor. Log construction was supervised by an experienced log cabin builder. He trained several five-man CCC crews who would lay up a log, scribe the lower edge to the log below, take it down and hand hew the edge to fit the lower log. Oakum (creosote hemp fiber) was used in joints and a mortar mix on the outside of log joints. Window frames were prepared and glass cut for each pane. Several windows were laid out on a bench before the glazing expert would complete the window. Those who remember say he drank coffee and spent quite some time preparing the glazing putty. Mixing linseed oil with his hands until it reached the right texture, he then would complete a six-pane window in minutes, doing each pane with one motion around the glass.

CCC members working in the Pigeon were mostly World War I veterans experienced in many trades. The home was constructed for a family and all modern. There are five bedrooms, one and a half baths, an office, large kitchen, dining room, and living room with fireplace built with cut fieldstone. There is a basement with laundry room, food and canning storage. The large hot air furnace was for wood burning, and a person could crawl inside to replace the firebrick. The fire pot would hold a log 30 inches long.

The staff building (educational unit) contains twenty bunks, a living-dining-meeting room combination, and a kitchen.

The center building, once a garage and then the office, is also the central water supply and central electric. It has an icehouse on one end. The water system was built with a 1,000 gallon tank underground with two-inch copper lines to other buildings. The original electric system, 32 volts from 16 glass batteries of two volts each, was powered by a single-cylinder generator primed with gasoline and run on kerosene.

The fourth building was a bunkhouse, since modified into a house.

The fifth building was a barn. Travel to Vanderbilt, the nearest town, 14 miles away, was impossible at times during the winter, so the forester kept a cow for fresh milk, chickens, pigs, and horses at the barn. Some of the openings along the river valley were fenced for pasture and hay. The barn is now used for fire and snow removal equipment and campground supplies.

On January 8, 1985, wildlife biologist Doug Whitcomb sat in the headquarters office compiling elk count figures when he and others smelled excessive heat. They phoned the Vanderbilt fire department and shut off the furnace power switch, then noticed a glow over the furnace. Fire investigators say wires in the ceiling ignited the insulation. While firefighters pumped water onto the fire, field workers moved file cabinets and papers, thus saving most of the files. The blaze heavily damaged the interior and roof. The office was relocated in the small residence. The headquarters foundation was saved, and the DNR decided to rebuild, using the original design.

When P. S. Lovejoy fought forest fires on foot and horseback in the West, he was incensed with the devastation he encountered. Later he encouraged legislation in Michigan for money to prevent and fight fires. The CCC program came at an appropriate time to build fire lanes in this remote area, construct fire towers and cabins for fire tower operators. The headquarters buildings were constructed and quarter-mile fire lanes laid out north, south, east and west for a two-mile radius. The entrances of some of these fire trails were blocked with logs to prevent unnecessary vehicle travel and reduce fire danger. Today, with modern firefighting equipment on land and in the air, towers are no longer used. Modern equipment can penetrate forests without fire trails. Old fire and logging trails create problems today, with many more people now using the forest for recreation by traveling in various types of motorized vehicles.

One fire tower about 100 feet tall was lowered to 55 feet and converted into an observation tower in 1977. It was closed for safety reasons in 1999. With no budget for an estimated $35,000 to $50,000 modification, the tower was taken out of the forest in 2000.

There are records of UM fisheries studies in Pigeon River Country dating back to 1929. Studies of both the Pigeon River and sinkhole lakes occurred each year. CCC crews mapped these lakes and constructed stream improvements. Some of their triangular submerged log rafts can still be found today. High eroded banks along the river were "riprapped," that is, vertical stakes held horizontal logs in place while the eroded area was filled in and planted. Several bridges were constructed from logs, which have long since been replaced by galvanized culverts and fill gravel.

Crews mapping the lakes measured surface areas and depth contours and obtained bottom samples of soil. Lake and stream research systems were developed at UM and a new Department of Fisheries was founded. In 1930, it became the Institute for Fisheries Research, which continues to be one of the best freshwater research units in the nation. The institute is on the UM campus in Ann Arbor and is part of the Michigan DNR.

There was a tremendous demand for college-trained limnologists in the next decade, and along with Michigan State University the University of Michigan trained many of the experts and teachers to fill this need around the nation. The first signatures on record for the education program at Pigeon headquarters date from April 12, 1937, when land use planners met there. P. S. Lovejoy is number five on the list. The county agriculture agents began a series of three-day conferences that continued annually for more than 40 years.

Most of the summer months were filled with conservation officer training and occasionally a small UM professors' group. In winter, hatchery superintendents, park superintendents, game area managers, and geologists each held one-week classes. Other groups that met at the headquarters in 1938 included members of Central Michigan Teachers College, Soil Conservation Service, ladies clubs, Western State teachers, Saginaw Teachers Club, Department of Public Instruction, vocational education coordinators, 4–H clubs, National Education Conference, National Resource Council, and the Conservation Commission. After World War II, use changed. Headquarters was used for trout studies after April 1949 under the Institute for Fisheries Research, while other meetings began to be scheduled at the new Higgins Lake Training School.

Biologists and professors from UM and MSU conducted fisheries and wildlife studies in Pigeon River Country, using the buildings for labs and living quarters. Occasional meetings and student projects in wildlife, recreation, and forestry continue today.

Over the years, forest management plans have changed to meet changing needs. Aspens, the fastest-growing trees, and jack pines, which mature enough to be cut in about 60 years, are used to make both pulp in paper mills and particleboard [glued wood chipboard] for [inexpensive furniture and] building construction. A few large [aspen and jack pine] trees are used for sawlogs (lumber). Where stands of [red and white pine] grow thick, they are periodically thinned to release the other trees for faster growth. They are also used for particleboard and paper pulp. Older stands of red pine are now thinned out of thick stands and used for utility poles. Some large pines are cut for lumber [and cabin logs].

Red pines as small as five inches in diameter are used for two-by-fours and landscape timbers.

Until [half a] century ago, 50 percent of mature trees were not cut and only the choice large-volume areas attracted commercial loggers. Most of the sales were for pulp. The major national forest product companies began to expand, and U.S. Plywood chose Gaylord for a new plant. This was constructed [in 1965] to produce a new product known as particleboard or chipboard, an industry that provided revenue in northern Michigan through a new technique of clear-cutting in the Pigeon River State Forest and elsewhere [by feeding] clumps of trees of all sizes up to 18 inches in diameter [into a] chipper. Semi trailers [carried] 35 tons or more to the processing plants to be glued into flat boards four by eight feet. Clear-cutting not only increases the yield for forest products but allows for new growth to increase and maintain wildlife habitat. Deer, elk, grouse, woodcock, and rabbits are important to the sportsmen whose fees paid for some of the land. Energy shortages and costs increased the demand for firewood over 100 times between 1975 and 1980 [though later it declined dramatically].

Hardwoods are also used to manufacture chipboard and cardboard boxes, but their greatest value is as grade lumber for flooring, cabinets, paneling, and furniture.

Georgia-Pacific, Inc., bought the particleboard plant in 1987 and closed it in 2006, citing the high cost of raw materials and energy compared with plants in Georgia, South Carolina, and Mississippi in a fiberboard market in which there is more supply than demand. The company's other four U.S. plants were using sawmill by-products, while the Gaylord plant used whole-tree chips, described as a more costly process. The company paid a $139,147 settlement to the state of Michigan in 2004 and improved its furnace *stack to reduce "excessive opacity" in an agreement with the Air Quality Division of the Department of Environmental Quality (DEQ) two years after Scorecard, a pollution information site, rated the Gaylord facility as among the "dirtiest/worst facilities in the U.S." for releasing more than 300,000 pounds of contaminants into the air per year between 1998 and 2002.*

The Pigeon River forester administers a plan that calls for [about 10,000] acres in a number of compartments to be inventoried each year. The compartments for each year comprise about one-tenth of the total forest area. A "prescription" is made up for each stand area and needed "treatment" follows. For example, a good stand of 25 acres of aspen is marked with paint around the boundary, the amount of cordwood and sawlogs determined, and the stand put up for bids.

The forester and his technicians determine the areas to be commercially cut, set the amount of wood, cords, and board feet for each land description, and sell the timber on bids. The forester works with wildlife biologists in determining treatments for wildlife management within these compartments. This includes maintaining openings and converting low-volume [poor lumber quality] hardwoods into aspen growth. Aspen regrowth is fast, as the tree sends hundreds of shoots from its root system. Sunlight is important to this growth.

The forester is also responsible for policing illegal timber removal, boundary surveys, land exchange requests, and recreational maintenance and planning. [In 2006, the Pigeon River Country and Michigan's five other state forests received national certification from both the Forest Stewardship Council and the Sustainable Forestry Initiative. After intense auditing, the Pigeon and other forests were found to be managed in responsible and sustainable ways. Many companies require that wood and paper products be from certified forests, including Home Depot, Lowe's, Nike, Johnson & Johnson, and the 3M Corporation.]

The Pigeon River Country [Management Unit] has an abundance of all types of timber cover and fresh water that attracts people for recreation in all four seasons. There is camping in the forest every month of the year. Hiking trails are marked. In spring, hundreds of mushroom pickers arrive from several states to hunt for morels. This is the time for spring flowers and freshly flowering trees in May. May also attracts trout fishermen on the many miles of the Black, Pigeon, and Sturgeon rivers. There are many openings and valleys filled with blossoms of the shadbush (serviceberry or juneberry), thorn apple (hawthorn), and wild cherries. The shadbush blossoms even before it leafs out.

Summer brings campers, hikers, and horseback riders. Wild berry picking starts with strawberries in June, followed by blueberries, raspberries, and blackberries. Blueberries are found in jack pine areas, and in some years the crop runs from early July into September, but generally late spring frosts kill the early blossoms. Raspberries and blackberries are abundant in some years, depending on moisture and frosts, and are harvested in August and early September. These are found in openings and slashings of hardwood areas. Cherries ripen in September. A good crop comes only about every five or six years, controlled by frosts. Chokecherries make good wine, as do pin cherries and black cherries. Pin cherries are small and taste much like cultivated sour cherries. Black cherries taste good eaten from the tree and make excellent jelly. Both grow on mature trees and chokecherries on shrub bushes.

Although fall is hunting season, the color attracts many in vehicles, on foot, or on horseback. There is a continuous change of color from the first red maple in early September to the last, bright yellow of the tamaracks before they drop their needles in late October. This is also elk mating season. White and red oaks are found scattered in the hardwoods; the eastern part of the Pigeon has many oaks, offering still another variation in beautiful colors of bronze, reddish browns, and deep brown mixed with evergreens. This is a paradise for the photographer. The colors seem to change daily.

We enter early winter with deer season in November, followed by the December rabbit and deer archery seasons. By late December cross-country skiing has begun and is enjoyed throughout the remaining snow season. A few enjoy winter camping and snowshoeing. This is another paradise for winter photography.

The Witness Tree and the P. S. Lovejoy monument are marked historical sites. Michigan was originally surveyed from about 1815 through the 1850s. Surveyors established a section corner each mile with a stake and used trees, rocks, and other landmarks as "witness" points, described in their field notes.

Perhaps the most famous witness tree in Michigan is a red pine marked June 17, 1850, during the original land survey of northern lower Michigan. The tree's diameter was eight inches at the time. The surveyor was William Burt, for [whose father] Burt Lake was named. Located in the middle of an open trail road, this tree marks the quarter section corner between sections 15 and 16, Corwith Township, Otsego County, Michigan. Each year hundreds of visitors stop to read the inscription marking the tree. A small parking area is provided.

Until 1975, the Witness Tree sat in the middle of a trail that was designated an Otsego County road. The trail split several feet around the tree. One winter morning that year Edward ("Ned") Caveney Jr., the new Pigeon River resident forester, discovered that county plows had cut some of the Witness Tree's roots. After a public hearing in which the few other people who attended all opposed the idea, he was able to convince the county to abandon the road. Only a portion remains in use, as access to the parking area.

Some motorists wanting access to blocked trails simply breach them and drive where they are not allowed. This has been an ongoing problem in the forest. Even the Cheboygan County Road Commission removed gates and berms in 1992, resulting in a court case, which ultimately confirmed, in 1997, the state's authority to close forest roads. For a few years in the mid-1990s, breached berms could not be replaced because there was no working dozer equipment and no budget for the work. In 2002, Joe Jarecki, who succeeded Caveney in 1990, and area biologist Brian Mastenbrook found $7,000 in outside grants to replace or reinstall about seventy-five vehicle barriers and put up some polymer signs that don't break when somebody drives over them. Jarecki explained that conservation officer citations will hold up in court when a sign remains as proof that the violator was notified the road was closed.

World War I veterans working in the forest were not the last CCC workers in the Pigeon River Country. In 1986, the state opened a pioneering Michigan Civilian Conservation Corps facility called Camp Vanderbilt. The half-dozen portable buildings were on the north side of Sturgeon Valley Road a few hundred yards east of Pickerel Lake Road. Young people staying there built 10,000 bluebird and kestrel houses, plus little residential enclosures for ducks and bats, installed throughout Michigan. They cleared trails and repaired picnic tables. Under instruction from a construction company and using a Scandinavian technique, they peeled red pine logs from within half a mile of headquarters, notched them, and in 1988–90 erected a headquarters building to replace the one that burned in 1985. They built an addition to the DNR district headquarters in Gaylord. They won a national award for erosion control on the Jordan River west of Pigeon River Country, hauling boulders and placing them along banks in a project that took several summers.

Some of those young Jordan River crew members later brought friends to show off their work. Arnold Morse, education director at the camp, said, "For most of them it was the first thing they ever felt they had accomplished. Now they are holding down jobs, paying taxes and mortgages. They recognize that those rocks were a turning point in their lives." The eighteen- to twenty-five-year-old men and women at Camp Vanderbilt came from families on welfare. Some 90 percent of them left welfare, getting jobs and paying taxes. The results were similar in camps throughout, with an estimated 70 percent of the young people joining the workforce. The new governor, John Engler, canceled the program suddenly in 1991.

Joyce Angel-Ling arrived fresh from Michigan State University's forestry school at the DNR offices in Gaylord in November 1985 and was almost immediately named the assistant director of Camp Vanderbilt. She began by procuring the modular buildings that came on site in the summer of 1986. Forester Scott Gasperin, the first camp director, spent much of his time recruiting across the state, offering the minimum wage plus bed and board. "I had to use people skills I wasn't aware I had," Angel-Ling says. She trained people entering the one-year program in communications skills and acted as a coach and job counselor.

She was struck by how resilient the students were despite their dysfunctional backgrounds. "They wanted to do the right thing, often talked to us, usually after hearing from home—good or bad or decisions about class or about telling on a coworker who didn't do their share. There was peer pressure in that setting—I often wondered about dynamics. It seems one negative person could bring down the group pretty quick. It was always a battle to keep things moving up and forward. You kept anyone idling for too long and things went downhill. Groups sometimes were highly positive, especially when Kim and Arnie arrived. There were individuals where you could see the light go on. They would want to work hard to get what they wanted. I don't think anyone ever told them they had a say in their own destiny. We told them you very much have a choice. They were usually around twenty years old. I call them kids, although I wasn't much older myself. Some left on a negative note, dismissed. But there was still a positive effect. Some called later and said it was a changing point in their life. Even though they were fired, they appreciated their time, they had some control, and didn't realize it until later."

Kim Lentz, a forester, estimates that about half the members stuck with the program despite its strict prohibitions against alcohol, drugs, violence, and swearing. Others couldn't meet the criteria, particularly the ban on alcohol. She remembers Bruce Marshall's ropes course, especially the flying squirrel. You jump off a four-foot by four-foot basswood platform about twenty-five feet up, harnessed with ropes controlled by other corps members on the ground. "You have to trust." One member grew so confident that she announced she was going to become a successful model, a businessperson. "She did all that," Lentz says, "broke her pattern of bad guys. At least five [former corps members who] I know were successful I see sometimes." The young single mom on assistance flew through the air in the Pigeon, came down, became a professional traveling model, married happily, and has a successful family business.

"When the governor canned the program," Lentz says, "we were given two weeks notice. We had to find places for people to live, write letters of recommendation, close the facility. It was a nightmare." Most of her work was administrative. Only occasionally was there an opportunity to impart forestry knowledge, showing the students the types of trees when they were building trails. In the Jordan Valley, they were told all about wetlands and why we should protect them. The outdoors was a new experience for a lot of them. "Some were never in the woods before. Some of the kids were from the city; all they knew were street smarts. They never interfaced in the natural world. We opened their eyes to team building, self-confidence, surviving, getting down a trail carrying a pack. Experience they never forgot. It was very disheartening when the program closed."

It was a time of cutting budgets, without consideration for whether that would cost more to society in the long run. A different program, opened under Michigan's parks department, continued to operate for a few more years at Camp Vanderbilt. When the camp was dismantled, most of it was pulled away on its wheels, like double-wide modulars. Only a pole barn and woodshop were stick built and had to be taken down.

One American Indian went on to Lake Superior State University after she left the camp. Arnie Morse helped her obtain financial aid as the first college student in the family. Another became a Charter Communications supervisor after arriving at camp just out of high school from Cheboygan, where the huge paper mill had just closed. He told Morse he cried a good share of his first night at camp.

Morse got members into the evening high school diploma program in Vanderbilt, which had a bigger budget than it had local enrollees in the General Education Development program and was glad to help. "I thought we were going to have to teach these people how to work," Morse says. "That wasn't it. They worked like dogs. What they didn't know was all the other things. Some of them we had to teach to take a shower. My conception going in was completely wrong. They were like sponges. They were needy for people who cared about them, helped them, imparted things to them. When I went to work, three or four would be waiting to talk to you about a range of things, as if you're their parent. It was an interesting thing for all of us to do, the kids and us."

The DNR moved the Pigeon's forester out of the residence behind headquarters in 2004 in what it described as a cost-cutting measure. Joe Jarecki and his wife built their own house just outside the forest boundary. The log residence sat empty. Joe retired in 2007. Laurie Marzolo, Atlanta unit manager, was told to manage the Pigeon River Country as well, nearly doubling her area of responsibility, with no end for that arrangement in sight. She began driving over from Atlanta one or two days a week.

Some people go to extraordinary lengths on behalf of the forest. Ken Mudget is one. Over more than a decade, he rallied other volunteers to build nesting platforms for loons, osprey, and other waterfowl; conduct experimental shrub plantings under the forester's guidance; keep the headquarters open on weekends with voluntary greeters from the Pigeon River Country Association and Retired Senior Volunteer Program; build a headquarters display case; build and put up 130 birdhouses in the spring of 1991 with help from students; clean up eleven fishing sites in a single season and more later. He and his Elkland Seniors Conservation Club paid to process donated deer and elk meat for needy people. The seniors continued picking up trash in the forest, set out more birdhouses, and converted an underground storage vault at Green Timbers into a bat cave with guidance from a habitat biologist.

The seniors and Vanderbilt schools started a nursery for chestnut trees. After planting more than 3,000 fruit and nut trees for wildlife habitat with local middle school pupils, Mudget observed, "We've got 80-year-old seniors with these 12-year-old kids. . . . When we're out in that environment, we're on common ground. It isn't just a matter of planting trees. We do our best to teach these kids how they can conserve and protect our natural resources."

7
Oil

When European explorers and settlers came to North America, the animal they called the elk was the most widely distributed of the deer, ranging across what is now the United States from the Pacific almost to the Atlantic. East of the Mississippi, they lived in Georgia, Illinois, Indiana, Kentucky, Louisiana, Michigan, New York, North Carolina, Ohio, Pennsylvania, South Carolina, Tennessee, Virginia, West Virginia, Wisconsin, and possibly other states. Highly adaptable, American elk can browse or graze; eat a variety of grasses, greens, buds, branches, and needles; paw their way through more than 30 inches of snow to the food beneath; and stand unaffected by severe winter storms. Yet they disappeared from all the states east of the Mississippi, and many to the west, victims of shrinking habitat and the pressure of civilization. The mammal of the genus *Cervus* (or true deer) and species *canadensis* (of Canada) was called elk by American pioneers, although the name was already used for a European animal that resembles what Americans call a moose. The term *elk* has persisted even though the Shawnee Indian name, *wapiti,* is also used. The subspecies *Cervus canadensis canadensis,* or eastern elk, is extinct, disappearing in the early days of settlement. *Cervus canadensis nelsoni,* or Rocky Mountain elk, was introduced in Michigan in the twentieth century near the Pigeon River.

A pile of papers arrived from Michigan's Department of Natural Resources in Lansing. The regional DNR office in Roscommon was already pretty busy. After some days, Lansing called. Review the applications right away and send them back, it said.

The applicants wanted to lease oil and gas rights on more than half a million acres of state land, the largest acreage ever offered for lease in one sale. It was 1968. Leasing had been routine since the 1920s. Roscommon staffers spotted a few state parks in the stack, marked them as unsuitable, and sent the material back to Lansing eight days after receiving it. Apparently no one noticed that among the lands leased to the oil and gas companies was 90 percent of the Pigeon River Country State Forest.

The foresters and biologists who managed the Pigeon River Country weren't consulted or informed. They found out about it after oil was discovered on private land near the forest and leaseholders began to apply to the DNR for permits to drill.

Ford Kellum was driving up the Osmun Trail in Pigeon River Country in May 1969 when just beyond a grassy area he saw an oil rig in the middle of a newly cleared acre of woods. He was the district wildlife biologist, whose territory included all of the northern Lower Peninsula from Traverse City to Alpena and north to the Straits of Mackinac. It was the first he knew of oil development in the Pigeon River Country.

Jerry Myers, a fisheries research technician who lived with his family at the headquarters complex in the heart of the forest, began to observe upward of 40 trucks a day coming out from Vanderbilt to conduct massive seismic operations. As many as a dozen trucks would gather in one place in what looked like a huge water-drilling mission that made a tremendous noise and shook the ground for miles around. The operators were attempting to locate deep pools of oil or gas by recording on a chart the echo of explosions. Campers complained of the noise, truck traffic, and removal of water from campground swimming sites for drilling.

Ford Kellum and Jerry Myers were both members of the Pigeon River Audubon Club. Ford and an exchange student from Holland, Abraham Vrugdenhil, had organized the club a year before. Their first program for 39 members was about birds in Greece. But the club soon plunged into a controversy that was to gain worldwide attention.

The oil companies were requesting permits from the DNR to drill on the lands where they had leased mineral rights. Kellum met with the director of the department, Ralph MacMullan, at Higgins Lake and told him and Jerry Eddy, who was chief of the geology division, that he didn't think it was fair for them to issue permits without the knowledge of the people who manage the land when the decision affected the land.

"They said, 'From now on we'll get your approval first,'" Ford recalled. "Well we—game, fish, and forestry—approved a lot of them where it didn't do any harm to the environment. But when it came to the Pigeon River Country I said 'No,' long and loud. Because that was an area that was unique. Not virgin but unique, and I didn't want them to drill in there."

As word spread about what was happening, it became clear that drilling even in the most remote parts of the north woods did not appeal to many others either. Even the local newspaper, the *Gaylord Herald Times,* which later supported what became known as controlled drilling, editorialized against the threat oil posed to tourism.

In February 1970, the Pigeon River Audubon Club took the first step outside the Department of Natural Resources to stop drilling with a resolution "not to allow any oil or gas drilling" on the state recreational lands northeast of Gaylord. The club expressed the hope that neighboring landowners would look on such drilling with disfavor. Members began mailing the document around the state, and resolutions of support arrived not only from nearby clubs like the Thunder Bay and Petoskey chapters, but from places like Jackson in southern Michigan.

In March, a gas well being drilled in Chester Township, several miles south of the present forest boundary, ignited and burned out of control for 12 days. The saltwater, barite, bentonite, and starch solution forced into the well to smother the fire exhausted the available drilling mud supplies in several midwestern states. Additional mud was trucked in from Oklahoma.

Two months later, the question of whether drilling could be stopped because of environmental damage came to a head. The first incident was a proposed well site near the Dog Lake Flooding in the far northern forest along the Pigeon River watershed in Cheboygan County. Field men were told they had no right to deny a drilling permit, even if they considered it a threat to natural resources or beauty.

The second incident was an oil company request to drill what became known as Charlton 1–4, meaning the first well in section 4 of Charlton Township in Otsego County. The site was next to the trackless wild of the Black River Swamp in the southern forest just off a tiny dirt road known as House's Lost Cabin Trail. The local game, fish, and forestry people went out with regional people and Warren Shapton, a deputy director from Lansing. The local people said no to this well proposal. Ford Kellum relates, "I told Shapton, 'We're turning it down.' He said, 'We're favoring it.'

"And I said, 'If you ok this and it happens to be successful, I'll retire and give you a fight because I don't think it's right.'"

On May 15, 1970, the department issued a permit for Charlton 1–4. A drilling crew began operations on May 27. As the drill bit descended into the earth, casing was placed around the sides of the hole. Down went the swirling bit through gravel, sand, and clay, through layers of sandstone, shales, limestones, dolomites, anhydrites, cherts, and salt. It was a journey back through time. It took the Colorado River 10 million years to cut a mile into the earth and create today's Grand Canyon; the drill bit at Charlton 1–4 took 33 days to go nearly that deep. It cut through the Wisconsin drift from the Pleistocene period, disturbing rock that had been in place for upward of one million years during the four glacial ages. It cut down to the original surface of the Michigan basin, some 345 million years old, the age when giant insects dominated the forests and the first reptiles appeared on earth.

The drill bit inched down, about one foot ahead of the newly placed casing, through mud that had eroded from the Appalachians and sunk in the sea that covered eastern America from Canada to North Carolina 350 to 400 million years ago. In those millions of years of the Devonian period, coral reefs grew and fragments broke off; in the waves of Lake Michigan many millions of years later, the fragments were polished into what are known today as Petoskey stones.

The drill bit descended into the Silurian deposits that accumulated some 425 million years ago when much of the east was inundated by a salty inland sea and volcanoes were active in New Brunswick and Maine. It was the period when primitive animals like scorpions and millipedes began to live on land. The Niagara Escarpment, a coral reef, formed during the Silurian period in warm, shallow, and clear waters along the edge of the Michigan basin. It slowly grew along the enormous shoreline from Wisconsin northeast to the Garden Peninsula (southwest of Manistique in the Upper Peninsula), into Ontario, and south to Niagara Falls, where the Niagara River drops over the escarpment. It was formed by lime-secreting organisms like algae and corals. Its main ingredient, limestone, hardened into dolomite, which is resistant to erosion. The Niagaran is exposed at the surface today as Drummond and Manitoulin islands on the north edge of Lake Huron. In some places, the Niagaran is more than 400 feet thick.

When the drill bit entered the 400-million-year-old Niagaran reef 4,671 feet below the drill pad next to the Black River Swamp, the drilling crew began to take samples with a device called a barrel. Lowering the barrel to the bottom of the hole, the crew would close the top and bottom and lift out a core sample, then examine it inch by inch. The first piece, seven feet long, was analyzed as dolomite, brown and fairly dense. Three samples later, at a depth of 4,686 feet, the crew found slight bleeding gas throughout the sample, a strong indication that they had something.

Unlike Hollywood movies, in which oil erupts from the earth and covers joyous men and women with dripping black liquid, the discovery of fossil fuel in the Pigeon River Country, as in other field operations, was a more subtle drama. Each subsequent core sample pointed to the presence of oil. Up came reef rock, described as vugular, meaning that it was laced with holes. The crew logged the presence of oil and gas odors, fluorescence, and sugary textured zones.

The core sample from 4,753 feet dropped on the floor and fell apart. The crew was unable to piece together the rotten, crumbly rock but recognized it as reef material bleeding oil and smelling of hydrocarbons. The next sample broke apart in the hole, and the crew recovered only a foot and a half of oil-bleeding, highly fragmented rock.

Such was the first oil discovery in the Pigeon River Country. Drilling continued to the bottom of the 224-foot-thick reef through a zone of rock that sweated water, which is heavier than oil, and into a layer of gray Niagaran. Drilling operations stopped at 4,966 feet on June 28, 1970, and the first Pigeon River Country oil well was put into operation.

"Well, I retired all right," Kellum said. "I counted my shekels to see that I could live on what I had. I was 62."

The week after the first oil strike, the DNR conducted a public hearing about oil and gas leasing on state lands in Petoskey. More than 700 people attended, the largest such hearing in history. Most of the audience opposed the drilling. One was Martha Reynolds, an executive of the United Auto Workers (UAW) union from Detroit. She spoke only hours after funeral services for Walter Reuther, the UAW leader who had personally supervised the design and construction of a large executive retreat on Black Lake at the mouth of the Black River. Mrs. Reynolds announced that the union's 400,000 Michigan members were opposed to any further oil leasing on state lands. The previous week the DNR had authorized an oil well in the upper Black River drainage area near the UAW retreat.

By the Monday following the Friday night hearing, the department's top executives in Lansing were talking about modifying policy. Warren Shapton, the veteran game biologist and deputy director who was one of the more candid senior officials, said publicly that if the DNR executive office had known what turmoil would result, he did not believe all the land would have been leased. But once the property was leased, he added, the department had to allow exploratory drilling in every leased parcel. That belief was to govern the department's conduct in the controversy from then on except for one test case called Corwith 1–22.

In October 1970, Governor William Milliken declared a moratorium that stopped fossil fuel drilling on state land in the forest altogether. But then Michigan's attorney general ruled that the state could not deny permits when requirements were met except under extreme circumstances.

The moratorium was rescinded, and drilling resumed in June 1971 with stricter controls. Without testing the concept in court, the assumption was made that the Michigan Department of Natural Resources could not actually protect the forest from degradation of its chief value, solitude.

Aesthetics was scarcely a value in hydrocarbon operations of the time. Sam Titus, invited out to look at her first oil facility, stood looking at the mounds of dirt and trees on top of what used to be a patch of orchids, listening to someone brag that the equipment had been painted green to blend with the environment. "With all your money and resources, you could never match the green you tore up," she thought.

The small, winding House's Lost Cabin Trail was straightened and widened into a year-round high-speed truck road. Otsego County required that the road be widened to 50 feet, and the department cleared another 50 feet next to it for pipeline, creating a vast opening for some two miles where a scenic trail had been before. All that for one well, Charlton 1–4.

After the moratorium was rescinded, the department approved more wells in the area of Charlton 1–4. A road was cut into the Black River Swamp and a 300-foot by 300-foot square bulldozed into a drilling pad, but the well was dry. The department required that other attempts to reach oil under the swamp be drilled on a slant from the higher ground near House's Lost Cabin Trail instead of straight down from the swamp. Nineteen test wells were drilled and five productive wells soon in operation. Pumps to move oil along pipelines, heaters to help the oil flow more easily, and storage tanks were installed. Fans whined, and workers came and went in trucks where the loudest sounds had been woodpeckers, the wind, and the call of coyotes. The oil industry announced plans to drill as many as one well per every 80 acres, which would have meant up to 1,000 wells in the remote acreage of the Pigeon River Country.

"We figured this problem of oil drilling was too big for our little Audubon Club," Ford Kellum said. "So I got together with Jerry Myers and Dave Smethurst to organize to oppose this oil drilling. Dave looked like a potential leader and a smart man. So I asked him, 'Will you chair this outfit, whatever we call it?' and he said, 'Sure, I'll be glad to.' We called it the Pigeon River Country Association."

At the time, Pigeon River Country was undefined. All state land in Otsego County was identified as Pigeon River State Forest. The idea that oil and gas wells would be placed indiscriminately on state land left ordinary citizens with the impression that the whole north woods might soon be full of wells.

From its first meeting in January 1972, the Pigeon River Country Association concentrated on defining a central forest area that ought to be protected as a semiwilderness, not preserved in its natural state but managed for multiple uses that are compatible with each other. Oil and gas development and the growing use of ORVs (off-road vehicles—which have been prohibited in the forest since 1988)—such as trail bikes were considered incompatible with other, quieter uses. In a statement before the Natural Resources Commission, which set policy for the state's Department of Natural Resources, Dave Smethurst noted that "hunting with hounds is almost impossible with the noise of trail bikes and snowmobiles in the background" and warned of the damaging effects of wildlife harassment and indiscriminate gouging of the landscape. In other words, the Pigeon River Country Association began to deal with the fundamental question of forest management at a time when the DNR was a collection of divisions that often went their own ways. An extreme example was the relationship between geology division and forestry, game, and fish divisions.

A direct confrontation occurred in June 1970 when field men inspected a new drill site northeast of the headquarters near the Elk Hill Trail Campground. The site is a major winter browse area for deer and elk. When district supervisors Ford Kellum (game), Steve Swan (fish), and Ralph King (forestry) objected to the drilling site, the geologists told them it was a waste of time to discuss the issue because the three had no say in the matter. The field men were told the only reason they were asked to inspect oil well drilling sites before permits were issued was to determine the value of timber that would be destroyed and to decide if the driller would use existing trail roads or build a new road. The geologists said they would issue a drilling permit 110 yards from the Pigeon River if they wanted to and that the objections of fish biologists would not stop them. The geologists produced copies of the state lease to confirm that the field men had no authority to protect natural resources. When the decision process was eventually changed, the regional geologist claimed that the other divisions knew nothing about drilling problems and should not participate. He called the DNR director a "ding-a-ling" for listening to the others.

During the period of intensive development along House's Lost Cabin Trail, Amoco Production Company applied to drill an exploratory well just north of the Black River Swamp. The site was a mile west of Hardwood Creek and about two miles southeast of forest headquarters. The proposed well was subsequently known as Corwith 1–22, or the first well in section 22 of Corwith Township.

Amoco assigned 50 percent of its interest to Northern Michigan Exploration Company to do the drilling, and the two companies applied together for the drilling permit in April 1971 while the moratorium was still in effect. A full field review of the application followed, with field personnel from each division making their recommendations.

The department turned the permit down on October 11, 1971. Director Ralph MacMullan stated: "Oil and gas operations at [this] site cannot be conducted without causing or threatening to cause serious damage to animal life and molesting or spoiling state-owned lands. Development for oil and gas has not yet reached this secluded area. The nearest producing well is two-and-one-half miles southwest."

Vance Orr, one of the six members of Michigan's Oil Advisory Board, let the two oil companies know that the denial didn't mean they couldn't drill. Orr, who was also president of Michigan Oil Company and a vice president of McClure Oil Company, approached the two Corwith 1–22 companies, indicating he could obtain the permit even though he was aware that it had been denied and no alternative site could be considered.

Orr secured an assignment of the lease, transferred it to his Michigan Oil Company, and on May 31, 1972, applied again for a permit to drill Corwith 1–22. He later signed an environmental impact statement and other documents that denied there were any streams or drainage ways within 300 feet of the site. That was in direct opposition to earlier, uncontradicted expert testimony that there was a drainage way 150 feet from the site.

Michigan Oil's permit was denied on July 21, 1972. Michigan Oil appealed.

David Smethurst walked into the office of attorney Peter Vellenga in Gaylord and asked if Peter could help. There was a hearing only a few weeks away. Vellenga got the Pigeon River Country Association into the Corwith case as a voluntary participant on the side of the DNR against Michigan Oil.

Sam Titus recalls that members of the association began to spend five, six, and seven hours at a time in meetings. And she remembers Peter Vellenga as a lawyer who was unsurpassed in finding legal material to advance their cause. You could never find his desk, she said, because the floor and surface were forever stacked with paper; if the phone rang, he'd have to hunt for it.

"I loved that guy," she said. Yet he seemed to her to be stronger in research than when he was talking in the courtroom. "He took forever to get to his point, and by then you might forget what the point was." His partner, Lowell Blumberg, was a different story. "When he spoke, you got the point right away," Sam said.

Peter Vellenga did the association's legal work on Corwith 1–22. It was the first time anyone could remember that someone had won a case against the oil and gas industry. While the Department of Natural Resources grew increasingly committed to drilling, this local lawyer, who represented a handful of local people, sustained a victory in the Corwith case that went to the Michigan Supreme Court. Vellenga was recognized as a bright man who could see the big picture in a profession that emphasizes the opposite, the detail, the fine points of distinction between one thing and another.

There were virtually no precedents in law for the case, since what they were doing was so new. So he dealt with what he felt was right and wrong. The department's case centered on whether the lease gave the industry the right to drill. Vellenga brought in environmental issues. Every time he brought something up, the oil lawyers objected because they were not issues originally raised by the department. What had been expected to be a two- or three-day hearing stretched to 23 days, the longest administrative hearing ever heard of.

The hearing officer, attorney Fred Abood, was experienced in oil contracts, but he struck Vellenga as a man who had not the foggiest idea of the environmental issues. Near the end of the long hearing, an oil lawyer showed Abood a picture of an elk. "That's a big animal," Abood exclaimed. And who could dispute it? Elk calves weigh 200 pounds six months after birth, heavier than most full-grown deer. Abood ruled that the oil permit should be granted. But from then on, Michigan Oil lost the case at every level.

During the next three years, Vellenga spun out massive amounts of information, and his legal secretary, Linda Darnton, edited it. He recruited members of the Pigeon River Country Association to help. Sam Titus, who was retired and living in Gaylord, had time to proofread, looking up word after word in the dictionary. In the early 1980s, a computer at Linda Darnton's desk in the Blumberg law offices turned out legal documents at high speed, printing every other line from right to left to save carriage return time and supplying standard language, such as addresses, from an electronic file. In the days when Vellenga and Blumberg had a partnership and Peter was working on the Pigeon River case, Linda didn't even have a photocopy machine. She had to carefully type each document onto a stencil and run it off on a mimeograph. Peter worked many more hours than he put on his billings. Yet, even with volunteers doing what they could, the legal bills piled up. The association asked for contributions, which were made through the Michigan Wildlife Federation and the Michigan Environmental Protection Foundation. It paid many thousands of dollars from its legal fund and eventually hit bottom in 1976.

Waiting to help was a young lawyer who had grown up in Texas and studied environmental law under Joseph Sax, the internationally respected UM professor who was described by another protégé as "a visionary, the most exciting thinker I have ever known." That protégé, Zygmunt Platter, became a teacher himself at Wayne State University and triggered the national controversy over the snail darter at the Tellico Dam in Tennessee. The Texan, on the other hand, moved to Grand Rapids as executive director of the West Michigan Environmental Action Council, a coalition of about 100 organizations with the motto "Translating Concern into Action." The translator was Roger Conner. "When he talked, everybody listened, even the judge," Sam recalls in awe.

In the early days of the controversy, August 1970, Ford Kellum had proposed to his department that a 120-square-mile area, the heart of Pigeon River Country, be set aside as a semiwilderness. The Pigeon River Country Association modified that proposal two years later, presenting to the Natural Resources Commission a proposal for a 129-square-mile area to be recognized as "a place of great natural beauty, not to be found anywhere else in the lower peninsula." The members declared, "We are not just an anti-oil group. We see the oil and gas activity as a major threat but in no way the only threat." Dave Smethurst handed the commissioners resolutions and letters from about 12,000 Michigan citizens saying they supported the Pigeon River Country Association's goals.

Within a few months, the first appeal of the Corwith 1–22 case was under way, and it was becoming clear that the Department of Natural Resources had not been able to come to grips with how to manage this extraordinary forest. A nine-year forestry division veteran, Lee Ekstrom, who prepared a detailed management plan, was laid off and his report scrapped. Ekstrom was known as a highly competent professional, a stickler for detail. The DNR apparently was not ready to make the hard decisions his report required about how the forest should be used.

At the same time, oil company lawyers and witnesses began to focus their Corwith testimony on the argument that oil wells are no more disturbing to an ecosystem than snowmobiles, motorcycles, and unlimited recreation. In fact, when Fred Abood, the hearing examiner, sustained Michigan Oil's contentions and recommended that the drilling permit be issued, he cited that very argument.

Finally, in December 1973, a "Concept of Management" emerged from the department and was approved by the Natural Resources Commission. It called for "prudent exploration and development" of oil and gas in the forest, noting that in "portions" of the area drilling might be denied or deferred depending on how it would affect other objectives in that area. The document put the Natural Resources Commission on record that: "It will be the policy of the Department of Natural Resources to manage the Pigeon River Country to protect and maintain the natural beauty of its forests and waters, and to sustain a healthy elk herd and wildlife populations. To manage activities so that those activities are in keeping with the unique and wild character of the Pigeon River Country; and to protect the area from overuse and overdevelopment." New forest boundaries were drawn along the lines suggested by the Pigeon River Country Association.

When Ned Caveney came to Michigan from northern Virginia, he noticed that people didn't seem to walk or hike as much in the auto state as they did back east around the Appalachian mountains. Ned thought the Sand Lakes area of northwestern lower Michigan would be ideal for that kind of recreation. It was remote, pretty, and quiet. It was also in the path of a proposed highway and under scrutiny by oil and gas developers.

Ned, who was an assistant forester in the Traverse City area of northern Michigan, urged the DNR to draw up a plan to set Sand Lakes aside as a quality recreation area. He was told to write the proposal himself. It was a new concept for the department, and it met some opposition within the department as being unnecessary. But citizens found the proposal appealing and through a flurry of letters convinced the department to establish the Sand Lakes Quiet Area.

When the management concept for the Pigeon River Country was approved, Ned Caveney was moved with his family to Pigeon River headquarters as resident forester, placing him in the center of the remote forest and at the center of one of the most deeply rooted controversies in the history of natural resources management in Michigan. He was to show his mettle as a professional who cared about what he was doing and could accomplish it with a minimum of upset to any of the interested parties.

The management plan took a bold step by creating a citizens advisory council; the director appointed the principal actors in the drama to the council as advisers who would guide the department in managing the Pigeon River Country. Key members of the Pigeon River Country Association were appointed to the advisory council, including Ford Kellum, Sam Titus, Doug Mummert, and Dave Smethurst. John Hood, who had taken 17 of his students from Interlochen Arts Academy to Pigeon River Country for a six-day campout in late winter 1972, was elected chairman and Smethurst vice chairman. Oil, commercial forestry, local planning, and business interests were also represented. Department officials attended as nonvoting ex-officio members.

From the start, the Pigeon River Country Advisory Council tackled the whole complex structure of forest management. Members struggled, for example, with the new concept of closing roads to help isolate portions of the forest. As Bob Strong, the district wildlife biologist, told them, "It is a matter of educating people that they will have to walk the extra mile. We are going to hurt some people's feelings in the meantime, but in the long run, they will say it is a good thing." Some 38 miles of roads were closed, leaving 109 miles of county roads and seven miles of state roads open.

The council took up a recommendation by fisheries biologist Steve Swan that the Pigeon and Black Rivers be designated natural rivers under a new state law. It took ten years to get the Pigeon under the law's protection.

The Pigeon River Country Advisory Council proved to be an experiment of great significance. The major elements are apparent in how the council dealt with the department's proposed "Plan of Development for Hydrocarbon Resources."

Dave Smethurst, who was elected chairman of the council after the first year, had for some time been asking, What if drilling takes place despite our efforts to stop it? Is it better to try to control it than to lose all say? Doug Mummert, who roamed the Black River Swamp every week and saw and heard how mineral extraction changed things, was as firm as anyone could be: no drilling, period. William Baute was an oilman. The job of evaluating the hydrocarbon resources plan was assigned to Doug Mummert, Bill Baute, Sam Titus, and Dave Smethurst.

Mummert reported: That the oil committee met last night, and it was hard to come up with a decision to try to point the council in any one way. Two of the members wanted to study the plan further. One was for the plan, one against.

The council decided to tackle the plan page by page, asking questions and making recommendations. During the day of intensive deliberations, what emerged was a pattern of forthright talk coupled with a willingness to be accommodating without sacrificing principles. In retrospect, it was a demonstration of the ability of people to work together. Some of the changes the council made include the following.

One sentence read "The extraction of mineral resources, including oil and gas from the forest will serve a vital public service and will be compatible with the other purposes of such lands, such as recreation, wildlife procreation and forest management."

The council suggested it read "The extraction . . . will serve a vital public service BUT MUST be compatible with other USES."

Another sentence read "No drill sites will be constructed in swamps where sensitive ecosystems might be endangered." The council suggested that it read "No drill sites will be constructed in swamps BECAUSE sensitive ecosystems might be endangered."

Smethurst suggested new language: "Any new road to serve a well site or facility will be gated and locked under the concept of a service road." Bill Baute, the oilman, opposed the motion. Discussion involved the feasibility of having too many keys. Ray Pfeifer, a department executive from Lansing, suggested a one-key system or some method devised to keep the public from driving the roads. Baute said he would be happy to try this since he would be glad to keep the public away from the equipment. Ford Kellum seconded the motion, and it passed.

On the suggestion of Rupert Cutler, a professor of forestry at MSU, the council prefaced its recommendations to the department with this language: "If in fact, oil exploration, production and transportation are to become a reality in the Pigeon River Country, these are our recommendations, believing that they will strengthen the plan. . . . The plan should be viewed as a minimum set of regulatory guidelines and, if development is to proceed, should be adopted as a preferable alternative to no plan."

Another amendment involved noise. Mummert initiated a discussion of the noise generated by the Charlton well. Baute claimed they had the noise level as low as they could get it and said it could be heard not more than about a quarter mile away. Mummert said he could hear it five miles away. A motion was made to monitor noise and odor levels and minimize them to the extent practical within the state of the art as determined by the state and the oil companies. Baute opposed this as unrealistic. The motion passed.

The major elements of this advisory council meeting on February 1, 1975, were the Department of Natural Resources struggling to balance its role as environmental protector with its assumption that industry had a legal right to drill, opponents of drilling having to accommodate the possibility that drilling would occur, and the oil companies having to accommodate an environmental viewpoint. It was not easy for any of them.

At the next meeting, the tension reached a flashpoint. Smethurst suggested adding a statement that oil and gas exploration would seriously disturb existing human and wildlife activity. He recommended the oil development plan not go into effect until adequate staffing for the forest took place.

Bill Baute stood, saying there were fewer people there than at the last meeting and they were not accomplishing anything by going over what had already been decided, so he was going to withdraw for the day. He and Chairman Smethurst talked awhile. Smethurst said the agenda called for an hour to discuss the plan and they were still within the time limits. He suggested Baute sit down as his influence and knowledge were vital to this issue. Baute stated he didn't want to walk out but that he had a lot of things to do and felt his time was valuable. Rip VanWinkle said there was nothing more important to them than this oil and gas program and the fact that they spent eight hours the last time didn't mean they hadn't had time for further consideration and reading since. "We could discuss it for two more days and still do some good," Rip said. Baute said he would rejoin if his time could be used more effectively and sat down.

The mix of opposing points of view gave the council a vitality that made it effective beyond its role as an adviser. Several landowners attended the next meeting, on April 26, 1975 at headquarters, because of the proposed road closings. Smethurst said he thought the council had antagonized a great many people. "They told us what they thought should be done but we never really discussed what they were saying," he said. "When the committee proposes something and sends it to the department, most of the bugs should be out of it by that time. When we send something to the director, it seems important that it reflect everybody's opinion."

Bill Baute responded, "I sympathize with what you are saying, but no matter how much time is spent on this thing, everybody is going to come in and want their own little road open. The council just has to make the tough decisions. We have to have the willingness to do that or we won't get anything done. We have to balance all those things and make a recommendation."

For its part, the DNR paid attention to the council. Ray Pfeifer from Lansing attended regularly. When asked about what was happening to the hydrocarbon plan, Pfeifer was candid enough to reply, "This plan, which is not off the typewriter much less the press, is in a stage of not having been through the process of final review by the director. He read it in rough draft form last week. It incorporates most of the recommendations of this council and many received from other sources."

The new director, Dr. Howard Tanner, attended a special council meeting in August 1975. He described drilling and no drilling as two extremes and said, "Our solution is to put the environmental impact into the overall decision-making process. As far as your role . . . I hope I have indicated the significance of public review, of public understanding, of substantial public support. I don't think a state agency in this day and age can proceed without it. I think it's already evident that the oil companies realize this and the oil companies are not anxious to pursue any other option but cooperating with us."

Smethurst got to the heart of the matter: "We have word at the council from the wildlife division that the elk can't make it. Fisheries division states that sooner or later there will be a catastrophe in the trout streams in the Pigeon River Country. Who has made the decisions about these tradeoffs? What kind of thought has gone into this?"

Ultimately, there were no answers. Director Tanner commented that "it is far more complicated than just oil and gas development. Right off, all kinds of human impact are areas that I expect we can work together on."

Smethurst asked, "When you get around to selecting field sites" for drilling operations, "who is going to do it?" The answers from Tanner's staff made it clear they were struggling with the issue, that it was a new area for all of them.

Rupe Cutler asked, "How can the institution" of the DNR "address itself to this need, divided, as it is, with all these divisions which sometimes disagree and sometimes agree?"

Tanner replied, "The Pigeon River Country can serve as a device for bringing about the kind of managerial development that [we are] talking about." He added, "I pledge you will be closely listened to. I can't guarantee that what you suggest will be gospel."

Nonetheless, the Pigeon River Country was unique in having an ongoing advisory council at all. Not even the Porcupine Mountains in the Upper Peninsula had such a council. When Rupert Cutler left the advisory council, he went on to the state's Environmental Review Board and then was appointed by President Carter as assistant U.S. secretary of agriculture for conservation, research, and education. He had been a chief advocate on the Pigeon River Country Advisory Council for forest management. With members as versatile as Cutler, the council was able to participate at every level of the DNR in working out management plans. In early 1976, Pfeifer made it clear the council could sidestep the bureaucratic maze that frustrated people inside the department. "When you finally arrive at something you want as an action," Pfeifer told them, "I think it is illogical for that recommendation to be ignored. If the message doesn't get the response that you want, it should be followed with a letter stating we would like at least a response . . . whether they can or can't be done and if not, why not. The director thinks this group is very important but he is just too busy."

When Bill Baute left the area, his replacement, Dale Fairbanks, immediately proposed that the department be asked to implement the council's recommendations and that the council be disbanded as having fulfilled its primary charge. During discussion, Fairbanks asked forester Ned Caveney, "Has the advisory council been of assistance to you, Ned?"

Ned replied, "Yes, I certainly feel that the council has been a help and is becoming more help all the time." The motion to disband the council failed 10 to 1. In his 1983 annual report, Ned wrote, "Pigeon River Country Advisory Council of 18 citizens gave unselfishly of themselves for 43 meetings on 61 days. This advisory council has truly become a model of public involvement in resources management."

Dave Smethurst appeared before the Natural Resources Commission meeting in April 1976 and was told by a commissioner later, "I didn't know you fellows were doing so much."

Forestry division chief Hank Webster told the council later that month that in helping to define key values and improve comprehensive management, "You can do something to apply to all the state forests—all 33 of them." Webster touted his idea for a temporary planning group to be "begged, borrowed or stolen" from among department specialists. If the idea "seems to be important, it probably wouldn't hurt if you, as a group, say so."

Chairman Smethurst replied that a field trip the next morning would give Webster a chance to apply his idea to the forest on a practical level. "I think I understand the concept and believe it, but I hope that tomorrow you can make it a little more meaningful to me in trees, birds, or whatever," Smethurst told Webster. "Maybe the whole thing will start to fall into place more." The council continued to maintain a practical, down-to-earth approach to big concepts, enhancing its role as a grassroots organization as opposed to being yet another arm of the department itself.

Director Tanner attended another council meeting in October 1976. It was shortly before Rupe Cutler left for his federal appointment. Cutler asked how the department would conduct detailed forest planning without the money that federal agencies had to work with. "Are you asking for help from outside the DNR staff? Are you preparing . . . inventory assessment of various kinds that could be done by students or whoever, or local people?" Cutler asked.

"The situation is worse than you have described it," Tanner said.

We are fewer this year than we were last year; we were fewer last year than we were the year before. We do everything less well, less intense. We are stretched mighty tight. We will continue to be the best we can . . . .

This state faces a shrinking income. We are not looking at a temporary situation. The movement of industry and population is southward. The likelihood is rather meager. General Motors is now the largest single employer in the State of Georgia. Automobile companies have not built new plants in Michigan. Our welfare costs are among the highest, our labor costs among the highest. Forty percent of our natural gas goes into industry—no other state does this. I think there are some ways we can make efficiency and we will make some gains with the people we have, but they will not be noticeable to the public at large. We will generally try to stay with what we have.

By 1984, the budget was just as tight. Caveney's annual reports had complained for some time that cutbacks in personnel to save money were actually costing money because of the loss of timber sales. "Nearly all timber stand improvement can now be done through timber sales if only we had the manpower to set them up and administer them," he said. "A forester could more than pay for himself and improve land management while making a product in high demand available." Ned said the student aide hired each summer by the Pigeon River Country Association was keeping the forest solvent with the help he or she provided in forest cover management. Even so, more than 700 acres went untreated in 1983, representing a loss of more than $42,000 in unsold timber. And 1984 was yet another year when the forester was unable to meet the goal of harvesting as much timber as there was new growth that year.

Yet in 1976, when economic hard times were first settling in, the attention given to the Pigeon River Country was leading to unprecedented coordination of effort within the multifaceted Department of Natural Resources. At Cutler's suggestion, the advisory council commended Tanner and Webster for creating, with the limited resources available, an interdivisional and interdisciplinary planning team "to do the best comprehensive planning job that is possible as evidence of some kind of a breakthrough and new approach to state land planning."

Tanner commented, "I have a different set of pressures demanding the plan for the Pigeon River. The fact that I have no plan at all places me in a difficult position. My question to Dr. Webster was: Can we combine two goals—the goal for me to have a good plan to use in laying out some of those fine things that are going to happen in the Pigeon River Country, and at the same time use it as a prototype [for] other forests? The alternative is to take a forest that is farthest removed from public controversy and just go on and do a more relaxing job over a long period of time. It is a difficult choice."

Webster added, "The pressure here for a good management plan is so intense, it may be that no plan will ever satisfy anybody." He was able to report to the council 10 months later: "I do want to emphasize again the importance of the council in the new management planning process which will end up being statewide. If, somehow or other, the Pigeon River Country State Forest went away, you still would have done something of very great importance—that is, the development of a more comprehensive management planning process with a good deal more citizen input."

The February 1977 council meeting was to be one of the hardest for those who were emotionally committed to keeping oil out of the forest. It was the night they had to vote on 10 well sites. Shell Oil had designated 10 suspected reservoirs of oil or gas. A team of field personnel selected a location on the surface where they thought the least environmental damage would occur. Now, to participate in the process, people on the council had to vote in favor of wells in certain locations when they felt in their hearts there should be no wells anywhere.

The council first adopted a statement that read, "Although a majority of the Pigeon River Country Advisory Council members do not support the management option of developing the Pigeon River Country State Forest's hydrocarbon potential, we do adhere to the belief that it is our role to assist the department in minimizing the environmental impact . . . rather than washing our hands of the issue."

On Charlton 1–10, the committee that selected the site reported "no particular problems." Ford Kellum spoke. Claw marks from bears climbing for beechnuts were visible on the bark of the stately beeches, he said. "This site is in almost the exact center with deeryards completely encircling it from one to two miles away." Doug Mummert stated that a well would change the character of Tin Shanty Bridge Road from a scenic route to a major roadway. The vote was 6 to 3 in favor of drilling with Kellum, Titus, and Mummert voting no.

When the well was drilled four years later, crews struck oil. Three years after that, the driver of a private automobile elected to pull off Tin Shanty Bridge Road onto a turnoff because an oil truck was approaching from behind at such a high speed that it appeared unsafe.

In a surprise move, the council voted 5 to 4 against drilling Corwith 1–35 in the largest uninterrupted wildlife route in the Lower Peninsula. The well was never drilled.

And on Corwith 1–26 Smethurst pointed out it was only five feet beyond the quarter-mile no-drill zone surrounding the Black River. It's a small island surrounded by swamp. The vote was 8 to 1 against drilling. The well was drilled in March 1982 and was dry.

The rest were all approved. Only one was drilled that year, during a temporary legal victory for the oil companies as the fight against drilling continued in the courts. Wildlife biologist Gary Boushelle told the council in October 1977 what was happening at the trial in Lansing. He related this story.

During tense questioning, a little old gentleman broke in and said, "Hold it, you're wasting your time." The judge expressed his displeasure, and the man was escorted to the gallery. During a recess, Boushelle talked to the man. The man said he was psychic, waved a vial of mercury over a Pigeon River Country map, and declared that they were wasting their time because there was no oil in the Pigeon River Country. This broke up the courtroom, Boushelle said.

In those years of the 1970s, the legal battle was fought through two cases. One was Corwith 1–22, in which the department's right to deny a drilling permit at one site was sustained by the Michigan Supreme Court. The other was fought against the department because it would not deny the rest of the permits even though the environmental damage would be the same.

Joe Sax believes the value of Michigan's wilderness and recreational lands is far greater than the potential value of any development that might endanger that land. "Uncluttered environment and natural beauty will become the most important resources we have here," he told the *Detroit Free Press*. "This state provides very high quality recreational opportunities very nearby. You won't find anything like it in Ohio, Illinois or Indiana."

Working on a law to regulate pesticide use in Michigan, Dr. Sax realized the state needed a general statute that would recognize a public right to deal with environmental concerns. He wrote a law unlike any in the United States. It focused on issues, like whether damage is really necessary, instead of procedures like hearings and impact statements. It offered an inexpensive avenue of appeal to almost anyone who felt a project might cause environmental damage. The bill won some key legislative support, attracted many supporters to public hearings, and in July 1970 became a state law. Experts considered it the best environmental law in the nation.

One of Joe Sax's former law students in Ann Arbor, Roger Conner, claimed a public right under that law to protect the Pigeon River Country from hydrocarbon extraction. The inexperienced lawyer took another lawyer with him for the first courtroom challenge on October 28, 1976, but over the next three years Roger demonstrated to friend and foe that he was a force unto himself. When he would drive up from Grand Rapids for a meeting that lasted until midnight, he would prepare to drive back so that he could resume his hectic schedule in the morning. "Oh, no," Sam Titus would tell him. "We don't want to lose you on the road somewhere. You're too valuable to us. You're sleeping on my couch." She would wake him at 4 a.m., give him some coffee, and send him on his way.

Conner challenged the oil and gas industry and the Michigan DNR to protect the Pigeon River Country from further drilling. He filed suit seeking an injunction against further drilling on behalf of the Pigeon River Country Association, East and West Michigan Environmental Action Councils, Detroit Audubon Society, Michigan Council of Trout Unlimited, Michigan Student Environmental Foundations, and Michigan Lake and Stream Associations.

Thomas Brown in Lansing, judge of the circuit court in Ingham County, ruled that plaintiffs had not proven pollution, impairment, or destruction. Three drill sites were immediately cleared and one well completed before the Michigan Supreme Court issued a temporary restraining order in early 1978.

On February 20, 1979, the Michigan Supreme Court banned drilling in the forest. All seven justices agreed that drilling would damage the area's natural resources. Four of them ordered a permanent ban on exploratory drilling; the minority favored sending the case back to circuit court for retrial. In a footnote, the court quoted the testimony of Ford Kellum that the Pigeon River Country was the center of "unique, almost endangered species, elk, bear and bobcat, osprey and bald eagle . . . where it looked like if they were going to survive the human race it's gonna be here."

The annual Pigeon River Country Association meeting held on June 23, 1979, was a victory dinner. Joe Sax spoke.

When those who are supposed to administer the law do not do the job that they ought to do; when other institutions, such as the governor's office, or citizen expressions of opinion, are unable to bring about needed change; when the law needs to be vindicated; then, with great reluctance, citizens have no choice but to go to court. The whole enterprise known as the Pigeon River controversy got started because ultimately the source of environmental rights lies in the people. . . .

The Pigeon River case demonstrates something that needs to be demonstrated over and over: ordinary citizens, people without a lot of expertise or political influence, who scrimp and scrape for every dollar, can win despite enormous odds. . . .

The Pigeon River case is not only important as a kind of David-and-Goliath victory and because the Pigeon River . . . is worth saving, but because it now stands as part of the body of legal precedent to which others will look. It is significant that the case was decided in 1979. . . . It's the first case in the energy crisis era, in which so many people think strong commitments to environmental protection have been severely diminished. . . .

The court made clear in this case that the mere judgment of an administrative agency about what's best for the resources of the state cannot stand as a final . . . decision. It's very important to keep sending a message back to Lansing saying that decisions made there, whether they are made in good faith, whether they're thought to be scientifically correct, whether they are politically expedient—cannot and will not stand as the final, conclusive judgment about how the resources of the state are to be managed. . . .

If the oil companies or DNR had sought to make a showing of . . . public need, they would have really had to come out into the open to justify what they were doing: what other oil development they were allowing, why they needed the Pigeon River Country, what benefits they expected, how important they were.

They would have had to share with the public and with the court all their thinking and all their decision-making. And that's one of the things bureaucracies are disinclined to do; they like to work in the darkness of their own offices. . . .

This case isn't over. . . . The oil companies have the resources, the staff and the money to keep fighting this case for a long, long time. There will be efforts made at the administrative level and at the legislative level to overturn these victories. There's a saying among developers—especially true as the value of the resources at stake rises—"Money can always wait."

It had to wait only one year. By April 1980, a bill was gliding through the Michigan legislature that would have not only allowed drilling but would have repealed the central provisions of Sax's Environmental Protection Act and all other Michigan environmental laws—air, water, waste disposal, toxics—in regard to oil and gas activities. It had 29 cosponsors among the state's 39 senators. And a number of new court decisions indicated the Supreme Court's decision would not apply to the rest of the forest. On behalf of the coalition of environmental groups, the West Michigan Environmental Action Council entered negotiations with the oil companies and the DNR to allow controlled drilling.

Conner's successor, Ken Sikkema, met in Gaylord with the Pigeon River Country Association, asking for an endorsement of the compromise. He explained that the Michigan Senate was not malicious, simply incapable of dealing with the Pigeon River controversy with vision and purpose while facing a depleted treasury, severe budget cuts, and rising welfare costs. Since the leadership was not coming from politicians, he said, it was necessary for the coalition to exercise leadership.

To Pigeon River Country Association members, that meant allowing oil development in the forest. On Sunday, November 9, 1980, members voted to not accept the compromise, reaffirming that oil and the Pigeon River Country are incompatible and drilling in the forest is unconscionable. There was much public reaction to the vote. The oil companies said they would not participate in the compromise plan unless the association agreed to it.

On Wednesday, the association's executive committee met with Gary Rentrop, the coalition attorney who had been doing legal work on behalf of the association. There was a mood of frustration, resolve, gloom. A conference call was placed to Roger Conner in Washington, DC, where he had gone to head up a new immigration reform organization. The people in the room were struck by his precise, philosophical, and optimistic approach to an overwhelming problem.

The executive committee then voted unanimously to drop out of the coalition and directed Rentrop to execute what is known as voluntary withdrawal with prejudice from the lawsuit. The action allowed the others to proceed with efforts to protect the forest through compromise. It rescinded the association's right to go to court over drilling.

In a letter to members, the executive committee said, "We are not deluding ourselves that there will not be drilling, but it is very important to us to be able to hold our heads high and to remain firm in our beliefs, however unrealistic and idealistic they may seem to some. . . .We are perhaps freer . . . to push in those forums open to us for more well-informed and responsive leadership. We also may still be, by our saying no, the standard-bearers for many people in the state of Michigan and elsewhere whose hearts are heavy right now and who, deep inside, cry 'No!' with us."

After a decade of struggle, the legalities began to blur and Sam Titus remembered the little things, the excitement of those times. Like when

Peter Vellenga called her early in the morning to say he had just learned there was a Natural Resources Commission meeting in Sault Saint Marie (also known as the Soo) in the Upper Peninsula and it was vital that the oil companies not be the only ones attending. He picked her up at seven a.m. and drove north to the Soo at excessive speeds while she read aloud from the documents Vellenga had to know about when he got there.

"They were real surprised to see us," Sam said. Later he took her to the hotel cocktail lounge and stationed her at a booth. "I have to talk to three people at once," he said, "and as I round them up you keep them here." When he brought the third one, she slipped into the next booth and tried to listen.

Her involvement in the Pigeon controversy was Sam's first close look at how men conduct business. Her own business had been dress designing in Ohio and Texas. When she retired, recently widowed, to northern Michigan, she found that the fight to save the Pigeon River Country gave her a renewed sense of hope despite the sometimes bitter disappointments. She became the telephone contact, getting calls from such people as Martha Reynolds, head of the UAW's environmental arm, who always wanted to know in detail what was going on and if she could help by sending out notices to the UAW's mailing list of industrial movers and shakers.

Dave Smethurst remembers being asked on the witness stand to explain what was special about fishing the Pigeon and the Black. Roger Conner had subpoenaed him because Roger wanted to demonstrate that there were values other than hydrocarbons involved. Dave paraphrased a passage from *Anatomy of a Fisherman* by retired Michigan Supreme Court Justice John Voelker, who, under the name Robert Traver, wrote such novels as *Anatomy of a Murder*. Some years later Dave heard Voelker speak and asked him to autograph *Anatomy of a Fisherman*.

Voelker opened it to the inside cover. David recalls the conversation this way: "No," David said, "could you sign it back here next to the testament to a fisherman?" Voelker asked why, and Dave told him the story.

"You mean," said the towering Voelker, "what I wrote got into the court record of the Pigeon River case?"

"Yes," Dave said.

Voelker looked at him closely, and with a twinkle in his eye said, "We got the sons-a-bitches, didn't we?"

In retrospect, they were exciting times, when ordinary citizens began to sit in rooms with the highest-level policymakers and representatives of one of the most powerful industries on earth, not making speeches but talking to each other. In some ways, none of them was ordinary at all. They took a hard look at things as they really were, measured them against what they felt ought to be, and did what they could. There were tears when the effort to stop drilling failed, but there was a sense of determination in people doing the best they could and finally hope that maybe what they did together had some value despite the frustrations. Even in the darkest days, when the Pigeon River Country Association faced overwhelming evidence that there was no way left to prevent drilling, there was humor.

It was the fall of 1980, and the West Michigan Environmental Action Council was in the awkward position of trying to get the Pigeon River Country Association to endorse drilling because the proposal offered the best controls that could be worked out. The spokesman, Ken Sikkema, explained the role he wanted the association to take by asking this question, somewhat rhetorically.

"If there will be drilling, how would *you* have it done, rather than how DNR would do it?"

Sandra Franz answered, "With spoons."

The major provisions of the compromise were that Shell Oil, which had a reputation for professionalism, would do all the oil and gas development and share the wealth with each company according to its share of land, thus minimizing environmental impact; and the advisory council would be an official adviser to the DNR in Pigeon River matters. The drilling was to proceed in stages from the southernmost part of the forest, with the northern portion designated a nondevelopment area, meaning that those companies holding leases there could not drill unless existing policy changed. The nondevelopment leases were to expire in 2001.

In a press release announcing its withdrawal from the coalition in November 1980, the association pointed out that the Department of Natural Resources had been unable to regulate chemical pollution in Michigan. "We are only now beginning to discover the awesome dimensions of our chemical wastes." It asked that the priorities of petroleum use be addressed as deposits dwindle, that there be some kind of public agreement on those priorities, and that the DNR be given adequate time and enforcement to get control of brine and chemical pollution.

"We can't even be sure that the public health is protected in the day-to-day operations of industry," the statement read. "It certainly makes no sense to use an area as sensitive as the Pigeon for our first demonstration of a compromise worked out only on paper and under the most pressing circumstances."

Extensive drilling resumed in February 1981. On August 6, 1982, Shell completed drilling Corwith 3–31, a producing oil well northwest of the

Black River Swamp and less than a mile from the mainstream of the Pigeon River. Thirteen months later, brine pollution was found in groundwater at the site. By January 1985, six tons of brine contamination had been removed from the groundwater.

Among the contaminants that go in and out of the hole at a single drilling site are an average of 78 tons of salt solids. About a third of that comes to the surface when the drill bit passes through salt deposits far underground. The rest is brought to the site, mixed with other additives into a drilling mud, and circulated into the hole under pressure to keep pressurized gases and liquids underground from shooting to the surface.

Some of the brine is liquified and hauled away on trucks. An average of 36 tons of salt solids are left at each drill site in a pit as large as a house. Under the compromise, all brine was to be removed from the Pigeon River Country. But after the seventh new well the industry convinced the department and the Pigeon River Country Advisory Council that it had made enough strides in brine storage to more safely store it at the site than dump it somewhere else.

Shell was allowed to store brine solids at each site wrapped in a plastic liner and buried four feet below the surface despite the fact that a department task force on oil field brines had recommended in 1980 that on-site disposal of salt cuttings and brine muds should not be allowed because the danger of pollution was so great even with a plastic sheet. The procedure used in Pigeon River Country became the state standard.

Following the discovery of brine leakage, in the spring of 1984 Shell began to test the 29 new well sites for brine pollution, to pump out whatever contaminated water it found, and to find, dig up, and place an extra plastic liner over each 60 by 80-foot brine storage pit. The first eight pits examined were those nearest to sensitive areas in the forest. Brine was found in the soil at each of the pits, attributed to a variety of causes such as spillage and the use of contaminated soils for backfill. One of the pits sat directly in the water table 800 feet from the Black River.

The first purge well installed to remove contaminated groundwater took about 30 gallons per minute, meaning that at just one site a four-month purge operation would remove up to 10 million gallons of freshwater and put it down an oil well, entombing it far below the flow of groundwater. A spokesman for Keck Consulting Services explained that groundwater and streams operate in cyclic balance to maintain the water table at certain levels. He said the amount of water taken from the groundwater channels would be replaced during the first spring thaw and the impact of purging would be nondetectable.

In a 1984 white paper, the staff of Michigan's task force on brines made it clear that procedures followed in the Pigeon River Country were far above standard brine disposal operations throughout the state and a majority of other states. Many brine pits were lined with neither clay nor a plastic sheet. And waste hauled from the drilling sites was sometimes dumped at random in remote areas of the county according to information obtained by the *Gaylord Herald Times*.

The report to the task force recommended that the brine pollution problem be corrected statewide. It pointed out that Michigan contains a greater amount of subsurface salt formations than many states and the freshwater system is extremely fragile. "On-site disposal of drilling muds, even with the strictest of controls and the optimum in pit liners, is still only a temporary solution," the report said. It recommended that in-ground pits and on-site disposal be stopped in favor of rigorously controlled disposal in which groundwater contamination is minimal. Shell itself told the advisory council that there is a sensitive situation in northern lower Michigan because the groundwater is close to the surface and the soils are so permeable. In January 1985, Shell offered to collect future cuttings and haul them away in steel bins to an approved disposal site such as one near Saginaw. Later oil operators and the state agreed on innovative procedures developed from the Pigeon experience for separating salt and liquid, putting the salt in pits and liquids into disposal wells far below the layers of groundwater. Eventually, the state further refined the requirements for drilling pits wherever new wells are drilled in Michigan.

More than 7,000 wells have been drilled into the Niagaran reef across northern lower Michigan since 1966. With the detection of brine pollution in the Pigeon River Country, close attention given to the problem there contributed to advances in environmental procedures. Shell sunk more than 20 monitoring wells at some sites, trying to locate sources of brine pollution. The more closely Shell looked, the more complex a picture of conditions beneath the surface emerged.

At Corwith 1–10, investigators found a layer of silt 12 to 30 feet thick that lay like a rumpled tarpaulin some 20 or 30 feet below the drill pad. Water rolled across the silt layer in all directions and collected in pools. Beneath the silt, water ran in other directions but principally north or east. Before the well was drilled, the advisory council was told the groundwater appeared to run south, away from the sinkhole lakes. The information from the array of monitor wells showed that the two Twin Lakes, both sinkholes, or Hardwood Lake, might be directly in the path of brine contamination.

There were 20 oil and gas wells operating in the Pigeon River Country by 1984, including the five drilled a decade earlier. But the companies had not found as much as expected. Of the 13 drilled in 1981, six were productive and only three of those tapped new pools of hydrocarbon. Of the 20 wells drilled in 1982, eight were productive and again only half of those tapped new pools. Oil and gas development in the forest during 1983 alone generated more than 5.7 million dollars in state revenue from fees, taxes, royalties, and rentals. Twenty years later, the Pigeon's wells were generating about a million dollars per year for Michigan's Land Trust Fund. Shell engineers estimated in 1994 that production would be over by about 2004. When 2004 came, however, Shell sold its interest in the wells to Merit Energy Company, a firm that buys and manages existing wells but does little or no exploration for new wells.

By then, oil personnel were estimating about 15 more years of operation for the 18 active wells. Don Spence, North Division general manager for Merit Energy, told the advisory council, "We do not have any plans to do any drilling in the Pigeon River Forest Area." Spence said he understands that when a well becomes marginal Merit has a contractual obligation with the state to plug it and restore the surface location. In oil industry practice, what is marginal has depended on oil prices: the more the price rises the longer a company can cover the cost of operation and still make a profit. A negative cash flow was showing up occasionally, at four wells in October 2005, for example, but the 15 oil and three gas wells in the fiscal year ending in June 2006 generated a cash flow of nearly nine million dollars, meaning profit above the cost of operation. The agreement Merit signed stipulates no future exploration or drilling for oil or gas.

Merit inherited eight contaminated production sites statewide, including the Charlton 4 central production facility in the Pigeon River Country, where it found BTEX in the groundwater seven to 14 feet below the surface. BTEX is benzene, toluene, ethylbenzene, and xylene—what are known as volatile organic compounds from petroleum hydrocarbons. The advisory council didn't know about this contamination until Merit found it and reported it at the September 2006 meeting. Merit's operations manager, Randy Sanders, said the company was cleaning up the sites. Smethurst urged Sanders to also investigate the abandoned facility north of Hardwood Lake, as well as all the pipelines running through the forest. Sanders said Merit took action quickly, because it would rather clean up now than face worse problems later, but admitted it was first tackling the worst situations, including Charlton 4.

Concerns that the wells should have been shut in 2004 instead of being sold were somewhat offset by evidence that Merit was meeting the higher operations standards that had been established in the Pigeon amid some unfortunate experiences, such as an incident that occurred in early 1985.

In February 1985, gas penetrated the casing of Charlton 1–4 some 900 feet beneath the surface, seeped through the glacial drift, entered the water table, and bubbled to the surface, leaving a crater 12 feet across. Sediment from the bubbling crater washed into the Black River Swamp. Shell claimed the leak was unlikely to occur elsewhere since Charlton 1–4 was the first productive well site in the forest and wells sunk since the 1980 compromise had triple casings designed to prevent leaks. Standards from the compromise were written into the 2004 contract allowing Merit to continue Shell's operations.

As part of that 1980 compromise, the industry began contributing funds for wildlife research. A great effort was made to render the fossil fuel facilities as invisible as possible to the casual Pigeon River Country user.

When the oil people told Ned Caveney they would use new equipment to push a pipeline under Tin Shanty Bridge Road rather than dig it up, Ned asked them to dig across the road and instead push the pipeline under a stand of trees to leave a vegetative cover between the road and the pipeline opening. They did so, and now a thick stand of trees blocks access to the pipeline opening. Where the pipe was laid along Tin Shanty Bridge Road, only a narrow 10-foot opening was cleared, the pipe laid, and the surface seeded. In some places, the pipeline crew left large pines standing in the right-of-way. It struck observers as a vast improvement over the days when the first pipelines were laid next to House's Lost Cabin Trail.

"By questioning those who would change the face of the land," David Smethurst said, "by forcing the decision-making process to go public, people concerned about Pigeon River Country have demonstrated that public participation makes a difference in our society. It has at least resulted in an unusual agreement between environmentalists and the hydrocarbon industry which goes to unprecedented lengths to protect a forest."

One of the wells, Corwith 2–31, caught fire in the early morning of April 10, 1995. Shell responded immediately and took out three dozen trees at the well site and along the Black River Trail to get water trucks in. Thirty-two hours later the fresh water had put out the burning casing gas leaking from a gasket and Shell began restoring the site, mostly by regrading, adding gravel, filling ruts, and reseeding. No trees were scorched, and the only residue left at the site was the clean water used to douse the fire. Members of the advisory council later commended Shell for the way it had responded to its first fire at a producing well in Michigan. That year Shell removed its Corwith 11 central production facility, leaving just one, Charlton 4, on House's Lost Cabin Trail.

Over the years it became clear elk were not really affected by oil development. They provided a symbol of an unusual place that deserved special attention. Advisory councils were never established in any of the 14 other management units in Michigan, but in the Pigeon the council continues to meet to this day, and it has been a recent model for snowmobile and off-road vehicle advisory committees for the DNR. The DNR itself was broken apart to manage natural resources while a new Department of Environmental Quality was established to implement natural resources laws and for a time was directed to find acceptable ways to hand out permits to whoever sought them. Shell drilled the last two new wells in 1988. Oil and gas leases in the northern, nondevelopment two-thirds of the forest expired in June 2001, meaning that this part of the Pigeon River Country was no longer at risk from the leasing that started the whole controversy. Pipeline corridors have filled in enough to be undetectable to many visitors. Dave Smethurst estimates there has been perhaps a 20 percent increase in activity and access in the southern third of the forest due to oil development but only 3 or 4 percent in the forest overall.

It turned out that brine leaked in the 1980s because the rathole, mousehole, and cellar were unsealed. Sealing them is now standard practice statewide, as is placing a liner under the drill rig and use of a tough, 80-mil liner for all secondary containment. Rock cuttings are separated from brine and put in a pit. The brine is pumped far underground to the Traverse limestone or Dundee formation. Merit, the new oil operator, impressed Rick Henderson, the district geologist, as a proactive company that makes decisions faster and at lower levels. Wells are fitted to start and stop pumping automatically by reading when enough oil has seeped into the system ready to come to the surface. Monitoring wells are in place down gradient of any potential source of contamination.

Yet hydrocarbon development pressure at the forest edges has reintensified with Antrim gas activity. In October 1999, the Sturgeon ran cloudy when Mercury Exploration ran a 1,000-foot directional bore some 15 feet or more under the riverbed. Clay and water slurry being pumped into the bore under pressure forced its way out of a fracture and rose to the surface eight or ten feet from the bank and drifted into the river. It was contained away from the Sturgeon a short time later by silt fencing. The bore was in preparation for laying a gas pipeline.

Otsego County is in the middle of a huge spread of gas wells, the largest amount of oil and gas well activity in Michigan. The 1970 oil discovery in the Niagara Escarpment was replicated in a 1980s discovery of natural gas both in shallow Antrim shale and in deep strata known as the Prairie du Chien formation. Yearly gas production in Michigan rose from 40 billion cubic feet in 1975 to 170 billion in 1990. Michigan was America's thirteenth-largest gas producer in 1994, ahead of all the other midwestern states. The Pigeon River Country is in the center of the Antrim shale surface deposit, which runs across the northern Lower Peninsula in a curve of similar bedrock. Where the shale is exposed, all the gas leaked out long ago, so drilling has taken place along the southern edge of the curve, where the shale is buried near the surface and still contains gas. Antrim gas drilling has had better than 90 percent success, most of it in Antrim, Crawford, Montmorency, Oscoda, and Otsego counties.

After drilling, the well is dewatered for six months, removing liquids accumulated in the well and allowing the gas pressure to stabilize. Then the brine water is pumped back into the rock from a nearby storage well to force out the gas. Brine, a potential contaminant, is salty water. Oil and gas form from organic materials decomposing within rocks in ocean-bottom sediments. When they become the oozes and liquids known as hydrocarbons, they migrate until they reach places that are impermeable. After Antrim gas was discovered in the northern Lower Peninsula and tax breaks put in place, a flurry of drilling began. By late 2004, there were about 8,100 Antrim wells producing in Michigan, all in the north. Drilling peaked in 1993 and began to decline but not disappear. The pressure on the forest has been unrelenting.

As an example of what has been happening in and around the Pigeon River Country, two 40-acre parcels of state land straddling the Sturgeon outside the area covered by the 1980 consent order were approved in 2001 for lease to Antrim gas developers, who agreed to drill on an angle from adjacent private property. An Antrim flow line along the east side of Fontinalis Road in Green Timbers was approved in 2004. A driller received a permit in 2005 to snowplow and temporarily improve, but not widen, a Pigeon road for access while drilling an Antrim well just outside the boundary. Compressor stations are placed at regular intervals along Antrim gas lines to provide pressure. A typical type of compressor station emits low-frequency noise audible for miles, creating what sounds like trucks idling for hours at a time in previously quiet woodlands.

Half a dozen environmental groups formed a statewide initiative in 1995 to reduce environmental and economic harm from Antrim drilling.

The issue came to a head over proposed drilling in the Jordan Valley, a remote and scenic watershed about 35 miles west of the Pigeon River Country. The application to drill was eventually withdrawn. But the Michigan Land Use Institute (MLUI) said hydrocarbon planning as developed for the Pigeon River Country was never adopted as a model for other sensitive areas. The result, MLUI, said, is that Antrim drilling has "disfigured hundreds of thousands of acres of forest and damaged rivers and streams." At the end of July 2005, the U.S. Congress approved a ban on oil and gas drilling in and under the Great Lakes, thanks in part to continual efforts by Representative Bart Stupak, whose First District covers all of the Upper Peninsula and a good portion of the northern Lower. Michigan had given permission in 1979 for drilling what came to be 13 oil and natural gas wells beneath the lakes at an angle from shore. Seven still produced energy in 2002, including one under Lake Huron and six under Lake Michigan. As late as May 2001, two months after Stupak first introduced his bill in Congress, the Michigan Senate had approved drilling beneath the Great Lakes.

In the summer of 2006, the *Traverse City Record-Eagle* said in an editorial that a proposal to allow 19 Antrim gas wells in the Pigeon's Blue Lakes area was a good idea because we need the energy. The drilling applicant was Aurora Energy, also of Traverse City. Mineral leases had already been purchased when the area was annexed to the forest. "[M]aking the DNR toe the line will be up to environmentalists and Pigeon River lovers," the paper said.

The state considers itself legally unable to stop drilling where it doesn't own the mineral rights, but where it owns the surface rights the state may be able to negotiate conditions for drilling consistent with those applied in the rest of the forest. Such options include drilling from the point of least impact to natural features and making compressor stations as quiet as current technology allows.

The Pigeon River Country Association learned in summer 2006 that Schmude Oil, Inc., of Traverse City, had leased the mineral rights for drilling up to ten gas wells near the heart of the central forest at the Song of the Morning Ranch, private property lying north and south of the Lansing Club Pond along the Pigeon River. The company applied to the Michigan Public Service Commission to run a pipeline along Sturgeon Valley Road about six miles to an existing gas compressor west of Fontinalis Road. The association voted to authorize legal proceedings against any such drilling.

8

The Dam

From above, trout appear dark and serpentine, curving and twisting like olive drab shadows through the water below. Removed from water, trout lose their iridescence and turn dull. Yet, as they break through the surface or twist into the air to feed, particularly males in autumn, trout show a spectrum of color, with glimpses of cream on their bellies: the silver blue to dark green of brook trout, dotted with red and blue spots in a halo of light; brown trout the golden bronze of sandy streambeds, spotted with red or orange, brown or black; rainbow trout the color of sunlight refracted through clear water.

In the summer of 1984 their waters in the Pigeon River turned black. Brook, brown, and rainbow trout died in several miles of the Pigeon River, tens of thousands of fish and a whole chain of aquatic life forms.

Pigeon River trout are in a real sense a form of the cold of the north woods. Trout thrive in cold water, even water at the point of freezing. Water warmer than 77 degrees Fahrenheit is lethal to brook trout; the lethal limit for rainbow and brown trout is in the low 80s. Cold water dissolves more gas than warm water can, so it holds more oxygen. Warm water, on the other hand, smothers trout.

The Michigan DNR as a general policy opposes impoundments on northern streams. One reason is that a dam backs water up onto the floodplain, where it heats up in the shallow pond and loses oxygen before continuing downstream. The temperature of the water at the one dam on the Pigeon River mainstream, built before the department exercised control over dams, would sometimes rise during the summer to 80 degrees. Forester Ned Caveney once watched 17 trout stack up like logs at the mouth of a tiny spring feeding into the heated Pigeon, trying to get enough oxygen to survive. There are some 700 such dams in Michigan; more than 10 fail each year.

Early in the morning on June 25, 1984, Ned Caveney got a call from Richard Armour, the maintenance man at Song of the Morning Ranch, informing Caveney that the yoga ranch was opening the dam on the Pigeon River to make repairs. The yoga retreat had occupied the private property for a dozen years, but it was still identified on local maps as the Lansing Club. Armour said he was making the call as a courtesy because the Pigeon River Country State Forest was downstream from the impoundment.

Did anyone at the ranch talk to the Michigan Department of Natural Resources about the drawdown? Armour said he had talked to someone in the district office in Gaylord who didn't seem very interested. Had he talked to Steve Swan, the fisheries biologist? No. Wait for a call back and don't release any more water until you hear from the department, Caveney told him. The forester then called Swan, told him the Song of the Morning Ranch was opening the only dam on the Pigeon to make repairs a week before the Fourth of July weekend without a permit.

Swan then called Armour, told him he had no authorization to draw down the pond and should close the gates immediately. Swan said he was concerned about siltation and the potential danger to fish in the river. They discussed structural problems at the dam.

Jim Hayes, an engineer from the Water Quality Division of the DNR, drove up from Lansing that afternoon. Hayes found the gates out of alignment and in danger of breaking loose. He filled out an application at the site for a permit to draw down the pond and repair the dam.

Three days later, on Thursday, Caveney got a message from regional director John MacGregor in Roscommon, ordering him to evacuate two campgrounds downstream. The Pigeon Bridge Campground and the Pigeon River Campground were already beginning to fill for the holiday weekend. The permit to conduct repairs was delivered the next day to Song of the Morning Ranch by the engineer Hayes. The permit stipulated that the pond was to be drawn down slowly, at a rate of no more than six to 12 inches per day, to avoid bank damage, flooding, and siltation. The owner was responsible for preventing such damage, the permit said.

Jim Hayes periodically inspected the dam all weekend. On Sunday, July 1, the turbine that supplied power to the Song of the Morning Ranch slowed to neutral. The river was still running clear, and the drawdown was within the limits of the permit. The 60-acre impoundment was down two feet when Hayes left Sunday night, satisfied that the requirements of dam safety had been met.

A river transports particles continuously. The particles include decomposing vegetative matter called organic detrital material, as well as sand and other inorganics. A pond on a river is a huge sediment trap. Water slows down as it enters a pond and particles sink to the bottom. At the upper end of the Lansing Club Pond, the largest, heaviest particles dropped out first. Then the smaller sand particles dropped, silts next, and finally clays, the finest, settled to the bottom.

The blood and body fluids of trout have a salinity of about 0.6 percent, higher than that of freshwater. So the Sturgeon, Pigeon, and Black rivers constantly diffuse into their bodies, mostly through the thin tissues of gills and mouth. They compensate by excreting copious amounts of very dilute fluid. In this sense, trout are a form of northern river that incorporates all the simpler organics, including the water itself, into one organism.

A running river is a complex environment in which life forms balance with each other and all the conditions of the river. Mayflies spend their nymph stage in silt beds. Yet more than 300 parts per million of fine particles in water will kill fish. The usual sediment concentration in northern Michigan streams is about 50 parts per million. The gills of trout have rakers on the forward edges. The rakers act as strainers to prevent large particles from washing over the delicate gill filaments.

Vegetable matter transported by a river is part of the food chain; benthos, or the invertebrates and other bottom organisms, feed on it. But in water behind a dam vegetable matter sinks in the heated water, accumulates, and feeds algae. When Ned Caveney inspected the dam with Richard Armour on June 29, algae had grown so thick on the water behind the dam that it covered a large portion of the pond like a thick mat. This mat bobbed against shore and dam on top of water that upstream and downstream from the pond ran so clear you could see three feet down to the river bottom.

Below the algae, the pond was virtually full of black vegetative material. On Monday morning, this material began swirling downstream in the Pigeon River. Jim Rubin, a conservation officer, called the DNR regional office in Roscommon, and Caveney called the district office in Gaylord. By four o'clock, they had not been told what to do. Caveney then contacted Hayes and Carl Hosford, chief of the Land Resource Programs Division in Lansing.

"We talked about a number of alternatives that might stop the silt, but we decided we couldn't do anything that afternoon," Caveney said. "We decided that Hayes was to call and tell them to stop the drawdown and close the gates to three inches. I was to see that was done. I asked who had the authority to go in there and do that. I don't think that question was answered, thinking back. I assumed the authority when I went in there and told them to hold the head" at a point visible on the dam. "It was the only alternative that made any sense."

Hayes called the ranch telling Armour to close the gates to a three-inch opening. Caveney arrived between 5:00 and 5:30 p.m. with Dave Smethurst, chairman of the Pigeon River Country Advisory Council. They watched the water in the pond rise against the dam. When it reached a spot on the dam that was 20 to 26 inches above the river level, Caveney told Armour to hold the water at that level or higher. When Caveney left the dam, he felt the situation was under control.

When he stopped at the Pigeon River bridge the next morning, the river was running like coffee grounds. Something had gone terribly wrong.

Trout in the Pigeon River take in oxygen about 50 times a minute, faster when stress or water temperature increases. Sediment escaping from the Lansing Club Pond filled the river from bank to bank, bottom to surface, as it moved downstream. Unlike the fine silt normally found in small quantities in the Pigeon, this black detrital material was thick and coagulated. It swept over annelids, mollusks, crustacea such as crayfish, insect larvae, and fish, including minnows, members of the perch family known as darters, and sculpins, a northern cold-water fish that rests on the bottom of the water, moves forward a few inches, and then comes to rest again.

Trout get oxygen in a beautifully coordinated movement. As the mouth opens to take in water, covers at the back of the gills close momentarily so that the water pauses in the gill chambers. A mere few thousandths of an inch of gill tissue separates water passing through the chamber from the trout's blood in a double row of delicate filaments. Such a thin separation allows dissolved oxygen to diffuse into the blood even as wastes diffuse out.

The detritus escaping from the pond clogged their delicate gill chambers. It plugged the esophagus, a tube leading from the back of the throat to the stomach. And it entered through the lining of the mouth and skin. In addition to the sediment itself, the water that moved with it was of such low quality that it could not sustain life in the trout stream. Organics in the water use up oxygen. Dissolved oxygen in the Pigeon River dropped from its normal level of six to nine parts per million to less than one part per million. The fish smothered.

As the detritus moved relentlessly along, trout must have sensed the disaster even from far downstream. Trout have two olfactory lobes in the front of their brain, corresponding to huge cerebral hemispheres in humans. Trout and others in the salmon family have such a refined sense of smell that they apparently use it to locate the stream in which they were born. Even to a human nose, the black sediment in the drained pond smelled dank and foul.

Trout also have a well-developed sense of touch, enabling them to detect small changes in pressure at distances analogous to our sense of hearing. Taste buds all over their bodies apparently enable trout to perceive the chemical nature of materials passing by them.

In the stress and temperature of the fouled water, heart rate and breathing rapidly increased. Water has one hundred times more viscosity than air, and aquatic creatures are streamlined enough to move through that heavy medium easily. Trout, among the fastest creatures in this dense medium, quickly move to their refuge positions when frightened. It is likely that is where many of them died. Trout are known to emit sounds to warn others; those that sound to humans like thumps are believed to come from muscular movement and those that sound like squawks from air movement. What people along the Pigeon River remember is that large numbers of fish appeared near the surface, gasping and flopping. Richard Armour saw thousands of fish downstream from the dam. One man counted 470 dead or dying trout floating past the Sturgeon Valley Road bridge in three hours.

Some 4,000 trout lived in the first mile downstream from the dam, counted in a routine program in which fish biologists in a boat attract the fish with electric current, shock them, take them aboard, count them, and return them to the water. Two weeks after the spill began, there were 339 trout in that mile.

In the days following the spill, seagulls fed from the Pigeon River. "Usually we never see them," Steve Swan said. The gulls were feeding on dead trout. Few trout carcasses were ever found. When trout die, they tend to sink instead of float. Swan said they rolled into the silt and decomposed in three or four days. Some were probably eaten by raccoons, which suffered a severe loss in their food supply as the fish population plummeted. Beaver, mink, muskrat, and otter all live in the watercourses and wetlands. Osprey and bald eagles frequent the drainage system. The impact on the whole food chain was beyond accurate measurement.

The total damage assessment was so complicated that it took the department months to conduct it. The loss of fish in the six research sections (each about 1.2 miles), starting at the dam, was 91 percent in the first section, 74 percent in the next section, and 25 and 20 percent in the last two. Farther downstream, the loss was 43 percent at Red Bridge, 34 percent at McIntosh Landing, and 59 percent at M-68, which is 17 miles from the dam and only a few miles from Mullett Lake. The dam was constructed without fish ladders, so fish on the downstream side could not get to the upstream side. There were no losses upstream from the spill; in fact, the fish population had increased since the last count. No lost fish were found in the Pigeon River's tributaries, and there was no indication that any of them escaped all the way to Mullett Lake. The capacity of the river to support surviving and new trout had been diminished. Those not killed were believed to be severely stressed and subject to disease.

The Pigeon River is one of the most studied rivers in Michigan. From 1949 to 1965 fisheries biologists lived at the river conducting continuous research and requiring fishermen to register and bring their catch to the office for counting, measurement, and identification by species and sex. Even barometric pressures were recorded. In the 1960s, some 1,000 trout were being caught each year in the six miles of research area beginning just downstream from the dam. At that time, about a quarter of the game-size trout were browns and three-quarters brooks. In 1984, a trout stream researcher, Gaylord Alexander, estimated that the Pigeon contained a third each of browns, brooks, and rainbows but that browns were the dominant trout by size since they grow faster than brook trout and the rainbows swim to Mullett Lake while still young. Browns are native to Europe; they were introduced to American waters in the Pere Marquette River in Michigan, southwest of Pigeon River Country, in 1883. The browns introduced much later to the Pigeon could get no farther upstream than the dam, so the waters upstream continued to be populated chiefly by native brook trout.

Many renowned scientists did fieldwork at the Pigeon River. The first trout stream improvement in the United States was conducted in Michigan in the 1930s under the leadership of Dr. Albert S. Hazzard, who credits Edward R. Hewitt, Dr. Carl L. Hubbs, and Dr. Clarence M. Tarzwell as being responsible for its growth in America. Tarzwell, Hubbs, and Hazzard all did fish research at the Pigeon in the 1930s, and Tarzwell wrote his doctoral thesis in 1936 on environmental improvement of the Pigeon River as a problem in applied ecology. Dr. Howard A. Tanner, who from 1976 to 1983 was director of the Michigan DNR, worked out of the Pigeon River Research Station while doing fieldwork for his doctoral thesis. In fact, most fisheries experts in the department have some firsthand knowledge of the Pigeon River, as do many at UM and MSU, which cooperated in studies at the station.

By all accounts, the Pigeon River is considered one of the outstanding trout streams in the Midwest. It is fed by both surface and groundwater. Groundwater is the principal source of water during rainless periods and a major control of water temperatures. Parts of the river fed mostly by springs of groundwater are cooler in summer and warmer in winter than parts where groundwater discharge is small. What is known to many as a premier trout stream is a natural balance of factors like water temperature and photosynthesis. Springs feeding the Pigeon River contain no dissolved oxygen, but in summer by cooling the river they allow it to hold more dissolved oxygen. During daylight, plants in the river give off oxygen; at night, they use a small amount. At midday, when the rising water temperature reduces oxygen, the submerged plants increase it and so maintain the balance. In fact, dissolved oxygen in the Pigeon typically increases to nine parts per million at noon from a before-dawn low of six parts per million.

The Pigeon is considered normally safe for wading; most of it three feet deep or shallower and the velocity is about three to four feet per second in the shallow riffles at midstream, much slower in the deeper pools. Under Michigan law, navigable streams are public property and can be waded or navigated even where property around the river is privately owned. Fishermen since the early 1970s complained that the water level suddenly rose due to increased discharge at the dam, preventing them from wading immediately downstream. The U.S. Department of the Interior considers wading to be safe when the stream velocity multiplied by depth in feet equals 10 or less. By that rule of thumb, the deepest safe water moving at four feet per second would be two and one-half feet deep. A one-foot rise in water level would endanger even a tall, heavy person. In each case in which the complaints were pursued with Song of the Morning Ranch, caretakers said the change in water level was due to routine operation of the dam and was in no way meant to harass fishermen.

The highest water level, or stage, of the Pigeon usually occurs during the spring snowmelt; even then, the water does not rise high enough to damage campgrounds. The highest stage on record, however, occurred May 15, 1957.

The night before, an inch of rain fell on the watershed of the upper Pigeon River. By the next morning, the caretaker at the Pigeon River dam saw water rising in the 60-acre impoundment and went out to open the dam gates. It was standard procedure after every moderate rainstorm. But this time a log jammed the spillway gate. Unable to free the log, the caretaker placed an emergency phone call to the Pigeon River Trout Research Station three and a half miles downstream. Jerry Myers, fisheries research aide, received the call at 10:00 a.m. and rushed with Dr. Leonard Allison, a fish pathologist, to the site after notifying the district office of the DNR in Gaylord.

Other department workers alerted state and county authorities about possible trouble downstream and began to search for persons who might be in or near the river.

Myers and Allison removed the log less than 15 minutes after the caretaker's call, but the waters had already gullied through the earthen roadway on the dam and were rising rapidly despite the increased spill through the gates. Roiling water eroded into the downstream side of the dam and began carrying away the earthen fill behind the 150-yard-long dam. At 10:25, the bank on the east side of the dam toppled into the water. Five minutes later the concrete wing dam on one side of the spillway, with the supporting earth behind it gone, crashed into the Pigeon River and a 12-foot head of water thundered downstream. It uprooted huge trees and dropped them on the high banks. It peeled sod back from the river's edge like rugs. It piled stumps and logs on the banks high above normal water level. It flooded the river valleys, destroyed woodcock nests, and ripped out natural cover. A mile and a quarter downstream a stump jam formed against the concrete Sturgeon Valley Road bridge, damming the high waters, which overflowed the road and washed part of it away. Three and a half miles downstream the U.S. Geological Survey gauge reached more than four feet above normal and could not record any higher.

The water washed through the six miles of experimental trout stream in about six hours, at 10 to 20 times the normal flow of the river. It left thick layers of sand and muck on the inside banks of river bends. On the bottom of section E, the 1.2-mile experimental section immediately downstream from the dam, it left a wide, flat ribbon of shifting sand on top of what had been gravel riffles. There were no reports of human injury from the flood. Unlike the spill in 1984, this flood deposited most of the detrital material high up on the floodplain where the flow was slowest.

For two weeks after the 1957 flood, the Pigeon River was virtually unfishable. Two trout were caught the first week. The catch in the four weeks following the flood was 175, compared with the average of 395 for the previous three years. This low count in 1957 was attributed primarily to poor fishing conditions.

The fall fish population study was ordinarily a routine, though interesting, chore. When heavy rain brought high, roiling water or there was early snow or sleet, the population study was an uncomfortable job, but usually it was exhilarating in the crisp, sunny days of early fall. In 1957, there was a feeling of apprehension because of flood damage. Several local residents were on hand to watch and lend a hand almost every day.

A crew of five men makes two complete runs through the six miles of research waters, electrofishing with a direct current shocker. One current draws all the fish in the area like a magnet. A second current immobilizes them. Workers wave the six-foot wand around logs and under banks, draw the fish along, then scoop them into a tub where they swim freely. Some 10 to 15 percent of the fish manage to swim through the current without being caught; the bigger they are, the easier it is to capture them. After proceeding 100 or 200 yards, the crew stops, turns off the generator, and measures and counts the fish. They remove two or three at a time from the first tub and place them in a tub of mild anesthesia, which acts like ether on a human, so they can handle the fish without hurting them. They remove a few scales from the lateral line in front of the adipose fin and clip a tiny piece from the tail, which regenerates within a year.

Fisheries researchers say only about one fish out of 500 dies during this procedure and that the mortality probably occurs because there was something wrong with the fish to begin with. Trout bump into things and lose scales regularly, especially during spawning. Brown and brook trout in northern Michigan spawn in the fall, rainbow trout in the spring. A female brown will select currents and gravel sizes for a satisfactory nest or redd, often in a riffle above the swiftest water at the tail of a pool, where currents readily percolate through the gravel and provide silt-free, aerated water. When a male in brilliant breeding colors arrives, the female digs a pit by turning on her side and cutting the gravel with vertical sweeps of her tail. Clouds of silt rise. The female sometimes moves away, then returns to test the depth and contours with her anal fin. Sometimes the male approaches to snuggle next to her or to repel another male. Within an hour, the female creates a pit about six inches deep and 12 inches in diameter. The two trout then arch their bodies into the pit, quiver and release eggs and milt at the same time, clouding the area until the current clears the water.

Then the female buries the eggs to a depth of eight to 12 inches by vigorously flipping her tail. The scene is repeated a few feet upstream several times until the female has released all her eggs. Then she spends hours placing gravel over the eggs, which protects against invaders yet permits water to percolate through to the eggs. When she is finished, the nest looks like the rest of the stream bottom and the eggs are four to six inches down. The adult brown trout enter winter looking smaller and less healthy following spawning because it takes so much energy and body weight. Sometimes during spawning the outer edge of the scale may actually erode before the trout resumes normal growth.

"It's like the bull elk not eating, running around chasing cow elk," Jerry Myers said. "The bull elk goes into winter looking pretty sad. That's animal life."

Experienced researchers can count how many times a fish has spawned by examining one of its scales. Fish scales under a microscope look like fingerprints. They are comprised of swirls of growth rings. The distance apart tells how fast they grew, as tree rings do, and the number of close bands (winter slowdown) tells their age. Trout counted on the Pigeon River often have scars from encounters with other fish. Jerry Myers has seen holes in live fish inflicted by great blue herons who lost their prey. Pigeon River trout get bumped around pretty well in winter by anchor ice, crystals that form during extended cold along the bottom of the river and rise in chunks during the warmer daylight, moving downstream, eroding banks, disturbing the streambed, and knocking into fish. Researchers feel that fish counts are less stressful than natural stream conditions.

After "processing," the workers return the fish to the waters where they were captured. Trout are territorial and defend their feeding areas against intrusion by other trout. The population is believed to remain relatively stable in a quality stream like the Pigeon. Survival of eggs beyond the fry stage is extremely low. Fry are trout that have emerged from the redd but have not reached fingerling, or finger-sized, length, which takes about 18 months. Many are consumed by adult trout. The older trout get, the more likely they are to eat young trout. The process recycles their own species in a hierarchical system that sustains a healthy fish population. Mature Salmonoidea, for their part, in the classic migration cycle, fertilize their young with their own decaying bodies, returning the nutrients that have washed to the sea back to the redd.

More than 90 percent of brown trout are lost between fry and fingerling stage, and yearlings and two year olds suffer 50 percent losses each season. Of a thousand eggs that may originally appear in one brown trout nest, only three or four trout will survive to their fourth year.

Researchers waiting for results from the 1957 Pigeon River population study feared that the flood would have a devastating effect on the trout population. But, as Dr. Thomas F. Waters put it later, no one was left unsurprised. The figures showed the population was slightly larger than it had been the previous year. Only in section E, closest to the dam, was there a noticeable reduction—some 1,000 fewer young of that year. Those were the brook and brown trout hatched in January and February from the 1956 spawning. They average about 2.8 inches in length by the September count. It was unclear what happened to the spring 1957 rainbow spawn.

Waters, who was in charge of the Pigeon research station in 1956 and 1957 and later became an assistant professor of zoology at the University of Minnesota, noted that there were well over 1,000 more trout in the other four sections. In his evaluation of the results, Dr. Waters pointed out that shifting sand at the bottom of section E had obviously reduced its capacity for spawning and food production. But the ability of wild trout to withstand a destructive flood, he added, was clearly demonstrated. Yet fisheries experts said privately that the ecosystem was only just beginning to stabilize after the 1957 flood when the 1984 spill occurred.

The first dam was built during logging operations in the late 1800s according to local residents who fished in the pond in the 1920s. The historical record is incomplete. The Michigan attorney general's office says it has been unable to find an original permit in the files. According to a report in the DNR files, the dam that collapsed in 1957 was repaired or rebuilt in 1923 by the Lansing Club, which acquired the property from previous owners. Darrell Fleming worked on the Lansing Club dam when he was about 16, which would have been in 1926. The dam had washed out around the edge, and a crew of workers widened it. Fleming used a two-handled slush scraper to gather fill and place it behind the concrete extension, "real hard work," he recalls. At the time, Lansing Club members would come up on weekends to fish and swim in the pond. Others remember the dam being worked on about 1927. In a newspaper account of the 1957 dam collapse, Leo Marlatt, a conservation officer, was quoted as saying that in 1927 a "gentleman in his cups who liked to see rushing water sneaked out around Labor Day and pulled the dam. Fish were flopping all over the banks and it was a mess."

Under Michigan law, permits to construct dams across navigable streams reposed in the county board of supervisors, which provided that petitioners, their heirs, successors, or assignees could construct a new dam without applying again to the board. So the dam activity of the 1920s was not reflected in official county records and is now a matter of faded memory.

Another event in the 1920s, better documented, was the arrival in the United States of Paramahansa Yogananda, the first great spiritual leader from India to live for a long period in the Western world in the modern era. During the 1920s, Paramahansa Yogananda conducted yoga classes in several large cities. Tens of thousands of Americans attended. *Yoga* is a Sanskrit word meaning union, or joining together. It refers to an individual's search for knowledge of his or her relationship with the universe. It involves meditation, in which intellectual mental activity is quieted while awareness is heightened. Yogananda emphasized the common thread in all religions as activities that seek out divinity. J. Oliver Black, a millionaire inventor and auto parts manufacturer from Detroit, met Paramahansa Yogananda in 1925. He said Yogananda "ruined my life," turning everything upside down and J. Oliver Black into a disciple of yoga. He eventually became Yogacharya Black, a teacher of yoga. As far as Yogacharya Black was concerned, most people walk around "stupid" and unaware of their potential.

He began to hold classes in the Detroit Institute of Arts every Sunday, teaching people how to clean themselves up mentally and physically through diet and the yoga techniques he had learned from Yogananda. In the 1950s, he purchased a half interest in a northern Michigan property that belonged to the widow of his friend Jim Jackson. Soon afterward, he owned the property outright. It comprised some 800 acres in the Pigeon River Country, including the Lansing Club Pond and dam. J. Oliver Black was the owner when the dam collapsed on May 15, 1957.

He told the DNR that he intended to have a dam built that would regulate the flow and control water temperatures better than the old dam had done. He recalled spending $110,000 on the water study and dam construction, including a turbine to generate electricity.

Local residents recall a plan to bring a monorail up to the Pigeon River from southern Michigan and develop the land there owned by J. Oliver Black and Alan Gornick, an attorney for the Ford Motor Company. The plan, hatched as a joke over a few drinks in about 1962, grew in local folklore into a serious venture, but never materialized.

Eventually Mr. Black began to bring yoga students up to the Pigeon River property. In the early 1970s, he organized Golden Lotus, Inc., a Michigan nonprofit corporation, and a yoga retreat called the Song of the Morning Ranch. By 1984, Golden Lotus had a mailing list of 1,200, the ranch had a staff of 16, and Mr. Black was still the resident yogi at age 90. Song of the Morning Ranch attracted people from as far away as Holland, England, and India. A Swiss who was 94 stayed at the ranch in 1983, and a 14-year-old girl stayed there with her parents' permission in the summer of 1984. Members have had backgrounds in osteopathy, chiropractic, law, chemical engineering, teaching, writing, theater arts, and religion, including Lutheran, Catholic, Jewish, and Unitarian.

One member of the staff, Nirmala-Devi Shanta, who assumed her name after hearing suggestions from various spiritual communities she has visited, said the setting of the ranch in Pigeon River Country enhanced studies there. In moving away from the intellect and toward intuition, students try to experience God in their daily life rather than creating an image of God as some sort of bearded autocrat. They find nature a more purifying experience than they do city life, she said.

Mr. Black commented that people need to get away for relaxation far from their worries and cares. Yet he perceived the destruction of aquatic life in the summer of 1984 principally as a controversy harmful to the work the ranch was trying to do with humans. "Humans need as much consideration as some little goofy fish," he said from his living room overlooking the dam. He was a small, thin man who looked directly at his visitor even when saying things he had said at other times to other people. He remained direct, practical, embellishing nothing, talking about spiritual matters in such a clipped fashion that he made ordinary conversation sound dreamy by comparison. His own conversation involved esoteric matters, but in no way did he sound esoteric himself.

One of the stories he told to illustrate the difficulties in understanding God involves fish. The teacher gathers all the fish together to tell them about water. "It's above you, below you, in you and all around you," the teacher says. The fish look around. After they swim away, one fish says to another, "I still don't understand what water is."

Looking forward to his ninety-first birthday on September 1, 1984, Mr. Black said he had a vision of the dam being restored to look the way it had for the last 27 years through the windows of his house. An old boathouse refurbished into a dwelling, the house is perched at the edge of the pond, with a view upstream toward the high pines owned by Alan Gornick, and downstream past the dam, waterwheel, office, and dining quarters and domes where Sunday services are held. The domes sit along the western side of the river, on the floodplain, glistening with the gold glitter that Yogacharya preferred as decoration on all the buildings of the Song of the Morning Ranch. The gold glistens even at night from the electricity that lights the buildings and paths through the woods. Members said Yogacharya used electricity in abundance because he believed members should be part of the ordinary world, not apart from it. Now the source of electricity was threatened.

"If it weren't for the DNR," Mr. Black said, "we wouldn't have had this trouble in the first place."

The Michigan Department of Natural Resources had 12 divisions that by description or title could have had responsibility for the problem at the dam. These included Surface Water Quality Division, Waterways Division, Groundwater Quality Division, Fisheries Division, Environmental Services Division, Environmental Enforcement Division, and Water Management Division. But the one with the most areas of related interest was, in fact, the Land Resource Programs Division, which was responsible for dam permits, wetlands, dredging and filling inland waters, submerged lands, the natural rivers program, cleaning out and dredging ponds, riparian rights, river channel digging, construction in or adjacent to rivers, physical alteration of rivers, and soil erosion and sedimentation control permits, among other things.

The Song of the Morning Ranch, on the other hand, had Richard Armour. His wife, Carol, a counselor in the state's social services program, was the resident with the most seniority at the ranch (10 years). Carol Armour acted as a spokesperson during the early days of the controversy. She complained privately that it took only one day to repair the dam but the department refused to let them close it and refill the impoundment afterward. As a result, sediment continued to wash downstream. Department employees were openly blaming the ranch by this time, pointing to destruction of the fish and food chain that occurred on the first day. Yet, Carol noted with sarcasm, when asked how much destruction had occurred, the department said it still didn't know. One ranch member said it looked like the department was unwilling to take any heat. Others who have worked cooperatively with the department said that when things go wrong it is standard procedure for the department to place all the blame and take none.

The feeling among members of the ranch seemed to be that the department should have advised them on how to repair the dam without damaging the river. The feeling in the community was that the mistakes of the yoga ranch could have been avoided if the department had acted with more wisdom. For all its interest in environmental affairs, the department neither provided a consultant nor required the ranch to use one, despite the obvious danger of a detritus spill.

In the first weeks after the incident, officials in Lansing had to struggle with how to handle the ongoing environmental disaster while making candid assessments of how it happened. At the same time, they sought to protect their position in case a solution had to be decided in court.

Four weeks after the siltation incident, a *Detroit Free Press* reporter, John Flynn, quoted an authority on aquatic insects as saying the worst damage to insects, particularly to their habitat, occurred in the 10 days after the initial spill. "Insects are amazing," said Richard Merritt, a professor of entomology at MSU. "They can recover, but when you say 10 days, you'll cause a lot more damage in those 10 days than in five hours or so when the first slug of silt escaped."

Steve Swan said, "Everyone agrees that the 10 days were a bad situation."

On the first day, as the ranch completed repairs in preparation for closing the dam and refilling the pond, there was no clear decision from department officials in Lansing about what to do next. It was Tuesday, July 3; the next day would be the Fourth of July holiday. Late that night Dave Smethurst finally called DNR director Ronald Skoog at home. Skoog called Ned Caveney and others, and on the morning of July 4 the ranch was handed a cease and desist order that said the gates were to be left open. The Pigeon River ran free for the next 10 days.

Ron Skoog, in his first year as director, said the decision to leave the dam open was his. It was clearly a decision supported at the time by field personnel. On the first day, detritus flowed heavily from before dawn until the I-beam was welded at 9:00 p.m. By that time, there was overwhelming sentiment that the dam should never be closed again. In fact, Steve Swan said the river had begun to clean itself out by the tenth day. Those familiar with the situation, outside of ranch members, felt that it would be a matter of only a few weeks until airborne pollens would vegetate the organic material drying on the exposed bottom of the impoundment. The river was flowing in its original channel, winding through the black, cracked bowl that had been the Song of the Morning Ranch's recreational lake.

There was also the question of safety at the dam. To allow the dam to be put back into operation would be an admission that it was safe. The department's engineer, Jim Hayes, found a whole list of things wrong with the dam when he inspected it on July 4. He described the welding as "poor workmanship" because it looked sloppy and unsmooth. The welding had been done to repair the sides of the gates, but Hayes said the gates were also extremely worn at the bottom and he doubted they could hold a seal. He found the upstream concrete wing wall severely deteriorated, one downstream slope eroded two to three feet, trees creating possible internal erosion, and channels upstream cracked. Finally, he told the informal fact-finding hearing held by department in Gaylord on the sixth day the river ran free that the dam spillway was designed to accommodate a maximum 857 cubic feet of water per second but needed to accommodate 900 if it was to hold the estimated peak discharge. Peak discharge means a storm that theoretically would occur once in 100 years.

J. Oliver Black, who had been silent up to this point at the other side of the table from Hayes, spoke up. "This dam will take care of 50 square miles. I got the best engineer available to design that dam and spent $110,000. It has held for 27 years. There have been no fish kills. We have given you clear water all that time. It will hold for another 27 years."

The engineer replied that there are 53 square miles of watershed contributing to the drainage area at the dam. The hydrology figures had been collected and refined over many years, he said.

Richard Armour described at the hearing what he said he knew of the events. On Sunday, he had been following the guideline of a foot per day drawdown. On Monday, July 2, there were reports of silt downstream, and he was ordered by telephone to close the gates to three inches. He made the adjustment. The water by then was down to the last few acres. Sandbars near Mr. Black's boathouse were showing. While Ned Caveney was there, the water against the dam rose six inches in half an hour. He made further adjustments as Caveney was leaving. He checked the dam periodically until 10:00 p.m., then went to bed. No adjustment was made through the night, he said. On Tuesday at 6:00 a.m., the water "was right down," he said. "The gates were in the same place."

Ron Powers, attorney for and a member of the ranch, brought up press reports that the ranch had raised the gates against orders. "We are dedicated to protecting the environment. Why would we open the gates in the middle of the night?" The implication from Armour's testimony was that the pond leaked out through the opening between 10:00 p.m. and 6:00 a.m.

Except for a turkey dinner every Sunday, the ranch serves no meat. Members are not allowed to smoke, drink alcohol, or use drugs. Staffers feed deer that frequent the area and have chased hunters off their 800 acres. Some members said they were uncomfortable knowing that people catch fish in the river and so were especially embarrassed that they were suspected of purposely causing thousands of fish to die. Members who attended the informal hearing looked uniformly healthy, clear-eyed, and trim.

The question that lingered at the hearing was whether the gates were deliberately opened or whether the water had simply drained out during the night due to a misunderstanding about what was required of the ranch. The department, after all, had half a dozen people giving instructions to the ranch and nobody specifically assigned to oversee the whole operation. It was no secret that the impoundment was loaded with detritus, yet the department's only safeguard against polluting the river was a stipulation in the permit that the water be drawn down slowly. When the silt first appeared downstream on Monday, the department's response was to stop everything until a decision could be made about how to proceed. As Phil Hendges of Shell Oil pointed out at an advisory council meeting, the DNR had no contingency plan for dealing with pollution. The only person specifically assigned to monitor the drawdown was Jim Hayes, who left before the siltation began because his responsibility was the safety of the dam not water quality.

If the cause of the spill was still a mystery, there was one more clue. It was a series of figures collected by the U.S. Geological Survey (USGS).

Since 1950, the USGS has operated a gauge at the Pigeon River headquarters complex that measures the height of the river above sea level. By periodically taking other measures, such as the width of the river and flow rates, the agency has been able to prepare charts that accurately calculate how much water is flowing past the gauge for any specific river height.

The measuring station is a box fed by a pipe leading from the river, a float that rests on top of the water undisturbed by waves or wind, and a digital recorder that punches out the elevation of the water at each reading. A reading is taken automatically once an hour.

The readings show that the lowest river flow during the whole drawdown period occurred at 9:00 p.m. on Monday, July 2, after Ned Caveney watched Richard Armour raise the level of the pond. The station is three and a half miles downstream from the dam. At an average river velocity, the gauge would be reading what happened at the dam about two hours and 45 minutes earlier.

In other words, when Ned Caveney saw a 20- to 26-inch head on the dam and left shortly after 6:00 p.m., under the impression that the situation was under control, the flow at the dam was at its minimum, 40 cubic feet per second. The flow gradually increased for the next four hours, which would have been until 10:15 p.m. at the dam, then dropped for the next three hours.

At that point, about 1:15 a.m. at the dam, the Pigeon River began to flow more rapidly again. It went from 54 cubic feet per second to 89 in the first hour. In the next hour, it rose to a peak of 90 cubic feet per second. That would have been water that left the dam at about 3:15 a.m. That peak was 2.73 feet above datum; it was the highest reading during the entire incident.

To Ned Caveney, the figures meant one thing: somebody had opened the dam. David Smethurst, who accompanied Caveney to the dam on July 2, before the spill, said he found no interest in or understanding of river ecology there.

Members of the ranch looked to Yogacharya Black for guidance in the situation. In the conversation in his living room a month after the spill, Yogacharya had said he didn't believe that water heats up in the pond. He didn't believe that the water slows down or particles drop out; the water goes out of the pond just as fast as it comes in, he said. Nor did he believe that any fish died while the dam was being repaired.

Asked how the ranch would deal with a state agency that could sustain a long legal battle, Mr. Black responded that he would sue for damages. The dam would not be removed, he said. Golden Lotus filed suit a month later, claiming that the DNR was responsible for the damage because it had assumed control of the drawdown and that the ranch had done only what it was told to do by the department.

The department prepared its own suit. In fact, the fact-finding hearing held in Gaylord was a technicality meant to ensure that all further steps would be legal. Several days after the hearing, Director Skoog issued a ruling that the dam was to remain open permanently.

On the tenth day on which the river ran free, attorneys for Golden Lotus appeared before Francis Walsh, acting Circuit Court judge in Gaylord. The dam was their source of electricity. They asked to close the dam because it was costing the ranch $1,000 a week to operate an emergency generator run on propane gas to service their heavy electrical consumption. Walsh ordered the dam closed. The department, claiming the dam was unsafe, closed the two campgrounds downstream. Jack Deming, a local merchant and member of the Pigeon River Country Advisory Council, complained at a council meeting that the shutdown was hurting tourist business. He was told the department would clearly be liable if the campgrounds remained open and the dam failed. Subsequent inspections convinced the department that the welding was adequate, and the campgrounds were eventually reopened. When the dam gates closed, water rose over the muck drying along the floodplain and left it floating in the pond again.

Even after the river water cleared downstream, detritus clung to quiet pools near the banks, washing into the stream with every rain, too buoyant to fall into sediment traps and too thick to disappear in month after month of continuously running water.

Members of Trout Unlimited and the Michigan United Conservation Clubs were so outraged by the incident that they lined up a battery of lawyers in defense of the world-class trout stream. In the first months after the spill, they watched events closely, letting the Michigan DNR know they were prepared to step in with their considerable financial and political clout. When Michigan's attorney general filed the suit against Golden Lotus on December 18, 1984, the Michigan United Conservation Clubs and the Michigan Council of Trout Unlimited joined the DNR as plaintiffs.

For its part, the Pigeon River Country Advisory Council asked the department to review whether legislation existed to adequately prevent environmental damage and whether it had rules of its own and adequate personnel to prevent such damage from happening again. The department was issuing hundreds of permits every year without adequate funding or personnel to monitor any of them. Dr. Don Inman of the environmental enforcement division in Lansing said that the department in 1984 had good control over construction of new dams but not over maintenance of existing dams. By the time of the Pigeon River spill, it had been trying for 20 years to strengthen legislation without success. The Pigeon River case was recognized as a turning point in protecting the quality of Michigan rivers.

The state finally enacted legislation in 1986 to adequately control dam safety and maintenance. But the program itself has been more precarious than expected.

The quality of northern Michigan streams is a reflection of the quality of their environment. Water in natural vegetation runs clear. The Pigeon River originates in a fan of streams that course through heavily wooded, isolated hills around the small settlement of Sparr.

In 1983 Melling Resorts International purchased Sylvan Knob, a small ski resort in the hills southwest of Sparr. Melling began clearing hundreds of acres, opening the dense forest for ski runs, resort buildings, and golfing. Nearby residents were soon talking about the high prices Melling was offering for land adjacent to the renamed Sylvan Resort, and later Treetops. As the holding grew, some landowners nearby expressed relief that developers would not be able to subdivide and sell off the vast acreage for private homes.

In September 1983 Steve Swan recommended to the DNR that Melling's application to reconstruct a 100 by 150 foot pond on a creek of the Pigeon River be approved. "This pond appears essential to the operation of this ski resort," Swan wrote. "Therefore I feel we should compromise our 'no ponds on trout streams' position. I recommend this permit be issued with the stipulation that the pond be impounded only during snow making operations with normal unimpeded stream flow allowed during the balance of the year." An earthen dam 8 feet wide, 55 feet long, and 4.8

feet high was constructed on the creek to impound water for snowmaking. The resulting pond was just off a graded dirt road that wove past a shop building and up a steep hill to a restaurant. The next summer more ski slopes were cleared down the far side of that hill, exposing a wide strip of beige northern Michigan sand that ran down the slope into a valley of cedars and spruces adjacent to more of the Pigeon River headwaters. The resort made plans to build a golf course with five of its 18 holes in the wetlands. It was the same summer of the spill at Song of the Morning Ranch several miles downstream.

On the Fourth of July, 1984, a husky man approached what are known locally as the tubes, the huge cylinders that carry the Pigeon River under the bridge at Pigeon River Campground. The river was running black from the spill that had begun the day before. He talked quietly about the mess. There seemed to be no words adequate to describe what was before us. We watched my dog drink from the river. At least it's not toxic, we observed. He talked about his days as a captain on Great Lakes vessels. He lived now, retired, about an hour away. His family came to the Pigeon every summer because it was so pretty. He said his son-in-law loved to fish there. Today, he said, his son-in-law was so upset that he didn't speak.

I remarked that when I was in New York City three weeks earlier the condition of the rivers and surface waters in the city, where there are so many bright people, had saddened me. When I stood on a footbridge in Central Park, I fantasized with my brother-in-law about obtaining a grant to study the effects of cleaning up the water there for a year or two. I said I thought people would respond to clean water, that most of them would try to keep it that way. My brother-in-law reacted with skepticism. It might plant a seed, I said. I recalled the story of the magic geranium in which a woman places the flower in her house, then cleans the room to match the beauty of the geranium, and eventually cleans the whole house to match the beauty of the room. It makes a nice fantasy.

Following the spill, brown trout from the lower reaches of the Pigeon moved in where most of the original trout had died, and within three years fishermen were catching 18-to-20-inch browns, as well as smaller brook trout; and steelheads were spawning new rainbow trout in the upper reaches below the dam.

Richard Armour told the rest of his story in the court proceedings.

Golden Lotus had the impression the DNR recognized the dam urgently needed to be fixed yet couldn't agree how to proceed with a river running constantly through the pond. Even though the permit had allowed one foot of drawdown per day, Golden Lotus had been ordered on July 2 to close the gates enough to bring the pond level back up.

In the hours before dawn on July 3, taking his directions from J. Oliver Black to open the gates and fix them, Armour let out enough water to put the river level just below the iron tracks of the wooden gate so welding could begin. He said it had been clear to him and Hayes when the permit was issued that the drawdown would drop the pond to the normal river level. It was the only way to make repairs. He understood from Hayes early on that they should act quickly, before the dam broke open.

The master welder reported that he had doubled the gate channels to 10 inches and the thickness to three-quarters of an inch. The court accepted and Golden Lotus carried out the DNR's eventual list of other modifications considered necessary to make the dam reasonably safe, including increased spillway capacity, a secondary gate system, and removal of trees where it was feared their roots might weaken the surrounding earth.

The DNR never detected sediments in Mullett Lake. It said mayfly and midge densities declined downstream, but no other aquatic animal counts downstream differed from upstream. Circuit Court judge William Porter found Armour and Black knowingly violated their permit but found no grounds to order removal of the dam even though evidence showed it made the Pigeon less productive for trout than similar streams. He noted there were 22 percent fewer trout than average, though also that the Pigeon's trout were larger than average, and that the Pigeon's water quality, stream bed diversity, and trout cover were comparable to those of other quality streams studied. He said the plaintiffs had failed to show that the dam was likely to fail again or that the original dam construction—whenever that had occurred, sometime around 1875—had been done without a permit. Golden Lotus was ordered to retain "on a continuing basis" a trained person to implement a dam safety and management program.

In 1986, during a rainfall of eight to 10 inches, 19 dams in the state failed. The legislature finally passed a dam safety act, bringing the state up to par with most states. It called for periodic inspections by licensed engineers. It gave Michigan the authority to require repairs, maintenance, upgrades, and permits.

But on March 23, 2005, the Michigan legislature ceased funding the state's dam safety program on the recommendation of the Department of Environmental Quality, which administered it. The move was akin to having a highway with a speed limit of seventy miles per hour but not posting signs or assigning troopers to enforce it, as Jim Pawloski saw it at the time. It left Golden Lotus still responsible for maintaining the dam and reporting to the state about it but made no provision for personnel to check the dam or read the reports. Partial funding was enacted on October 1, 2005, restoring the dam safety program.

Pawloski, who had been the DEQ's area dam safety administrator when funding suddenly ceased, said Golden Lotus had been complying with the requirement for inspection reports every four or five years. In November 1993, it paid the fifth and final installment of a $90,000 civil penalty in the dam case, which was deposited in the state's fish and game fund.

Through the years, the yoga retreat obtained approvals for a Planned Unit Development under Otsego County's zoning ordinance. The ranch envisioned members gradually erecting separate houses for visiting or retiring there. In the dozen years since approval, four houses have been built. Thirty other lots have been leased through a separate for-profit organization, Clear Light Community Management Company, Inc., a subsidiary of Golden Lotus. Clear Light pays taxes on its income. The residences pay property taxes even though it's a spiritual community.

Carol Armour, who lives in one of the four houses and was working in Gaylord's post office, says the tax arrangement is satisfactory. "The town needs money, too," she said. Clear Light can sell only to an approved member so Golden Lotus can ensure that "people have a spiritual purpose for being here." Drugs, for one thing, are not allowed. "We can buy back property if a drug dealer is found," she said, and "if we stick to the highest principles, we get the best results. . . . So we ask people who fall in love with the place to come to retreats for a year [and] get to know whether the spiritual life is appropriate." Residents own only their houses; the land remains under the control of Golden Lotus.

She says it will certainly remain a spiritual community. "Let's say Golden Lotus" dissolved. "It would go to another of our type of organization. Self-Realization Fellowship (SRF) is our mother organization, so a different philosophy coming in won't happen." Golden Lotus asked SRF in Los Angeles to send a spiritual director to carry on after Bob Raymer, who over the years since J. Oliver Black's death had himself become ill.

Mrs. Armour added that the improvements made to the dam had been a good idea: "Five years ago or so we had a hundred-year storm. We would have lost the lower domes and the main house if we hadn't been forced to make those changes." More than four inches of rain fell in 20 hours August 17 and 18, 1995. It raised the Pigeon more than four feet above normal, washed out the road at the Pigeon River Campground, and cut a new channel 20 feet wide and three feet deep. The Pigeon River crossed the road near Tin Bridge. The Black flowed across Tin Shanty Bridge Road for nearly two days. But the new emergency spillways at Song of the Morning Ranch kept the dam intact.

The money that paid the penalties imposed by the court was donated by Golden Lotus members. Yogananda, Armour said, taught them to see through to higher truths. Learning how to behave is basic to all religions and moral codes and the basis of all civilization. "Behavior involves responsibility. Is it not stealing if I don't pay my debt?" she asked. Yogananda balanced development of body, mind, and soul through yoga. Respect is due them all, she said.

Joseph Robert Raymer is listed as the president of Golden Lotus, Inc., and Carol Armour as resident agent. She was asked about the impression among DNR field staff that members of the ranch wanted to work with water quality experts to reduce negative impacts short of removing the dam, perhaps by reducing the pond area so temperatures would not rise so high. Her response was to ask where that information came from. She said the ranch would never remove the dam and that all the research about the Pigeon was suspect because it was motivated by a desire to remove the dam.

Golden Lotus, Inc., and Song of the Morning Ranch applied in 2001 for permits for two construction projects that needed the approval of the Natural River Zoning Review Board. They asked to place a seawall in the lake next to the boathouse building and fill behind it. The board denied the request. They also asked to repair erosion caused by the hundred-year storm of 1995, a repair required by the Department of Environmental Quality. The board approved that request.

DNR's Fisheries Division continues to characterize the dam as a problem for trout fishing, blaming it for fluctuating temperatures, sudden increases in water flow, and periodic release of detritus from the pond. Graphs generated by the USGS do show peaks of suddenly rising water flow in most summer months. However, the peaks come right after heavy rainfall. And, while the Pigeon River temperature averaged one to three degrees warmer below the pond than above it in summer 2005, it was not any warmer than the Black River. Still, the pond remains full of dark, floating particles and vegetation poised to flush downstream whenever water starts moving rapidly through the dam.

Part 3 🌿 Voices

9

Hemingway

The most famous person of letters known to have spent time in the Pigeon River Country is Ernest Hemingway. His experiences there occurred just as the area was being set aside as a state forest. He was a young man just back from the war, but as his writing developed he used what he knew of the area to serious purpose.

In his "Up in Michigan" short story, Hemingway described three young men coming back from hunting with rifles on "the pine plains beyond Vanderbilt" carrying "three deer in the back of the wagon, their thin legs sticking stiff over the edge of the wagon box." In "Now I Lay Me," his central character mostly gave up thinking about the girls he had known and concentrated instead on trout fishing "because I found that I could remember all the streams and there was always something new about them, while the girls" after awhile "blurred and all became rather the same."

In a July 26, 1919, letter to a friend, Howell Jenkins, Hemingway talked fondly about the Pigeon River Country. He called it the Pine Barrens and said they could "nearly drive across" it "without any road just by compass. It is so free from under brush." He told Jenkins "that Barrens Country is the greatest I've ever been in," and that "there are some great camping places on the Black" where he guaranteed they would catch all the trout they wanted. In a September 15 letter, he told Jenkins that Ernest's group of five people caught 23 fish the day before on the Black even though "it rained like hell."

Hemingway, who had defective vision in his left eye, was carrying cigarettes, chocolates, and postcards for Italian troops as a member of the Red

Cross in Italy when an Austrian fragmentation bomb exploded along the ground July 8, 1918. The injured Hemingway carried a more severely wounded Italian soldier 50 yards when a machine gun round tore into his right knee; he staggered but got his man another 50 yards to safety. Hemingway was 18. A year later, after convalescing in Milan, he was at his parents' summer home on Walloon Lake some 25 miles west of what is now Pigeon River Country. His fishing trip in early July was his first in nearly two years, according to his biographer Carlos Baker. He said Hemingway and his friends drove southeast to Vanderbilt, then east past the Sturgeon and Pigeon to the Black, where they spent seven days and "took more trout than they could eat."

The road Hemingway traveled from Vanderbilt still exists as a narrow dirt road, closely lined by woods. It is now called Old Vanderbilt Road and runs roughly parallel to the newer, paved Sturgeon Valley Road. In an unpublished letter July 15, 1919, Hemingway said they had seen the bear on "the Pidgeon river" and that the trip was "a peach."

Hemingway took the Vanderbilt road again in August 1920 and camped at the Black River. He and four friends were gone for six days in a rented car with a trailer. "We had a marvelous time this trip," he said in a letter. "Brummy [Ted Brumback] . . . can play the mandolin wonderfully and in the evening he would play after supper in the dusk and 'side the camp fire.

"And before we went to sleep we'd all be curled up around the fire. Often a wonderful moon . . .

"Brummy and Dick [Smale] were wading down the stream and Brummy was tired and wet and about two miles below camp. Brum's beard was blond and curly and Dick sez, 'Gosh, Baugh, you do look like Jesus Christ!'

"'Well,' the Baugh comes back at him, 'If I was I wouldn't wade. I'd get right up on the water and walk back to camp!'

". . . It was great in camp lying all rolled up in the blankets after the fire had died down to coals and the men were asleep and looking at the moon and thinking long long thoughts."

In October, Hemingway met Elizabeth Hadley Richardson, and by spring 1921 they planned to marry. On April 28 that year he wrote to Bill Smith that he would "sometimes get thinking about the Sturgeon and Black during the nocturnal [night] and damn near go cuckoo. . . . May have to give it up for something I want more—but that doesn't keep me from loving it with everything I have. Dats de way tings are. Guy loves a couple or three streams all his life and loves 'em better than anything in the world—falls in love with a girl and the goddam streams can dry up for all he cares. Only the hell of it is that all that country has as bad a hold on me as ever."

The week of his September 3, 1921 wedding, Hemingway spent three days at the Sturgeon River for a bachelor splurge at the end of fishing season. In 1924, he wrote "Big Two-Hearted River," a short story based in part on a 1919 fishing trip to the Fox River at Seney in the Upper Peninsula. He used the name of the river north of the Fox because of its "poetry," and it is apparent that he drew on other Michigan experiences for the story, which is about a wounded man battling for inner recovery. In a coda, Hemingway said the character Nick Adams "wanted to write about country so it would be there like Cézanne had done it in painting. You had to do it from inside yourself." The story describes Nick watching a long time as trout held themselves steady in the fast water, the biggest at the bottom "in a varying mist of gravel and sand, raised in spurts by the current."

In 1992, Jack Owen, a member of the Pigeon River Country Advisory Council, donated to the state for display the end of a white pine log his wife found washed up on Lake Superior beach near the mouth of the Two-Hearted River. On it was an original log mark from when it was cut about a century ago. The pine was about two feet in diameter and had been growing about 200 years when it was cut down.

10

Berdine Yuill

Tom Yuill's son Stanley and Jim Yuill's son Berdine were lifelong residents of the Pigeon River Country area. Berdine was a supervisor and justice of the peace for many years. In 1975, Sam Titus taped interviews with Stanley and Berdine.

Berdine Yuill: [When] my father come, there was no railroads here or anything, just a vast amount of timber. They come and they started in the logging business. Them days it wasn't so much logs, they cut wood, called a coal kills. They used this wood on the railroad instead of coal, fired the engines with that, you see? And they hauled it then to the railroad tracks, then they would have places to pick it up. Well, then it advanced into lumbering days. My Uncle Tom and Uncle John were the mainstays in the lumbering business. My father pulled out and went farming. My uncles established lumber camps in the forest out here.

Sam Titus: Did they have a name for all this area?

A: No. Camp Two was out here in the forest; they had their own railroad, and they hauled their logs on these railroads to a mill in Logan.

Q: And that's about two miles south of Vanderbilt?

A: Yes. The hardwood timber was shipped to Bay City to W. D. Young & Company; they manufactured it there. After Camp Two was finished up they established another camp at Merkle Springs. That's where the Hidden Valley [resort] is.

Q: Oh, you called it what kind of Springs?

A: Merkle Springs. There was a spring in there and they called it Merkle [for the adjacent John Merkle farm]. After that was finished they established a Camp One, and lumbered all these vast acres. And in time to come the mill burned [in 1920]. A big fire went through, just sweeped the country. I remember that: it got so smoky you couldn't see. After that the people commenced to farm the land, then it grew up the second growth that they're lumbering today.

Q: When you were young, what did you do for fun?

A: Well, I was the fellow that had to work. I had chores to do. I milked the cows and farmed and went to school, and that was it.

Q: That was it. How far did you go to school?

A: Eighth grade.

Q: When you were young, did you think you were going to see what has happened to this . . .

A: Never thought I would get old.

Q: Really?

A: Yeah. I can remember when I got twenty-one, how proud I was. No, I had no forethought of what would happen. It's like running in debt, there's always payday.

After farming started, what the people raised for a cash sale was potatoes. There were warehouses here, [and] everybody that farmed raised potatoes. And they had contractors come in to contract them for so much a bushel.

Q: Did you have any close friends that you have kept track of all these years, that you still know, that still live here?

A: No. I'm about the oldest person in this county.

11

Stanley Yuill

Sam Titus conducted this interview with Stanley Yuill in 1975.

Stanley Yuill: We didn't float anything on the rivers; they were used for pine. Our main business was hardwood. We sawed in our mill in Logan, brought hemlock in on our railroad [from] that big [logging] outfit east of Gaylord. We shipped the hardwood down to Bay City.

Sam Titus: It got on a boat down there?

A: They manufactured it. Hardwood lumber for flooring. My folks came here originally to farm, and they farmed a lot of timber. We had our first automobile here in 1910.

Q: What kind?

A: Cadillac. They shipped it up from Bay City, on a boat to Cheboygan. It took them all day to come down this road where the sand—you know, they got stuck. A good many people had their first ride in that car. . . . The first year we took a trip back to Ontario—go down through Port Huron and up that way [into Canada]. But gee, it took us three days to go.

Q: No wonder, there were no roads.

A: I know it. It was all down through the jack pines, the sandy roads. No markers. You stayed where you left off. They didn't have any maps. They kind of made signs that people put up.

Q: Now getting to animals, birds, and wildflowers and that sort of thing. How much was here that you can remember?

A: Just outside of town a ways there was all kinds of forest and the wild berries were around most every place. Never went far before you got blackberries, and we still get them. I one time got the urge back in, I forget what date it was, we started to—30 acres of raspberries, gosh, as a crop we couldn't sell them.

Q: Now you get 90 cents a quart for them.

A: I guess so.

Q: Now if you had 30 acres of red raspberries you'd be a millionaire.

A: Yeah, I guess if we would have held onto all our land we would have been millionaires ten times over. But that's gone; we sold it for nothing, give it away, lots of it.

Q: Can't worry about it now.

A: No, I didn't make it so I don't care, nothing to me. My father was pretty well off when I come along.

Q: Did he hunt?

A: He never hunted a day in his life. He owned thousands of acres of land to hunt on, but people from Detroit come up and they never asked permission to hunt. They did everything, burned everything up.
   There were quite a few different people out here once. They logged hardwood and made broom handles. I think originally somebody had a stave mill, they made out of elm.

Q: Were there a lot of shingle mills?

A: We had one in town. And then Kellys had the little mill in the Pigeon. They made little mills someplace near where they were getting the timber.

Q: And whenever one of these little mills sprung up there would be a little community.

A: Yeah, a little settlement. They'd have a blacksmith and a cook. Our camps were all larger as we got around.

Q: How many did you have altogether before you quit?

A: We had four, I think.

Q: Going at once?

A: Yeah. See, we had two railroads, one that come out from Wolverine and another one at Logan. We had four locomotives.

Q: Whatever happened to all that stuff?

A: We sold it when we got through with it. Sold the rails.

Q: And took them up. That's where the roadbeds are now.

A: You'll see where railroad beds have been all over the country.

Q: How big was Vanderbilt as a town when you . . .

A: About the same size. Mostly pretty good class of people. They bought out east of Gaylord where we lumbered, we sold them the land. I know a fella down there to Roscommon, he, I forget what his name was, he brought them in by the trainload from Chicago. And sold them farms out there they couldn't raise anything on, and they would get out there and they just about starved to death. They would move back, find some other job. Boy, I tell you it was bad.

Q: Was this your family home?

A: No, ours burned. It was up there on a farm about a mile out. We owned all the land on both sides for miles. I don't know, we owned too much land, that was the trouble.

Q: It was hard to keep track of probably.

A: Oh, gosh, when tax time come, we kept track of it all right. They ruined us for about $10,000 a year, so I don't know, maybe it was a good thing after all. But my uncle years ago, he said, "Someday"—he was talking about his land out east of here, we had so many acres—"Someday you'll get $10 an acre for this." We said, "Holy smokes." Now we're taxed that much. We owned a lot of lakes, rivers—Sturgeon River over the full length from Gaylord to here. And then we had the west branch of the Sturgeon, we owned several miles on that, and Pickerel Lake, we owned that.

My father, he could make money anyplace.

Q: Because he could see ahead.

A: Yeah.

Q: That's what the spirit of the people who did this land, that seems to be what I find out, that someone came in like a father who had this foresight and just went ahead and did it.

A: Yeah, they bought up this timber, then they got in with an uncle. He would go down to Bay City and go to the banks in Saginaw and borrow money for him to keep him going.

One of the first settlers' cabins in Otsego County, photographed sometime after 1883

John Yuill next to virgin white pine in 1916

Logs floating in the Black River during the lumbering era

Camp 2 in the Pigeon River Country, 1917

Foreman Bob Moore, Harris Smith (*seated*) and his older brother, chore boy James G. Smith Jr., at Cornwell's Mill on the Pigeon River in 1908. The boiler was used to clean a larger boiler.

Interior of a mill that rendered virgin timber into lumber

Pigeon River State Forest original headquarters buildings in 1930

White pine cones near the Sturgeon River

Cornwall Flooding in the central forest

Rocking horse oil rig in the southern forest

Tree limbs in a sinkhole lake

Two calf elk with their mothers, one collared

Fly-fishing on the Pigeon River

A new conifer takes root in
an ancestor stump near the
Black River

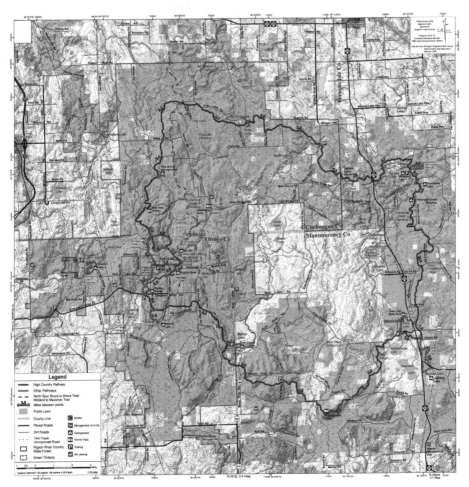

The Pigeon River Country as it appears on a 21 × 22 inch map of the High Country Pathway available from the Pigeon River Country Association, P.O. Box 122, Gaylord, MI 49735, or at http://www.pigeonrivercountryforest.org

Q: Was your mother's family from around here?

A: My mother was born in the Upper Peninsula. They moved down to Berryville here.

Q: That was another little village?

A: It was before Vanderbilt started. They thought the railroads were going through there. It didn't do it, they came through here, and so that shut them all up. So they moved here, and he built a store here, John G. Berry, that was my mother's . . .

Q: Your mother's relative, her family . . .

A: Yes.

Q: Where did they pick up the word *Vanderbilt?*

A: Long story. When they organized the town here, they thought they would give us a good, rich name and so they named it after Vanderbilt, that owned the railroad, and when he went through and saw it he went sailing right by.

Q: He wasn't impressed with a town named after him.

A: No, he didn't leave anything either.

There were four family Yuills living here, but most of them are gone, I'm about the only one left.

Q: You and Mr. Berdine.

A: Yes. His father lived right across the road from him, and he was the only Yuill that farmed. He thought he could make more than he could by working for his brothers, so there was only the three Yuills that did the lumbering business, and he did the farming. But my folks did probably one hundred times as much farming as he did. As soon as their teams of horses were done in the wintertime, we put them to work in the farms here. We had two or three farms.

Q: Who supplied you with your horses?

A: I think my dad bought the first carload of them down in Bay City.

Q: The great big wagons you used to pull, where did you get those?

A: With the big wheels? We made them. We always had a blacksmith. He made everything. They had to. You couldn't run and buy one. We had two stores, one in town, a grocery store, and one in Logan. Did quite a business. I looked over the books one time before everything burned.

There was about a half million—stuff that was gone out to people who needed. My father was generous; he was always giving someone something.

Q: What type of social life did you have? How many churches were here?

A: Just the one. My father, when he left Scotland, his father said, "When you get to this country, when you get settled, built a kirk." And that's what he did.

Q: What denomination was it?

A: Congregational.

Q: What did you do for social life, I mean besides the church?

A: We had lodges, the Masonic Lodge, the Star. We would have a ball game. We tried to have a band. We paid all expenses on the ball team and the band. Every town always had somebody for supporting the whole town.

Q: I suppose that's the only way it could survive.

A: Well, yes. He had to supply work.

Q: Did you feel that when you were here in Vanderbilt you were going to a bigger town [in Gaylord]?

A: Well, yes. Gaylord was the county seat. We didn't go to Gaylord much.

Later Mrs. Titus and Mr. Yuill talk about poverty.

Q: You mean they had a poorhouse?

A: Oh yeah, poor farm, they called it.

Q: And the people who were left without anything went to the poor farm to live, was that it?

A: Yes, if there's nothing, but most of the people would support them, you know, their . . .

Q: Their own people. But once in a while there would be some more people left with nobody.

A: Yeah, yeah, that they had no one that cared anything about them, so they sent them there.

Q: It might be good if we still had those kind of farms, rather than nursing homes like they send old people to now, which is death. It's the most horrible thing there is in the world. How far did the grades go in those days?

A: Tenth grade. I had to go to Big Rapids to school.

Q: To finish out?

A: Yeah, that was a privilege to go to school.

Q: Do you remember who any of your teachers were?

A: My teachers? Oh, yes. There was Miss Leachman, Miss Jennings, and Armstrong.

Q: Were they native girls or did they import them?

A: They were all from outside.

Q: When you had all these camps around, what did you use for a doctor?

A: We had a doctor in town, Dr. Weiner. He was the doctor that delivered me. I forget the name of the doctor before him, but he was in the same place. Dr. Weiner took his place; he was here for quite a few years. He was a pretty fair doctor; I don't suppose he went to any great college.

Q: But he knew what to do.

A: Yeah, he saved a lot of people during the flu epidemic.

Q: Now, when you had an accident out to one of your mills, what would you do?

A: They'd die . . .

Q: It took too much trouble to get them into town?

A: Yeah. They'd fend for themselves, they'd go on home and . . .

Q: Do whatever they needed to do.

A: Yeah.

Q: There wasn't anything like a hospital, I suppose.

A: No.

Q: The doctor would take care of them in his own home if he needed to.

A: Yeah.

Q: Of course, every woman was a nurse in those days.

A: Oh, yes, everybody had to do something, they knew something, they all had a doctor book.

Q: And now there's hardly any woman knows how to take care of anybody, any young woman in her home anymore . . .

A: No, it's all done. Yes, we didn't have any unemployment or insurance or anything like that.

Q: No, when someone had a bad time everybody pitched in and helped them. How old was your father when he came here?

A: About 25.

Q: Did his father ever come over here to see him?

A: No. Father and his father and mother stayed together later in Canada for a while when we first got our car. His mother had her first ride, and she said, "They'll all be killed, they'll all get killed."

Q: I expect that looked pretty frightening to her.

A: Oh, it did.

Q: How well did you know Dr. Hoobler's father?

A: We sold the land to the Hooblers—I think my father used to, when they would come up on the train to town, why he would take them out there with the horses. That's [how] the Lansing Club started, too. They come up on the train, and someone had to take them out.

Q: Did you like to be in the woods? I mean, were you fond of the woods, or did you think of it as a livelihood?

A: I don't know. I never thought a thing about it. I just thought—it was woods.

Q: You didn't think about it in those days like we're thinking about it now. You know, it's so fast going that . . .

A: Well, they come to a different section every year. You moved the camp every once in a while, every two or three years. We had teams and wagons. They would load it all on, and then they made tar paper and just cut a slab.

Q: Was it dirt floors?

A: No, no, we always . . .

Q: You always made a floor.

A: Yes. Cook camp was always clean and nice and fixed up with a maple log table there, and everyone sat down there to eat. That was probably the most interesting sight. I met a fella in Idaho, I was standing up against the bank there just resting and looking around and I had my car out in front and the fella come along and said, "Are you from Michigan?" I said, "Yeah," and he said, "What part of Michigan?" I said, "Northern part." He says, "I used to work up there." I said, "Where did you work?" He said, "Yuill Brothers."

Q: Young guys migrated camp to camp to camp?

A: Yes. They went out there in Idaho to work in their woods, but it was a different sort of a deal entirely than here.

Q: But the people who worked for you were not residents, they . . .

A: Generally they weren't. Well, they might have lived some place near here. Of course, all the men stayed in one building, so they wouldn't have any family there. Well, this is quite a town, quite a country.

Q: Yes, that's why I think it's so important to get all the little things that you people can remember that lived it. This has been your life.

A: Yeah, this is where I lived all my life.

Q: What's gone on here has shaped your life, your way of thinking and everything else, so it's an important thing. That's why we want to get it on paper if we can. Because now it's a little late.

A: Yes, because the ones that participated, they've all gone.

Q: But maybe we can salvage enough out of it by digging deep in your memories. Were the people all friendly? I mean, did you ever have any cantankerous old stinkers you had an awful time getting along with?

A: Well, drunks.

Q: Was that a problem then?

A: Well, once they would come in from camp . . .

Q: They would go on a drunken spree?

A: Yeah. They had five or six saloons here, you know, so they must have drunk a lot. That was mostly the woodsmen.

Q: They were really rough guys probably.

A: Well, not exactly, they wouldn't be until they got drunk. Had a little money and saved it up.

Q: What was the wage in those days?

A: Dollar a day, $30 a month.

Q: Flat. Now they got food with that, didn't they?

A: Yes, and that's all. Most of them brought their tools with them, just their ax and saw.

Q: They always had mounds of flapjacks and potatoes?

A: Pork 'n' beans. We had meat. Cause we raised the hogs right on the farm, right in the camp.

Q: They had three heavy meals a day.

A: Oh, yes, they fed good, too; they fed good, always had cake and pie on the table, that was natural.

Q: And these guys that did the cooking, they didn't do anything else but cooking.

A: That's all they did was cook, that was . . .

Q: . . . a big job, they didn't have electric can openers . . .

A: No they didn't. They had a helper, the cookee. They didn't set and talk at the table. When they sat down, they sat down to eat, no talking.

Q: If they talked, they'd lose . . .

A: They'd throw them out. They was pretty strict, you know, these cooks.

Q: You were there to eat, so eat. Did you have dishes or did you have tin?

A: They had tin.

Q: Big stoves.

A: Yeah, big stove, and they washed [dishes] in the big tub.

Q: Did you always put your camps close to the rivers so you would have water?

A: No, we . . .

Q: . . . or did you make a well?

A: A well. I can see them yet—the cooks. After Sunday school, kids would go out to camp and they'd feed them. But I know people would go out there just for Sunday and think nothing of it, get the meal; they never thought about paying for it.

Q: Good heavens, really?

A: Oh, yes, hundreds of people.

Q: You just trotted out with your horse and buggy and had Sunday dinner and come home.

A: Yeah.

Q: And for free.

A: Well, of course my father never thought anything about those things; he'd just feed them and that was it.

Q: And still he made money . . .

A: Money, gosh, he made so much he was a millionaire at one time.

Q: A lot of people wouldn't have done that.

A: No, I know lots of camps kicked them out, couldn't get anything to eat, wouldn't feed people. That was no good; we weren't like that. We had lots of wood to put into the stove 'cause they had somebody out there that split the wood for them.

Q: I can't relate to a forest, but I lived on a farm with my grandmother and I can relate to a big farm.

A: Well, not many years ago we lumbered the last piece we had. We had a half an acre left out right behind our house there, and that was what was supporting that school; then they done away with the school.

Q: Did you ever have women cook at these camps?

A: Once in a great while, but not very often. [Cooks] did all their own baking, made the pies, cakes.

Q: And I think it's terrible if I have to make two pies in one day.

A: Oh gosh, yeah.

Q: Was a dollar a day the highest wage you'd ever paid? What did you pay your cooks?

A: He was a little better paid; he was kind of a special man.

Q: Would he usually have a family with him?

A: Not very often. He just cooked, was a bachelor.
    We had men killed out there. One time they had those big wheels, and they were coming in with a load of logs and the thing broke off the tongue, where it attached to the horses. It just flopped right back over and the tongue hit him on the head and smashed him all to pieces. I know my dad went out there, where the fella's wife was; oh, gosh, he sent a couple of thousand dollars. That was big money those days.

Q: Sure was.

A: But they didn't have too many accidents. They cut themselves once in a while or a tree would fall on them.

Q: The only means of cutting down a tree in those days was a crosscut saw and an ax, wasn't it?

A: A crosscut saw.

Q: With two men on it, one on each side, and an ax.

A: Well, an ax was just for trimming the limbs.

Q: How many trees could a good lumberjack cut down in a day?

A: Well those big ones, about 15 or 20.

Q: Good Lord.

A: If they couldn't cut enough, why they would get another bunch of sawyers. But we always had quite a bunch of sawyers.

Q: No wonder they needed three meals a day. Did you have whistles you blew?

A: This camp man had a long horn. He would blow that.

Q: And that was supposed to be quitting time.

A: Well, they generally looked at their watch. And, of course, the foreman would tell them when to quit.

Q: And they worked how many hours a day?

A: Oh, all the time; hours didn't mean anything. They would quit when they thought it was about time.

Q: Or weather. It poured down rain, I suppose they came in. You didn't work in the wintertime, though, did you?

A: We worked all the time in the winter. See, we had the sleighs and the teams. The easiest way to take in the timber was on the sleighs.

Q: You slid it on the ice and snow?

A: On those bobsleds. They would build them up, and it would haul quite a load. It was easy going.

Q: Was there more snow than there is now?

A: Not any more, I don't think. There was snowplows, of course.

Q: What kind of snowplow?

A: Handmade up in Cheboygan. They called them the Cheboygan plow, but they had runners and they had two wings that come out.

Q: And the horse was on the front end?

A: They were on the front. You had to have two or three teams maybe.

Q: And they would go through the drifts and drag this thing.

A: Yeah.

Q: Maybe that's what we ought to have now. That sounds marvelous.

1 2

Chore Boy

In September 1969, James G. Smith Jr. left a sign along the Pigeon that said, "I worked in Cornwell's mill on this spot in 1908 . . . age 16, now 77." District game supervisor Ford Kellum found the sign and communicated with Mr. Smith. In 1975, Sam Titus and Ned Caveney went to Alma, Michigan, to interview Mr. Smith in his home.

James Smith Sr. was the engineer at the Cornwell mill on the Pigeon around what is now Section Four Lake north of the headquarters. His son worked at the C. S. Bliss lumber camp on the Tittabawassee River in 1907, when he was 15, then joined his father on the Pigeon as chore boy from October 1908 until July 4, 1909. Young Jim built the fires in the men's camp, cook camp, and office and called the cooks. That work was done before the foreman and the men got up each day. He got $20 per month.

James Smith Jr.: There isn't really much to talk about—only get up real early in the morning and go to bed late at night. I traded horses up there one time, and I was pretty smart. I was going to beat this fella at a horse deal. I never saw the man before. I just came out of the men's camp, he stopped and talked, a perfect stranger. He said, "Is there anybody around here who wants to trade horses?" I said, "What kind of a horse do you want?" He said, "Any kind." I said, "Well, I'll trade with ya." So, I said, "What kind of a horse do you want, a workhorse or a driving horse or what?" He said, "Just a horse." Well, I said, "All right, come down and get it." I said, "I'll trade ya. I haven't seen your horse and you haven't seen mine. So call it a deal."

So, we had a sawhorse laying up against the barn with one leg broke off of it. So I was real smart, and I went down. I said, "Well, here's your horse." "Boy," he said, "it's just right." He picked it up and put it on his shoulder and started out across the dam. I said, "Now just what is this?" I wasn't as smart as I thought I was. I hollered at him. I said, "Where is my horse?" He said, "The other side of the mill, right around on the road." So he went on across the dam. I went around back of the mill, followed the road. There lay a dead horse. Well, it was my horse, so I had to bury him. Afterward I found the sawhorse. He just carried it across the dam nicely and threw it over in the swamp. I buried the horse with the shovel. I did wiggle him around and get him in a hollow spot and I threw the dirt over top.

Sam Titus or Ned Caveney: It's beautiful country up there.

A: Yes, it is. I would love to have a little house right up in there where the mill used to be, right on the stream, and I wouldn't care if I never saw another person. [Pointing to his hand-drawn map:] And this is your pond where they used to hold the water.

Q: Floated the logs.

A: And the sluiceway. The water would go right through.

Q: What was the sluiceway made of?

A: Just wood, very crude. Then this jack ladder was a conveyor; went from here up into the mill. The saw was in the upper part of the mill, the upstairs.

Old Tom Manning—old Tom, he was 66 and I am 83 now, yet he was old Tom (laughter). Tom's job was to sort the logs and send them up the jack ladder. One day Charlie Cornwell, that was the big shot, was in there. Tom made a mistake where a log got ahead of him. He sent the wrong kind of log up. All they had to do is roll the log off and wait till they were cutting that kind of timber. But Charlie wasn't satisfied, he had to go down there and blow a little. So he went down and jumped Tom about it and said, "What's the matter with ya, Tom? Don't you know anything?" Tom said, "I'm not supposed to know anything. I work for the Cornwell Lumber Company. They know it all," and went right on pushing logs. So Charlie just walked down the line and let him alone.

Q: What was your job?

A: I was a chore boy. I took care of the store and the post office. That was a big city. I had to call the cooks in the morning, build the fire. Here [points to map] was the blacksmith's shop in the barn. Any horses that wasn't working right at the time, I had to take care of them and milk the cow, feed the pigs. I had to keep the camp clean.

Q: Two men's camps?

A: Yes. One was right next to the river. They called it the old soldiers' home—the old timers stayed in that one, that was the best camp.

Q: How many men were in this [whole] camp?

A: About 30 when the mill was running in the summer. It was down to 12 or 15 in the winter. All they did was lay out the lumber in the winter. The mill didn't run. But in the summer the mill ran and, of course, took a bigger crew as the logs came down the river. A lot of them came in here by rails and they dumped them in the pond.

Q: How did the forest look, how did you feel, how big were the trees?

A: The pines were gone at that time. There was hemlock and maple that they were lumbering at that time, but most of the pine was gone. See, the pines were big ones. The stumps were there.

Q: Four feet in diameter?

A: Yes, right around three or four feet, but the hemlock, of course, they run about that big around.

Q: That's two feet.

A: The other thing I thought of about the hardwood swamp, how probably I'm the only one in America knows where that is. It was east of the river and back a little ways toward the south from the mill. I think I went farther in there than anybody ever went. Yes, I'd find a tree, then I let the tree bend over like that so I could get to another tree and then I would go up that one and let that bend over and skip to another one. I went probably two blocks back into the swamp. Where nobody ever walked in or went in before. You couldn't walk in there, it was too wet.

Of course, I'm woods crazy anyways. I love nature. . . .

We had a real good foreman up at the mill. Bob Moore. He was 25 years old. The old foreman died. They wanted to put another foreman in, but none of the crew liked it. So my dad and a couple of the old timers said that if they put him in why they'd leave. Well, of course, my dad was quite important there: the engineer's running the whole thing. So the boss said, "What am I going to do? I need you on the engines, need him on the scaling, need him here . . ." My dad said, "Put Bob in." Bob was keeping books. The boss said, "Bob is just a boy." Dad says, "That don't make any difference. Put him in. We'll see that he goes through." Bob had brains enough, so they made him foreman. About once a week he had these old timers come in the office and they talked for a couple hours. He always took their advice. And he made an awful good foreman.

Q: Your father was an engineer, so he traveled from mill to mill to mill. Were the rest of the people who just worked there, were they travelers or did you hire them from the area or did they follow the mills around?

A: They followed the woods. Of course, a lot of these camps didn't have mills. They cut the logs, then shipped them out to the mill.

Mr. Smith talks about the beaver dam northwest of Ford Lake near the mill.

A: There was a big pine log. We cut notches in it. I think three V-notches and one long one, and we lay behind there and we watched the beaver work. When we got tired of it, we'd just raise up and you would hear his tail come down on the water and you wouldn't see any more beaver for an hour or so.

Q: Beautiful!

A: The watchmen would set out on the point, and they always had one there. So when my wife and I was up there I found the log with the notches in it, where they dug out the gravel to build up the road on top of the dam. There was a piece of log with the notches in it, but it was only about that thick; the rest had burned and rotted away.

Q: Did you ever go back camping to the Pigeon River with your children?

A: The youngest boy and I did [in 1969], three days and nights, rabbit hunting. Most of the time we were exploring. Showing him around the country. We didn't hunt much. I showed him the beaver dam and things like that. We wanted to see some elk, but we didn't see any. Our tent set there out towards the burner from the mill, and this elk come right out there. And he bugled four or five times. The next morning I looked out there and his runway come right down where our tent was. That's what he was bugling for.

Their tent was near the well by the original men's camp.

A: That barrel is still there.

Q: It's pretty well caved in.

A: When the boy and I was up there, we had to have water. So we went down at night. I never dreamed that the well was gonna be there yet. But here you could see the sand bubbling up the bottom of the barrel. So we cleaned it all out, stirred it all up, and let it run out, dug a little trench there. The next morning went out there and it was just as pure and nice. Boy, I'd like to have some of that water right here.

I used to have to come down where the bank was low, fill the barrel, bring it up on a hand sleigh to the men's camp, and dump it in the barrel there for the men to wash with. Well, the foreman thought he was awful cute one day when I got up here. I had the barrel probably about half, two-thirds full of water. He sneaked out and tipped it over. I grabbed it, probably two or three pails full in it yet. I took it over to the door of the office, dumped it right there and gushed in all the dirt and sand and everything. His wife made him clean the floor. But there was always something like that going on up there; that's what made it livable.

My dad and [my three brothers] and my sister lived in one house. The section boss lived right beside the little stream. Let's see, there was one, two, three, four houses there besides the one on the north side of the railroad.

Q: What did these little houses look like?

A: They were just shacks.

Q: Like one room?

A: No, there was generally a couple bedrooms and there was . . .

Q: A big living room, kitchen?

A: Yeah. There wasn't any fancy work.

Q: Did you have a porch on them or anything?

A: No.

Q: Fireplace?

A: No, they was lucky to have a roof on them. They didn't pay any rent. They were just owned by the company, and if anyone wanted to bring their family in why . . .

Q: Cornwell owned them?

A: Yeah. Paul White was the hunter for the camp. That's why there wasn't many deer around there. Every campground had a hunter. They used to furnish meat for the camp.

Mr. Smith looks at some old photographs.

Q: Is this a typical building?

A: Yeah, that's the men's camp. This is Burt Lozo. That's Paul Campferd, Jake Gray and Charlie White, John Smith, Paul White, these two were brothers, and George Dixon and Hank Williams, Dave Fisher. [Points to another man] I never liked that guy; him and I had a fight once.

Q: You were this size and you fought with that one?

A: Yeah, and I knocked him flat. Another guy, he stepped in and stopped it; he just hauled the devil out of the guy for hitting a kid that size. He said, "I hadn't ought to stop it. What I ought to do is just let him beat the devil right out of ya." Al Beatty his name was. He was the Beatty that first run lions and tigers together in the circuses. You probably heard of him.

Q: Oh sure, Clyde Beatty.

A: Clyde Beatty is his brother.

Q: Would somebody be coming through and just take pictures?

A: Oh yeah, they come through there quite a lot, some local photographer.

Q: How long did your father work there? Just that one year?

A: Oh, no, he was there several years. And when that mill shut down he went to Vanderbilt at the Yuill Brothers mill.

Q: How long did the Cornwell mill operate?

A: I think it only operated the following year [after] I left. But it had been running quite a long time then. That was a good big mill; they used to cut 50,000 feet a day.

Q: You said you got up early in the morning. What was a normal day? How many hours did it last?

A: All I had to do was get up about 4:30, call the cooks so they could get up and get breakfast ready. Outside of that I had a pretty good night's rest. And then I had to put the lights out in the camp at 9:00. Everybody went to bed, and I had to stay up till 9:00 and put the light out.

Q: Kerosene lanterns?

A: Yeah, we didn't know we had any electric lights then. It was my job to clean the chimneys and fill the lamps and trim the wicks. I had plenty to do. I had to carry water. We had big barrels in the corner in the sink, and I had to fill that barrel, keep that filled so they could wash. I had to keep wood piled in there, had a box stove, used to call the cooks. Then I'd go out there and feed the horses that wasn't working. Then I'd come back up and call the foreman. The crew would eat, then him and the cooks would eat.

Q: What would you have, pancakes and stuff?

A: Always had pancakes. If they didn't, why they couldn't have had a crew.

Q: What kind of pancakes, buckwheat or what?

A: I don't know, just flour. The cook always had some special deal of his own. They had a little griddle there about three feet long. It held 12 pancakes. There were three and four this way. You had your batter in a big pitcher. You poured it out like that, then down this way and back this way, then you set your pitcher down and you turned this first pancake. By the time you got them all turned you started back here and took this off. That would be done. That griddle was almost red hot. It didn't take long.

Q: I bet they were good. Did you have maple syrup?

A: Yes, part of the time. But part of the time we used oleo and sugar. Of course sugar didn't cost a dollar a pound then. And corn syrup; used to get that in big drums like.

Q: Did you have eggs and meat?

A: Very few eggs. We used to have a few up at the mill because we had a few hens there. Had a cow, so we used to have milk. Of course, I had to milk the cow. One thing I always used to enjoy when I'd milk the cow was there were four kittens about that high. Whenever I sat down to milk, they'd come running by there and I'd squirt milk at them and they'd sit up here and drink. It was a wonderful life. I get quite a kick out of reading articles now about lumberjacks. I was a lumberjack. I wasn't up at the mill what they considered a lumberjack, but at Bliss camp I was because I worked in the woods. I swamped and I sawed and I drove team, hauling logs. But the way they explain the lumberjack now wasn't the way I saw it.

Q: Mr. Smith was talking about his recreation on Sunday—the only day off they had.

A: All we had to do was wander around the woods. I remember, my two youngest brothers, they were just little gaffers, and I was writing to a couple of girls I went to school with down north of Saginaw. I wanted to send them some trailing arbutus. I asked the kids if they knew where there was some, and they said yeah, they knew. They took me out about a half mile up through the woods and found some trailing arbutus. They were little bitsy kids, but they knew that whole country, every foot of it. I don't know if there's any of those flowers left or not.

Q: There's a lot of them.

A: Boy, they were a beautiful flower. They used to come right up through the snow. And my daughter-in-law said, "Why, they're just weeds." I asked her if she knew any flower that wasn't a weed at the start. Lilacs—they're all over that woods up there. Any place you go, why you see a lilac bush.

Q: Yep. Did you ski? How did you get through the heavy snow?

A: We used snowshoes.

Q: You never thought of skiing?

A: Well, yes, we used to use barrel staves and put a strap over them. Go walking around that way. Come down the big hill right in back of the mill. We'd take a barrel stave, nail up a two-by-four, and put a little board over it for a seat. We'd sit on there and come down and balance ourselves with our arms and legs. I hit something one time; it steered me over. They had built a doghouse, and they cut the back end and I come right close to the doghouse, so I dropped right off. Went ker-plunk! You couldn't steer it very good. It's a wonder some of us didn't get our necks broken.

Q: Did the men do that too or just the kids?

A: Oh, just the kids. Of course, they didn't grow up then till they got to be about 40. The foreman used to do it: he was 25 then. The older guys used to make the stuff for us, and we'd use it. Like that sleigh that my dad built. I went up there quite a few years afterward and found the sleigh down where the garden was. It's a wonder somebody didn't haul it out of there and use it. Of course, it's pretty heavy. He made it out of two-inch beech. Foreman used to generally steer it. The time I changed horses on it I didn't stop to think that horse wasn't trained to follow the thing like the other one was. I just jumped on the sleigh and said come on. The sleigh started down, and the horse started the other way. I had plenty of trouble then, wading through snow, following him back. He'd wait until I got pretty near to him, then he'd take off. Took about two hours getting him back.

Q: Did you play cards, anything like that?

A: The other guys used to, but I never did. Sunday we'd hunt. We went out one time with the foreman east of the river. He wanted to go off in this direction. I said, "No, it's this way." "No," he said, "it's like that." I said, "No, it's this way." He said, "Well, go ahead if you want to." I said, "That's what I'm gonna do." So I started that way, he started the other way. Pretty soon he hollered. He come over. He said, "I'm not gonna go over that way in case you get lost and [I] can't find ya." So he followed me, and I took him over to the mill.

Q: How much of that country had been cut over in 1908?

A: Pretty much all of it. Just the hardwood was left. We were just starting to lumber the hardwood when I was up there. There was hardwood northeast of the mill. We used to hunt in there. On the west side of the river there was a swamp, and we had the dog in there, a cocker spaniel. He was running rabbits, and I shot five rabbits [while standing on] the same tree. They were all snowshoes. I didn't see a cottontail all the time I was up there.

Niser's camp was to the east. And I remember Lena Michli was the cook. When I was a kid, I thought that was such a funny name and I always remembered it. She was from Bay City. Most of them had men cooks. They did at the mill. In the winter, why, they could get along with a woman because she could handle it. But you get 40 or 50 men in there, it's quite a job for a woman. I used to have to cut the meat—the whole carcass. This Ermine Campford, he was a butcher, and he was chore boy before I was. He taught me to cut meat. I could go in there and carve up a quarter of beef. Now we've got a boy, the oldest, all he's ever done in his life is cut meat. He's in Chicago.

Q: Did you use the spring for refrigeration? How did you save anything?

A: We didn't. We ate it!

Q: How did you cool your milk? In the spring?

A: If we wanted to cool anything in the spring, we could set a pail in there or drop it in the river. Now you'd take butter and put it in [the river] and it would stay hard. I know when you fell in it was cold, too. The foreman pushed me in there one time off of the dam. The dam was open, so water was falling through, and I had quite a job to keep from going through that. So one time Charlie Cornwell and his wife and daughter came in. The daughter wanted to know if there was any fish in the river. Bob, the foreman, said, "Yeah, there's a lot of them. Come on out and maybe we can see some." So I went out with him. We went to the up side of the dam, and he was looking out like that. He couldn't see any. I said, "There's some right there, Bob, back under the bank." He got out like that, and he said, "I don't see any." I said, "Lean out a little farther." So he leaned out a little farther. As soon as he got off balance, why, I just give him a start and in he went. Mrs. Cornwell says, "What in the world did you do that for?" I said, "He knows what I did that for." But he wasn't as lucky as I was. He went down through that sluiceway just rolling like this. He went down farther than from here to the middle of the road before he could get himself squared around and over to the shallow. He come back, and he said, "Well you got even, didn't you?" But there was something going on like that all the time. That's what made life worth living. Even the old guys was pulling things on people up there.

Q: When you cut up a carcass, how did you keep that meat fresh?

A: We had what you call a meat house, just a little shack off the cook camp. It just hung in there. We'd take a quarter of a beef at a time; they didn't last long.

Q: I suppose with that many big, healthy eaters.

A: All husky young guys, you know, and they ate a lot. It's just like the pancakes. We'd put a platter up like that, what they call camp platters. We'd pile the pancakes right up like that before we let them start eating or we couldn't catch up to them. It took a lot to feed that crew. Peeled three bushel of potatoes for a meal.

Q: How much wild meat did you have?

A: Quite a little. Deer was the only thing. We never monkeyed with anything small because it wouldn't go far enough. But this Paul White, with two dogs, he'd bring in a deer every little while. Before I started to stay down at the camp, I was working in the lumber yard, and old Tom Manning brought me a great big sandwich, real nice and warm. I started to eat it, and he said, "Do you know what that meat is?" I said, "Venison." Later he brought me a sandwich of bear meat. He pulled the same thing on me, brought me a nice warm sandwich. I said, "Boy, bear meat, eh?" "How in the devil did you know that's bear meat?" I said, "Well, because it tastes like bear meat."

Q: There was a school right there where the shingle mill was, along the Pigeon?

A: Yeah. At the time, there was only a couple families there besides this one that owned the shingle mill. One time there was a girl, can't think of her name now. They used to bring the mail in from Wolverine. Lloyd Meeker used to carry the mail. I was out there one time and rode back in with him. This girl was coming out to teach that school. Can't think of her name. I knew her well, too. It was a mile and a half up the river. I remember telling her it was a mile and a half for her to walk right up through the woods. So I told her to wait and I'd go hitch up a horse, take her up there. "Why," she said, "never mind bothering." She could just as well do that. But I didn't feel like seeing a young girl like that walk up through the woods.

Q: You were a young man, and she was probably pretty.

A: Oh, yeah. I was 17 (laughter). I told Bob I'd take care of the mill when I come back. So I went and hitched up a horse and took her up to the shingle mill and come back—Ethel Perry was her name, Ethel Perry; she lived in Wolverine. My three youngest brothers went to that school at one time.

Q: Can you remember when they first quit using horses and started using mechanical conveyances in the woods?

A: After I was out of it. It was still horses whenever I was around there. I used to take special delivery letters to Camp Niser. Jump on a horse and strike out through the woods. Never paid any attention to the road. I'd just go through the woods riding one horse.

Q: Was that the end of the post line? Did all the guys from Niser's Camp come over . . .

A: Oh, yeah. From McDade's Camp, too, they'd come over. That was the only post office around there outside of Wolverine. There was an old Frenchman there, I can't remember his name. He couldn't talk English. He was over in McDade's Camp, and he had a little grandson, just a little fella. The snow was way up like this, ya know. He used to come over after the mail and buy a few things from the store. The little kid was too small to walk in that snow, yet he was too heavy for the old man to carry that much. They were both all done in by the time they got to the mill. So I told the kid, "You tell me how to say this in French." I used to know quite a little French from being around the Frenchmen along the Saginaw River. I finally told the old man not to bring the kid over anymore, that I would figure out what he wanted. So I did.

He told me how to trap mink. I told him about one great big mink there. I seen the track a lot, but I couldn't catch him. He said, "How do you set the trap?" I told him, "I just set it." So he told me to put some bait up about that high on a limb of a tree and set four or five traps just under it. He said the mink will come along and smell that and can't get it so he'll jump up to get it, and he'll land in one of those traps. Well, I caught that big fella.

Q: Mink are supposed to be real smart.

A: Yeah, they're hard to trap, but you couldn't fool that old guy and I caught quite a few of them after that. Bob and I used to go hunting when we was working in the yard before I went to choring. We'd go out in the morning, and it would start to snow and we'd call off work. "Can't do anything now, it's storming too hard. We can't work." We'd tell everybody to go to the camp. We'd go and get our coats on and our snowshoes and the guns and we'd go out hunting. It was too stormy to work up there, but we'd go out and hunt all day.

Q: Go out and play in it.

A: When I was running the plant in Merrill, in the butcher shop there they had a ten-horse Fairbanks Morris engine. I was working on that engine one day, and I heard somebody talking in the front. I recognized Bob's voice, the foreman I had up at the mill. It was several years after I was up there. He was working for the Bay City Grocery Company. I hollered to Trayhan, the butcher. I said, "Don't pay much attention to that guy. He's just a windjammer. He loves to tell you most anything."

I didn't hear a sound for a minute, then I heard Bob say, "Who was that?" Trayhan says, "I don't know. Somebody out in the back room." So Bob come peeking around like that. "My God, Jim!" he said. He come over, and I thought he'd squeeze the hand off me. He wanted to know where Dad was and where my brothers were and everything. I said, "Dad's down in Pontiac." He said, "What's he doing down there?" I said, "He's in that asylum down there." "My God," he said, "his mind gone haywire?" Says, "Where are the boys?" I said, "They're down there, too, in that same place." He said, "All of them down there? What's the cause of it?" I said, "I don't know unless they pay better wages down there than they do any other place" (laughter). Dad was running the engines down there, and two of the boys was working down there.

Q: That's right, your father being an engineer, he would work everywhere.

A: The foreman and I used to fish quite a little, and I've seen three of those big camp platters piled right up with trout that we caught. But we never saw a big one. But millions and millions of [smaller trout]. Boy, when I wasn't fishing, I'd sit there and watch them. Every chance I'd get, I'd sneak down to the river and watch those fish. I don't think there's anything on earth nicer than trout to eat. Brook trout. My oldest brother's from Saginaw. I come down from the mill into Saginaw, and I met him. He said, "Come on over, we're gonna have perch for supper. You always liked fish so well." Well, I used to like Saginaw River perch, but I went over there and they had perch and I never tasted anything that tasted so much like mud in my life as I did those Saginaw River perch after eating those trout up there out of that [Pigeon River] stream.

Q: There were still a few Michigan grayling, at least in the Black River. Have you ever seen any of those?

A: In the Pigeon. Bob Moore and I each caught one. Old John Tinland told us they were grayling. That's the last I ever saw them. We didn't even eat them. We were fishing for trout. We got trout, so we threw [the grayling] away.

Q: Do you remember where you caught them?

A: Just below the dam.

Q: How big were they?

A: About the size the trout were running. I don't even remember what they looked like now.

Q: They look thin.

A: Yeah. They had a long dorsal fin, I know that.

Q: Yeah. A long dorsal fin. Michigan grayling. They were good to eat. Other fish were introduced into the streams. Brook trout was more competitive than the grayling. Some say the water warmed up a little bit. Logs were floated down the river and that disturbed the riverbed.

A: I never got over to the Black River. I got, of course, around the Sturgeon more from when we went through Wolverine. I was within a mile or two of the Black but didn't need to go over there so we didn't.

And then there was Pike Lake. There was two guys there. They used to go over there and spear pike. Well, this game warden, I can't remember his name now, was trying to get them, but they kept dodging him. He'd be out there with a light and he'd come in from the east side of the lake and their light would go out and they'd land someplace and disappear. He couldn't get them. So this one time they were out there spearing, and he made a noise of some kind so they'd know he was coming.

He was getting in his boat or something like that, and they doused the light and decided to cross the lake. So he went around, and when they pulled up on shore he said, "Here I am boys." He had them right there.

Q: What kind of stuff did you grow in your garden?

A: We used to grow about everything. Radishes and lettuce. Tom was quite a gardener. Quite a few potatoes.

Q: Would you say how many acres that garden was?

A: I don't think it was over half an acre.

Q: That would make quite a lot of green stuff.

A: That was quite a crew, too. There was quite a few to eat it. It wouldn't last long.

Q: No, and the growing season's short. What month was it you left the mill? You came in October of 1908.

A: And I left the first of July 1909.

Q: The mill was going then, wasn't it?

A: Yeah.

Q: When did they start it up in the spring?

A: It would be May because they'd have to wait till the snow was over with. Of course, they couldn't have very many logs in the stream. They dumped them in afterwards when the snow was gone. They would cut in the winter, and in the spring the trains would bring [the logs] in and the mill would start. Took my dad quite a while to get the mill in motion. Just like overhauling a car, they'd have to overhaul everything in it. Dad was always fussy about the engine. The engine had to be running right.

Q: How many horses did you have at camp?

A: . . . I think, three teams.

Q: You just used them around the mill and in the yard?

A: One on the dump cart; they used to haul the wood for the stoves. Then they had the sleds. They had one horse to haul the tram cars out. That darn bay horse. I've forgotten his name now. When it was time to quit, we couldn't get him to haul that car out of the lumberyard. If you forced him to go up there, he'd go a little ways and he'd jump off the tram. The darn tram must have been about ten feet high. I'll be darned if he wouldn't jump off that thing on the way up. When it was time to quit, he was gonna quit. Hy Green was supposed to be hauling it out there one day. The horse got away from him. So he run down, got him, brought him back. He was gonna make him haul that load out to the yard. He went back to hitch the tugs and the horse jumped ahead, run over, jumped off the tramway and went to the barn.

James Smith put some of his recollections in a letter.

The railroad ran from Trowbridge to Cornwell and ended at the river. One car was shunted down to where it was to be loaded with lumber. A brakeman was on it to stop it. But when he tried to set the brakes there were no brakes, so it wound up in the river. The water wasn't very deep but deep enough to give the brakeman a good bath.

On Thanksgiving we were emptying the water barrels on the tramway so they wouldn't freeze. Being a holiday, most of the crew were partly oiled up. My father and one of the fellows got into an argument as to who could run the fastest. Dad bet a dollar that he could run to the dam and jump in the river before the other fellow got to the dam. I said, "Dad, are you crazy?" He motioned for me to keep still. I was to be the starter and when I said go, the race started. I noticed that Dad, though a good runner, was behind. The other fellow beat Dad and jumped in. The water was ice cold and he crawled out nearly frozen and put his hand out for his dollar. Dad gave it to him and said, "It's worth a dollar to find out that all the damn fools aren't dead yet."

The crew loaded lumber on flat cars to be hauled out to the main line to be shipped to Bay City, Saginaw, and other places. Sometimes the snow was so deep the train couldn't get through and it would take a couple of days to batter a hole through, but eventually they would make it and haul the lumber out. Only the #1 clear lumber was saved. That with knots or knotholes was cut up for firewood.

13

Walter Babcock

After cutting the pine and hardwoods, lumber companies went into the wetlands for cedar, spruce, and tamarack. In April 1982, Jerry Myers interviewed Walter Babcock about the logging days on the Sturgeon, Pigeon, and Black rivers.

Jerry Myers: Where did your family first settle?

Walter Babcock: They come to Trowbridge about 1895 or 6. Trowbridge was about four miles south of Wolverine.

Q: And right on the Sturgeon. Your father and mother had quite a large family.

A: Eleven children. [I had] eight brothers and two sisters.

Q: What year were you born?

A: 1909.

Q: When did your father start logging?

A: When he worked at Bungtown in the lumber mill, about two and a half, three miles east or upstream on the Sturgeon from Trowbridge. [He worked for] Metrim-Belcher Lumber Company. When he came, they was cutting about 100,000 feet every eight hours. The pine was the most accessible, and the best was gone by the early 1900s. I saw pine cut in different stands after that, but the biggest share was gone.

Q: Do you remember the diameter of the logs?

A: When they was haulin' some elm out there on a flatcar, they put two tiers of logs on them and three logs to a tier. They had quite a good size logs. I would say six foot. And maple, my God, four feet. Sometimes they'd roll off the cars. We'd just saw 'em up for wood—they wouldn't pick 'em up.

Q: Do you remember seeing any pine that was left over, that it would go four-five foot in diameter?

A: Oh, yes, but not a lot. In isolated spots, they'd cut 'em and bring 'em out after they started to cut the hardwoods. There were some monsters.

Q: They floated some pine down the Pigeon, down what we call Cornwall.

A: Yeah, and they floated the Sturgeon. But when my dad first went in they'd float a lot of it down to the mill in Bungtown. And he had a mill in Bungtown later on, a [railroad] tie mill. And they floated a lot of that, mostly maple and beech and oak.

Q: Oak seemed important through Michigan, the days of the passenger pigeon—white oak, especially. Now we have scattered red and white oak in that area, especially over toward the Black on the east side of the Pigeon River Country.

A: My dad lumbered more in the swamps—cedar and spruce and tamarack. He cut a lot of tamarack. He'd take the larger part of the tree; they'd make ties out of it, then the top, they made mine props. They cut mine props all the way from eight foot to two foot.

Q: And most of your brothers worked with your dad in lumbering?

A: We all did.

Q: You said your mother cooked a lot in the camps. Where were some of your camps located?

A: We had a camp just east of Lance Lake or Wolverine on the Little Pigeon—I guess we was about three years in there—and then we had a camp on Dog Lake, two years in there, and then we were in on the Black, where the Tin Shanty—where the railroad originally went across the Black.

Q: That's what we call the Tin Shanty Road now.

A: We lumbered four years in there.

Q: You took timber out of the swamp—balsam, spruce, and cedar.

A: Mostly spruce, but there was cedar and balsam.

Q: Pretty big white spruce?

A: Oh, boy, beautiful. Maybe 14, 15 inches. We'd get eight 8-foot sticks out of a tree [100 inches to a stick]. But that all went for pulpwood. The

Fletcher Company had the paper mill over to Alpena. They went from wood right into paper.

Q: This was in the twenties, wasn't it?

A: We was in that camp from 1921. Moved out of there in '25.

Q: The Tin Shanty site is important in the Pigeon River Country State Forest because it's fairly well in the center. It's really the only bridge that crosses the Black in that area.

A: The first two years we was on the Black down in the swamp them Yuill Brothers was cutting hardwood, that would be east across the Black, because we used the same banking ground right there where the Tin Shanty is.

Q: Banks and camps are different.

A: Yeah. These banks were all on the Pigeon River railroad branch, but that's just where they banked their timber until they moved it out.

Q: *Banking* means storing it, piling it until shipment on the railroads. You said you were at this Tin Shanty area about four years. What age were you then?

A: Twelve, 13, 14, and 15.

Q: What were your daily duties?

A: Just workin' cuttin' timber, and loadin' it out. They didn't even have Finn fiddles then; you used a cedar saw, they called it, one man.

Q: For the swamp. Did you run teams and harness them?

A: Oh yes. We only had two teams of our own, but then my dad would hire other teams when the haul started.

Q: You did some skidding?

A: Oh yes. The first year I was 12, but this brother of mine who died with cancer when he was young—I was 20 months older'n him—he drove team. I'd help him harness the horses in the morning—

Q: 'Cause he wasn't tall enough—

A: I was big enough—I could throw the harness up on the one I'd harness. He had a box he'd stand on to harness his horse. And he drove the team.

Q: Did you use drays to load logs on or what?

A: Logging sleighs. He would go to the woods in the morning, and boy we loaded 'em up when we started to haul. He would blow his lantern out when he got back to the banking ground in the morning. He'd be back there with his first load—

Q: Just at daylight.

A: —He wasn't 11 years old yet. Nowadays, parents wouldn't let their child that old go to the woods, let alone work all day.

Q: How did he get his schooling, or how did all the family, for that matter?

A: We took some schooling, missed a lot of it.

Q: Did you study some while you were living in the camp? Did your mother help you with this?

A: Yes, my older sister helped, too.

Q: Your mother was kept pretty busy. How many did she cook for in these camps?

A: We had about 20 then.

Q: And how big a lady was she?

A: I don't know just what she weighed then, but when they were first married she weighed 102 pounds.

Q: And could she handle horses and logs?

A: She could handle ANYTHING. She was terrific.

Q: She had quite a good sense of humor, too, didn't she?

A: Terrific. Never lost it.

Q: You mentioned one time she was kind of scuffling with your dad—

A: (Laughs) Upended him in a rain barrel!

Q: Your dad was a pretty big fellow, too, was he?

A: About 175 pounds.

Q: What about food in camp? You mentioned the wild berries were plentiful. You had probably strawberries, raspberries, and blueberries. How'd you handle those?

A: Blueberries, she would can a thousand quarts some years.

Q: Pack them in glass jars—the old blue Mason jars?

A: Oh boy, yes. Never quart, always two quart.

Q: And who picked these?

A: We picked 'em. When they were right at the best, we'd just shut down all operations and pick berries.

Q: How about strawberries?

A: Never strawberries but raspberries. I've seen her can 300 quarts of raspberries.

Q: In a season.

A: Yeah. That took a lot of pickin', I'll tell you. And blackberries, she'd can a lot of blackberries.

Q: How did you provide potatoes and things like that—in the fall when they were abundant?

A: Yeah, just get a truckload of potatoes and bring them in, pit 'em. We had big cellars. Put potatoes, apples, and stuff like that in and keep 'em . . . what they called root cellars. Nothing would freeze in them. If it was gonna get real cold we'd hang a lantern in there—you'd have a door, and then three or four feet another door, and between the doors we'd hang a lantern. It'd keep the frost from getting in there.

Q: You maintained about 20 men in the winter, and that was a peak time, I suppose, when you could skid logs.

A: When the sleigh haul started, if you didn't get your timber out it stayed for another year because you didn't have trucks or tractors to haul it out with.

Q: Did you water some of the . . .

A: Ice the roads? Oh, yeah.

Q: And they had barrels or places where you could dip the water?

A: And just sprinkle it along.

Q: A tank wagon drawn with horses?

A: Yeah, right on a set of sleighs. You could haul about twice as much after you iced your roads. It made a tremendous difference.

Q: How did you put brakes on when you go down a grade?

A: Didn't. The roads pridneer* level along—if there was a little dip, the horse'd just have to run a little. Course, we had them horses shod with sharp shoes.

---

* This word is similar to the expression "pretty near" and is spelled phonetically. Walter Babcock doesn't say "pretty near."

Q: Did you have somebody there in camp who could take care of the blacksmith part?

A: Generally there was somebody. Pridneer every camp had their own blacksmith.

Q: Did you have cleats on the horseshoes for ice?

A: No, regular horseshoes. The shoes were sharp. We never did use cleats. In the swamp, those horses could step on theirself pretty easy and cut theirself.

Q: [There were fires] over quite a few years—15, 20 years of burning, wasn't there?

A: God, I remember from our old farm all you could see was black stumps as far as you could see. It wasn't very pretty.

Q: Did you have any fish?

A: We didn't fish too much. The Black was full of trout then. You'd go across a foot log, and always, there'd be 15, 20 brook trout in a pool. The only body I ever saw fish there was one of the brakemen off the railroad. He'd go catch their lunch when they'd park there. While the others were switching, he'd go down to the river and catch a mess of fish and they'd cook 'em there in the coals. Our supplies, everything, come in on the railroad.

Q: Didn't have very good roads then, did you?

A: Terrible.

Q: Probably horse-drawn . . .

A: That's what they were built for, for horses. But we had cars. Model T Fords.

Q: Can you remember Bungtown?

A: All I can remember is there was probably a dozen families there when I was a kid. There was a lot more people [during the pine days].

Q: Did they have saloons and hotels?

A: No. They had a big general store and mill. When I was a kid, we used to shear sheep in the old dance halls. That was in 1918, 1919. [Earlier the Cornwell Ranch in Bungtown] brought cattle in and run 'em before there was any fences built. I don't know if it didn't pay or what, but they switched and brought in sheep by the hundreds. Trainloads. But that only lasted two, three years.

Q: Too cold winters and springs for the lambs.

A: I think so. [It] wasn't the Cornwells that done this. They leased that land to this company that brought in the cattle and sheep. Then Cornwells, when they started to run cattle, why my dad built all the fences.

Q: Your father owned quite a little property just to the north.

A: About 400 or 500 acres.

Q: When he put fences in, he'd trade 40 here and 40 there.

A: (Laughter) Yes.

Q: And he sold some of it, too, didn't he?

A: He did later, yes. He was what we called land poor.

Q: I suppose there wasn't much demand for property then.

A: There wasn't.

Q: There was a Richardson farm after the Richardson lumbering.

A: Yes, that was at the old headquarters where the CC [Civilian Conservation Corps] camp was. They farmed there. That was a veterans camp [in the 1920s]. World War I veterans. That was quite a camp. You can still see sidewalks and the opening, the shrubs. We used to go out there and play ball. We had a baseball team in the camp.

The elk were unloaded at what was old Bungtown in 1918. If I remember, there was 13 or 14 elk brought in there.

Q: They brought them in by railroad cars?

A: No, brought them from Wolverine, but they were trucked from there. I don't know why because the railroad was still in there.

Q: But they unloaded them from railroad cars at Wolverine onto a truck?

A: Yes. We saw elk every year after that. Didn't seem to increase too fast.

Q: The people in the community were interested in them.

A: Oh, yes, at that time. Something new. When they did take hold they seemed to increase pretty fast, but for several years they didn't increase fast.

Q: There was a pair of big wheels at the Pigeon River headquarters in 1949. They have been reconstructed.

A: I think I saw the last big wheels operated in southern Michigan near Hardwood Lake in 1922 or 1923. The Richardsons finished lumbering right around Hardwood Lake, and they used the big wheels to get their logs to the railroad.

Q: The big wheels we saw at headquarters were repaired and sent to Hartwick Pines [State Park] where they are on display in the museum area.

A: They could move logs with them.

Q: What did they use, one team?

A: One team. They were dangerous, too. They balanced those logs underneath so they'd just drag a little for a brake, and if they didn't going downhill, it had to be a fast team to keep out of their way.

Not too far from Bank 3, near the old grade, there was this Norway pine. About halfway up it had branches completely around it, then not a branch again for 20 or 30 feet and [then] the top. They called it Hell 'n' Heaven, and it was there, oh, through my childhood, and they referred to that as a landmark.

Q: That landmark was cut between 1930 and 1935. Did that cause controversy?

A: Well, yes, a lot. The old timers were pretty sore about it.

Q: This parallels the Witness Tree. A benchmark indicates it was used by William Burt, the original land surveyor. The county at one time was going to improve that road and take the tree out. They finally left it there.

A: Yep, I know where that is.

Q: There are similarities—one was a landmark and the other a survey mark.

A: Yes, and you know, when they cut this pine, what it was worth then didn't amount to anything. It was a shame it was done.

14
Living at Headquarters

Four years after the original Pigeon River Country headquarters was built in 1919, the third forester to live there arrived with his family. William and Bertha Horsell brought their daughter, Janice (born 1917), twins Geraldine and Gerald (born 1919), and Bob, who was six weeks old when they arrived in 1923. Later, their son William D. (Bill), daughter Norma, and son Lyle were born at headquarters. The family lived there 13 years, then moved as first occupants to the present headquarters site a mile upstream in 1936 and remained until 1949. When young Bill was born, the nearest hospital was in Grayling (more than 50 miles away), so the doctor came to the Pigeon River Country to attend to the delivery. On November 12, 1982, Jerry Myers sat down to talk with Bertha Zettle Horsell, her daughter Janice Horsell Boyd, and her son William D. Horsell.

When young Bill was about five years old, evening came and they couldn't find him. The men started down to the river, into the woods, and around the barns. Behind the garage, where a boat was stored upside-down across logs, they saw Bill's little arm beneath the boat. They found him sound asleep. Mrs. Horsell says she seldom worried about her children in the woods.

"Can you imagine raising seven kids on the bank of a river?" Bill asked. "We were in the river half the time." They would walk half a mile upstream to a sandy depression in the Pigeon where the water was up to their necks near a clay bank just below what is now the P. S. Lovejoy monument. "It was real calm going through, it was deep and beautiful," Janice recalls. "There was just us kids. I was the oldest one."

"The river wasn't very wide and they weren't far from the bank anyway," Mrs. Horsell said.

Bill said, "If you jumped into one of those holes, the current would carry you to shallow water in just a few seconds."

One Sunday mother and children went for a walk beyond the barn going south. About half a mile later their dog Cubby came charging down the trail toward them pursued by a black bear.

Bertha: The CC boys had saw that bear and cubs just a few days before. The dog probably got too close to the cubs. He started to bark. When the bear started to come after him, he didn't have time to bark. If she'd ever caught him, she'd have tore him all to pieces. We got out of the road when we saw them coming. The dog ran right up to Bill, Lyle, Norma, and I. The bear was not very far from us when she saw us. We was all yelling and hollering. I think it scared the bear so bad [that she stopped].

Bill: I was about 12 years old. And that bear was at least as high as this ceiling here. It stopped, and I stood there looking at it. She just kind of hunched right down and slid to a stop. You could have reached out and touched your hand on her head—Mother could have; it was about 12 or 14 feet for me to reach up there. At least it seemed that high. Mom was within switching distance, and I was right alongside of her. She just reached out with a switch and slapped it in the face. [The bear turned and went back up the fire lane.] Then we turned and went the other way at a pretty good clip.

Bertha: It seemed to me its eyes just bugged out, you know, when it saw us. I said to Norma, "Did you see that bear's eyes?" She said, "No I could just see it's teeth."

Janice: We were out there last summer, stood on the bank, and couldn't believe how the trees are grown.

Bill: I remember P. S. Lovejoy when he was an old man. He'd go around the building and pull up milkweeds, but he didn't want anything else pulled out of that lawn. He wanted it left just like it was in the woods. I always remember him as a tall, lanky man.

P. S. Lovejoy was recovering from a stroke when the new headquarters was constructed by Civilian Conservation Corps workers in the mid-1930s. "Mr. Lovejoy had the big say about that building," Bertha Horsell said.

Bill remembers that a sick elk was butchered behind the barn: "They opened it up, and around his neck was a solid mass of worms." He recalls his father taking porcupine quills from the nose of one elk in the middle of the road near Pick-

erel Lake: "Big cow stood right in the middle of the road. Dad got out, and she had a nose full of porky-pine quills. He got his pair of pliers out and walked right up to her and pulled a bunch of quills out of her nose. She finally took off in the woods."

Jerry commented that some local authorities wanted to cut down the Witness Tree but Bill's dad had saved it. The tree was marked in the original 1850 land survey and survives today.

The Horsells were in Pigeon River Country on February 9, 1934 when the thermometer reached 51 below, the coldest day on record in Michigan.

Janice: I remember we didn't go to school that day. We always followed the CC trucks; they opened the road.

Bill: The kerosene froze in the cans.

Bertha: It was kind of a thick, milky-looking stuff. The moment it got indoors in the heat it turned liquid again.

Janice recalled that the river froze that year.

Jerry Myers: I remember one year in the early sixties half of December the minimum temperature each day was zero or below. All of January, all of February, and half of March. That year I walked to the river just to look for otter. I found two or three places where they could get out, where a spring or something would leave some open water.

Jerry walked the river from Vanderbilt Road Bridge to headquarters and several miles north and only sunk his foot into a hole once. Janice recalled skating on the river.

Jerry: I remember those old furnaces, combination fuel oil and wood. Along toward morning, when the fire would die down, the furnace would kick on.

Janice remembered carrying an oil lamp up to bed when the bottom broke off. She stood yelling. Someone came to take the lamp from her. Plans were being made at the time to install electricity because of the fire danger from oil lamps.

The forest electrical system included a generator for 110 volts DC and a whole wall of glass batteries, which stored two volts each. Once, after maintenance work, the terminals were not retaped. When Bill's father stepped behind the board to throw the switches, the room exploded with sparks, glass, and acid. A dozen batteries were destroyed, but Horsell was unhurt.

Bill: Yenk Marlatt, conservation officer, was at the Pigeon one time. Couple carloads of hunters came in. One car had a small buck tied to the fender. Two guys were practically fistfighting over that deer. Old Yenk was there. He wanted to see the deer, so out they went. They were going back and forth. This guy said it was his deer; he shot it. The other said he shot it. Yenk took his knife out and cut the ropes. The deer fell off on the ground. One of the guys said, "What are you doing?" Yenk [looked at the size of the antlers and] said, "Well, it's an illegal deer. Now, who shot the deer?" Neither one of them shot it. They got right back in their cars and away they went. No more argument.

Chuck Rich, Kenny Yuill, and Bill cooked for conservation commissioners one weekend when Bill and his friends were 14 or 15 years old. Bill's parents were away. He tells the story.

Three came in. Said they were going to stay in the staff house. We told them, "There's nobody here to cook." They said, "We expect you guys to cook for us." So we cooked for them. And they were some meals we put on, I'll tell you.

They were drunk all the while they were there. One fellow was so crippled up he could hardly walk, and he insisted he was going fishing. We thought he'd never come back, but he did.

We mixed them up a salad one day. We put everything we could find in the kitchen into that salad. We mixed up a great big bowl of it. We threw all kinds of spices into it. We even found a bottle that had a little whiskey in it; we poured the whiskey into it. We stirred it all up . . . [with] vinegar and put it on the table. There were only three of them, and they ate every bit of it. There wasn't a bit of salad left in that bowl. We brought that bowl back in with the big spoon into it and put it on the cupboard. And before we got ready to do dishes the spoon turned green in that bowl. We thought maybe we killed those guys. Didn't hurt them any. They really liked it.

When they got ready to leave, this one old duffer came staggering out in the kitchen. He gave me five dollars for a tip. Then back he went in the dining room. A little while later back he came again. He said, "Did I give you five dollars?" I didn't know whether to tell him or not. And I said, "Yeah, you gave me a five-dollar tip." "Well," he said, "I want it back." So I reached in my pocket, got five dollars out, and gave it back to him. He took it, then pulled twenty dollars out and gave it to me as a tip.

The Horsells had cows, horses, pigs, and chickens. Bertha said some campers took some of their best chickens, but wild animals never did. Jerry said such campers are known as "white skunks." Bertha said someone shot their first horse right in the eye while the horse was in the pasture by the barn.

"If they shoot a horse, you can understand how they can shoot an elk," Jerry said.

Hunters once shot at a tame deer, which ran to the house and dove through a small window into the basement but suffered only a few scratches. Bertha walked her up the steps and out.

Jerry recalled that in 1949 or 1950 someone chased a deer behind the house and shot a hole through the metal frame of a guy wire on the house. "You never know what they're going to shoot," he said. Bill said they posted the area around the buildings "No Hunting."

One of the most intense experiences in the woods is disorientation. It's what we call getting lost, but it bears little resemblance to being on a wrong road in a car. Despite the trauma humans experience when lost in the woods, they usually get out without serious incident, although many old Pigeon River hands recall encountering people on the verge of hysteria. In retrospect, the experiences can seem almost funny.

Bill: We ran across a guy that was lost. He was from the South, but he was working in Detroit. On the fourteenth [of November], the night before deer season, three other guys picked him up. He got in the car and went to sleep. When they pulled into the woods out there, all he knew was that the car was parked underneath a big tree. He had no idea where he was because he slept all the way up from Detroit. He got out of the car, went out in the woods with his gun, hunting. About noon the first day we ran onto him. He had no idea where the car was except it was parked under a big tree "with needles on it." We couldn't find the car. Finally we took him to the police station in Onaway [and] told him eventually somebody looking for him would contact the police. We never saw him again.

Once when CCC workers brought in trees to plant, they knocked the ball of dirt from the roots getting it off the truck. Bertha's husband, the forester, told her the tree would never grow. "It's one of the biggest ones there now," she said.

15
Camping along the Pigeon

One family that remembered the early days of recreation in the Pigeon River Country, the Motots from Fostoria, Ohio, began camping in the forest 15 years after Hemingway's last visit. In August 1982, Jerry Myers interviewed Kathryn Motot, her daughter Doris, and their friend Florence Parkinson, who all had camped along the Pigeon with Kathryn's late husband, Roy, years before.

Kathryn Motot: We left our home in Fostoria, Ohio, in June of 1936 to take our vacation in northern Michigan. We come up first east of Grayling on the Au Sable and stayed two nights there. That's where Orlo done his first fly-fishing. Then we come on up north.

We cut in to Vanderbilt and cut out—we didn't know where we was going, just nicely running around with our old Model A. Finally, Roy said, "There's a row of pine trees down there. There's got to be life because they're too pretty to be just growing out in a field." So he said, "Here's a little cow path."

Q: You had a two-wheel trailer with a tent?

A: Yeah. So we turned down that little road, and that's where we come to the old bridge, big old planks with big cracks in them, and it teetered up and down, no side rails or nothing on them. We just fell in love with the place. I said, "Let's stay here a few days." We went to work clearing off a space big enough for the tent. The boys got out of the car and saw two big snakes on those logs under the bridge.

Q: Water snakes, I assume?

A: They were water snakes. We pitched our tent, no toilets, no tables. There was one old table the loggers had made out of great big round logs, so I got the hammer out and the nails, hunted up some twigs, sticks, and whatever and nailed it together. It did wobble back and forth, but we used that to put the camp stove on.

The boys wanted to go wade. I didn't know anything about the river, so I even went out wading so the kids wouldn't get out over their head. We stayed about 10 days. The next year Roy said, "We're going back up on the Pigeon." The kids could hardly wait. I think that was the year Joanna and Joe Coon come from Detroit. They were across on the other side where that spring crosses the river. He cleaned that spot up for his little tent. And that's the way any of us met, and every year we'd make out our plans to be up here together. We set on the old bridge, hang our feet over. We'd watch the trail come down to the bank where there would be a great big long string of deer. They would all wade out there in the river and drink. We'd sit with all the kids and watch.

Q: When you first came up here, the country was quite brushy and short shrubs and short trees . . .

A: Yeah, it was brushy on the roads from Vanderbilt out. Nothing like it is now. Dusty and full of chuckholes, and you'd just about lose your car in one.

Nancy was born in 1940, so we come up here when she was ten months old. We camped on the other side of the bridge, put our tent up. The [jack pine] limbs was clear down on the ground. She had learned to creep. She'd get out there and get her diaper hung up on the lower branches of pine trees and she'd just scream her head off. I'd go out and back her up and away she'd go. . . . Nan was two years old when [Kathryn's son] John fixed up his fly rod. He carried her on his hip and taught her to fly-fish, and she was left handed.

Q: Two when she was first fishing. That's got to be a record. Now, didn't Roy tie all his own flies?

A: Tied all his own flies, made his own clothes.

Q: And Joe Penxa, I believe—Joe had one of the biggest hands, at least double of mine, and of course he was a great big burly cop from Detroit, very interesting stories he used to tell. . . . And Anna, as I remember, used to do a lot of cooking, like you did.

A: She fed everybody that come down here camping. The three-C boys would come down there. They had a little shanty, and they had the fish tagged, metal tags through the gill. She cooked for the boys or baked them a pie. They come down and set in that little shanty all day and the big shot out of the three-C camp never brought them nothing to eat. So she'd feed them.

[One night] Roy slept in the back and I slept in the front to get up to look after [Nan in her baby buggy] in the night. I took my shoes off, and I set 'em down side of my bed. I had the flashlight because she was taking her bottle. I looked down, and I thought, "By golly, old man, you can just aggravate me all you want and razz me, but I'm not going to let on one dang thing what you're trying to do." Because he knew I was afraid of snakes.

So I kind of dozed off, and I opened up my eyes and I looked down again, and I thought, "I don't care if you just move my shoes. I ain't going to say one darn thing because then you'll laugh at me." So I looked down a little closer and I thought, "That thing's still moving." So I ranged him with my elbow in the ribs, and he wanted to know what was wrong. I said, "Get up. Look down here." It was a cow [milk] snake. It couldn't have been over a foot long, if he was that. He was crawling back and forth over my shoes. So Roy takes the flashlight and flicked it over to the door of the tent. We had that little threshold. It lit under that threshold. I said, "You get that thing out of here. I'm not meaning outside, but out of sight, because I don't want to see that snake when I get up in the morning." He had to get up and go outside in the night to put the snake outside.

We had a bobcat. There was a bunch of guys camping out of Detroit. They was laid off from the Hudson Motor Car Company in 1945. They had to cross the bridge, and they had a great big tent up. They had a generator where they run electric lights. There was a little guy in the outfit called Harold. He was a cute little guy. We used to have a lot of fun with him. Him and I always got stuck doing dishes. The tables were close together, and I always called him dish rag darling.

Well, one night the guys, they come in with a big mess of fish. I had a great big cooler. They put them in, set them right outside our tent. We heard they were around, because we knew there was animals around, but it didn't bother me any. Got up in the morning and there had been a bobcat that tried to get into that cooler. He [left] great big streaks. Man, he was a wild big thing. Well, poor Harold he set up the next night, but [the bobcat] never come back.

Orlo and Donna got married in 1948 in March; then in July they come up. I had Orlo and Donna, my two girls, and John, and I had my nephew and Donna had her sister. They was all up there in that 12-by-14 tent. We had one of these folded picnic tables, the legs all fold under;

we had that setting right in the door. Orlo and Donna was in the tent on my right, I was back in the corner, and I heard a noise. I got really awake.

I said, "There's something here in the tent, I can hear it." Roy said, "Just be quiet." So we kept real still. So he rolls over and picks up the flashlight, and there sets this big coon on that table where we had a square box that kept the cookies and crackers and bread; we had doughnuts and stuff. There he was a-settin' up on his haunches and he was rolling that cookie around and his eyes were just flashing around, and he was nibbling cookies for all he was worth.

So Roy got him down and he run under Orlo and Donna's cot. There was no floor; he just scoops under the wall. Everything was quiet. About 15 minutes later, I said to Roy, I said, "Here comes that darn coon again, right back up to the cookie sack." So we got him down off from the table. Roy picked up Orlo's shoe and he threw that shoe out behind that coon. Orlo got up in the morning and he hunted, half asleep, no glasses on, he was hunting, hunting for his shoe. I said, "If you go out around the tent you'll find your shoe." He said, "How did it get out there?" They never knew that coon come under their cot and got up there in the cookies. Boy, I'll tell you his ol' belly was all puffed out, he had about all the doughnuts.

The kids and Charity's kids, they was all around the campfire on the other side of the bridge. And they was an old coon, she kept coming to the woods on the other side, and following across the bridge. She'd go way out around the jack pine, set back there and watch us. So Al, he said, "We're going to fix her a plate for supper." I said, "She's awful skinny." We fixed her bread and molasses. We put lettuce and stuff on a paper plate, and we pushed it under the jack pine. Each night she'd come back we brought it a little closer out. She kept coming a real closer, real closer. So she cleaned up her plate and she'd sit down, she'd spread her fingers apart, she'd lick each finger on each hand, she'd set there a little bit, back she'd go way on around. So she'd come back another night, and we still had her plate fixed for her.

Judy, their oldest girl, she was just at the inquisitive age, she said, "Daddy, what is that, a mama or papa coon?" He said, "I don't know." She set there until the coon sit up again and the feet spread out. "Judy," he said, "that's a mama coon, 'cause she has six breast buttons." And she had six little coons, so when they got bigger, by golly, she got those all over to camp, so we fed all of them.

We would take trips to the headquarters. Around about the second bend from the camp we saw a bunch of fox a-playin'. An old fox and a bunch of kittens. They was fighting over a wild animal somebody hit in the road. One was pulling one way and the other, and they was just a-growling, so we took pictures.

The Motots camped every summer in the Pigeon from 1936 until Roy died in 1974.

Q: Joe came in [to headquarters] one day, and he had a bag of mushrooms. He threw them all out; he said, "I ate a little of this one last night, I ate a little of that one, and two or three of these and one over here." He said, "I kind of got sick on this one, but it wasn't the blame of the mushroom, it was probably I had a couple too many beers and kind of upset my stomach." I sure got a bang out of the way—we enjoyed his visits.

Doris: One year he even went out and picked tender milkweed and come back and had Mom fix it, and he sat there and ate that.

Kathryn: Yeah, the milkweed plant, when you first come through and you get two or three little fresh leaves on it, the little tiny leaves, you pick those off and cook them just like green peas. Serve them in butter or cream, whichever way you want. And they're good.

One week we all went out and come in with 2,500 [mushrooms]. A lot better then than it has been the last few years.

Q: I think they are pretty well covered now, and probably there's some effect on not leaving some for the spores to start new ones.

Q: When you first came, there were very few—one or two other campers. Then it grew. Finally, they were putting rules on camping, you only stay 15 days, you know. Along about the mid-sixties was probably a peak camping year. But you've seen the up and down of camping. You've seen the enjoyment and you've some that misused it.

They talk about fishing in the Manistee River. Roy was never keen about that river. It was too swift and deep for the children to be around. Fishing on the Pigeon was different.

A: Orlo's dad had went fishing, and he told Orlo, "When I come back over the bridge, you get in behind me." He was trying to teach Orlo about the river and how to get along on his own and still have the sense of direction to come back to camp on his own. Roy went on down to the bridge and around that first curve, it's a meadow down there. Well, that's where Roy got out, but he didn't tell Orlo he was going to get out. Orlo was only 10 years old, and the kid kept going and going and going. After you get down there where the river's all spread out there's a lot of little tributaries. All bear country. The kid got way down there in all that swamp. I said to Roy after an hour or two, "Why ain't Orlo here, didn't you see him?" He said, "No, I didn't see him." We waited and waited and waited and he still didn't come and it was getting supper time. Roy said, "I'll go out and hunt him." So he got his boots on and he goes back down the river and here the kid got clear down in that swamp where the river all split.

Q: Down at the county line area.

A: Down there at the tributaries, where there was all. . . . He didn't know which one to take to fish, it was all swamp. And here the kid ran across a big bear down there. When he got back to camp, he said, "The water pushed me down and I knew I had to walk back against it." So he turned around and he was on his way back when his dad found him.

There was a man got lost. He was down at the old iron bridge on the Pigeon. . . . He was gone two days and two nights. The state patrol and sheriff was all out. They stopped and wanted to know if we had seen him, and I said, "Yeah, he was here in camp [but left] before I could take him down to where he belongs." He was long gone. Boy, he was really out of his mind when he had come to my camp.

Once Roy went down a little path and pretty soon he come rushing back, and I wanted to know what was wrong. Pete and Joe and Roy, they took off and they got up there, just stood there, their mouths gaping open, here a little baby deer lay. So they came back and got us women and the kids so they could see that baby deer. And he come up and sucked on Roy's hip boots. Joe said, "There's no doe around." He picks her up and puts her in his arms and totes her back down to camp. She didn't have any fear. We were afraid she'd fall in the river and drown. All of us campers took turns buying milk to feed that baby deer. We kept her the whole summer and dropped her off at headquarters. Bill Horsell said he'd keep her for us because she didn't know anything about the woods, she couldn't go out and forage for herself. He would go out in the forest and cut aspen and stuff and feed her at the barn. He kept her that winter, called her Dandy.

Q: That's the one that Horsells told us about. It used to walk down the outside basement steps.

A: Yeah. She tore the screen door off and come in and went to sleep. She wouldn't stay out in the barn in the stall he had fixed for her. When anybody strange come down, she would stand back behind these big tall breaks. If there was nobody there but a bunch of friends, she'd come out to get her pat.

Q: Do you remember the albino deer?

A: I saw that down there on that meadow. Somebody shot it.

Q: Somebody shot it in deer season that year. That was before the antlerless season, so it was illegally shot.

A: We've had elk go through camp, and we've had bear through the camp, the bobcat, and I've seen coyotes down on Webb Road.

Q: You've probably heard coyotes at night yelping.

A: Oh yeah. I love to hear them. Last year we saw a coyote right there near camp.

Q: Big coyote right there; you saw it, too, Mrs. Parkinson?

A: Yeah. The coyotes all—their howling sounded so pretty coming down through that valley.

Q: One of the interesting things I think, during our life, I had my family out for a drive one afternoon. We were down on the pipeline. And here's a cow elk and two yearlings, and we stopped, shut the car off, and watched them. They didn't hear us, didn't smell us. And all at once they started playing, the two yearlings played like young colts. They even kind of danced around and finally ended up scratching each other's neck—you've seen horses doing it.

A: One year we brought my mother up. We was driving up one road and down another so she could see the animals because she was a great one for outdoors. They was five deer and they were bucks and they were having a fight and they had their horns locked and Mom got a real bang out of that.

Q: That's very unusual to see.

A: There used to be a lot of porcupine too because they always chewed up the toilets in the campground.

Q: I have had people tell about chewing tires.

A: It was chewing Joe's one night, on his trailer.

Q: One thing, they ruined a lot of good rods that people leave outside up against the tree, chew the handles. You know they used to get on those log buildings there. They didn't sleep at night. Two o'clock in the morning. It's kind of a rhythm. They would get on one of those logs outside, and that just echoes like a violin inside . . . crunch, crunch, crunch, crunch, crunch, crunch . . . you know, there really was a rhythm to their chewing. It wasn't just a bite then another bite.

A: Nibbling, nibbling.

Q: Yeah. Did you can any berries while you were here?

A: Yeah, I canned berries, made jam, canned blackberries. Made apple-sauce.

Q: Camp 2 and Camp 7 always had a good tree on them and some down there on the Tin Bridge.

A: We got apples [one] year and had a pie.

They talk about storms and then about Howard Tanner, until June 1983 the director of the Michigan DNR.

A: One storm we went through, we had our big 12-by-14 tent, oh it was a terrible storm. The hail was up on the road, way down in the valley on the rivers. Hail was as big as headaches.

   They had the old-fashioned gasoline pumps with the big black bowl on them. It broke them all up in Wolverine and Vanderbilt. These old timers around here were scared to death; they'd never seen a storm like that. Roy and I went out sightseeing after the storm. We was down on the Hardwood Lake Road. The deer was just froze to death with the hailstones. They were as big as eggs, and I said, "Do stop. I want to get some." He laughed at me and said I was crazy 'cause there wasn't no hailstones that big. I got out and picked up three and they filled my hand.

Q: That was in June or July?

A: July, but I can't tell you the year.

Q: I had somebody say, "Boy, that Howard Tanner, somebody is always in controversy if you're in charge of something." I didn't say anything to him, but I know Howard Tanner could outfish nine out of 10 people.

A: Oh, God yes, he could catch fish where there wasn't any fish.

Q: You take 10 percent of the people that catch most of the fish, he's included in them. He was an excellent woodsman. He was born and raised in the north. So he understands a lot of these problems, and he's been quite sympathetic with our program at Pigeon and retaining the buildings there. At one time [other people in the department] wanted to tear those down. He's the one that really helped save these because of the enjoyment he had at the Pigeon River. His work was done on Section 4 Lake for his thesis.

A: One of the conservation men stopped and picked John up—he was little; we always warned the boys never to go in a lake because we knew nothing about them, but we knew they were deep. I never had no problems with any of the kids to run off and take chances. But the conservation man, he stopped in his truck and asked if he could take John with him in the boat on Section 4. I said, "Well, I guess." He had his paraphernalia—the rope and his stick with the bottle on the end that takes the water temperature, oxygen, and the whole works.

So he takes John with him. He warned him, and he went through all the rigamarole about safety, so set still in the boat and all, and John never did forget. He took his stick with this rope and dropped that down in the lake where the algae and stuff grow, and after so far down there's no oxygen and nothing grows for the fish to feed on. And he went down 92 feet in that lake, at that time, and John never forgot that. But I never had no problems with my kids doing something they weren't supposed to. They never cut down a tree, they never tore up a tree.

Q: We enjoyed having them around.

A: In my summers, in the years that I've been up here—you know I'm not that old—there's been a great change. The campers aren't like they used to be. People that's got kids, they destroy trees, tables, toilets, and a lot of them don't like to go into the state campgrounds. They go to the state parks so their kids got swings and everything. . . . We are now property owners. I can't say I miss the campgrounds, but I do miss the river.

We have done a lot, and I think it was in [the early 1970s] we was out here, camped at the gravel pit. People that was camped at the Grass Lake had a campfire. It was real windy; the fire got away from them. People come across the bridge, told us there was a fire—we'd better leave. My niece and I went to headquarters. There was one man on duty. I said, "We'll meet you there." He was going to tell me how to get there. I said, "Never mind, I know where it's at." We even led the conservation truck in. It burned off ten acres. My niece, her husband, and a friend of mine from Fostoria, we helped fight the fire. We was there until, I don't know, probably five or six hours that night. And they said something about it, and I said, "We enjoy it up here. We've always come up here and we want a place to come back to, that's why we did it.

Q: Over the years, though, fortunately we haven't had any real bad fires. We've had some near ones like the one you just mentioned.

A: In '41, in June, was when the big airplane cracked up over here towards Canada Creek [east of the Black River]. It was an army man out of California. He was 21 or 22 years old, and his bomber went over us. We was all at the bridge. I kept looking at that plane. I said, "That guy's in trouble." You could tell by the way it was too low and the noise it was making. It was a big one; it was a bomber.

I bet it wasn't an hour and a half before the word come back that he had cracked up over here. They had to make a road through to get back and—oh, my gosh, I ain't going to tell you how many feet around the trees that had been just all blowed up, you know. And the hole, well, you could have set up two of these buildings in the hole, and they picked his body up in a ten-quart pail.

Q: Probably he was practicing bombing runs or something because World War II was nearly there for us. Canada was already in it.

A: When we went back, his shirt, it was just like ribbons hanging in the trees, his pants, and the blood running down those birch trees, you could see where the blood was running down, and he was a young guy out of California.

The Motots were surrounded by fire at the Dirk Schreur camp.

Q: What did these fires look like or how did they start?

Doris Motot: Just past the Pigeon on that road going north was that big farm place, just old buildings. We seen the smoke rolling. We was running as hard as we could run to get home to tell our parents that there was a big forest fire. And our mother met us because they was afraid we wasn't going to make it home. For some reason or other my dad came home for dinner that day. He seen the smoke, so he sent my brother with Dirk Schreur's little pony up into the woods to call them in to fight the fire. Somebody over by Miss Dendler's, barefooted, had set a fire there. That was all brush, where they had cut the timber off. Pine and everything. And before they could do anything for the fire the fire was just a short ways from the houses, and they started backfiring it.

Q: In other words, it was within 100 to 200 feet of the buildings.

A: Yes. Houses, the men's shanty, and the horse barn and the blacksmith shop, the cook shanty and general store, icehouse. The train came. They said, "Load the children and the women into the boxcar and take them out." They had us all put our furniture out into the center of the roads, and they said they could take us out—the women and children. The men could fight the fire.

Q: You remember fishing; the brook trout probably were very abundant?

A: We'd take a piece of cord, tie it, take a branch off from a tree, put a hook on it, and that's what we fished with. . . . All worms. You didn't know what flies was then. . . . No, no limits.

Doris: Us kids used to take cans and pick raspberries on that great big pile of brush. After they would cut the hardwood, there would be these raspberries come up. I think there were eight of us. We got our pails full sitting out around on stumps. We heard a noise down underneath, looked down and there was an old bear and her cubs. We didn't even stop to get our pails.

Q: That presently is called Inspiration Point. I took my girls, that was back in the late 1950s, used to go up there in the spring and fly a kite. We would always get a breeze, and you could let it out for miles and wouldn't have to worry about it falling into trees or on telephone lines.

They discuss the Presque Isle fire of the early 1940s.

A: Owen Jack and the three-C boys got over there to fight the fire. Jack was a great lover of animals. He wouldn't destroy nothing. He wasn't any dummy. He used to live in Jackson, Wyoming. He used to be around some in Idaho. But I know he'd cry when he'd talk about the deer and little bunny rabbits—he saw them in the fire, trying to get out. But they would just get outside and stop right there in their tracks.

That's the way it was, the cattle, the pigs. . . . They took all the women and children from the wood camp out into their plowed fields, laid their mattresses down, and covered the women with quilts so they could breathe.

Q: Which way was it coming?

A: North. It came all the way up through to Vanderbilt, up through to Wolverine and up on through.

Q: Mrs. Parkinson and Mrs. Kathryn Motot, we've enjoyed . . .

A: We've been camping for 40 years together, and we've never had a fight yet.

Q: Isn't it great?

A: I told Florence the other night, we're sitting playing cards. I just laid my cards down and looked at them. I said, "Do you know, we been up here four months and we eat back and forth and pittle around this, that, and the other, no arguments and no crabbing." I said, "Why can't the rest of the people do that?"

Q: You know, I think it's the outdoor life that relaxes you.

A: I've had a lot of people look at me like I've lost my marbles. . . .

Well, I look terrible. . . . I don't know much of anything, only camping.

I didn't have tents always, either. My mother and dad couldn't afford it. We went out and we'd lay blankets out. There was a creek then, down at home, close by. We'd just go away on Saturday for supper, cook out along on the river and creek bank, lay a blanket out under a tree, and crawl on and sleep.

Q: That was down in Ohio?

A: Yeah, I've done it for 70 years.

16

Remote Places

The writer John Mitchell says that in preparing his book, The Hunt, *he found Doug Mummert to be one of the few hunters he had met who were directly involved with wild creatures in their natural habitat, who were sensitive to the circumstances of death, and who feel their methods are time-honored and respectful of their prey. Doug Mummert is one of two or three people who know the most remote areas of Pigeon River Country best. He regularly visits the forest two days each week hunting coyotes or tracking bear and training his dogs. He observes, in all kinds of weather, portions of the forest most people never experience. Here are some of his observations.*

You can only beat so much brush, and your feet will only stand so many miles on the snowshoes. But modern man's methods—all you gotta do is turn that key and tow enough gas and keep her going in a circle.

I think what I like about snowshoes is that I can penetrate country nobody else is in. Take the Black River Swamp—two miles wide and six miles long. The first time you go through that, it's a monstrous big place. But the more you penetrate it the smaller it gets. You have this inbuilt fear of big country like that. Just like with night.

[When you disturb a coyote, which sleeps during the day,] usually he'll run his feeding pattern. And the bear does the same thing. If you follow him, you see the wildness of the country.

Animals are very clever. I found where two coyotes killed two partridge at one time. A partridge is very alert. If there are two partridge sitting together and you kick one up, the other will automatically fly. He's alarmed by noises. I don't quite understand their system, but [the two coyotes] approached these two partridge [which were 10 feet apart] and they got both of those partridges. I never could figure out how they done that.

I would say that this area has qualities to hold wildlife, what I will term "sensitive animals:" elk, bear, coyote, and bobcat. They have thrived in this environment because of its inaccessibility to people.

Doug discusses specific locations, identified by their section numbers in Corwith Township (a section is one square mile).

Section 11, Tubbs Creek: On Sunday, January 16 [1977], our group of coyote hunters jumped [moved from their beds] three mature coyotes. They had bedded down in the thick area of swamp after their regular night's hunt for dead deer and rabbits. They selected this area because it was quiet. The male coyote that my hound ran that day circled most of the day, and at about four in the afternoon his escape route was to take to the deep snow in the slashing. His cunning and wild instincts saved his hide that day—due to the fact that he stayed in wild country with no roads.

Section 10, Tin Shanty hardwoods: This is one of the larger tracts of hardwood in the Pigeon River Country. Elk and bear use the beechnuts and acorns from the beech and oak to put a layer of fat around their body for the four months of winter. This area is rich in this type of food.

Section 35, Top of Tin Shanty Hill (east): This is a natural travel route of wild game. Coyotes I studied and hunted have come out of the Black River Swamp near the little unnamed lake north of House's Lost Cabin, crossed the Tin Shanty Bridge Road by the hemlock trees, and on to cross the Sawdust Pile Road about one mile south of the Tin Shanty Bridge on their path to the Tubbs Creek area. I'm sure they use this route [because] it has very little people activity.

Section 26, Tin Shanty Bridge: Where the tubes go under the road is the pathway on the Black River ice that animals use in the deep snow. The ice makes easier means of travel when an animal such as the bobcat wants to get from Black River Swamp to the Tubbs Creek Swamp. Coyotes, otter, beaver, bear, coon, muskrat, pileated woodpeckers also use this area.

Section 28, Black River Swamp: No place in the Lower Peninsula of Michigan is there such an uninterrupted piece of swamp. This is solitude to anyone that has snowshoed into her interior in the wintertime—or at least it was before the sound of the oil facility came into being in the 1970s. Bear, bobcat, and coyote like this type of area because of its size, because modern man is reluctant to penetrate into its interior, and because it contains thick vegetation.

Sections 14 and 24, Hardwood Creek: The Hardwood Creek Swamp is the most ideal bear habitat within the whole Pigeon River Country. Even though it is not real wide, it does contain thick vegetation, [and] is damp most of the summer to provide a cool spot for the heavy-coated bear. In the spring, when he first comes out of hibernation, dead deer and mush-rooms supply him until the Juneberries ripen. Then blueberries come next in the wet areas around Hardwood Lake, plus strawberries, blackberries in section 15 and 22 next, then the acorns and beechnuts on the ridges. Nowhere [else] in the Lower Peninsula do we have this exact condition.

Section 12: This area previously had very little use by people. The rail-road bed has been all but impassible for years. I have passed through this area many times following bear and coyotes. They like this area because of its solitude.

All the sections that Doug Mummert describes were subsequently approved as test sites and were drilled for oil and gas. A flow line was laid through the Black River Swamp to carry crude hydrocarbons through the forest.

Part 4 ❧ Directions

17

Ecology

Despite the usual calm evident in the forest, troubles run deep and wide. In their depth, they involve overuse and misuse. In their breadth, they involve the landscape in general, where the potential for catastrophic failure grows more likely by the day.

Our response has been mixed. We are so overwhelmed with bad news that we grow weary, looking for respite in places like the outdoors. As a human society, we are seemingly unable to deal with all this. Unfortunately, global warming is not something we can patiently wait for somebody else to solve. As we look for guidance in how to proceed, there may be lessons in experiences we've already had. The experience of the Pigeon River Country is that ordinary people can take on large and powerful challenges and make a difference. Whether that will be sufficient is not clear. If we are lucky, it will depend on what we do about it and when.

Toward the end of a Pigeon River Country winter, with the ground yet frozen and frost coming each night, new plant leaves begin to emerge amid the brown and gray litter. One of the first is skunk cabbage. Its leaves, ranging from wine red and maroon to yellow and green stripes, rise several inches high in spiraled hoods, resembling gnomes, that can poke up through thin ice in their wetland surroundings, generating heat by making and using oxygen.

The whole complexity of a living earth operates within bounds that sustain its health, keeping oxygen, for example, constant at about 21 percent of the total atmosphere. Below 15 percent, there is not enough oxygen to start a fire in dry twigs. Above 25 percent, there can be no forests because even the tropical rain forests would ignite and burn away.

Carbon dioxide, once dominant on earth, has been kept by the living earth at a mere 340 parts per million particles of air. A tree takes tons of carbon from the air and deposits them into its roots. Once in the ground, the carbon dioxide reacts with calcium silicate in rocks, forming silicic acid and calcium carbonate, which move in groundwater to streams like the Sturgeon, Pigeon, and Black, eventually reaching the sea, where marine organisms use them to form shells. Rainwater similarly dissolves rock surfaces by applying the carbon dioxide in the rain to the rock, thus making calcium bicarbonate, which again flows in rivers and streams to the sea. These methods of removing carbon dioxide keep the earth cool. The carbon dioxide that has remained in steady quantities in the atmosphere as a trace gas (about 0.03 percent) creates a kind of permeable greenhouse glass that keeps the atmosphere within a familiar range of temperatures.

As we entered the twenty-first century, this natural regulation had fallen severely out of balance. Carbon gases have thickened, trapping more and more heat from the sun. The earth has been drifting toward a state so hot that most living things will die. Already, more than half the quantity of carbon gases that caused devastation at the end of the Paleocene 55 million years ago have been put into our atmosphere. Climatic deviations, once begun, accelerate. The earth has survived such crises before, but most species living here have not. More than 99 percent of earth's species are extinct.

The current crisis is this. The sun is getting hotter, having passed the ideal for earth about two billion years ago. By putting carbon gases into the air—which trap more heat around the globe—and replacing forests and other natural ecosystems with cultivated and developed land, we have increased the temperature while removing so much of the earth's natural cooling capacity that the continued existence of human beings and most other species is in doubt, as is the life of the earth itself. The scientist who first looked at the earth as the single organism that keeps itself in balance declared in 2006 that there is a strong possibility it cannot survive this crisis. The direction we are going in has not eased. It has speeded up.

With all our attention to environmental sensitivity, each year we have fewer forests globally than we did the year before. About 13.7 million hectares of forest disappear every year (nearly 34 million acres). More than half of the tropical forests were degraded or gone by the time we entered the twenty-first century. One million plant and animal species are expected to vanish from the earth within two more decades. Scientists familiar with the warming crisis warn that we have to stop destroying forest habitat everywhere. Our forests are not only local: they are vital elements of the interconnected biosphere in which we live and breathe.

Whatever forest management we have conducted worldwide has not addressed planet health or imbalance, even locally. Michigan's forest managers have just begun looking at the forest from this perspective, starting with the red pine. It's a useful illustration. There are only half as many red pines in northern Michigan as there were in 1800, and the dry-mesic and dry northern forest communities where red pines thrive are significantly reduced. Much existing red pine is in plantations, an artificial condition convenient for harvesting but unfavorable for the diversity that keeps the outdoors healthy.

Dense fir forests in Mexico, the nesting sites of the world's monarch butterflies, have been decimated by loggers. The World Wildlife Foundation established a fund of more than six million dollars to pay people living near the 138,000-acre reserve in Mexico to report on logging instead of harvesting trees. But some take money from loggers as well and let them continue to cut down the trees. Armed gangs pay authorities to look the other way. Such a self-centered approach is not unusual; it's the norm.

There is evidence even among those of us who are not armed thugs that we are seriously disconnected from our biosphere, that we essentially treat other life forms as separate from ourselves. It's ironic that such treatment is said to be for our own betterment, for it's not much different from taking whatever we want from the land or putting whatever we think is necessary into the air.

In some 8,120 articles about pigeons and behavior in scholarly journals published between 1975 and 2005, there is a heavy emphasis on homing capabilities in which researchers damaged a pigeon's body to study the effects. They put plastic tubes up pigeons' nostrils and release them to fly. They administer electric shock. They feed the pigeons drugs. They conduct what they call "ablations," which are surgical amputations, removing parts of brains or apparently whatever else any given researcher thinks may be interesting for studying its effects. One-month-old homing pigeons were surgically deprived of either their right or left hippocampus, then tested for their homing abilities. Whatever qualms we might feel privately, publicly we recognize nothing unhealthy in conducting such experiments in the name of knowledge and our well-being.

There have been efforts to adopt guidelines for "assessing and monitoring the health" of such captive creatures. In evaluating laboratory mice, one report says, researchers should look for a variety of things. The listing offers a dreary view of what laboratory life can be like for mice. The problems include mice injuring other mice, poor weight gain, ulcers, vaginal or uterine or rectal prolapse, diarrhea, dehydration, hypothermia, lethargy, anemia, head tilts, abnormal breathing or movement, tremors, and paralysis. The report also notes that "there has been an increase in the number of investigators using mice; the number of mice used in biomedical research; the number of mice bred and maintained to their natural life spans; and the number of mice with potentially adverse or debilitating phenotypes."

To study whether birds learn songs rather than somehow knowing them through genetic programming, a noted University of California researcher gathered some white-crowned sparrow chicks in Wales, deafened them, and found they could never produce more than a scratchy buzz.

Entomologists trap insects and bring them, in alcohol, to universities and museums by the millions. It is from these dead specimens that much of the information about insects is derived, resulting in a heavy emphasis on body structure and hardly anything about how the insects live in the world.

Recent research has variously disabled such creatures as female meadow voles, prairie voles, golden hamsters, zebra finches (colorful songbirds), various other songbirds, rat pups separated from their mothers, marmoset monkey babies, adult rats fed cocaine while being strapped down and given tail shocks, rabbits, infant domestic dogs (otherwise known as puppies), infant wolves, infant coyotes, force-fed ducks who were then stunned with electricity, fruit flies who were systematically killed if they were females or daughters of females for 41 generations at the University of California at Santa Cruz, ants, caterpillars, wasps, butterfly larvae, some 881 butterflies trapped for a single study, honeybees restrained as 20 mg transponders more than twice the bees' length were attached to their bodies with double-sided tape or glue, snails and 30 peacock and tortoiseshell butterflies superglued with similar transponders, zebra fish (freshwater fish originally from the Ganges River), tiny transparent worms, hawk moths, and, sure enough, monarch butterflies, whose claws were removed so they wouldn't tear themselves while they were being held alive in glassine envelopes. Chimpanzees in the wild have declined to the point of being listed as endangered, while those in captivity continue to increase; about half of those in U.S. labs are still being used for experimentation, primarily for research on hepatitis, malaria, and behavior.

Granted, some research is now less invasive. Researchers put a collection of *Mesovelia* and *Microvelia* water-walking insects, both present in the Great Lakes region, into aquaria, videotaped them, and analyzed the digital images to see how they ascend the slope at the water's edge to reach land. Eagle DNA was studied in a six-year project that involved gathering their fallen feathers and analyzing them. Researchers characterized it as a "breakthrough" approach. A new phenomenon in 2005 was computer programs that let users, particularly high school students, dissect animals that are really just digital images. The images, of course, are pictures of a real dissection, in one case of a fetal pig that weighed three pounds until it was sliced apart.

The problem is that even in advanced civilizations we can convince ourselves that other living creatures are less than ourselves, less feeling, less important: bad for the bird but good for the research grant. We don't all act this way, but it doesn't take many to set us on courses for which we can later be profoundly sorry.

In Auschwitz in 1943–44, Josef Mengele tortured twin human beings to death in the name of scientific inquiry. Experiments included injecting chemicals into children's eyes trying to change their color, amputations and other brutal surgeries, and submerging people into boiling water to measure how much heat it takes to cause death. The subjects who survived such experiments were nearly always killed afterward. Other experiments on humans at Nazi concentration camps, according to Nuremberg trial indictments, included freezing, low pressure chambers simulating altitudes up to 68,000 feet, induced malaria infection and drug treatments, experiments with toxins and poisons, and bone, muscle, and nerve operations. These grisly recitations differ from current experiments primarily in the fact that one animal, *Homo sapiens,* is now left out. Purposeful disfigurement and termination of humans these days is primarily under the guise of political activity.

It's no wonder we think so little of the harm we do to our own earth. It may be for some of the same reasons that such activities continue to take place. Indeed, some in the life sciences consider the illusion of human independence from nature to be a sign of dangerous ignorance. A tendency to maintain such independence, in this view, will lead ultimately to our own death as a species and surely to massive death on, and possibly of, our planet.

Outside the laboratories, especially in dwellings in and around our more remote lands, many of us find it amusing that someone would worry about the loss of pugnose shiners or Hungerford's crawling water beetles. There are plenty of other fish and insects. We seem to be unaware that these species do vital work on behalf of a planet under constant threat of imbalance. It's like losing one after another of the thousand species in our colon until we finally notice some trouble with digestion. It is one thing to buck up and carry on but quite another when our system starts to fail from an inability to synthesize vitamins or break down sugars. At some point, we either recognize and begin to address the problem or we reach crisis. Our planet already has a fever.

Humans are only recent players in the rise and fall of individual species, but our track record is not good. Elk have made a comeback. In fact, the largest herd east of the Mississippi is no longer in the Pigeon River Country. Kentucky, which imported elk from the West in 1997–98, estimated that it had 4,500 elk in the fall of 2005, making them the largest elk population in the eastern United States, compared with about 1,000 in the Pigeon River area. Michigan issues about 100 hunting permits for its annual Rocky Mountain elk hunting season, as many as it believes will keep the herd at 800 to 900 animals.

In 2006, biologists at Rocky Mountain National Park were still struggling to get a plan accepted that would reduce the elk herd of 3,000 to a level that would not continue wiping out the aspen. The 400-square-mile park next to Estes Park, Colorado, has been steadily losing butterflies and beavers because of the imbalance. As authorities considered bringing in nighttime sharpshooters with silencers and others suggested reintroducing wolves, recreational hunting, contraception, or just letting nature take its course, various groups found each idea unacceptable. Some people, including a town planner, actually thought the elk would start hanging out in town to escape sharpshooters or hunters.

In 1985, Michigan released 49 martens in the Pigeon River Country State Forest, then 21 more in the Huron-Manistee National Forest and 15 in the Pere Marquette State Forest in Lake County. The marten populations were successfully reproducing but remained a threatened species. Osprey and bald eagles are recovering from near extinction nationwide, but the *Accipiter gentilis,* or northern goshawk, remains scarce in the Pigeon River Country, and its population is declining throughout the state. Goshawks are known to mate for life and to use the same nesting area for decades, usually 40 or 50 feet above the ground in trees much taller than that, mostly near water. Their eyesight is up to eight times sharper than that of humans. But there has been little systematic inventory of goshawks in Michigan and not much study of their productivity, abundance, impacts from forestry, competition, predation, or habitat. Goshawks are in the same family as bald eagles, osprey, red-shouldered hawks, and Cooper's hawks, all of which are of concern in Michigan due to their low numbers.

Organochlorine pesticides thinned eggshells and directly killed many raptors, including goshawks, through direct contact and by concentrating up the food chain. Such pesticides are still used in the Tropics and brought north in migrant songbirds, which are among the goshawks' prey. Our pine siskin, for example, winters as far south as Mexico and summers as far north as Alaska. We're now finding mercury at toxic levels in songbirds; it spews from coal-burning power plants in midwestern states and enters the food chain in worms and other tiny creatures. The populations of 20 common birds in the U.S. have plummeted by half in the last 40 years, according to a 2007 report by Audubon Society. The evening grosbeak has declined by 78 percent, ruffed grouse 54 percent. We ride to the rescue of single species but miss the big picture.

Cooper's hawks in the Pigeon River Country and other northern locations migrate to southern Michigan in winter. Smaller than goshawks, Cooper's hawks are active in white pine and open deciduous forest areas, especially at edges and near streams. Widespread DDT use decimated them, and shooting, trapping, timber harvests, and golf courses and buildings reduced the birds or their habitat further. Scores of species of mammals, reptiles, amphibians, birds, and fish in the northern environment around Lake Michigan are listed by authorities as being in trouble.

The rayed bean, a freshwater mussel once common in the Pigeon River, is now largely gone. It is known to survive in only one Canadian river, apparently a victim of siltation, agricultural chemicals, and urban pollution. At the other end of the aquatic scale, the populations of large predators in the oceans are down to about 20 percent of their previous numbers. The weight of black marlins as recently as 1952, when Hemingway wrote *The Old Man and the Sea,* averaged 134 kilograms. Today it's about 35 kilograms. Blue sharks that averaged 52 kilograms now average 22. In 2006, the U.S. government closed 654,000 square miles of federal waters—about the size of Alaska—to fishing and particularly to devastating bottom trawling, as a response to alarming declines in fishing stock worldwide. The protections, enacted for areas off Hawaii, the West Coast, and Alaska, resulted from the various interests working together.

Bilge oil dumped from ships in the oceans kills at least 300,000 seabirds every year off Newfoundland—a loss greater each year than the one that followed the Exxon *Valdez* disaster. A drop of oil the size of a quarter will likely kill any bird it touches, either by damaging its insulation and causing hypothermia or by poisoning the bird when it ingests the oil while preening.

Much of the picture is poorly documented. Brian Mastenbrook, the Pigeon's wildlife biologist, said in late 2005 that pressure on the rare and secretive bobcats has been increasing. But he said the Department of Natural Resources doesn't have a good enough population assessment method to determine whether bobcats are decreasing, only how many have been taken. He sees truck after truck with a dog box in back hunting bobcat in the season from January into March but has no idea where they were hunting. People are guiding more hunts than in the past. They hang roadkill deer in trees where coyotes can't get them, check the woods later to see if a bobcat has visited the carcass, then start dogs following the cat's trail. Magazines carry ads for bobcat hunts, guaranteeing you'll get a cat for so many hundred dollars. All Mastenbrook can say for sure is that bobcat numbers do not seem to be increasing. The 100,000-acre Pigeon is only about one-fourth of the work area this one wildlife biologist has been assigned in this era of lean state budgets. The DNR, with half of one percent of the Michigan general fund budget, had 3,000 employees in 1975 and 3,003 in 1993, while the Department of Corrections, with 14 percent of the general fund, rose from 2,000 employees to 14,000 in the same period. The U.S. Forest Service was spending $2 to $4 per acre for forest recreation and Michigan about $1, described as the difference between high quality and getting by.

Natural resources people in Michigan have shown extraordinary dedication to the outdoors, especially field personnel, who tromp across the land doing their job whenever they can get out of their office cubicles. In a stroke of foresight, the department assigned an ecologist to the Gaylord office, Keith Kintigh. As the area's wildlife ecologist, Kintigh tries to see how every detail fits into the overall picture. He says that the "ecological approach is familiar to older foresters—it's the best of everything we've always done." The main differences are the intensive training and the new technology that allows anybody, the public included, to access old information about the land now stored in digital files, a lot of it online. Geographic information systems, remote sensing imagery, and powerful desktop computers allow sophisticated spatial analysis of watershed dynamics, energy flow, nutrient cycling, species presence, and site stability and resilience.

Small groups of personnel, all busy with many other tasks, are assigned to ecoteams in the northern Lower Peninsula ecoregion from Clare County to the Mackinac Bridge. Their big picture is one of landforms. They talk of landscape, by which they mean the whole ecosystem above and below ground, including species and habitats in greater breadth than a stand and looked at over long periods of time. They see a level to gently rolling ecoregion of sand and gravel, glacial outwash and moraines, dotted with swamps and bogs. Growing on these are five forest types, ranging from very dry to wet-mesic, meaning wetter than ideal but not a wetland.

Mesic, pronounced MEE-sik, refers to land that has a moderate or well-balanced supply of moisture.

There are many ways to classify things. One way is with terms such as *hardwood forest* and *mixed conifers.* The newest ways look more complicated but are simpler and more accurate. With only a handful of groupings, we can categorize the outdoors based on what usually grows on a site's understory. See white pine? Red maple? Blueberries? Witch hazel? We're in a PArVHa habitat, that is:

Pinus strobus	P
Acer rubrum	Ar
Vaccinium spp.	V
Hamamelis virginiana	Ha

It's very dry to dry here, with few nutrients. We're in recent glacier country (within the last 10 or 12 centuries), and possibly in the Pigeon River Country, where this habitat is common. If we dig, we're likely to find gravel or coarse sand less than four feet down. Red oak is the most common cover in current PArVHa stands. There's usually a moderate presence of juneberry along with the witch hazel and blueberries. Red maple and white pine often dominate among the saplings. Along the ground, we're likely to find bracken fern, wintergreen, wild lily of the valley, and false Solomon's seal and possibly sweet fern and spreading dogbane. But if we find blue cladina, reindeer lichen, or bearberry, we're probably in a different habitat, PVCd (first initials for the scientific names of white pine, blueberry, and reindeer lichen), in an even drier soil with even fewer nutrients where the dominant forest tree is usually jack pine.

The difference in this kind of classification is that it considers several things at once: soil, water, what's on the ground, the bushes, the trees, and what associates with what, all looked at from the perspective of repeatable patterns of understory vegetation. Such a view is leading to a whole new way of treating forest management: managing for overall resource health rather than individual forest resources in isolation. In the study of red pine in 2003 and 2004, several things were noticed. Red pine is mostly in plantations, where it doesn't much help wildlife. It's all maturing at about the same time—soon. Ninety-five percent of the red pine in the Pigeon River Country is more than 40 years old. The new guidelines let managers put red pine in nonplantation settings on sites that are naturally suited for it. Managers will take into consideration past, present, future, and the overall ecological context, as well as economics and social factors. They will establish similar guidelines for all the other managed forest types, such as the Pigeon's treed bogs, where two-thirds of the trees are in their eighties. They will also establish guidelines for its oaks, nearly half of which are in their seventies, as are more than a third of the white pine and paper birch, and for its mixed swamp conifers, half of them more than a century old and only 3 percent of them younger than 20.

This is quite a change when we consider that there's a lot more money in growing pure, densely stocked red pines all the same age. This is not to say that those days are gone, but no longer will the system ignore the ongoing and significant decline in natural red pine communities, with their mix of flora and fauna, or the disappearance of others.

All but one percent of the mature hemlock-hardwood forest is gone from the Great Lakes region. The hemlock that's left—less than half a percent of a landscape where it once was the dominant tree—is under increasing pressure with an artificially high deer population browsing young hemlock and a scarcity of the decaying logs and tip-up mounds that give hemlock a suitable substrate. Logging has traditionally not been managed to restore healthy, native conditions. As many as 90 species (such as ruffed grouse and rose-breasted grosbeaks) multiplied their numbers as northern Michigan's forests were drastically altered by logging, burning, and unbalanced regrowth. But overall the rich diversity of species has dramatically declined due to the loss of scores of plants, animals, and insects now in danger of disappearing from the region altogether. Their losses have deep ramifications for the health of the ecosystem. Even at the national level, advocates for endangered species don't challenge inadequate management of the overall landscape; instead they sue to protect a single species while the plans for national forests remain unbalanced, with many other species ignored.

Nor have we paid much attention to the long-term effects from how we tinker with the landscape. Garlic mustard was introduced from Europe in the late 1800s. Scientists have discovered it kills off fungi that help trees and other native plants get nutrients from the soil. Garlic mustard, which chokes out other plants and has no significant natural enemies, is slowly killing our forests wherever it spreads.

One tough issue ecoteams try to find time to discuss with the public is fire. Fire creates wildlife openings in a forest with much richer results for overall habitat than managed logging does. It gives native plant species a chance against nonnative, invasive ones and allows the best species for the site to become established through natural means while timber management makes arbitrary decisions about what will grow on the site.

"Sustainable forests were influenced by fire," Kintigh says. "It was there historically. It's not socially acceptable now. Thin stands get red maple back because there is no fire" on the site to give vegetation typical of the site a chance to become reestablished. Brian Mastenbrook describes the controlled burns the department has been doing since the early 1990s near Inspiration Point and on land recently added to the forest. Some 900 acres in Green Timbers are burned on a rotation of 300 acres per year. "It helps eliminate nonnatives," he notes. "Leafy spurge is coming in, cherries filling in. We're trying to keep mostly grass—savannah or open grassland with just a few trees. It increased a food source for at least a month afterward. Animals come from all over to eat regenerating growth." About 80 acres in the old Civilian Conservation Corps field off Osmun Road, where the forest has filled in about half of the 600-acre opening, was burned in spring 2000 to maintain some opening, and another burn set up for fall 2005.

Crews put a line around the area, plow and disc, and lay foam fire retardant at the edges so the fire can't escape. In big 300-acre burns, 25 to 30 people participate. They burn from the edges toward the center. The fire draws from its own wind and goes out on its own. "People complained about CCC last time because it was all black grass," Mastenbrook noted, "until it regenerated in about a week to 10 days. It starts to green up, and there's a carpet of green two weeks after the burn."

A serious problem remaining is how thin we are stretching these resource managers. One of Keith Kintigh's favorite moments has been watching nighthawks diving in the remote forest, an experience likely to be more rare for him than ever. By mid-2006 Gaylord's sole wildlife ecologist had to take on additional duties when the wildlife biologist in Atlanta retired. This has been the trend in recent years, with fewer people being assigned more responsibility but few new resources. The era, after all, is one in which voters seem to prefer spending on themselves instead of pooling sufficient money to act on behalf of such shared but distant concepts as natural resources. Since 1977, the Pigeon River Country Association has faithfully raised enough funds to provide a summer worker to help on Pigeon River projects that are underfunded by the DNR's Forest Management Division. In 1983, right after graduating from MSU, Brian Mastenbrook was such an intern, working with Arch Reeves. "It changed my life," Brian says.

Arch saw a young man who "has a feel for the out-of-doors." When Arch first had to pace off a mile from one survey post to the next for forestry measurements, after a few summers he could get within a few feet of the post. Right away "Brian could almost step on the next post" even though the mile went through the ups, downs, and detours of terrain. "It's an art," Arch says.

Mastenbrook, as the current wildlife habitat biologist, recalls a recent open house where resource managers sought public comment. "Gaylord," he said, like other urban places, "is like a city removed from logging and natural resource management. They're more sophisticated, less basic. There's less contact with what's going on around them. We hear instead more from small groups with a direct interest, not much directly related to the Pigeon River Country. Ruffed grouse hunters want us to cut every last stick of aspen, while Sierra Club says no cutting or at least much less."

Mastenbrook has tried to get consideration for pulling out Tin Bridge. "It's eroding," he says. "You would have to improve the whole road. That increases use—an infrastructure change we shouldn't be managing toward." Its removal would leave only the Webb Road and Sturgeon Valley Road bridges crossing the Pigeon. After thinking about it, the Cheboygan County Road Commission decided to replace the bridge in 2007 despite opposition from the advisory council. To get federal funds, the county would have to install a two-lane bridge where the seldom-used road is barely one lane. Wetlands on both sides would be disturbed and filled, making it questionable whether the county could get Michigan Department of Environmental Quality approval for anything wider than one lane.

Half a dozen miles southwest of Tin Bridge, Doug Mummert watched the Otsego County Road Commission haul 600 dump-truck loads of fill to both sides of Tin Shanty Bridge and put in free-flowing culverts to keep sand from running into the Black River. "I was opposed because it's a blue-ribbon trout stream," Mummert said. "You couldn't go much more than 35 miles an hour—now its over 50. No stream impediments were put in to provide proper habitat." It's one in a litany of what he feels are degradations over the last two decades. Hard surfaces for Tin Shanty, Clark, and McMasters Creek bridges and more of Sturgeon Valley Road, in some places between six inches and three feet of gravel applied. A pond eliminated on Hardwood Creek to accommodate a free-flowing culvert, ignoring in the process an eagle's nest that fed as many as five eagles from the pond, which was filled with roughage fish where it was too warm for brook trout. Gates blocking timber trails pulled out by authorities from other local governments. Quad runners, snowmobiles, and hot-rod motorcycles. Commercial operations taking over bear hunting, in which 80 percent of the bear harvested in Michigan are killed over bait piles, some rigged with timers and photo devices to register when the bear comes in. Interest groups staging special events in the forest. Traffic jams during elk viewing. Mature oaks 80 years old yet only halfway through their life cycles that provide acorns once every four years for bobcat, elk, deer, and bear being cut down "by mistake," including one oak 34 inches in diameter, and in the face of warnings that there will be no more oak in the Pigeon within 40 years. Hordes picking morel mushrooms, which bring up to $20 a pound in Indiana and Illinois. Snowmobile traffic driving many elk from the interior of the area. In summary, he says, conditions for bear, osprey, eagles, and bobcats, the most sensitive wildlife, are five times worse in the twenty-first century than they were two decades ago.

As Mike Koskus, an advisory council member put it, people who come to the Pigeon today say, "Wow, what a great place," but the people who were here 40 years ago would say, "What have you done?" Peter Gustafson, chairman of the advisory council, in 2005 listed certain changes as having a significant cumulative impact: horseback, snowmobile, and commercial use; vehicle access and road improvement; wildlife baiting; special events; and rising recreational use in general.

Baiting, or placing food to attract deer for hunting, was eventually banned, at least for a while to combat tuberculosis, on public land in Otsego and Presque Isle counties, plus five other adjacent counties outside the Pigeon area, but placing up to two gallons of bait on the ground per hunt site is allowed throughout the rest of Michigan, including Cheboygan and Montmorency counties. Baiting for bear is allowed in the entire state.

Ash trees in the Pigeon River Country's northeast corner were found in 2005 to be infected with the emerald ash borer (*Agrilus planipennis*), considered deadly to ash and untreatable. Michigan's Department of Agriculture cut some of the stately trees, and found more infested ash nearby, but put off a decision about how to treat the area. Like other state agencies, the agriculture department was experiencing budget cuts. In May 2005, it quarantined the area, meaning it announced that trees could not be removed from the area subject to a misdemeanor fine of $25 to $100, a civil infraction fine of between $1,000 and $10,000, or possibly a felony fine of up to $250,000 or five years in prison for actions damaging plants or natural resources. It was unclear how such a quarantine would be enforced.

The Pigeon River Country entered the twenty-first century in the midst of a several-year drought. In fiscal year 2000, rainfall was nearly six inches below the forest's 29-year average. While rainfall rose 1.67 inches above average two years later, the effects of drought continued to be felt in stunted growth and vehicles breaching barriers that are normally too wet to be passable.

As the globe warms and oceans rise due to melting ice and glaciers, freshwaters such as the Great Lakes are likely to drop. Global warming will disrupt the intricate patterns that continually replace freshwater. Winters won't disappear; they might be more severe as weather cycles reach extremes. But overall warmth will continue. Storms will continue to form as natural systems arising to reduce the imbalances.

Changing conditions have far-reaching effects. Water pollutants will concentrate in higher numbers as previously fresh water evaporates. Droughts in the Midwest will be more frequent and more severe, reducing water levels even further. Rivers like the Sturgeon, Pigeon, and Black would dwindle, reducing or removing habitat for trout and other cold-water fish species. Even a modest warming of 4.5 degrees Fahrenheit over 70 years would reduce rainbow, brook, brown, and cutthroat trout habitat by a fourth to a third nationwide. Balsam fir and other northern trees may migrate north or simply die out, maybe replaced by maple. Kirtland's warblers, which nest only a little south of the Pigeon River Country, would go the way of the jack pines. Freshwater would lose dissolved oxygen and begin to choke with algae. Silica, essential to some freshwater organisms, decreases in groundwater during droughts. Crayfish, snails, and other water organisms start to die off as temperatures rise.

Freshwater supplies have been falling for some years around the globe, while demand grows dramatically. In 2005, more than a billion of us lacked access to safe drinking water. The United Nations Educational, Scientific, and Cultural Organization estimates that the average amount of freshwater available for each person on earth will shrink by one-third before 2025. We know only the outlines of how our freshwater system works on earth and hardly anything about underground flows, to say nothing of how we should tackle rising heat and diminishing water supplies and rain.

Already at least 15 bird species in Michigan have begun arriving one to eight weeks earlier in the Upper Peninsula, apparently in response to the continually warming climate, a trend that began in 1965. As the land gets drier, grassland and pasture replace forest. If the severe climatic fluctuations leave the land wetter, oaks and other more moisture-tolerant trees would thrive at the expense of others. But if the land becomes drier, conditions will be ripe for wildfires. According to Environmental Protection Agency computer models, the shallow prairie wetlands of the north-central United States and south-central Canada—nesting sites for 50 to 80 percent of our ducks and other waterfowl—will experience stronger and more frequent droughts.

It's easier to get interested in a crisis descending upon us than it is to remain interested as life goes on and changes occur slowly and sporadically. We have other things to worry about.

Officially, we think so little of natural land that we treat it as a holding area for eventual economic gain through some kind of development. Even formalized zoning does not recognize undeveloped land as a final goal. When Ann Arbor drafted an open space plan for 2006–11, its treatment of natural land was an anomaly in a state where land use reform falls victim to midnight shenanigans in the legislature.

"Natural and cultural amenities are a necessary aspect of a balanced community," the plan reads, "and therefore must be considered a legitimate land use, along with housing, business and industry." It's the kind of thought that gets pushed aside when somebody wants to do something with his or her property. Almost all of the woods and open spaces one sees when driving in northern Michigan outside the Pigeon River Country are private property just waiting for somebody to start development. Only the parcels with groundwater too close to the surface to "perk" for septic systems have some measure of immunity, at least until somebody runs a sewer line.

In response, some of the people most familiar with the natural lands of northern Michigan have formed an organization called Habitat Initiative to help property owners surrounding the Pigeon River Country see the benefits of keeping their land undeveloped, including tax breaks and other funding already in place. It's an effort to treat habitats as natural systems. As one state forester put it, "Administrative boundaries are not recognized by species other than humans." Within the first year, the project had permanent conservation easements protecting 873 acres of private property near the forest boundaries from development and another 4,215 acres with stewardship management plans in place for helping wildlife survive in the area. One of its challenges was finding enough money to keep its outreach efforts going.

Recent close study of fossil time lines indicates that it was climate change that killed off most of North America's largest mammals some 13,000 years ago. As the earth entered its warm period between glaciations, woody plants appeared, which were unsuited to Eurasian wild horses and eventually mammoths, the two extinct mammals studied most closely through radiocarbon dating. The earth is more stable during glaciation and more vulnerable between ice ages to the continually changing patterns of pressure and temperature of a planet in orbit around a sun. It's the time we picked to run amok, trashing tropical rain forests and spewing carbon gases, all the while acting skeptical about the possible danger. Despite our capacity to love, shared with other creatures, we can act awfully selfish when we shouldn't.

In our cars, we treat one another as annoying clogs in our machine. We treat people jogging or bicycling along our roadways little better. It's time we all got out of our cars and looked around us, particularly up. There are more than a few dozen stars up there. We can see a vast array of them from places like the Pigeon River Country. Why can't we see them from our cities, our neighborhoods? What's blocking our view? We need to stop treating environmental concerns as if they were some lunatic fringe of special interests. We have deadly serious problems that need to be addressed. We can't afford to let some people paint these issues as kooky. They're real.

People who see such things clearly have made a difference. Not just wild-eyed environmentalists. First of all, people in the oil and gas business, road construction, and the building trades have repeatedly demonstrated environmental sensitivity, sometimes while denouncing tree huggers. Second, there's nothing wrong with hugging trees; some of them are our oldest—and tallest—relatives. Trees aren't people, nor do they think like us. It's unlikely they look down on us the way we look down on one another, though who could blame them if they did. But they are vastly complicated living beings that stay in one place doing wondrous things with water, air, chemicals, and sunlight in a kind of molecular wizardry.

Roadkill is not a joke waiting for a punch line. It's a sad symptom of a human enterprise that does not fit well with our natural world. It's one of many. We ought to consider doing something about it. We're problem solvers. First, however, we need to see the problem.

Yet people, with all their personal reservations, flaws, emotions, and whatever else we might think stands in the way of problem solving, stepped up to the plate in the Pigeon River Country Advisory Council, perhaps sometimes doing too little too late, or the wrong thing, but nonetheless improving the way we run the railroad. They brought their various views to the table but didn't let it stop there. Members of environmental groups alerted enough other citizens that things got attention and were addressed. Surely we can put such efforts into addressing our most serious challenges as a living planet. Our society has so intimidated the environmentally minded that they suggest dialogue instead of answers, as though the best we can hope for is not getting things done but trying to get people talking about what they might want, whether they know anything about it or not. Should we vote on whether our water should be clean enough to swim in? Apparently so. Should we dialogue about whether letting our children burn to a crisp is a good idea? Evidently.

Our societal ignorance is appalling. It festers as we watch reality TV, where the most realistic thing is the advertisements. Ask any of us to name the countries next door in Central America and see what we get. Surveys show that one out of every five American adults thinks the sun revolves around the earth and almost no American adults know what molecules are. Only half the Americans surveyed in 2005 labeled as true the statement "Human beings, as we know them, developed from earlier species of animals." It was a lower percentage than that found in Latvia, Croatia, Cyprus, or any of 32 European countries surveyed except Turkey.

Up north, we've had a cool ride—up to now. Jim Harrison, a northern Michigan poet and novelist who likes to poke around in the bushy country of the Upper Peninsula, mentions in his 2004 *True North: A Novel* the few birds (ravens, chickadees, and redstarts) "that could survive winter up here. [The redstart] lines the interior of its nest with a cushion of animal hair and grouse feathers, the warmest cocoon possible. . . . I was curious about how many thousands of years it had taken the bird to evolve this survival behavior." The American redstart sings high, sharp notes and, impressively, alternates between two different songs. His fellow warblers usually sing the same song over and over. Perhaps it's a melodic reminder that nature is not hardwood forests, tree stands, or landforms; it's irregular shapes, overlapping activities, interlocking patterns, snowflakes, calm here, turbulent there, jagged edges, sudden leaps, and beautiful melodies. And the whole cannot be derived from summing up its parts.

18

Sam

Sam Titus came north from Ohio when her husband died in 1968. She began calling herself Sam because she liked the name. Once a model and owner of women's clothing shops in Ohio and Texas, she took an interest in cultural activities and the northern Michigan outdoors. Sam and a woman friend named Herman Toms would get a state firewood permit each fall, drive a pickup truck to the woods, and cut up a truckload of fallen timber by hand with a crosscut saw.

Sam was asked to speak to a group of sixth, seventh, and eighth graders visiting the Pigeon River Country from their middle school in Cranbrook near Detroit. They got off their bus at a well site, and Sam stood quietly while a Shell Oil Company representative spoke first. He unfolded a series of flowcharts and spread them on the hood of the bus. Sam recalls that everything about the man was loud, "even his clothes." While he talked, the youngsters looked around and made square mud pies with their shoes.

When it was Sam's turn, the Pigeon's forester, Ned Caveney, walked over and handed her a battery-operated megaphone. "I can't use one of these," she whispered.

"Try," Ned replied.

Sam held the megaphone near an oil well, seven silver bracelets dangling from her arm, talking with a battery-amplified voice about the birds and animals that lived in the woods around them, about the clear waters and the flowers. She raised her other arm, eight more silver bracelets dangling from it, pointed to the oil facilities, and asked the youngsters if they wanted to see more of that in the forest. She says their response was heartwarming.

One girl even walked up to Sam, hugged her, looked up at her, and said,

"We love your forest, too." Among the cards and notes she got from the pupils later was a poem from the girl to "The Lady of the Woods" decorated with drawings of trees and wildlife.

A Woodland Concert
SAM TITUS

It was a beautiful fall morning. I pushed the button to open the garage door. The car started right off, and I felt great. I backed out of the drive, pushed the button to close the garage door and flicked on the radio. The announcer informed me I would hear Bach for the next several hours. Wonderful! I could turn on the back speakers and have the music as loud as I wished since I was driving to the forest alone.

I hurried along the blacktop, knowing I wouldn't see deer or elk until I was on the gravel road. Music I loved and bright color in the trees made living a privilege this morning.

About one-half mile onto the gravel I thought I saw animals, so I slowed down. There was a sizable group. They were elk! I went as slow as my car would go. One good-sized bull and eight cows. They stood like statues; not even an ear flicked. About forty feet from them, I stopped. Not a move. Then it struck me. They were hearing my loud Bach! I rolled down my window and slowly turned the radio as high as it would go. I prayed that a rattly old truck wouldn't come barreling along and frighten my concert patrons.

My feelings were bursting from me. I wanted the whole world to see what I was seeing and feel what I was feeling: those great animals listening. How were they hearing the sound I was hearing? Could they be pleased? They were not frightened. Not an animal moved as the announcer told us about the next thing we would hear. It was almost as if they expected the announcement. No trucks came. We stood in that place in this world and shared an experience. Finally the bull slowly walked into the trees, the cows following.

The road Sam describes as gravel has since been paved by the Otsego County Road Commission.

19

A Dancing Ground

FORD KELLUM

Ford Kellum went to work part time in 1933 as a fire chaser for the Michigan Conservation Department (now the Department of Natural Resources). He became a fire warden, and by 1937 was a wildlife biologist whose career over the years took him around the state. In 1964, he was transferred to Gaylord.

I saw the Pigeon River Country first in 1938. We had our first wildlife school there in June. The buildings were new, built by the CCC. It hasn't changed an awful lot since then. The trees are a lot bigger. In 40 years, jack pine and red pine get to a pretty good size. There was some hardwood that wasn't cut at all on the Fisherman's Trail. When I was there in '38, we were taken up to Inspiration Point. There was an opening, and the prairie chickens came to that country. In fact, they danced right there in that opening. A prairie chicken looks like a grouse, weighs about two and a half pounds. In the spring of the year, they have this orange sack that fills with air and they expel the air. They sound like a mourning dove. You can hear it for four miles on a still morning. It's a vibration to attract females to the dancing ground. About twenty were dancing there. They are a bird of the prairielike country, but that was about the last year because the state went in there, made furrows, and planted pine trees.

But it was getting better for deer and grouse. One thing we must remember: habitat always changes—it grows. And as it changes so changes wildlife. There were timber wolves in lower Michigan. They're most sensitive to man. The cutting of the timber and the people drove them out right quick. The same thing happened to the elk. The last wild turkeys and elk were seen in the Saginaw Valley in the 1870s. [Turkeys have been reintroduced and after some decades remain in precarious numbers in the region. They are particularly threatened by snowmobiles.]

I knew [Beaver Lake Basin in the Upper Peninsula] real well when it was virgin—up until 1938–39. The deer and moose experimental station I was running was only about three miles from the escarpment that went down into the basin. When I wanted a little recreation of fishing, or hiking or camping, I used to walk down there and stay overnight along the banks of the Beaver Lake Basin. We had wolves and moose and deer, and they were all getting along fine—no problems. No people. Then, in late '38 and '39, [the logging companies] built a road slanting down the escarpment. The moment they started working in there the wolves disappeared. I lived just a half mile from the camp, and in the wintertime you could go out my front door, which faced the swamp, and hear the wolves chasing the deer coming out of the Beaver Lake Basin. That's where they lived. Oh, it was a beautiful sound. You'll never forget the sound of a wolf chasing a deer. When they started cutting in there, immediately the wolves left.

The moose—well, they had accidents. They're curious. Come deer season, instead of running like a wolf they'd come toward you. And that big animal like that facing you and you've got a gun, you think they're going to eat you up or something. I was raising nine moose, as well as deer, and experimenting with their eating habits. Between accidents and shooting and various things caused by man, the wolves and moose both disappeared. The cutting caused an abundance of food from the tops [of the trees, which were left on the ground]. It's the mixed hardwoods, mostly, and some hemlock. A lot of good food. That combination in the Beaver Lake Basin was ideal for deer. The tops were chewed on by the deer. The following year a lot of sprouts came up from the cutting. It made it ideal for the deer. But there were no controls. No wolves. Eventually the trees grew up. Change. Changing of the habitat. As habitat changes, so changes wildlife. Trees grew up, self-pruned, browsed out, big flock of deer. Starvation—if you don't harvest them. Man, inasmuch as he raised hell with the countryside, he's got to compensate. He changed the face in there. They were getting along fine until he messed it up. Now he's got to compensate. How to compensate? He's got to take the surplus or they'll die.

One of my purposes up there at the station was to find out: is there a practical method of artificially feeding deer? We concluded, "No." You can charge $25 for a deer license, and only the rich people would buy it. And that would be money enough to feed the deer. But when you get a winter like this [1976], you couldn't get in. We tried all combinations of browses and grains, and we even mixed what we called a New York deer cake: soybeans and molasses. So living and working with nature and especially man, seeing how he relates to the countryside and wildlife, there's not too many people who understand it. I don't know why.

There's so many people now—and more and more of them. I was raised on the farm back in the teens. You get more appreciation for the outdoors, wildlife, plants, by living in it than you do by living on blacktop or asphalt or the streets.

We had wild elk, we had mountain lions, we had wild turkeys, we had wolves, we had lynx, we had passenger pigeons; I can even say we had prairie chickens. Well, now where are they?

Most of your big animals, unique animals, are in the Pigeon River Country. The lynx, the mountain lion, and the wolves, back into history, were right in Detroit. That's a big swamp area around there.

The wildlife—take the birds, for instance—is an indicator of the environment, good or bad. If the birds disappear, we will too. When I surveyed, I had the islands under my district—the Manitous and the Foxes—we had eagles all over the place. I counted 'em, osprey and bald eagles. While I was still here, they disappeared. DDT came into the picture. That's an indicator, by their absence, that something's wrong with the environment.

So what have we got in the Pigeon River Country? We've got bald eagles, a few osprey. There's some elk. There's quite a few bear. And according to research a bear has to have about 50 miles of semiwild or wild, almost roadless country, for the species to survive. They won't die out right now when you put roads in there, but eventually they will.

We know the coyote, the deer, and the red fox have adjusted to man's intrusion. In other words, it's the last big wild in northern lower Michigan. We got a lot of it in the UP [Upper Peninsula]. It's the last big wild down here close to so many millions of people. And if we can control it and put some guidelines down so we won't ruin it we can maintain something pretty nice for posterity. I feel we owe the next generation something besides taking everything for ourselves and leaving them nothing.

It's the last big wild, as Lovejoy called it. I knew P. S. Lovejoy; he came to see me when I ran my moose experimental station. A smarter man I never met. He was way out ahead. He was the first one to say, "Let's save the Pigeon River Country. It's the best we've got in southern Michigan." He was so smart I was scared to death of him. We had 55 deer in different kinds of pens, three or four moose runs. The chief of our wildlife, Ruhl, he came down there. He told me P. S. was coming and was going to put me on the spot. I was a young biologist, and I was scared to death. He came into the little oval office and said, "Well, let's go down and look her over." He said, "What good are you doing here with your experiment?"

I don't know how come I said this, but I said, "We aren't doing a damn thing that's any good."

"Oh, yes you are."

And I said, "What?" Then he got to going. I got off the hook right there. Ruhl said, "You're a lucky devil." I knew I couldn't answer because he was a philosopher, way out in the bushes.

The whole setting [in Pigeon River Country] is nice. You've got your free-flowing rivers, [the Sturgeon,] the Black and the Pigeon. You've got lakes that have no cottages around them. You've got trail roads that are just two ruts. You've got the big trees; virgin or not, they're big. You've got a good stand of white pine up on Webb Road at the corner of Fisherman's Trail. At Round Lake Campground you've got a vigorous stand of red and white pine with a winding two-rut trail through it. It's pretty. And you can get back into some of these places and have solitude. People need a little of that. You go nuts listening to the traffic buzz by your place all the time. You've got to have a little of this solitude someplace, sometime, to shake these other things off and settle down into nature.

It's easier going on a machine than it is walking. But, really, it isn't long lasting in your life. I've walked across the Porcupine Mountains from one end to the other and stayed in there a week with 20 below zero and four foot of snow. I'll remember it forever. If you hear a wolf when you're sitting at the Lake of the Clouds, like me and my wife did, you never forget it. You don't hear that with a snow machine. You don't hear that in an airplane. You get the broad view from an airplane, but you don't get nothing from a goddamn snow machine. And to think I spent one whole winter trying to invent one.

20

Wildlife

FORD KELLUM

In order to see or hear wild animals or birds, drive or walk slowly and pay attention to any unusual sound or movement in the woods. Wildlife know Pigeon River Country much better than you or I do. These wild animals have much better sight, smelling, and hearing ability than we have. Be cautious, and you may glimpse elk, deer, black bear, or any other of several species of wildlife here.

One of the first things is to know where and when to look for the animal you wish to see and possibly photograph, which is difficult without a telephoto lens. All animals have their own preferences for food and cover. Yet they all seem to stray from their normal food and cover habits during the mating season, when the young are being born, and again in winter when snows are deep and temperatures low. Some animals hibernate. The more common ones, like deer and elk, will concentrate in protective cover where food is available close by.

In order to spot wildlife, you should know what food and cover they like and where and when to make your observation. Keep a keen lookout for tracks on the roadside or in the snow. This will at least tell you that elk, deer, or black bear have been around. Know your tracks and who belongs to them. There are other signs, like fresh browsing on limbs, barking of trees, or where a buck deer has barked a small tree or bush while trying to rub his velvet off his antlers in September and October. Elk will find a larger tree, and usually their rubbing will be higher from the ground since they are taller than deer.

Most wild animals can best be seen at sunrise or sunset, that transition time when they are on the move. A good pair of binoculars and a map are almost essential. Have a compass along, and be sure you know which needle points north. I didn't one time and had to walk six miles through woods and water to get out. But I suppose most folks will be driving a car on the trail roads. If you do, go slow, stop every once in a while for 15 minutes, be quiet, and have your window open. In the spring, summer, or early fall you will be surprised what you will see and hear if you just sit there for at least 15 minutes to one hour. Surely there will be birds to see and hear while waiting for an elk or deer. Near a river bottom is a good place to spend some time. In the winter near or in a swamp or on the edge of a timber cutting operation; in September and October, early in the morning near an open area for elk bugling. It's their mating season. The old bull elk may have a herd of females that he is protecting for himself. Younger bulls may be nearby in the woods that would like to steal some of his cows, and the master bull elk isn't about to let that happen.

Deer, moose, and elk have antlers. Cows and antelopes have horns. The difference is simple: antlers drop off yearly while horns are a permanent fixture. Horns develop from blood flowing through the center while the antler, as it develops during the spring and summer, is fed by blood passing through the velvet, which completely covers the antlers.

The chemical composition of a deer antler is the same as that of body hair. The antler's size and shape are a direct reflection of his health during the past year. A good, healthy buck can support a six- or eight-point rack at one and one-half years of age, but if food conditions are poor he will not be in the best of shape and will have spikes from one to five inches long or a very small rack regardless of age.

Deer have their best set of antlers at age five to eight. However, as the buck gets older the bur or base of the antler each year gets larger and the points get shorter, maybe even deformed. He may wind up with just rugged spikes in his old age from 12 to 15 years. In lower Michigan, bucks seldom live that long because of hunting.

A buck in poor health or wounded may retain his antlers longer than a healthy buck, who may lose his antlers in December, January, or February. New ones will start to develop right away, be six inches in a month and fully formed by midsummer. The velvet covering on the antlers will gradually dry up and be rubbed off, usually in late August or September. That is about the time the fawns also lose their spots.

At birth, the spotted fawn will weigh from 6 to 8 pounds—about the same as a human baby—while the mother will average about 115 to 135 pounds—about what a human mother might weigh—and a buck from 135 to 200 pounds—what a man usually weighs.

Deer and elk have hollow hair, which makes for good insulation from the cold and makes them all good swimmers. Their hair is shed in spring and fall. Deer have what we call a red coat in the summer and a gray coat in winter. Elk hair doesn't have such a change in color. It's mostly light gray or tan.

Elk and deer, like most other animals that travel in herds, have a social order. A dominant cow elk or doe deer will be in charge of the herd; grown males live apart from the herd. There will be a bull or buck in command of all other males on down the line to the weakest bull or buck. This boss attitude will exist until the bull or buck gets too old to ward off a younger and stronger animal, which then takes over as boss. During the spring and summer before the rutting season, bull elk or buck deer have a tendency to travel together. There seems to be sort of a close fraternity in which big bucks or bulls with well-formed antlers will associate more than the smaller-antlered bucks or bulls. We have seen many times during the summer small bucks with spikes up to four or five points who run together.

When it comes to leading the way, it is usually the dominant cow elk or doe deer that will take the lead, followed by her fawn or calf elk, and last will come the big bull or buck. However, elk seem to have a tendency to travel in herds while deer seem to be found usually in small family groups. In winter, when the going gets tough, they will bunch up where there is food or protection from the cold available.

Elk are much larger than deer. A bull may weigh 600 to 800 pounds, a mother 400 to 600 pounds, and the baby calf from 12 to 25 pounds. When they are born in May or June, calves have a spotted coat like a newborn deer, which also is [usually] born in May or June [but] sometimes as late as September.

In 1916 Michigan secured a small herd of elk from Jackson Hole, Wyoming. They were released in various locations in northern lower Michigan, including the Pigeon River Country, but they all disappeared. In 1918, a small herd of elk was accumulated in a holding pen at the Houghton Lake State Forest, including two bulls and three cows. They were all released in the Pigeon River Country three or four miles southeast of Wolverine along the Sturgeon River. The elk we have now are the result of this release.

Michigan had elk dating back at least 5,000 years. We have found skeletons and antlers in lime lake bottoms that were given the carbon test by the

University of Michigan. The last remaining native Michigan elk disappeared about 1877 in the Saginaw Valley.

Michigan deer are natives, as far as anyone knows, but existed in much fewer numbers than today. Deer like a diversity of foods and may be seen browsing, but deer are browsers first and grazers second while elk are grazers first and browsers second. When Michigan and the Pigeon River Country were covered with virgin forest, there was lots of cover but not much food deer could reach. The forest was self-pruned. When forest cuttings and subsequent forest fires occurred, new trees and shrubs began to grow and so did our deer herd. Now we are maintaining a Michigan herd of around a million deer. About 100,000 to 175,000 deer per year are killed legally by hunters. The illegal kill runs about the same amount per year.

In order to hold the deer herd down in numbers, field wildlife biologists decide how many does and fawns should be harvested each year.

Deer have adjusted to our human way of life, while some animals like the mountain lion, timber wolf, and lynx cannot adjust to man's intrusion. These large predators have disappeared from lower Michigan. When they were here, they kept the deer herd in balance with the available food and cover. Now man tries to keep the deer herd in balance with the food and cover by allowing kills of what are computed to be surplus animals. Otherwise, starvation [rates] would be unbelievable. Severe winters with deep snow, wind, and zero temperatures will take many deer, especially fawns and old or wounded deer, and leave pregnant does physically incapable of giving successful birth.

In 2005, an endangered species specialist reported that gray wolves have been found in the northern Lower Peninsula and urged the Natural Resources Commission to manage for sustaining their population.

Pigeon River Country is semi-wild, fairly quiet with a large block of public land—148 square miles [164 in 2007]. Elk number around 1,000 animals. Elk have long legs and can get by in deep snow much better than deer. They can reach higher in trees for food, which makes it tougher for deer to survive in some areas. Here again people come in to help the situation by having a systematic timber-cutting program that furnishes food from the downed tree tops right away and a good crop of sprouting for several years following. That all makes food down where both elk and deer can reach it.

A rotation of timber cutting with forest reproduction is necessary along with scientific harvesting of deer. A big block of mature forest is not the best situation for most kinds of wildlife we are accustomed to but is ideal for arboreal wildlife like red squirrels, porcupines, chickadees, kinglets, and woodpeckers.

Over the centuries, deer have become immune to certain diseases and infectious parasites. However, they do carry with them a parasite we call the brain worm. Deer live a normal life with brain worm, but in the bloodstream of an elk brain worms settle into various locations in the spinal cord and affect the animal in different ways, sometimes causing death. The elk may become blind, walk in circles, or appear to have a broken back.

This brain worm has an adverse effect on other large animals like moose and caribou. Therefore, these large animals survive much better where there are few or no deer, as in northern Canada above the natural range of our white-tailed deer.

Human winter activity is especially hard on elk. We have found that when the snowmobiles were running all over the woods in the Pigeon River Country elk just about stopped reproducing, so we had to limit the off-road vehicles in both summer and winter. Our deer seemed to take this human activity in stride.

There are black bear and bobcat within the boundaries of the Pigeon River Country. Both of these animals require a large acreage of undisturbed heavy cover, swamps, streams, and river bottoms. Both will wander out of their home range for miles, hunting for food in the upland or during breeding season.

Some scientists claim the black bear and the bobcat need at least 50 square miles of wild country that is virtually roadless to survive as a species over a long period of time. We do not have many such areas in lower Michigan any more, but the Pigeon River Country is large enough if we can keep industry and other such human activities to a minimum.

When I was a young fellow in 1917, Michigan had many bear and bobcat north of a line from Muskegon to Bay City and of course in all of the UP. But now the bear and bobcat are a biological oddity in most of lower Michigan except for a very few isolated wild areas.

The Dead Stream Swamp in Roscommon and Missaukee counties is one of those food areas. Our own Pigeon River Country is probably the largest and in the long run will be the last stronghold in southern Michigan where these two wilderness animals can survive the onrush of civilization. Bear are seldom seen in winter because they hibernate when foods are covered by deep snow. They eat fish, carrion, fruits, and berries and like honey. Two cubs are born in January or February when the mother is dormant. They will weigh eight ounces or less each. Bear only breed every other year. The average weight of the adult is about 350 pounds.

In the Pigeon River Country, we have noticed many bear claw marks on the trunks of the large beech trees along the Fisherman's Trail. Claws leave permanent scars on the smooth gray bark when bear climb these trees hunting for beechnuts.

You must remember when you are camping that the bear were here first. They may come to your camp scrounging for food if they are accustomed to being fed bait, so it would be wise to keep your food in your car at night. Bear in their most natural state avoid human smells. If you deposit your waste foods in a pit or garbage barrel, they may be enticed to investigate that, too. Bear can be quarrelsome, so be careful. Usually when they hear a lot of noise they will take off for places unknown. Bear usually travel alone unless it's a she-bear with cubs. My advice is "Don't mess with them."

In parts of northern lower Michigan and all of the Upper Peninsula, we have enough bear to warrant a season on them to harvest the surplus. When too numerous, they can be destructive to beehives, fruit trees, or even, on occasion, livestock. A limited bear season is held to control their numbers and hold the nuisance bear damage to a minimum.

In the Pigeon River Country, we have quite a few night-traveling bobcats. They, too, are hunted in a short season, mainly by a few rugged hunters with dogs. When hunted, the wary bobcat will take the dogs and hunters through the thickest tangle of swamps and brushy river bottoms you could imagine. It's tough going. In the early 1970s, some of the local cat hunters would find a fresh track in the snow, put their dogs on it, and follow the track until the cat was jumped. Then the dogs barked, hot trail. Before long, the cat took to a tree. Hunters closed in, tied the dogs to a tree nearby, climbed the tree and shook the cat out. The other hunters tried to step on the cat with snowshoes, holding the cat firmly embedded in the snow, and reaching through the snowshoe webbing to place a tag in the cat's ear. This is a bit risky with a large cat. After the ear tag was placed, they let it go to run another day. The dogs would take after the cat again, but the hunters hold on to the dogs' leashes and take them out of the woods and home.

The deeper the snow the quicker the dogs will tree the cat. When hunting cats, dogs will frequently follow streams and travel on the ice. In many cases, the dogs will break through and fall into the river. Oh, it's tough, all right.

I can remember in 1939 bobcat hunting along the Creighton River in Schoolcraft County in the Upper Peninsula with Blaine Brannon, the Cusino refuge superintendent. We were following an old cat track on thin ice. I broke through into three foot of water. The temperature was zero. After I got out with the assistance of Blaine, my pant legs froze like two stovepipes. We hustled to our pickup truck, which was parked along the Creighton Trail a mile or so from the river. You'd better be young and healthy. Four miles later we were at my house, thawing out by the old barrel stove.

The bobcat is not a large animal, averaging from 12 to 25 pounds. The largest one we know of weighed 38 pounds. He had been eating from the previous deer-season kill.

The bobcat reflects the true wilderness. We love him. If you ever see one, you will never forget it. You would get the same thrilling experience seeing a wolf or mountain lion. They, too, once roamed the Pigeon River Country but not anymore. But we do have the wilderness atmosphere, and I hope he will be with us forever so on occasion our children will see one. We all must protect areas like the Pigeon River Country from being depleted of the wilderness species wildlife that we still have—elk, black bear, bobcat, bald eagle, and osprey, to name a few.

The bobcat has a short, six-inch tail, black at the tip. He usually carries it straight up. Color varies quite a bit, but usually bobcats are pale brown to reddish-brown with black streaks and spots. They have small ear tufts and resemble the lynx. The lynx, which once roamed Pigeon River Country, has much longer ear tufts, larger feet, and looks larger, but it is actually smaller than the bobcat.

One evening I took my wife, Wilma, for a ride up Tin Shanty Bridge Road. We crossed the Black River just past the Round Lake Trail. She said, "Look, Ford, there is a house cat in the road up ahead." I said, "Yes, sir, it is." Just then the cat turned off the road and we saw the short black-tipped tail sticking straight up. "Oh," we both said, "it's a bobcat!"

I've heard Wilma tell this little story many times to her friends. She will never forget it, and neither will you if by chance you see a bobcat.

Bobcats' main foods are snowshoe hares, dead deer, some birds, and many small rodents. They usually have three kits born in a den, log, or underbrush in early spring.

There is a fair to good supply of coyotes but few red fox in the Pigeon River Country. There was a time not long ago when Michigan paid bounties on bobcat, coyote, and red fox. This fact was hard to understand as these three predators do much more good than harm. They help control rodents. Without that control, rodents would become a serious problem to plant and bird life.

We have hunted coyotes. I was the cold trailer leading the hound dogs on a cold trail during December on fresh snow. Following a cold trail you can learn a great deal about the coyote's way of life. They hunt for mice by jumping up and pouncing. They have taken me through briar patches where hares had been feeding. But no hares this time, just a lot of tracks. The coyote was lying up on the south slope of a hill where he could see, hear, and smell anything that might be dangerous. We jumped him from his early morning bed. Our two Walker dogs were really howling in hot pursuit. We never once saw the coyote. He spotted us probably before we got within a quarter mile of him. There I was alone in the middle of a wildernesslike country, mostly upland and quite hilly. The coyote was running in a long, sweeping, three-mile-wide circle with the Walker hounds strung out behind.

A coyote can give most single dogs a battle for their lives, so we usually run two dogs. Generally one dog is faster than the other, which may be half a mile or more behind. In about two hours, the coyote may slow down and even sit and wait for the first dog to arrive, make a few very short circles until the second dog catches up, then off they all go again to complete his three-mile circle. I've observed these facts from the hillside looking across a valley at the coyote and dogs. It's most interesting and educational. Mr. Coyote would have to cross a trail road or fire line someplace. The remaining hunters hope to be located in the right spot to intercept him. Usually a run lasts three to four hours.

A male coyote weighs 20 to 30 pounds, sometimes more, and the female somewhat less. They run with their big tail down at a 30-degree angle. They are buffy-gray with rusty legs, feet, and ears with underparts whitish, nose and ears pointed, legs long, and the tail with a black tip. They run and hunt by night but are frequently active by day. They have a high-pitched bark and howl often in evening chorus. They eat berries, rodents, deer, and other foods. The den is usually hidden from view on a hillside where the mother will raise her litter of six to seven pups, which are real cute.

Years ago we saw coyotes with the mange in the Pigeon River Country. Sometimes they become almost hairless, but coyotes live with their problems and are doing real well here in the state of Michigan.

I have come face-to-face with a few coyotes in the Pigeon River Country and on three occasions, while deer hunting, have flushed them from the side of a trail while driving slowly by.

The red fox has similar characteristics to the coyote, but a fox track is very even, one step behind the other in a line. Fox like the open fields and orchards more than swamps or heavy woods because that's where they find the food they so dearly love—mice and rats. Many fruit farmers in the Grand Traverse area won't allow fox hunters or trappers on their farms because, as they say, a red fox is a living mousetrap that saves the fruit farmer thousands of dollars in rodent repellents. Mice girdle fruit trees under the winter snows. I have seen one red fox carrying 10 mice in his mouth at one time. When shot at, he dropped them.

The red fox has a white-tipped, bushy tail, red body on top, and white underneath. Their feet are black. They have a pointed black nose and small pointed ears and weigh from five to 16 pounds, sometimes more. Fox are around winter and summer, sleeping on stumps or a little knoll curled up like a red ball. The mother may have from five to 10 pups in a den. Pups are blue, their voice a short yelp ending in a "yurr."

If you are looking for fox, in the early morning or evening park yourself downwind from a marsh or grassy field and just look and listen. You may see a fox, coyote, deer, or elk and lots of birds of the open fields and marshes. An excellent spot to make this observation would be in the big CCC opening up the Osmun Trail five miles from forest headquarters.

Hunting fox is the sport of kings and queens. I have hunted fox in Michigan with dogs. Beagles are best. They are slower and won't drive the fox out of the country like a long-legged hound would. Tracking fox on new light snow without dogs is a real challenging sport. You must be a very careful hunter and a good tracker. You may see a red-topped stump that turns out to be the red fox. Old-timers used to hunt this way, but you don't hear of it anymore.

Beaver and otter have been around as far back in history as man can remember, and we have them in the Pigeon River Country. Both of them have valuable short fur. At one time in early American history, the beaver hide and fur was used as a medium of exchange for supplies. The beaver and otter were both overkilled in lower Michigan in the 1910s and 1920s to the point where we had them live-trapped in the Upper Peninsula and released along many lower Michigan streams. I took part in this program in Lake County, Baldwin District, in the middle 1930s. As the beaver and otter increased, the wildlife division of the Conservation Department set trapping seasons on both beaver and otter, regulating the take by area so as not to overharvest them. Beaver are good conservationists. They build dams on the ponds and streams, backing up water that makes good duck nesting and other shore bird usage. Beavers' main food is aspen trees, commonly called popple. They live off other trees to a lesser degree. They have been known to flood roads and cottage lawns, but the good they do far surpasses the harm caused.

In a beaver flooding, which may be several dams upstream, otter will fish and muskrats build houses that waterfowl and terns occasionally nest on.

Big river beaver live in holes in the banks, but in the Pigeon River Country they use the small rivers, streams, and ponds. Their life work and engineering ability are most interesting. They repair their dams whenever needed. They build large round houses made from bark, sticks, and brush. Sometimes these homes are 15 to 20 feet across at the base and 4 to 8 feet high. The entrance is a channel underwater. They come up inside to an earthen shelf above high water that the family will rest on. During the summer and fall, they cut trees down, drag the smaller limbs down into the water near their lodge, and poke these sticks into the bottom of the pond in order to feed on them during the winter months. The beaver lodge has a breather hole on top, and in winter the snow is melted off in this spot by body heat.

The beaver is our largest rodent and only land mammal with a broad, scaly, flat tail. An adult may weigh up to 60 pounds. Their fur is dense, brown, and waterproof. They have strong jaws, chestnut-colored teeth, and incisors which continually grow out as they wear off from cutting trees. They are most active at dawn, dusk, and night. When disturbed, they will slap the water with their tails, which sounds almost like a rifle shot, and dive under and swim away. Beaver may have two to four young born in April through July in the lodge. The following year, if the lodge becomes too crowded, the female will chase her older children out. At times we can see them wandering around hunting for a new area in which to start a family of their own. One good place to see beaver workings in the Pigeon River Country has been on Hardwood Creek. Meridian Road takes you right to it. There are many other dams and lodges in the Pigeon River Country, but they are a little harder to get to. Beaver will change their location if food becomes scarce.

Old experienced trappers can tell how large a beaver is by looking at the tree stumps it has cut. If the stump is over a foot high, there must be a large beaver nearby, especially if the cutting is fresh. The old trapper can tell if there are a lot of beaver at the lodge by the amount of cuttings. In building their dams, they push mud, sticks, and stones with their front feet and chest and carry small sticks in their mouths.

In an effort to increase brook trout in the Black River, the DNR launched a five-year program in the mid-1990s to remove beaver and their dams in the headwaters above Clark Bridge Road. In spring 1995 alone, an estimated 300 beaver were trapped. Volunteers began removing about 50 dams, slowly, by hand, to prevent silt from running downstream, and paused to trap any beaver trying to rebuild them. The effort was designed to lower stream temperature, increase oxygen, and improve the habitat for brook trout even at the expense of beaver and all the wildlife that benefit from beaver ponds. The advisory council asked that some beaver be left since they were also a valuable resource, but the DNR's Fisheries Division, which administers the program, claims some beaver will remain anyway, even though it's trying to eliminate them. By 2007, plans were under way in fisheries to take out beaver and their ponds on another Black River tributary, Milligan Creek. From other perspectives in the DNR, beaver ponds are an attribute, helpful for waterfowl and other wildlife. Foresters recognize that beaver in a relatively short time exhaust their food supply, then move on. Forests regrow, in what's called succession, filling in the pond, and returning it to a combination of higher, vegetated ground and cooler, narrower stream flows. Beaver are a responsibility of Wildlife Division, but Fisheries Division administers the stream programs and notes that beaver removal is an immediate tool to combat rising stream temperatures, which severely reduce brook trout populations when they reach an average 66 degrees Fahrenheit. Even in relatively cool 2004, some areas of the Black got above 80 degrees, and in the very warm summer of 2005 all 13 measuring stations on the Black topped 70 degrees and four topped 80 degrees.

Otter are valuable fur animals, fun loving, with the whole family taking part. They have slides from the river and stream banks. They all seem to enjoy sliding down into the water day or night, winter or summer. They catch fish and eat crawfish and frogs. Occasionally they will live in an old beaver house or in a riverbank. On a log or beaver dam, you may find a pile of fish scales or small bones where they have had their meal. The otter will weigh up to 30 pounds. They are very long with a long, round, pointed tail that is fur-covered. Otter have webbed feet. They are dark brown and light-colored underneath and are excellent swimmers. They like suckers and can catch them swimming.

I remember in 1940 watching a man fishing for pike from a boat on an inland lake in Schoolcraft County. He had just caught what he thought was a monster fish that he couldn't reel in. It was taking most of his line. All of a sudden an otter came to the shore, shaking his head vigorously, breaking the line. The otter went on, dragging the fish line. The otter is a powerful beast. On land or snow, they will push and slide across country to another watershed. They are weasel-like in appearance.

Otter do not make loud noises, but they grunt, chuckle, and chatter. If you are lucky enough to be near a lake where they are feeding, they will surface and you can hear them chewing and cracking bones. The price of their fur is usually a little less than that of a beaver. In the Pigeon River Country, we have seen them along the Black River, Hardwood Creek, Hardwood Lake, the Pigeon River, and the Cornwall and Dog Lake floodings.

The snowshoe hare is white in winter and brown in summer. They can be found almost anywhere in the forest. Their big feet allow them to travel easily over any type of snow. We all know them well, so we won't have to go into detail about them. Their numbers fluctuate greatly within a 10-year or so cycle. Bobcats, fox, coyotes, hawks, and owls feed on them and hold the population down to a healthy level. If we did not have this predation, their numbers would increase astronomically, causing great damage to young trees, shrubs, and fruit-bearing bushes.

When most other hunting seasons are over, the snowshoe furnishes some of the very best of any sport hunting. When the hares are thick, dogs sometimes run two at a time. Seeing the white hare on white snow is difficult. Thick young pine cover or swamps are ideal places to run a dog and jump the hares. Some hunters will hunt them without dogs, but it's harder that way. They sit still until you get real close, thinking they are hidden. Many times you may look at a clump of snow and all at once will see a red eye. Then you know that the clump of snow is a snowshoe.

The snowshoe hare population plunged in 1991 and has remained low for the 15 years since, appearing in only a few pockets during annual timber inventories. "We don't know what's wrong," Arch Reeves said.

The slow-moving porcupine can be found in almost any wooded area of the Pigeon River Country. They eat bark and small limbs in the treetops; they have sharp quills that are barbed. If you should get one in your body, your natural muscle contractions will work the quill inward. When molested, a porcupine will bunch up in a round ball with the pointed spines sticking out for protection. The porkie will not attack you but may swing his tail, also covered with sharp spines, at the intruder. They do not have any serious enemies in Pigeon River Country. A fisher is one animal that kills porcupines by flipping them over and getting at their soft underbelly, but we don't have any fisher in the Pigeon River Country; they are found in Canada.

A porkie will weigh 15 to 25 pounds. They make the weirdest sounds on occasion—short barks, groaning, and crying—sounds that could scare the liver out of you while camping out sometime. They live in hollow logs and snags or trees. You can usually tell by a large pile of droppings near their den. The porkie is one animal that the whole family can get close to, take pictures of, or just observe.

You will recognize the raccoon by his bushy ringed tail and his black face mask. They weigh around 30 pounds and are good tree climbers, living in hollow logs, large holes in trees, and old buildings. Raccoon have adjusted to civilization. They hibernate in cold winters and are versatile in the foods they consume, including green or dry corn, fruits, fish, birds' eggs, crawfish, most garden vegetables, and small grains.

They tame easily but are most mischievous. They use their front paws to get into our pockets and investigate anything. They like chicken eggs, too. They have long fur that the pioneers used for fur coats and coonskin caps.

On the Fisherman's Trail one August, grasshoppers were very thick on the two-track. A car ahead of us had killed many hoppers that were in the wheel tracks. We were slowly coming down a gentle incline and noticed five raccoon in the trail eating dead grasshoppers. They were so busy they did not see or hear our approach. We coasted with the motor off, stopped, got out with a camera, quietly walked to within 15 feet of them, and snapped a picture. The mother gave a warning grunt, and they were gone. Our picture was excellent with no telephoto lens. You never can tell what might be seen while driving the Pigeon River Country trail roads. Be ready; have your camera set. We've gotten pictures of snowshoe hares in the spring and ruffed grouse in the fall from our car.

There are many small animals, including chipmunks, squirrels, several kinds of mice, and waterfowl, especially on the Cornwall and Dog Lake floodings. Grouse, woodcock, and snipe furnish some of the best hunting opportunities in the state.

Many state university biologists have completed advanced degrees here studying grouse and woodcock. A team of research biologists, all PhDs from the University of Georgia, spent weeks studying our grouse and woodcock and claim our game birds are healthier and freer from parasites than at any place they have checked in the eastern United States.

Former President Jimmy Carter spent three days in the Pigeon River Country in October 1986 and bagged two woodcock. An intensive study of how hunting affects grouse concluded in 1999 that other birds took more grouse in the area than hunters did in four out of five years and that grouse survival was the same in hunting and nonhunting areas.

If you have questions about wildlife, ask the people at Pigeon River Country headquarters. The area forester, wildlife biologist, conservation officer, their assistants, and others have been protecting the Pigeon River Country since the early 1920s for you and your children to enjoy. We may need your help someday to continue to protect the Pigeon River Country from being exploited.

Be alert, enjoy our Pigeon River Country and its wildlife, trail roads, rivers, lakes, woods, and fields. Come back again. We would love for you to have fun seeing, feeling, and smelling our big outdoors.

Pigeon River Country species classified as threatened, rare, or scarce in 1985 were mostly still in trouble in 2006. The short-billed marsh wren, more recently called sedge wren (Cistothorus platensis) *is officially listed as in drastic decline by nine north-eastern states in its former range, though not Michigan. Badgers are thriving in the state, although they are not found much in woodlands. The gray fox prefers wood-lands, but Michigan is the northern edge of its range, and it is not common in the Pigeon, though it lives in unknown numbers throughout the United States and into Mexico. The pine vole, still in trouble, is now called woodland vole* (Microtus pinetorum). *Southern bog lemmings seldom live a full year in the wild and are gen-erally considered threatened, although they are not officially so listed by the state. The water shrew, while present only in low numbers, is no longer considered in trouble as a species. Barred owls, who mate for life and need large tree cavities, have been rang-ing successfully into the Pacific Northwest and are no longer listed by Michigan as threatened.*

Wood turtles are threatened or endangered in much of what's left of their range. Where they do survive, they have been known to live up to 58 years. Many die as road-kill. The five-lined skink is the only one of 3,750 species of lizards that ranges as far north as the Pigeon River Country, although it is one of the most common lizards in the eastern United States. Almost nothing is known about the behavior of lizards. The five whitish stripes along the dark skink bodies fade with age, as do their bright blue tails. Five-lined skinks stay within a circle of 30 to 100 feet most of their lives, particularly in moist, partially cleared wooded areas containing stumps, brush and sawdust piles, logs, fallen or loose bark, and rocks.

Michigan in 2006 listed four amphibian, 43 bird, 35 fish, six beetle, 53 butterfly and moth, eight cicada and hopper, 13 dragonfly and damselfly, 14 grasshopper and cricket, 10 mammal, 19 mussel, 10 reptile, and 34 snail species in danger throughout the state, along with 26 habitat communities, including dry-mesic northern forests. Our northern wet-mesic prairie, oak barrens, and oak openings are ranked as critically imperiled, meaning they could disappear anytime. Oak barrens and openings occur naturally in savannas on sandy and glacial ridges. With fire suppressed, many savannas have been taken over by ash and other trees except where it's very wet. Sinkholes are ranked as rare and imperiled.

Here is the 1985 list of threatened, rare, or scarce species in the Pigeon River Coun-try, followed by a list of resident mammals.

Mammals
badger
gray fox
pigmy shrew
pine vole
southern bog lemming
water shrew

Birds

black-crowned night heron
red-shouldered hawk
Cooper's hawk
goshawk
short-billed marsh wren
barred owl

Reptiles and Amphibians

wood turtle
five-lined skink
four-toed salamander

Mammals of the Pigeon River Country

badger
beaver
black bear
bobcat
coyote
mink
muskrat
otter
porcupine
raccoon
skunk
snowshoe hare
gray squirrel
fox squirrel
least weasel
short-tailed weasel
long-tailed weasel
woodchuck
red squirrel
northern flying squirrel
southern flying squirrel
little brown bat
silver-haired bat

cottontail
white-tailed deer
elk
gray fox
red fox
keen bat
striped ground squirrel
eastern chipmunk
deer mouse
white-footed mouse
bog lemming
red-backed vole
meadow vole
pine vole
meadow jumping mouse
woodland jumping mouse
prairie mole
star-nosed mole
masked shrew
water shrew
short-tailed shrew
pigmy shrew

21

Signs of Wildlife

FORD KELLUM

Look at the soft sand or snow by the side of the road for animal and bird tracks. It's hard to tell the difference between the small bird tracks, so we won't go into that. Elk make tracks similar to deer tracks except they are twice to three times as large. On snow, they both drag their feet. Both have divided footprints. The elk print is more round than that of a deer.

Elk sometimes feed on the bark of the larger Juneberry trees, aspen, and red maple. If you see that sign, you know elk have been there.

Notice along the outside edge of a swamp where cedar trees do not have any green foliage from the ground up to nine feet high. This is a browse line caused by the feeding of elk and deer. Especially during the winter, elk reach higher than deer. Therefore, they can compete for winter food.

If you look carefully where trees have been cut within the last two years, you may notice that the ends of new shoots, especially those of aspen and red maple, have been eaten off. These buds are nutritious for deer and elk. That's why timber cutting is considered so important for most wildlife. In a new cutting, before sprouting begins, you may see hundreds of deer, elk, and rabbit tracks where these animals have been feeding on the fallen limbs. If you find salt blocks, such as those placed by the local Northland Sportsman's Club, be aware that they attract elk, deer, and porcupines.

There was an elk hunt in 1964 and another in December 1965. The legislature gave researchers two years to study the effects of an open season on elk. The DNR held a drawing to see who could hunt for an elk. About

90 percent of the hunters got an elk. That was 269 animals felled by 298 hunters in 1964. In 1965, there were 183 animals taken by 298 hunters, a success rate of 61 percent.

The DNR allowed the two elk seasons because of elk damage to farm crops, overgrazing of the range, and competition for winter food that deer live on. There were many illegal killings of elk after the regular season. There were also mistake kills made during the two regular seasons, and some elk were wounded and died later.

Between 1965 and 1968, the elk herd increased by about 15 percent a year. Then, in 1968, off-road vehicles and snowmobiles began traveling all through the Pigeon River Country, adversely affecting the reproduction of elk, followed shortly by oil company seismic surveys with added people, machines, and noise. Poaching was another serious problem. The elk population was reduced to around 200 animals. The Pigeon River Country Advisory Council passed a resolution and sent it to the DNR asking for control of all off-road vehicles in the area except on county roads. It was done. The elk herd grew, particularly in isolated areas, to 600 to 1,000 animals. Growth of the herd was also attributed to the offer of a $500 reward for poaching convictions; seeding, fertilizing, and controlled access to hydrocarbon sites; and habitat improvement, which provided wider variety of food through selective cutting.

During the second week of December 1984, the department held another elk hunt in which 50 hunters were selected in a computer drawing from hundreds of applicants. All the applicants had paid $4; those selected paid an additional $100 for licenses. One hunter did not participate because of an illness in his family. The other 49 each killed an elk. One hunter was charged with killing four elk that stood together in a clearing. One of those four elk was a 16-year-old female, the oldest animal taken in the hunt. She weighed 360 pounds field dressed. The largest elk harvested was a bull that weighed 632 pounds field dressed, which is well over 900 pounds live weight. Two six-month-old calves were killed, one weighing 217 and the other 202 pounds. Field personnel counted 891 elk in the entire range in January, projecting a total elk population of 940. The department began a similar hunt annually, with success rates for hunters dropping to about 70 percent.

By 2006, Michigan was posting two elk-hunting seasons per year—one for nine days in August and September outside the Pigeon and the other for eight days in December in the forest and all the counties surrounding it: Emmet, Cheboygan, Presque Isle, Charlevoix, Otsego, Montmorency, Alpena, Antrim, and Oscoda—plus a third hunt reserved for four days the following January if needed. About 70 percent of the elk range is outside the forest boundaries.

Snowmobiles have continued to pose a challenge. In 2004, the advisory council saw and opposed a recommendation circulating through the DNR to run part of a statewide east-west snowmobile trail through the northwest corner of the Pigeon River Country. Field staff also declared it unacceptable since it would run through wet and sensitive areas. A route through the Pigeon was rejected by the DNR director, but there was a feeling that the other shoe could drop at any time. The Gaylord to Cheboygan Workgroup had recommended establishment of the Tuscarora trail, which would put thousands of snowmobiles through the Pigeon on a weekend, even knowing that the Concept of Management says no new snowmobile trails will be allowed in the Pigeon.

In August 1982, I estimate there were 3,700 deer, 40 bobcats, 30 or 40 black bear, and 50 coyotes in the Pigeon River Country.

A bear track resembles a print that can be made with your hand. Double your fingers up to the second joint, leave your thumb up high so it doesn't touch the ground, then press the heel of your hand into the soft dirt, roll your hand forward, and press your knuckle firmly down: you will have a bear track. We have fooled many a bear hunter by doing just that at our organized bear hunts.

Many animals like to walk on trail roads at night, apparently because it is a way to go from here to there quietly. A walking bear or bobcat will not show claw marks. A coyote and fox will show claw marks; the coyote track will be larger, the stride a little longer and more irregular than that of the fox. Bear will stand up on their hind legs and reach as high as they can to chew on a tree, thus marking their territory. Such marks are usually found on evergreen trees and generally in or next to a swamp. When black bear climb beech trees in the fall for nuts, their claw marks remain permanently on the smooth beech bark. In the fall, you may notice a juneberry bush or wild cherry tree with a lot of broken limbs, which could be evidence that a bear fed on the wild fruit and broke the limbs because of his weight. Look for bear droppings, which are usually full of cherry pits.

Squirrels will cut small limbs off oak trees, and the ground under oaks may be littered with small branches and leaves in the fall of the year.

Porcupines like to eat hemlock and aspen buds. They, too, will drop a lot of small limbs on the ground, which rabbits and deer will feed on, mostly in the winter when other foods are covered with snow.

The raccoon and porcupine will definitely show all their claw marks. They both are about the same size, both wander around a lot, and their tracks are hard to tell one from the other.

Fox squirrels, black [eastern gray] squirrels, and rabbits make similar tracks. Squirrel tracks usually show all four footprints while those of the rabbit usually show just three footmarks and are somewhat larger, particularly the tracks of the snowshoe, which is an abundant mammal in the Pigeon River Country.

Did you ever see a badger track in the snow? We did once. It looked like someone dragged a 14-inch-diameter log through the snow, with big claw marks at the bottom of the trail. I only saw one badger in nine years of working in the Pigeon River Country, so there couldn't have been very many. Biologists now estimate a more abundant badger population.

22

Streams and Lakes

SIBLEY HOOBLER

Dr. Sibley Hoobler's father was born in a pioneer cabin near Standish, Michigan, and as early as 1920 was camping and fishing with young Sibley on the Black and Pigeon rivers. Sibley's mother's father came to Michigan from the Maine woods to help lumber the white pine of the north country. Dr. Hoobler went to Ann Arbor after World War II and taught medicine at the University of Michigan until his retirement in 1976. He and his family visited their cabin on the Pigeon River every summer since its construction in 1928. One of his greatest joys was fly-fishing, which he learned in the Pigeon River Country. When he died in 1994, the advisory council made particular note that he was one of the first private citizens to react to oil development in the forest.

"The stream is brightest at the spring," according to an old saying. The waters of the Pigeon River Country surely qualify as the Pigeon and Black rivers both arise in a roadless swampland on the southern edge of the forest.

The Pigeon River is bright and clear as it emerges from the headwaters and remains so until reaching the Lansing Club pond and dam. Below this point, slight turbidity may be detected. The river is good for trout fishing but not for canoeing because of frequent brush piles even below Webb Road bridge. Below this point curves are sharp and the current swift.

This river flows north to its estuary in Mullett Lake. The Old Vanderbilt Road bridge crossing provides public access. Upstream of this bridge, wading is difficult but fishing is good. No access over public land is possible for about three miles until one reaches Kelly's Camp. The access road is a swamp trail, passable only in dry weather. This camp was the site of one of the last logging operations in the Pigeon River Country. Nothing can now be seen of the lumbermen's buildings nor of the old bridge; the wider, deeper stream perhaps still bears the marks of the lumbermen's enterprise. To the west is trackless swampland where cedars provide winter sustenance for the deer. The surrounding land, with a few exceptions, was owned for a time by the Nature Conservancy, which made a list of some of the rare flowers seen along the entrance road. It is now part of the Pigeon River Country State Forest, with the understanding that it will always be kept in a wild state.

North of the Old Vanderbilt Road bridge, the Pigeon River flows through private land until the Sturgeon Valley Road bridge is reached downstream from the dam [at Song of the Morning Ranch]. This dam and the [Lansing Club] pond above have an interesting history. It was one of a series of logging dams on the Pigeon, through which logs were floated to the mill in Cheboygan. This dam alone survived into the days when the author was entering his teens. At that time, the cabin beside the spillway was run as a fishermen's hotel by Mr. and Mrs. Mert Limbocher. The river above and below was divided into six segments, each representing about a three-hour fishing interval. The access roads to the east of the river were tiny sand trails, the ruts the size of the narrow tire on the old Model T Fords.

Mert would drive his guests to their appointed places each day, rarely touching the steering wheel as the ruts were deep enough to guide the vehicle around curves. After the daily delivery and pickup ritual, he loafed while the missus cooked furiously to keep up with the guests' appetites— usually serving trout stacked 25 to 30 on a serving platter. Mert's only other duty was to refill the larder on the days the fishermen did not bring in enough trout. He would catch 10 to 15 trout in 30 minutes in the pool below the dam. This is still a good place to catch trout even though all other reminders of the Limbocher Hotel no longer exist.

Below the Sturgeon Valley Road bridge and campground, the river flows for several miles north; banks alternate between forest cover and meadowland and are generally high and dry. Many fine holes shelter brown trout and some brookies. The meadow is particularly attractive at evening. It may be reached by walking north half a mile from the campground. The stream is easily accessible, and the grassland on the east bank provides a beautiful backdrop for camping or picnicking. This area was in the center of a research project from 1949 to 1973 to inquire into the advantages of bait fishing over fly-fishing and into size limits.

The next point in the river is the forest headquarters. The buildings were built in the 1930s; the surrounding area contains some of the most beautiful and mature pine forests in the whole area. The headquarters is open weekdays.

A quarter mile north on the road, the P. S. Lovejoy memorial stone stands on the left. This was his favorite lookout over the Pigeon River valley. Farther downstream along the road, a sharp left turn takes one into the Pigeon River Campground, which has many campsites all in relative seclusion. The bridge here is a lovely place from which to view the river and for family wading and picnicking. Because of such activity, trout fishing is less productive than upstream. Bank fishing is possible for beginners, and the trail to Elk Hill Trail Campground [a quarter-mile from the group camp] is easily followed. The river below is shallow and quite rocky. The scenery is lovely, especially from the bluffs to the east.

The next point of access is the Tin Bridge. The road to it is tortuous through the swamp. Here the river seems to become larger, and many a deep hole at the bends harbors large brown trout. The river then passes through several miles of aspen and tag alder until it reaches the Pine Grove Campground, where automobile access is again possible. The next entry is two miles downstream at the "Red" bridge (Webb Road bridge).

The Little Pigeon, a Pigeon River tributary, is chiefly outside state forest boundaries and privately owned, although public access occurs at the Webb Road bridge west of the main Pigeon River. This is primarily brook trout water. Cornwall's Creek, another tributary, has an interesting history. This small stream enters the Pigeon near the old Cornwall [originally Cornwell] dam. During one of the nation's recessions, plans for making a lake above the creek were dusted off to give some boost to local employment. The impoundment is shallow and the water warm, but it does support a fair panfish population. Bass are also present, and recently tiger muskies have been successfully introduced. Many waterbirds may be seen. One may fish directly off the impoundment, but with a boat the more productive waters are easily reached.

The Black River is smaller than the Pigeon River but is more varied and interesting. It is one of the few remaining trout streams harboring chiefly brook trout. It arises in the same swampland north of M-32 as does the Pigeon, but its tributaries come chiefly from the eastern portion of this trackless wilderness.

The first practical access point for fishermen is McKinnon's Bend [about a mile down the road running southeast from Round Lake], where the stream runs deep and slow among tag alders. There are many large brook trout in this kind of water, which continues past one other access point, but they require a skillful angler to take them. At the Tin Shanty

Bridge Road, the slow, deep portion of the river ends and its character changes to a bright, sparkling stream flowing over rocks and representing some of the most beautiful river water in the forest. An exceptional spot is at the turnout near the now nonexistent Chandler Campground. A second downstream access point is easily reached on foot. Wading the river between these points is a true delight.

Downstream the river swings away from the road: the next convenient access is just over the hill to the east of Town Corner Lake Campground. The river then leaves state forest land.

The addition of Blue Lakes in 1990 provided additional access to the Black along its west bank north nearly to Blue Lakes Road. With the Black River Rod and Gun Club property added later, the forest got another mile of frontage, where visitors can drive within half a mile and walk in to the Black River.

In 1981, after brown trout began to appear, an extensive shocking program was undertaken: brown trout were removed to maintain the Black River as one of the few "pure" brook trout fisheries of the state.

There are many small tributaries to the Black River, a few within the state forest boundary. Tubbs Creek and Hardwood Creek are small and inaccessible. Hardwood Creek drains Hardwood Lake; the valley down which it flows was once considered for designation as a primitive area. It is inaccessible except on foot. McMasters Creek is a small creek without access except at Clute Road. The dam on this brook has created the Dog Lake Flooding, a shallow man-made lake located in perhaps the wildest swamplike area of the forest. The land to the east is served only by Duby Lake Road. Otherwise this area is roadless and wild.

Many young fishermen caught their love of the sport by bank fishing with a worm dropped into some deep or secret pool. There are at least four such areas in the neighborhood of the forest. One is Trowbridge Creek, a tributary of the Sturgeon River. The stream is in a meadow and winds through tall grass harboring many trout. McMasters Creek is more accessible. Bank fishing below the road bridge is possible. A real adventure is to creep among the tag alders of Milligan Creek just at the northern forest boundary. Between mosquitoes, long grass, and potholes it is quite an adventure, sometimes rewarded by a big, fat brook trout for the creel. For the less adventurous, there are trails along the Pigeon from which the holes can be readily fished. This is the case along the meadow stretch alluded to, about half a mile downstream from the Sturgeon Valley Road Bridge. Another area of easy access is downstream from the Pigeon River Campground.

The small lakes within the Pigeon River country are varied and attractive. There is a campground on Pickerel Lake's east shore, well cared for and with a lovely view to the west. A stream leaves the south end of the lake; at its beginning the water is shallow and is a great home for turtles. The east shore provides the best swimming in the forest. A delightful sandy beach was made during the Depression days (the Civilian Conservation Corps had an encampment nearby). This shallow, safe beach is a delight for children as well as their parents. Fishing is not spectacular, but there is a boat ramp and trailer park. No motors are allowed. There is a trail around the lake that is varied and attractive.

Town Corner Lake has a very small sandy beach along the east shore where a primitive campground exists, with a boat ramp.

Another campground is on Round Lake, noted for its red pine and wooded shores fringed with water lilies. Many consider this the most beautiful campsite in the area. There is no sandy beach or boat ramp, but the proximity to the Black River is attractive for fishermen.

Hardwood Lake is the source of Hardwood Creek. It is very shallow but extremely wild and beautiful. There are two access points on the north shore, but the banks are thick with bushes and hard to penetrate. There are no fishing or suitable swimming beaches. Dog Lake is in a similar category. It is very wild and a place to get away but with some discomfort as access is difficult. Migratory ducks, geese, and shorebirds rest here in the fall.

Grass Lake has many attractive features. It is shallow and provides good feeding grounds for bass and panfish. The mixed forest cover and the proximity to the lake make it an excellent area for birding and for wildlife viewing. It is one of the few areas where poison ivy is rampant.

There are many other lakes in the Pigeon River Country. Among the most unusual features of the forest are the sinkhole lakes in its center. These represent erosions in the limestone floor of the forest. One of them shows the progressive sinking of the lake's floor. This is Section 4 Lake, incidentally one of the most beautiful of the group, with a wonderful aquamarine color. The other lakes are of similar origin; they are scattered on each side of Osmun Road. These lakes are closed to fishing and boating; they are being used to study various aspects of fisheries research.

All of these seven lakes are limestone sinks. The research projects in the lakes and the Pigeon River itself have contributed greatly to the success of Michigan's statewide fisheries resource management.

The fisheries division decided to open the sinkhole lakes to fishing in 2008 and stock four of the seven with thousands of fish every year. Some on the advisory council said these few lakes that had remained unstocked for more than 40 years should remain unstocked in the future. Fisheries personnel said the special research regulation was expiring in March 2007 (it was renewing the regulation at other sites outside the forest). Opponents replied the fragile lakes could be opened to fishing but should not be stocked. The fisheries people said their plans to limit access to a single footpath at each lake would prevent people from going down the steep banks and creating erosion. Eugene Horan, a member of the advisory council and Pigeon River Country Association, said he feared stocking the lakes would attract just such heavy use and asked why some lakes couldn't be left alone in their natural state. Tim Cwalinski, a fisheries biologist, replied that the plan would allow a camping father to take his children to a quiet lake for a little basic fishing experience.

Fisheries reported it would not stock North or South Twin Lake or Lost Lake because of severe erosion potential; those lakes contain no game fish, so, fisheries said, nobody would fish them even if allowed. It planned to put yearling trout in Hemlock, Ford, West Lost, and Section 4 Lakes in 2007 and open them for fishing in spring 2008, restricted to artificial lures only, from watercraft with electric motors, except for Section 4 Lake, where fishing could be only from single-user personal watercraft such as float tubes but not canoes or boats.

When Blue Lakes Ranch was purchased and added to the forest in 1991, fisheries biologist Jan Fenske described its three lakes to the advisory council. South Blue Lake was the best of the three, 55 feet deep and 19 acres in size but containing soft water, which is not productive for fish: it contained eight- to nine-inch bluegills and 11-inch largemouth bass. North Blue Lake, also 19 acres, was only five feet deep, its soft water containing three- to five-inch yellow perch. Robarge Lake, near the headwaters of Stewart Creek, which empties into the Black River, was 18 feet deep and contained slow-growing hammer-handle pike. Fenske said the plan was to eventually replace the pike with brook trout for a catch-and-release walk-in fishery.

This enumeration of the lakes and streams of the Pigeon River Country tells only half the story for the nature lover. It is a great delight to drive the forest roads and discover these gems of natural beauty, still clear and cold and pure. To approach one's favorite spot as the sun sinks in the west is to feel a sense of personal renewal and a mystic delight. The color of the darkening sky and the voices of the night will long linger in the memory. As Shakespeare wrote:

The setting sun and music at the close
As the last taste of sweets, is sweetest last,
Writ in remembrance more than things long past.

Infrared color photography, viewed in three-dimensional stereo pairs, shows the sink-hole lakes looking for all the world like somebody poked a giant pencil straight down into the forest, leaving perfectly round holes that filled with water. Jerry Myers lived in the Pigeon River forest in 1951 when one of the sinks demonstrated to observers how the lakes actually formed. He supplied the following report.

One of the most unusual features of the forest is the limestone sinkhole lakes. Seven of these lakes are located near the center of the forest. They are North and South Twins, Lost and West Lost along the Osmun Road, Hemlock at the county line, and Ford and Section 4 west of the Pigeon River. These lakes are part of a cave formation, cone-shaped, three to four acres in diameter at the surface, with depths from 30 to 60 feet.

The lakes were formed by surface soils falling into underground limestone cavities. Such cavities outcrop in Presque Isle and Alpena counties and are called Michigan caves. Evidence of the formation of the lakes occurred on Section 4 Lake during the winter of 1950–51, when the west end caved in, pulling trees with it, including a red pine 150 years old. A large log on end that was pulled down by the suction during this cave-in is still visible.

These bowl-shaped gems of emerald beauty attract many photographers, especially during the fall. The lakes were mapped during the 1930s by CCC workers when fire trails and roads were developed. This was an ideal area for fisheries and aquatic study with residences and lab facilities nearby. The Institute for Fisheries Research established the research area of six miles of stream and the seven lakes for intensive trout research from 1949 to 1964. A checking station was opened at headquarters whereby anglers obtained daily permits for fishing a designated stream section or lake and were required to return to headquarters to record angling information.

Trout, which do not reproduce in most lakes, were planted annually. Some 1,000 to 1,500 fingerlings (five to six inches) were planted in each lake in the fall. If more were planted, the trout would become stunted because of the lack of adequate food. Brook trout live four or five years, reaching nine to 11 inches in length by the end of the first summer. Fifty percent of the trout were caught during the study period.

Quiet, scenic shoreline fishing offered many families enjoyable outings. A trout season from the last Saturday in April through Labor Day (the season was later extended), for example, recorded more than 3,000 individual fishing permits for people from 35 counties of Michigan, 23 states, four Canadian provinces, and five other foreign countries. Some 10 to 12 percent of the anglers caught 80 percent of the fish.

What follows is a brief list of what fish were in some of the forest's waters in 2001.

Pickerel Lake: Rainbow trout, largemouth bass, perch, some bluegills
Town Corner Lake: Bluegills, some bass
Round Lake: A few panfish
Dog Lake: Northern pike (prone to winterkill)
Grass Lake: Bass and bluegills
Mud Lake: Bass, perch, bluegills (subject to winterkill)
South Blue Lake: Bass and bluegills
North Blue Lake: Perch
Robarge Lake: Small pike
Cornwall Flooding: Tiger muskellunge, bass, bluegills, sunfish, perch
Pigeon River: Brown, rainbow, and brook trout
Sturgeon River: Brown and rainbow trout
Black River: Brook trout

Gas motors are forbidden on Dog and Pickerel lakes and Cornwall Flooding; North and South Blue and Robarge lakes are catch and release only, using artificial lures.

23

Trails and Camping

SIBLEY HOOBLER

There are several trails of varying length for both the casual walker and the serious backpacker. From Pickerel Lake Campground one may walk entirely around the lake, a distance of several miles.

The Shingle Mill Pathway has several loop trails. For shorter walks on the pathway, it is possible to select destinations where the walker can be picked up by car, such as the walk from Pigeon Bridge Campground, paralleling the river on its east bank. Or one may walk to Ford Lake, which can be reached by roads on the west side of the Pigeon River.

Two lengthy trails are available for the backpacker. One is the Riding and Hiking trail, which runs from Empire to Tawas. Elk Hill Trail Camp is an overnight stop with fresh water and campfire sites available. The more lengthy trail is called the High Country Pathway. The trail goes north from the Pigeon Bridge Campground along the Shingle Mill Pathway. It continues up to the remote northern forest, passes above Dog Lake and east into Thunder Bay River State Forest before circling back through the southeastern Pigeon River Country to its starting point at Pigeon Bridge Campground.

SNOW SPORTS

The various loops of the Shingle Mill pathway are used throughout the winter for cross-country skiing. An effort is made to clear a parking area at the point of origin at the Pigeon Bridge Campground.

There were six campgrounds and one group camp open in summer of 2007. Pigeon Bridge Campground and Johnson's Crossing group camp were temporaryily shut in the state's 2007 budget crisis, Pigeon Bridge because there was no money to fix a failed water well. The campgrounds are available first-come first-served and cannot be reserved. The fee ($15 per night) is placed in a local receptacle and a permit must be posted and left up after departure.

The two group camps are used mainly by groups with horses and are available only for groups of 15 or more people and only by reservation through the unit manager, Pigeon River Country Management Unit, 9966 Twin Lakes Road, Vanderbilt, Michigan, 49795. Telephone: 989-983-4101. The group camps are gated and locked when not in use.

Campers with horses are limited to 10 sites at Elk Hill Trail Campground, to groups of 15 or more with reservations at Elk Hill or Johnson's Crossing group camps, or to one of 15 designated offsite camping locations in the forest. Headquarters maintains the list of locations.

Pickerel Lake Campground has a substantial sandy beach for children. Designated spaces are large enough for trailers, and there is a landing site for boats.

Several campgrounds are on the Pigeon River. At the Pigeon River Campground, a swimming hole near the bridge is attractive to youngsters. The site is a nexus for forest trails. The only campground with access for launching small boats is Town Corner Lake. A hiking trail is nearby. Round Lake Campground is in a red pine grove looking out on a small scenic lake. The Black River is not far away, and this point is a center for many scenic roads.

It is also permissible to camp anywhere within the state forest that is not posted closed to camping. However, the camper must first secure a free permit, which is available at most DNR offices, including the forest headquarters, where a supply is provided on the front porch when the building is closed. This permit must be posted and left at the campsite after departure. Such camping in remote areas offers its own special rewards and also carries special responsibilities.

Keep food, toothpaste, soap, and all cleaning activities 100 feet away from wells, streams, and lakes. Pack out all your trash. Gather firewood only from dead and down trees and shrubs. Secure food to keep animals out of it. Keep campfires small, attended at all times, and left only when the ashes are cold or damp.

Water in the lakes and streams is not guaranteed against pollution. Large containers may be filled with fresh, clean water at the hand pumps at the forest campgrounds.

The major north-south road through the forest is Osmun Road. This road, an old railroad grade, proceeds north from near the forest headquarters along the east bank of the Pigeon River. There are many points of interest. A quarter mile north of forest headquarters look for the Lovejoy memorial marker, where the founder of the forest enjoyed a westward view over the spacious Pigeon River valley. Farther north on both sides are the sinkhole lakes. At the Clark Bridge Road intersection, a short trail to the west reaches Inspiration Point, which overlooks the Cornwall Creek valley and flooding. Where Osmun Road intersects Webb Road, the forest is thick and beautiful.

Between Pickerel Lake and the Pigeon River Campground there is a network of two-track trails leading to Ford Lake, Section 4 Lake, Grass Lake, or Devil's Soup Bowl. Some roads are hardly passable, and caution must be exercised not to get stuck in the sand. Such a risk adds to the adventure and rarely leads to trouble if the driver is prudent.

Fisherman's Trail in the northwest portion of the forest originates near Grass Lake where there is a dense stand of hardwood trees. There are two straight east-west routes. The southerly is an extension of Sturgeon Valley Road crossing ridges covered with hardwood trees; the northerly leads to Hardwood Lake and continues to [Blue Lakes Road, which crosses branches of] the Black River. About one-half mile [east on the unpaved continuation of Sturgeon Valley Road] a marked turnoff leads the visitor to the Witness Tree.

Leading away from Round Lake are several forest trails. The one going east to the Tin Shanty Bridge road skirts the north shore of the Black River Swamp. About one-half mile from its eastern origin there is a stand of tall red pine trees. Beneath them on the forest floor in springtime wild lady's slippers may be seen. They are a protected species not to be picked.

A trail going due west from Round Lake ends at the Upper Pigeon Bridge. A great variety of conifers shade it; be on the lookout for a half mile of almost pure jack pine stand. This regenerated from a fire in 1933. The seeds in jack pine cones lie dormant until exploded by the heat of a fire. Thus, jack pine is frequently the first tree to appear in a fire-ravaged area. The trail north from Round Lake to Sturgeon Valley Road has a special sylvan beauty, partly the result of selective cutting of pine trees. It is difficult for the present day traveler to realize that nearly the entire forest regenerated in 50 years; in 1920, it was called the Pine Barrens, and trees above shoulder height were rare.

24

Animals and People

We benefit not only from time spent outdoors. We have a rare and mostly unappreciated connection with animals. Temple Grandin points out that we evolved living alongside them but now live in separate worlds unless we have dogs or cats. After 40 years of working with animals, Grandin wrote *Animals in Translation,* in which she discloses revealing details about how they perceive their world.

Her particular insight comes from being autistic. People without this disorder of the nervous system think in complex ways perhaps dominated by the ability for abstraction.

We see a dense stand of trees, we think *forest.* Autistics think almost exclusively in images. So, Grandin says, do animals. And it's not exactly that they're seeing birch here and maple there: they observe details like a white cylinder of trunk dotted with black marks and horizontal black lines. Animals apparently see in such detail that they are startled by movements, things out of place, conditions we humans never notice. Grandin says animals remember this highly detailed information. That's the way you get food in the wild, by being attuned to what's around you. "There's a great big, beautiful world out there that a lot of normal folks are just barely taking in," she says, not because we don't want to but because we put things in categories, blurring the specifics. In a lab experiment, people were told to watch a basketball game videotape and count the passes made by one team. Half the people later have no memory of seeing on the same tape a woman wearing a gorilla suit who walks up, looks toward the camera, and pounds her fists against her chest. Her appearance wasn't part of our concept of the game. Grandin says verbal people can't just turn themselves into visual people because they want to, any more than visual beings can will themselves into verbal ones.

We verbal beings have our most complex cognitive functions in our top layer of brain. Below that, animal and human brains look about the same. The lower-level structures of a pig brain and human brain look identical. Not that we are identical by any means, but we have a lot in common with animals. Brain structures tend to be passed along, added on to, not reinvented. Virtually everything animals do is driven by some kind of feeling. Being frightened, startled, intrigued, or curious is a motivator for them just like for us. Each of our three different human brains has its own memory and intelligence. The newest one, on top, is one that all mammals have but is largest in primates. Researchers no longer believe the top one is in charge of the other two, where we share more closely the electromagnetic and chemical characteristics of our fellow animals. As Grandin puts it, "[Y]ou have your lizard brain to breathe and sleep, your dog brain to form wolf packs, and your human brain to write books about it."

Our neocortex on top ties things together, makes connections. For animals, separate things tend to stay that way. What we characterize as a walk down a dirt trail, they might experience as dark grayish-brown grains underfoot, crumbly, interlaced with many fine roots, and with a strong acid smell.

The human cognition system smooths information into one story that leaves out many details, especially those that don't fit. We storytellers can fail to notice the precision in perception even of animals we know better than others.

Dogs can be trained to respond to their owner's seizure by bringing medicine or a telephone or lying atop the seizure victims so they don't hurt themselves. Some dogs actually alert their owners ahead of time that a seizure is coming, seeing signs invisible to the owners themselves. Dogs are sensitive to motion, even potential motion, in other living beings.

Dogs can distinguish between the breath of a person with lung cancer and one without. Grandin observes that autistic people and animals see things even when not paying attention to them, while humans are "built to see what they're expecting to see." Fluorescent lights flicker; autistics and, apparently, animals see it, but our advanced neocortex combines the flashes we experience into a solid light.

What's going on among forest animals is apparently familiar to us at deep levels that reach our consciousness only in modified, generalized form. Looking at the simplest animal life, even an ancient, formless creature shows a profound and little understood connection to the rest of us.

Sponges, the most primitive animal known, have no brain, no gut, no apparent back or front, no eyes, gills, heart, other organs, or even nerves. In adulthood, sponges pump water through a canal system and cavities, extracting food. More than a hundred species of sponges live in freshwater, where they can freeze or dry out. Yet they survive. While the parent may disintegrate, little buds called gemmules, which start off inside adult sponges, have thick shells, are resistant to adverse conditions, and become new sponges when conditions improve. They can be carried by the wind or water or on the feet of birds to other streams and ponds.

Sponges live throughout Michigan's freshwaters, growing as a crust on hard materials beneath the surface such as sticks, rocks, pebbles, the underside of aquatic plants. They have been attaching themselves to, and killing, zebra mussels in the Great Lakes, though only on a local scale (zebra mussels, accidently introduced to the lakes, filter out almost all the phytoplanktons that support fish and other animals).

Freshwater sponges can live even in stagnant pools but not in muddy or highly sedimented water since solid materials clog their pores and kill them. Their bodies are a watery jelly of cells that have a strong will to live. Even when squeezed through a cloth after being ground up, the fragments of sponges creep together in water and rebuild. Some of the cells take silica in freshwater and make a sponge skeleton out of it. Some cells form a skin, some become eggs and sperm, and some digest food by applying the oxygen they carry around. Sponges are like the first animals of 600 million years ago, when single cells began cooperating in the ocean in the presence of rising oxygen levels. These cells get water pumping through the sponge in a rhythmic motion that we're still trying to understand, involving what scientists call mesenchyme condensation in choanocyte chambers. Not so simple, after all. But somehow familiar, these little rhythm sections.

Rhythm can be catching. Fireflies in certain quantities and locations, specifically observed along rivers, flash on and off at once by the thousands. It's a synchrony shared by many others on earth, including pendulums and people. A Dutch physicist in the seventeenth century observed that when he put two pendulum clocks close together and set them in motion to swing out of rhythm with each other within half an hour they synchronized and continued to sway back and forth at the same time. A footbridge 1,000 feet long over the Thames River began to wobble side to side when authorities opened it in 2000 to thousands of people streaming across. Engineers saw that pedestrians adjusted their pace to the swaying, making it wobble even more. London added two large shock absorbers to stop the wobble. Researchers from Cornell University studied the phenomenon and found that mathematics describing synchrony in two pen-dulums and 1,000 fireflies also applied to more than 160 people walking across a bridge.

Not only do we tend to move in synch; we operate in units. Ducks placed in a row for one study all went to sleep for awhile. But the ducks at each end slept with one eye open—the eye facing away from the other birds. Every so often, the end ducks would stand up, turn halfway around, and sit again, allowing them to alternate their open eye. Several bird species, including ducks, keep half their brains on full alert in threatening situa-tions, yet can, like humans, sleep with their whole brains on standby. Many birds demonstrate what we humans would consider friendship: they often help a breeding pair of their species feed fledglings and protect the nest from predators. The point is not that humans and other animals are alike, but that even among our many differences there are many similarities. We benefit from an understanding of them.

Caddisworms, who live on the bottom of rivers, build walls, as humans across the globe have done, with natural stone fitted together. The caddis will reinforce its silky funnel of a home with a wall of small pebbles and sometimes construct part of it from reeds or wood. Most of the 1,000 species of caddis flies in North America spend a year in their larval homes before their brief stints as adults.

Insects, in all their variety, are "builders in clay, weavers of cotton goods, collectors of pieces cut from a leaf or the petals of a flower, archi-tects in pasteboard, plasterers mixing mortar, carpenters boring wood, miners digging underground galleries, workers handling goldbeater's skin and many more." One scrapes a ball of wadding from a wildflower stalk and out of it makes cotton satchels underground for storing eggs and honey. Another tracks the chemical scent of a female of his species from as far as eight miles away. Some sing their cricket songs in megaphones they have dug for that purpose. Another directs her hundred nymphs from one leaf to the next with her long antennae and rebukes any little one that straggles. Another remembers her several digger wasp nest locations and how many offspring she has in each, bringing the right number of cater-pillar meals to each nest every day. Others start clustering around their queen when temperatures drop below 55 degrees Fahrenheit, with a dense skin two-bees deep at the perimeter for insulation, and thus keep the colony alive through a northern winter.

The American bittern, undertaking a defensive posture when alarmed in the marshes of the Pigeon River Country or elsewhere, stretches its neck straight into the air, so that it looks like a cattail or reed, and sways from side to side in time with the reeds if there's any wind.

To really understand our differences, it's quite helpful to know something about our similarities. The forest resonates with activity familiar at basic levels, from sponge fragments seeking each other out to birds saying hello.

When a new species arises, the change is small. The new one is nearly identical to the one it evolved from. Over time and distance, vast differences appear, yet some characteristics hardly change. Reptiles have kept many of their ancestral fish brain circuits such as their swallowing controls. Fruit flies, like their human cousins, need about 10 hours of sleep a night and produce low-frequency electrical activity, slow-wave sleep, during part of their night. Honeybees and crawfish sleep, too. Birds and mammals, including humans, have rapid eye movement (REM) sleep. Birds and mammals use similar greeting rituals.

It's interesting to imagine that mosquitoes might provide a tangible connection today between us and our distant past by putting our own inherited codes back into circulation. Female mosquitoes mate only one time, storing the sperm for a lifetime in their abdomens. Once or twice in the female's life, she takes in a meal of blood, then produces 125 or so eggs, which are laid and hatch into larvae when the site floods, sometimes years later. Mosquito larvae feed on microorganisms in the water, then start the cycle over again.

If it happened to be you that mom first drilled, your genetic code, your DNA, goes on a merry adventure to who knows where. Her proboscis plunges quickly into a surface capillary and begins to take up our blood, which in each white cell contains our whole pack of DNA. A yard-long DNA string or strand is usually in a convenient cube one-millionth of an inch on a side. On this thin strand is the code for eyes and hair, bone density, stature, and all the other traits that come in a genome. The mosquito flies off to a quiet place where she can concentrate the proteins in our blood and dispose of the watery remains. Microbiologists say our blood would be broken down to its basic building blocks, meaning none of our genetic codes would survive. But there are many, many codes in there, and isn't it fun to speculate that mosquitoes might just perpetuate parts of our genetic instruction book even when we don't have offspring of our own?

There's lots of information around about dealing with the pesky bites of mosquitoes but precious little about how our DNA fares in the process. A similar blind spot is evident when investigating what happens to our bodies after official death, especially since we are teeming with organisms, some of which presumably go on living. Most of that literature talks about rigor mortis and, if it mentions bacteria at all, characterizes them as evil creatures that attack the corpse. One professor, typically, calls them "saprophytic organisms," which means death-loving, and raises the question of what he would call beings who attack their chops and drumsticks weeks after the animal has "passed on." One researcher into the science of decomposition, Arpad Vass at the University of Tennessee and Oak Ridge National Laboratory, reports that he quickly had to abandon his assumption that bacteria attacked the corpse in stages, like insects. "I was inundated by the sheer numbers of organisms" and eventually concluded that "every micro-organism known is involved . . . from *Acetobacter* to *Zooglea*." Even he doesn't say exactly how the complexity that makes up a human being goes on living in any of its various parts, even bacterial, but talks instead about how the human decomposes.

There are hints between the lines of research papers that parts of rats and rabbits, such as lung cells, continue to function hours and even days after "death." Some research even mentions, in passing, that bacteria already inside insects at death keep other microbes from invading the nutrient-rich environment. In any case, partnerships such as muscle fiber and heart valves may break up, to say nothing of the vast well-ordered community that constitutes an individual plant or animal organism. But life goes on, rebuilding and rearranging with the same codes, traits, and raw materials. Some bacteria have been known to wait out bad times in suspended animation as spores—tough little one-celled beings—for 250 million years until the right conditions emerge, in this case when biologists dug them up from 2,000 feet down in New Mexico.

Bacteria's larger cousins, the insects, tell us even more about sharing. They are necessary links in essentially all terrestrial food chains. Insects eat plants, making nutrients available to animals who don't eat plants but do eat insects. These insectivores range in size from other insects up to bears. Mosquito larvae feed on microorganisms too small for fish, which eat the larvae instead. Some spiders feed specifically on female mosquitoes who have just had a blood meal.

We welcome some tiny life forms more than others. Researchers have identified a special class of cells, known as mirror neurons, that let us animals experience actions as our own even when we are only seeing or hearing them. The mirror neurons fired the same when a monkey opened a peanut or heard somebody else open one. Humans have such elaborate mirror neurons, researchers say, that we can feel what's in somebody else's mind. They're related to how we respond to music, art, dance, spectator sports, faces, and body language.

Fish have been found to behave honorably when being watched, then cheat a little when other creatures aren't watching. Not only that, but when the observers spotted a cheater they stopped being nice to him but not his fellows. It happened with a wrasse, which eats parasites from the skin of bream. The wrasse, who likes skin mucus better than parasites, would go after the mucus if other bream weren't watching. If bream saw a wrasse cheating, they would not approach him for cleaning. Monkeys, too, consider the visual perspective of others. They will steal a grape when a researcher looks away but not when the researcher is watching. Researchers at Yale took this as evidence that monkeys reason in complex ways about what others know. Many animals use sticks and other natural materials as tools. Beaver in the Sturgeon, Pigeon, and Black rivers plant poles for their dams at an angle against the current.

Crows have whatever tiny genetic code it takes to spontaneously use tools when needed to get a job done such as prying food out of crevices. Two crows raised without seeing such a thing did it on their own. When they're in the wild, around experienced tool-using crows, young crows improve their technique.

Deer wearing wireless video cameras on their antlers may have been showing off but nonetheless nudged each other in what surely looked like kissing. One deer kept drinking water out of a crevice in a tree, perhaps knowing she would surprise the research team. Other people, fortunate enough to watch deer moving precisely on their slender legs in the woods, have seen them groom each other. It's better than a video. Deer place each foot as they move so that it sticks exactly where they place it. Movement glides from miniscule motion through fluid shifts to exuberant and rapid leaps.

Some elk in the Pigeon wear collars that broadcast where they are, helping technicians learn about their wild ways. About 46 of the roughly thousand animals have the collars, five of them with Global Positioning System (GPS) capability. The other 41 are tracked by triangulation, which has an accuracy of about two to 20 acres and isn't precise enough to pinpoint which habitat the elk is frequenting. The GPS collars, on the other hand, are accurate within a circle of 10 feet and provide data three times a day.

When the DNR first started putting collars on elk years ago, it asked Arch and Douglas Reeves a question. Arch grew up hunting in the Pigeon River Country and began working as its wildlife and forestry technician in the early 1970s after a dozen years as a fisheries technician for the whole northern Lower Peninsula. His son, Doug, grew up, like his dad, hunting the area and experiencing the outdoors. Members of the elk-collaring team asked how many elk they would be able to collar in a week. "A week?" Doug replied. "It'll take that long to find your way around. You might get one in a month." The team ignored the advice and found out for themselves that Reeves was right.

Soon Arch and Doug Reeves were asked to help. A young man from Lansing arrived, went out to the forest with them, saw an elk a long way off, and tried to shoot it with the tranquilizer dart. It missed. "We can get you closer," Arch said. "Let's do it my way," the young man replied. So they drove along in a vehicle, with him standing up until he decided they were close enough. He banged on the hood so they would stop the vehicle, and he fired. The dart bounced off the elk.

"Now it's our turn," Arch said. "You sit by that basswood over there, and we'll get an elk to come over to you." He recalled, "We went around, slowly moving the elk. He eventually got over by the basswood. There was no shot. Suddenly the elk took off like a horse."

The Reeveses went over and found "the boy in the weeds, his head hanging down." Doug asked him, "Did you shoot?" No.

Doug asked why. There was nothing in the gun.

Why not? The young man replied, "I didn't think it would work," paused, and added, "And he damned near stepped on me."

The young man was from MSU, hired for the summer, working on his graduate study program. Doug Reeves is now the assistant chief of wildlife for all of Michigan. Arch retired in 1994.

Arch learned from his father, a conservation officer, that you can approach deer and elk if you don't walk right at them. "I whistle and walk around like I don't know they're there. Kind of crowd 'em. They'd move, then stand and watch. They're curious. If you move right toward them, they leave quick."

These days, elk get a collar if a helicopter pilot can get within 40 to 50 yards of the animal while flying over mixed cover. One skilled pilot guided an animal through the woods to an oil pad, flew below the tree canopy, dropped a net over the elk, and backed out so he wouldn't fly into the trees. A netted elk is restrained with a hood and hobbles on the feet until collared and released. Technicians don't use drugs or anesthetize them. After nine months, a little explosion from a .22 caliber squib breaks the collar and it falls off, still broadcasting so technicians can find it. It's an improvement over the days when they had to capture the elk and anesthetize it to take the collar off.

Elk began getting these GPS collars in 2003. Only half a dozen collared elk are in the Pigeon; most are at the eastern end of the range, handled by technicians in Atlanta. Three with collars were killed in the 2004 hunting period.

Years ago, when Arch Reeves realized that bobcats might not survive the pressure of hunters killing every one they see, he began shooting pictures instead of weapons and convinced many other hunters to release at least some of the treed bobcats to be hunted another day. Many bobcats have since been captured, held down with a pole, given an ear tag, and released. Yet hunters never report shooting a tagged bobcat. "They don't want to say they caught a cat somebody else once handled," Arch says. Instead, they tear off the tag and throw it away: "It's something in human nature." Others find tagged cats and release them. It's purely happenstance, Reeves says, whether a tagged cat will be found again.

Collaring is considered a scientifically defensible method for accurately surveying the elk population and tracking not only habitat choice but health issues. In one 1999 study of social patterns in Michigan's elk, they were found to have much less social cohesion than "sedentary herds in stabilized habitats." In other words, they act like wild animals, roaming, trying to find food, and staying away from hunters. A 2002 study found calf production as high as any ever recorded for North American elk, with survival rates higher than elsewhere, indicating their northern Michigan habitat is of high quality. Further study in 2003 confirmed habitat quality, showing an average 10 percent larger body mass in the Pigeon area than elsewhere among elk herds.

Western elk have been reintroduced in Arkansas, Kansas, Kentucky, Minnesota, Pennsylvania, and Wisconsin and live in 17 western states. All of them are descended from one subspecies. Twenty-five elk were shipped from Gaylord to Wisconsin in 1995, where they were fitted with radio collars and released into the Chequamegon-Nicolet National Forest just south of Clam Lake. A decade later Wisconsin estimated its herd at just over a hundred. Pennsylvania's elk population grew from an estimated 38 in 1974 to 622 by 2001, then began to decline because of extensive hunting, dropping to 552 by 2003. Of the six subspecies of elk in early North America, two are believed to be extinct and two survive in small numbers in the Canadian prairie and North Dakota and in protected California enclaves. The other two are Roosevelt elk (*Cervus elaphus roosevelti*), estimated at 117,000 in Pacific coastal forests, and Rocky Mountain elk (*Cervus elaphus nelsoni*), estimated at 850,000 living in many places in North America, from intermountain New Mexico to north-central British Columbia, and, of course, in the Pigeon.

Deer habitat in the Pigeon is shrinking, particularly where small gaps and forest edges are closing. Managing for high densities of deer hurts many other wildlife, although it favors the familiar indigo bunting, chestnut-sided warbler, and even predators like bear and bobcats because of increased numbers of snowshoe hares and other prey, along with the deer themselves.

Red oaks, maples, and white and red pines are large in the Pigeon; pin oaks are dying out. Glen Matthews, a district wildlife biologist, says it takes more understanding each decade to know what is needed to keep systems sustainable, hence the hiring of an ecologist planner to go beyond the custom of looking at one patch of ground. The objective locally is to analyze the habitat of the whole elk range, including parts of Presque Isle, Montmorency, Cheboygan, and Otsego counties, to determine whether more openings are needed, how the range is moving, and how it fits into the overall picture in compartment planning. Elk have an impact on juneberry, bigtooth aspen, and oak. Managing a forest that favors elk by providing lots of cuttings and slash doesn't appeal as much to the eye as a quiet forest with big trees and a parklike understory.

Gray fox, though scarce in Michigan, are more common in the Pigeon, having migrated from southern Michigan. The badger is not scarce. There's not much wildlife in the Pigeon River Country that can't be found elsewhere. Bobcats are found in Presque Isle, Alpena, and Arenac County swamps and are expanding as far as Kent County outside Grand Rapids and toward Lansing, though not necessarily in sustainable populations. Some public land is more isolated than the Pigeon River Country, where publicly fought battles have led to many visitors. Its special features are special features elsewhere as well.

"It's risky to say this pipeline or trail will destroy wildlife," Matthews observes. "It rarely does. What it creates is erosion. You can say it is likely to have a harmful effect."

Small changes can seem less important to us generalists than it might to other species. Ants passing a pebble landmark on a return trip are known to stop, turn around, and look at the pebble from the same spot they saw it heading out. The ant is apparently making sure it's the same pebble. Grandin says this suggests that ants don't necessarily put pieces of sensory data into one whole as humans do. For us, it's the same headquarters building whether we're heading one way or the other on Twin Lakes Road, even though it looks different from one side than the other. Ants and other forest creatures see each change in sharp detail: this bed of clover, perhaps, covered over now with a pile of hay.

Horses are supremely sensitive to the shifting, balancing humans on their backs. A good rider and horse work as a team, responding to each other in ways that can resemble the fluid movements of a single organism, a circling hawk, say, or a dancer. Trail riders like to take that special relationship into the forest. Many have been coming to the Pigeon River Country. There are an estimated 9.2 million horses in the United States, 2 million more than a decade before. Nearly 4 million horses were being used for recreation in 2005.

During a late 1980s budget crunch, the DNR started closing campgrounds in Michigan or giving some to townships. The Michigan Trail Riders Association helped renovate the Elk Hill Campground and turn an overflow area a quarter mile away into a gated group camp, using part of federal grant and volunteers.

Michael Clark regularly brought his quarter horses up to the Pigeon from Charlotte, Michigan, more than 30 years ago, originally going to Elk Hill. "It got crowded, so I moved out, camped in the woods." In the late 1980s and early 1990s, he began to see piles of manure all around and too much hay. "Flies were eating us alive. I cleaned it up a lot." He sees the problem as large groups coming to ride together. Clark prefers browse for the horses, or hay cubes, which are compressed pieces. Otherwise, he says, hay scatters around and people don't haul it out: "It lays and rots. They tie their horse on a picket line close to a tree. Horses gnaw on the tree," eventually killing it by girdling. Some riders fill a hay bag—half a bale. "The horse is gonna pick out the best and leave the rest. Rotting hay kills what's on the ground. It leaves a mess, like tin cans. It's unsightly. To the extent you can, you should leave it in the condition you found it. To me, it's an aesthetic thing, the way things are done."

When an elk bugles, there is a deep rumbling in his chest. "You hear it up close," Clark says, and "it'll raise the hair on the back of your neck." Arch Reeves, experienced at listening to the softest sounds in the forest, reluctantly agreed to take a turkey hunter along to hear elk bugling. "It got quite dusk. I'm starting to head back out. A bull came quite close. One was shaking a tree back and forth. Two came together. Antlers crashed. I enjoyed it. Then I heard squeek, squeek of the man's blood pumping in his neck. He was standing directly behind me." Arch got him behind some stumps until a third bull came and took the cows and the other bulls left.

On the way out of the forest, the man started banging two sticks together. "What are you doing?" Arch asked. "I want them to know I'm here," the man said. Arch said, "You're doing the wrong thing. You sound like antlers. That will attract elk. Just talk. He dropped the sticks and talked my ear off." Reeves says the sound of bugling "is so powerful, you feel they could do anything to anybody."

Mike Clark says, "I saw two bulls sparring. They push each other around; they don't really fight. When horses are grazing, it's a sign to other grazing animals that it's okay. One satellite bull came right in to us while we were watching a bull and cows."

Once, at the south end of Cornwall Flooding, all four of Clark's horses walked off and disappeared. He had put big bells on them. So he tracked them for a mile and brought them back to camp. The thoroughbred was accustomed to being ponied, or accompanied by another horse. Off Sturgeon Valley Road near Tin Shanty, a pan rattled and the thoroughbred took off again. "I tracked him a long ways. Thought I lost him. Thought I'd have to get an airplane to find him. I rode into Elk Hill to water my horse. There was old Tommy." Then Tommy ran away one more time. "If I led him, he'd be alright, but that was enough packing." He started coming to the Pigeon with hunting dogs.

Clark grew up in the country. His dad was an outdoorsman, camped out, grew up in a log cabin. He once camped in the Pennsylvania woods every day for a year. Clark's dad was in the Eighty-second Airborne in World War II. He never told scary tales, and "I never saw him kill anything." Clark's maternal grandfather had English setters. Clark began raising them and by 1985 was taking his out for about 30 days of fall hunting in late September and early October, mostly in the Pigeon River Country.

Raising setters you pay attention to genetic traits. His latest pup was from different lines. Clark owned both parents, so he knew them well. The pup got biddable traits from her mother, that is, she would do his bidding, stay with Clark. Her bolder temperament and desire to point birds came from the male's championship stock. When she was a year old, Clark put her on the ground in a setter preschool. "She went to work, a joy to watch. She had energy, desire, enjoying it herself. She made some mistakes but pointed 26 birds—13 each grouse and woodcock. She had composure. She ranged as far as 300 yards."

"A bird landed near me. I knew it was there. She came in, pointed, stayed on point." Usually a dog will move at the sound of gunfire, but she stayed because she also had another bird pointed. She pointed woodcock in the same area where grouse had been, showing her maturity.

"She's a culmination of all the dogs I've bought and owned." Dog handlers call it "nick" when genes from both lines "nick together. You get the best of each. It's like when an opera singer marries a football player and the kids can sing opera and play football." Clark calls her Nicky. He and his wife live at what they call Sycamore Farm. Nicky's registered name is Sycamore Indigo. Her black and white mixed fur is kind of blue, Clark says.

Nicky's characteristics are far past his expectations. "For some dogs, getting the bird pointed—that's it. In trials, form counts heavily—the way they run, how they handle birds, heads and tails up, standing on top of their toes, how they handle. I make a sound, nod my head, she goes where you want. Dogs read you." He says blue healers, a cross between the wild dingo and a collie, and border collies are especially good at reading people.

People should handle dogs, Clark says, by overcoming resistance without using force. Dogs handle well by nature. "It's difficult to train something they're not bred to do such as herd cattle." His setters want to point birds. "They know to stop, not go in to the bird. 'Whoa' means stay still, not become still. It comes from stalking." If you use force to overcome resistance one place, it builds up somewhere else, he says.

Mike Clark took Sycamore Indigo into the Pigeon River Country for the first time on 26 September 2005. She was two. "This was a really big day," he allowed when he got back. She pointed and continued to point after he shot. "Very rare. Most dogs will move at the shot."

He was obviously lost in thought about his day in the Pigeon. He had been a cop in Ingham County for 27 years. Finally, standing near the bank as the Sturgeon rushed by in the dark, Clark said, "Some hunt for the game. Others of us hunt for the dogs. Not only do they have to point, they have to do it right. Like in ballet. It's hard to explain, but it is really something to see."

In the outdoors, dogs can do certain work spontaneously that reminds us of our special relationship with them. Pete Clapp made his first trip to northern Michigan with a minivan containing his wife, four kids, and a recently rescued dog. The previous owner had tied the dog up in one place all day. "He was crazy," Clapp said. He ran away every chance he got. Pete and his family sat in the minivan unsure of what to do with the dog. They finally decided to find out if he was going to be their dog or not. They opened the door. The dog took off, ran way out and circled all the way around, then ran out farther, circled around again, and a third time farther out. Then he returned to the van, laid down by the door, tongue hanging out, exhausted. He never tried to run away again. After the Clapps got a cabin up north, the dog would arrive, inspect the perimeter before settling down, then continue to investigate within that perimeter.

As people come north looking for quiet recreation, we sometimes find more activity than we want. The way Dave Smethurst puts it, "For about a month every fall, the Pigeon is loved to death by horseback riders. It's Grand Central Station. At the same time, there's bow hunting for deer, grouse and woodcock hunting. All of a sudden, hunters come across two horse trailers." The Pigeon River Country, unlike many other horseback sites, has no dirt bikes or four-wheelers (ORVs are permitted on a few county roads but not off them), and there is a quiet air space agreement with the nearby National Guard. The number of horse camps at Elk Hill rose from 84 in 1984 to 329 in 1990. By 2000, there were 1,000 more horseback use days than 20 years before. The North Spur of the Michigan Shore to Shore Riding and Hiking Trail passes through the Pigeon River Country. There were more than 200 horses in the Elk Hill group camp one summer weekend in 2004.

The DNR has implemented additional recommendations from 2002 about user conflicts, but there are fewer resources every year to enforce them. A checklist circulated by Joe Jarecki, the Pigeon's unit manager, shows proposed actions for pages' worth of situations, many of which remained undone unless he did them himself. Some await action by trail riders, who participated in the meetings and made several site improvements. Others require funds that have not been forthcoming from the state. It's a dilemma we face with our public wildlife areas all over the country: we all feel we have some right to use them, but relatively few are prepared to pay what it costs to repair and protect erosion sites, police conflicting uses, and so on. Some suggest that people should love the Pigeon by staying away.

When, in 2005, the advisory council began to participate in updating the Concept of Management to, as DNR Director Rebecca Humphries had asked, remove ambiguities, council chairman Pete Gustafson suggested certain tests for proposed uses: Is it of low impact, leaving no footprint? Does it degrade the forest's wild character, its wildlife, aquatic, or plant communities? For some time, the council itself had been facing the delicate issue of placing restrictions on some traditional uses rather than simply trying to regulate how such uses are conducted. It began by considering quantitative database measurements as an objective way to determine if, for example, usage was exceeding the capacity of horseback facilities. Such a database would help in deciding whether to expand facilities or perhaps require permits, as with other recreational uses, such as hunting.

Russell Sherman suggests an alternative to us packing up for the forest. "To play the piano is to consort with nature," he writes in *Piano Pieces*. "Every mollusk, galaxy, vapor, or viper, as well the sweet incense of love's distraction, is within the hands and grasp of the pianist." Another musician observes, "[W]ell-crafted music creates the very world it travels through, meeting every anticipation with a graceful resolution, and raising new anticipations at every turn."

The connection with the Pigeon River Country is not as tenuous as one might think. It's a relatively vast space on this busy earth, where mechanical sounds are not ever-present. It's a place, like some others, where we're more likely to hear the rich repertoire of cicadas rubbing their knees in song. Those who wish can practice what musicians do as part of their training: focus utterly on what we hear as though our lives depend on the next sound. When we listen to the vibrations in the cavities and rib cages of an animal, we can be led out of our skins into the life around us.

Listen to a fly. It buzzes for about a second, starting at one pitch and ending at another, which might be related to its takeoff, flight path, or landing. Animals take sound as seriously as any musician. Mozart's starling picked up a phrase the composer had written but changed a G-natural to a G-sharp. Mozart wrote "Das war schon!" (That was beautiful!) in his notebook. The musical phrase appears at the beginning of the last movement of his Piano Concerto in G Major, K. 453. The European starling, exported to North America a century later, resides spring, summer, and fall in the fields and woods of the Pigeon River Country, singing its array of calls and songs. It uses whistles, rattles, snarls, clicks, and screeches. It also takes the themes of other species and weaves them into long soliloquies and can imitate our speech as well. In chorus, a flock of starlings is called a murmuration because their vocalizing is constant.

Not much is really known about their complex music. In one study of starlings in captivity, it was noted "the starlings' vocal capacities defy simple categorization." They imitated phrases rather than single words, recombined phrases into new phrases, and only rarely preserved a melody as they had first heard it. They tended to sing off-key, fracturing phrases at unexpected moments, and stood intently listening when they heard new music, moving their heads back and forth but remaining quiet until it was done. One of them repeated, "Does Hammacher Schlemmer have a toll-free number?" a day after hearing it once. It appeared that they thrived on mutual companionship, chatting excitedly among themselves while humans in the homes where the starlings stayed talked to one another. The researchers said starlings in natural settings quickly learn new whistles for social interactions such as entering new flocks. Parent starlings and their young use what science calls vocal exchanges, as do young starling siblings.

Captive white-crowned sparrow males learn songs heard on tape recordings until they are 50 days old, then only from other birds with whom they interact. White-crowned sparrows, a woodland bird in the Pigeon River Country, are among the majority of songbirds who do not mimic other species. Starlings in the captivity study did not imitate recorded songs or prose, but one began imitating the tape hiss. The researchers said interaction among live beings seems to be more important than the quality of a tutor's voice in birds learning new material. For his part, Mozart wrote after his starling died:

Nur war er etwas munter,
Doch auch mitunter

[He was not naughty, quite,
But gay and bright]

At least two researchers suggest that Mozart's *A Musical Joke,* K. 522, with its "awkward, unproportioned, and illogical piecing together of uninspired material . . . grotesque cadenza which goes on far too long and pretentiously and ends with a comical deep pizzicato note," sounds just like the kinds of things a starling might have sung to him, as does the abrupt ending. These researchers also suggest that we study bird interactions more deeply, looking for example at why only certain links are made between sight and sound. They propose that birds sometimes use sounds as probes into the properties of their environments, gauging effects and sharing. Bernd Heinrich, after studying ravens in the field for many years, observed, "A raven is expressive, communicates emotions, intentions, and expectations, and acts as though it understands you." He describes watching a pair rise from their nest and soar in tight formation, wingtip to wingtip, among the beech and oak.

Another observer, a clarinetist, is convinced that a thrush interacted with his clarinet playing, changing his song in relation to the musician's notes. He thinks birds "sing for the same reason people do: because they can. It's part of their essence." Heinrich says mutual communication is the source of attachment between beings.

Mice, it turns out, also sing. Their music, sung too high to be heard by human ears, has been recorded, slowed down, and compared to the songs of whales. The clarinetist, who is also a professor of philosophy, says researchers couldn't make sense of sperm whale clicks until they recruited an African drum master, who heard patterns, rhythms, and signs that they were listening and responding to one another. Mice use syllables in phrases and motifs. Researchers have analyzed recordings of male mice responding to contact with female pheromones by vocalizing hundreds of chirpy syllables at 30 kilohertz and higher. Individual mice sang different songs.

Birds gotta sing, bees gotta dance. We might figure they're just communicating basic stuff, like here's my territory or there's the nectar. But then there are wrens who sing four-part songs. Two male plain-tailed wrens trade phrases with two females for up to two minutes, using split-second timing. Others sing in groups of seven, with males singing A and C patterns and females B and D in rapid succession with no overlaps, as if the whole thing was a single song. Two or more males sing the same phrase in synchrony even though they know up to 20 different phrases.

Birds can produce two different notes simultaneously. Their voice comes from deep in the chest, where one channel produces high notes and another the low ones. Even short songs can carry complex messages. A cowbird uses more than 40 notes in his songs, some higher than we can hear, and may take two years to perfect one of his cowbird concertos of high notes, low notes, and combination notes.

Researchers are puzzling through what it all might mean, sticking to scientific rather than aesthetic interpretations, as researchers tend to do, such as speculation that the birds are synchronizing reproduction or defending territory. Those who know music better than scientists might, give us a much richer idea of what might be going on. Sounds in music move along in a structure. They contain emotion, that is, they engage our feelings.

Identifying tone intervals, or the distance between two pitches, is physically a complex task. A tritone, such as a C and an F-sharp played together, is considered the most dissonant sound in the musical scale. People once considered a tritone to be the devil appearing in music. Moving one of the two notes a half step up or down brings resolution, a feeling of "Ahhh, that's better."

These are essentially two electrical vibrations. We aren't the only ones who hear them. The bill of a platypus, for example, detects the tiniest electrical currents that are constantly given off by living things. Music is tones occurring over time. Everything we do, one musical authority writes, starts with "a kind of fleeting hypothesis that is confirmed or disconfirmed." If what we anticipate is slightly different from what actually happens, we adjust the next anticipation. Music is closer to perfection than is the movement of a body. While we have moments of inelegance in preparing a meal around the campfire, music meets every anticipation with resolution, sometimes different from what we expect and always raising new anticipations as it goes along.

A cry comes from high above, a KEE-ah penetrating the beech canopy half a dozen times, like the shrill whistle some humans make blowing across a blade of grass held just so over the mouth. Except the power of this cry echoes through the forest. The hawk floats beyond the sugar maple and beech, looking like a stretch of orange with fluttering white dots and a semicircle of thin white and thick black stripes.

The bird makes half a dozen quick wing flaps and repeats its cry, then soars, flaps, and glides silently. It is a red-shouldered hawk, once one of the most prevalent hawks in the eastern United States but decimated since by loss of mature forest habitat and perhaps the fallout of heavy pesticide use. The U.S. Fish and Wildlife Service lists the red-shouldered hawk as a rare/declining species. It appeared in only 12 percent of the blocs surveyed recently in the north-central states compared with 76 percent for the red-tailed hawk.

Yet the red-shouldered hawk has been moving north into the Pigeon River Country out of its former range. Most red-shouldered hawks migrate south out of Michigan, Wisconsin, and Minnesota in late fall, returning by March or April to their nesting areas in mature, wet hardwood forests that have closed canopies and extend over wide acreage. When timber managers open canopies as part of their standard practice, red-tailed hawks tend to displace red-shouldered hawks.

Red-shouldered hawks mate for life. One pair claims as its territory in good habitat anywhere from half to nearly five square miles. The hawks' kee-yah cry, easily recognizable among raptor calls, is lower in pitch than the shrill hiss of the red-tailed or the clear, keen cry of the broad-winged hawk. At one and a half pounds, this raptor is less than two-thirds the size of the red-tailed, though a third larger than the broad-winged. Yet the fierce head of an approaching red-shouldered hawk could strike fear in any heart. With beak open, the face is a collection of pointy-cornered shapes in the form of eyes, beak, and mouth, accented by radiating dark marks surrounding the black openings on a white field.

Red-shouldered hawks live up to 20 years on a diet of small mammals, amphibians, reptiles, and a few insects, crawfish, fish, and small birds. The *Buteo lineatus* has five recognized subspecies in the United States; the largest, *Buteo lineatus lineatus,* is known as the eastern or northern red-shouldered hawk. That is the one that hunts over the Pigeon and elsewhere in

Michigan, Wisconsin, Minnesota, Ohio, Indiana, Illinois, and Missouri. It breeds in the eastern United States and southern Canada as far west as Nebraska and Kansas and as far east and south as Maine, eastern Arkansas, North Carolina, and Tennessee.

Hawks have eyesight four to eight times as good as humans have and see small objects clearly at great distances. Red-shouldered hawks studied in Michigan took a variety of prey, depending on what was available, getting mostly mammals during a drought and mostly amphibians and arthropods from the same territory when there was lots of standing water.

On the ground, hawk prey, such as chipmunks, talk a lot, flicking their tails in what seems dramatic emphasis. Actually, chipmunks are usually perched above the ground in a bush or tree when vocalizing—to whom is unclear since they live alone, filling and guarding their underground larders of seeds and nuts. They are fairly tolerant of people, however, so they are an easy accommodation when we want some wild animal contact and a little chatter.

And we mustn't forget our dogs, who don't fit too well in the forest but fit precisely with humans. Recent research indicates that dogs and humans have been together 10 times longer than previously supposed. Back when they were wolves, 100,000 years ago, *Canis lupus* and the newly evolved *Homo sapiens* teamed up, possibly before humans began talking in sentences. Humans, according to some anthropologists, learned from wolves about hunting in groups, complex social structure, same-sex loyalty, and nonkin friendships—things wolves had, humans didn't, and few primates apparently have even today. Dogs may have been why early humans survived while Neanderthals, who had no dogs, didn't.

Even more fascinating, the brain structures of early humans and early domestic dogs both changed in a symbiotic relationship. That is, the forebrain of domestic animals shrank while the midbrain of humans became 10 percent smaller. The forebrain has the frontal lobes, where we do all our abstract thinking. The midbrain has olfactory bulbs, where we handle smells. As Grandin puts it, "[H]umans took over the planning and organizing tasks, and dogs took over the sensory tasks. Dogs and people coevolved and became even better partners, allies, and friends."

She adds that as we became human we gave some things up. "Being close to animals brings some of it back."

25

The Birds

HAROLD D. MAHAN

Harold D. Mahan, director of the Cleveland Museum of Natural History and later the San Diego Natural History Museum, has been a consultant to government agencies, industries, and private organizations in environmental interpretation and planning and is a former research and teaching fellow at UM, a National Science Foundation Faculty Fellow at MSU, and a professor of biology at Central Michigan University. He was coauthor of An Introduction to Ornithology *in 1975. In 1992 he and his wife, Laura, opened a store in the southern Appalachian mountains for nature enthusiasts, The Compleat Naturalist, in Asheville, North Carolina, where he is also an adjunct professor at the University of North Carolina at Asheville.*

If you lived in the Pigeon River Country year-round you possibly could identify over 200 different kinds of birds, nearly every species found throughout Michigan. Why such variety? Well, the country along the Pigeon River has a great number of different natural habitats: mature beech-maple woods, wild and agricultural fields, streams, lakes, and several other types of wetland areas. Like all animals, birds are a reflection of the kinds of habitats that exist in an area, hence the rich variety of birdlife. The following are a few examples of this.

BIRDS OF THE WETLANDS

Streams. Along the Pigeon and Black rivers, campers and fishermen may encounter a solitary great blue or green heron stalking fish in such streams, while overhead the rattlelike call of the belted kingfisher may be heard. During summer evenings whip-poor-wills, which have a habit of calling their names over and over just before and after dark, will be perched on low limbs along the waterways. Some trout fishermen associate such calls with the appearance of large brown trout moving out into the more open stream from their secluded daytime hiding places.

Smaller bird species include the golden-winged warbler, alder flycatcher, and winter wren. The latter, with a sleigh-bell-like song, sounds nothing like the more familiar house wren. Listen for it in deep woods where large pine trees have been blown down. Its nest is built in among the exposed roots of such trees.

The golden-winged warbler, with its low, buzzy song, nests in the alders and willows along most of the streams. In the same areas, you will find the common yellowthroat, a diminutive bird whose song phonetically is "witchity-witchity-witchity." Look for the black mask on the male of this species.

Another common streamside bird is the chestnut-sided warbler (song: "see, see, see, Miss Betcher"). It, too, is an alder nester.

Marshes. In the more open, still-water areas where cattails and reeds occur, you will find another of the Pigeon River Country's wrens, the long-billed marsh wren. The males of this species arrive in late May and sing their territorial songs from daylight until after dark. The song sounds very much like an old treadle sewing machine, and these males build many fake nests to which they attract females. When the females arrive a few weeks later, they build the real nests.

Also present are red-winged blackbirds and common grackles, both of which use cattails to support their nests. Short-billed marsh wrens also are found in wet meadows. American woodcock and the common snipe, both shorebirds sought by hunters during the fall, will be found in such areas probing the wet soils for earthworms. In the open waters of these wetlands, you will find the black tern, which builds a nest on a floating mat of marsh debris.

In the marsh edge, wherever mud flats occur, several species of plovers and sandpipers will be found during the spring and fall. Only the spotted sandpiper and solitary sandpiper will be common in such areas in the summer nesting season. The spotted sandpiper is one of the easiest shorebirds to identify since it is the only shorebird in the region that pumps its tail up and down as it walks.

Lakes and Ponds. In this area, especially during migratory periods in the spring and fall, one has a chance to see a larger percentage of those species of swimming birds than are possible to see in any other part of Michigan. Included are loons, grebes, and bitterns, as well as many species of ducks and geese. Loons occasionally may be heard and seen on Grass Lake and other small, backwoods lakes in the area during the summer, spring, and fall. Along the edge of such lakes may be found many species of shore-birds, as well as gulls and terns in the open water. The time of year and nature of the shoreline and surrounding vegetation will determine to a great degree the species present. To be expected are such insect-eating species as chimney swifts and all of the swallows; in fact, all species of water-associated birds may be found at least for short periods of time, especially during migratory periods.

BIRDS OF DRY HABITATS

Second-Growth Fields. Throughout the Pigeon River Country, there are numerous dry, sandy fields with a distinct assemblage of bird species. In such areas, look for prairie warblers in Christmas-tree-sized jack pine stands where there are open fields, the savannah sparrow in the wetter agricultural short-grass fields, and field sparrows wherever there are fairly tall grasses with some shrubs.

One of the most interesting birds of the dry fields is the upland sand-piper. This species often nests on the tops of fence posts. Its song (a "wolf" whistle) and behavior (an upward raising of its wings when it lands) helps to identify it.

Woody Fields. A variety of birds will be found in those areas that are changing into forest lands but still predominantly contain herbaceous veg-etation. Occurring in such habitats will be both species of cuckoos and the grey catbird, brown thrasher, eastern bluebird (especially where there are large dead trees providing woodpecker holes), loggerhead shrike, and American goldfinch. The latter, also called the "wild canary," is one of the last to nest in a season since it nests only when such plants as the thistle have developed seeds to feed its young.

Mixed Forests. In those areas where such forest trees as poplar, small pines, cherry, and birch are found, we find mourning doves, ruby-throated hummingbirds, several species of woodpeckers (if dead trees for nesting cavities are available), eastern kingbirds, great crested flycatchers, blue jays and crows, chickadees, titmice, nuthatches and creepers, house wrens, robins and other thrushes, cedar waxwings, vireos, and a great assortment of warblers. Ovenbirds and American redstarts are especially common.

The ovenbird, a large warbler that resembles a thrush, nests on the ground where it builds a nest resembling a Dutch oven. Its loud daytime call, "teacher, teacher, teacher," may be heard in nearly all of our woods. It is in such areas, too, that the northern oriole (formerly called Baltimore oriole) often builds its pendulous nests in poplars, willows, and tall birches. The scarlet tanager, the only woodland bird with a red body and black wings, also is found in such areas.

Coniferous Forests. In the more mature spruce and pine forests, especially in extensive areas of such species, you may find nesting sharp-shinned, Cooper's, red-tailed, and red-shouldered hawks. Broad-winged hawks, short and broad in appearance contrasted with other native hawks, are fairly common nesters. Since the larger hawks are somewhat similar in appearance, it is wise to learn their fairly distinct calls if you plan to iden-tify them.

Also found in such areas will be roosting and nesting owls (screech, great horned, barred, long-eared, and saw-whet). Utilizing the sandy, leaf-covered ground for nests may be whip-poor-wills and in the openings nesting common nighthawks. The pileated woodpecker will be present, as will kinglets, northern parula warblers (nesting in areas where usnea lichens, their favorite nesting material, is found), and blackburnian and pine warblers. Evening and pine grosbeaks will use such areas in the win-ter, as will red and white-winged crossbills. Purple finches will be found associated with the taller spruce trees, along with the black-throated green and blackburnian warblers. Of all these species, the evening grosbeak is one of the most interesting since it probably does not nest in Michigan's Lower Peninsula at all yet is here during the entire summer. Most people who feed sunflower seeds will continue to attract this species during the entire year.

Mature Beech-Maple Forests. In the mature climax vegetation of the Pigeon River Country, still other bird species will be found. Included will be such species as pileated woodpeckers (and the possibility of all other woodpecker species if suitable dead trees occur), great-crested flycatchers, eastern wood pewees, chickadees, titmice, nuthatches and creepers, house wrens (and winter wrens, especially in areas where uprooted trees occur), wood and hermit thrushes, red-eyed, solitary, and warbling vireos, and many species of warblers (black and white, yellow-rumped, black-throated green, blackburnian, blackpoll, ovenbird, Canada, and American redstart). Scarlet tanagers and cardinals will be found in the openings of such woods. Do not expect to see many cardinals here, however, since this is nearly the northern end of their range.

GAME SPECIES

A number of bird species that occur in the Pigeon River Country may be legally hunted. Included are ducks and geese, ruffed grouse, American woodcock, common snipe, American coot, and rails.

The most important game bird species are the woodcock and grouse because of the presence of extensive second-growth vegetation (alders, willows, poplar, and birch). Although the ruffed grouse is found in the area year-round, the woodcock leaves for more southern climates shortly after the first killing frost. Success in hunting the ruffed grouse largely depends on the cyclical nature of their populations; hunters should check, therefore, with local game biologists for information concerning their population status at any particular time. Of course, the hunting of all game species is controlled by state and federal laws, and licenses are required.

LISTING THE BIRDS

In order to provide a summary of all birds species found in the Pigeon River Country during every season, a list of the birds of the region is on pages 278–83 with space to check off the species you see in the area. This checklist also indicates habitats where each species is typically found. Some species on this checklist pass through the Pigeon River Country only during migration. Some occasionally appear in other habitats than listed. Hawks and owls, for example, often visit several habitats in their search for food, gulls may be seen flying over fields, and during migration certain species will move through a number of different habitats.

BIRDING EQUIPMENT AND REFERENCES

To maximize the enjoyment of looking at birds in the Pigeon River Country, the following suggestions are made concerning equipment and books.

Binoculars. To fully appreciate the fascinating color and behavior of birds, it is necessary to acquire a good pair of binoculars. For most children and adults, a pair of 7 × 35 binoculars is required. The designation 7 × 35 refers to the magnification (7 power) and size of the front optical lense (35 mm). Adults, certainly, can handle a pair of 8 × 40 binoculars, but binoculars of a higher power are not recommended because they are too difficult to hold steady; binoculars of a power of magnification below 7 are usually

Checklist of Birds of the Pigeon River Country

(✓) SPECIES	SPRING	SUMMER	FALL	WINTER	WETLANDS	FIELDS	WOODS
Common Loon	•	•	•		•		
Horned Grebe	•	•	•		•		
Pied-billed Grebe	•	•	•		•		
Great Blue Heron	•	•	•		•		
Green Heron	•	•	•		•		
Least Bittern	•	•	•		•		
American Bittern	•	•	•		•		
Canada Goose	•		•		•		
Mallard	•	•	•		•		
Black Duck	•	•	•		•		
Pintail	•				•		

(✓) SPECIES	SPRING	SUMMER	FALL	WINTER	WETLANDS	FIELDS	WOODS
Merlin	•	•	•		•		•
American Kestrel	•	•	•			•	•
Ruffed Grouse	•	•	•	•			•
Ringed-neck Pheasant	•	•	•	•		•	
Turkey	•	•	•	•			•
Sandhill Crane	•	•	•		•		
King Rail	•	•	•		•		
Virginia Rail	•	•	•		•		
Sora	•	•	•		•		
Common Gallinule	•	•	•		•		
American Coot	•	•	•		•		
Semipalmated Plover	•	•	•		•		
Piping Plover	•	•	•		•		

Species						
Green-winged Teal	•			•		
Blue-winged Teal	•	•		•		
American Wigeon	•			•		
Wood Duck	•	•		•		
Ring-necked Duck	•			•		
Canvasback	•	•		•		
Greater Scaup	•	•		•		
Lesser Scaup	•	•		•		
Common Goldeneye	•	•		•		
Bufflehead	•	•		•		
Hooded Merganser	•	•		•		
Common Merganser	•	•		•		
Red-breasted Merganser	•	•		•		
Turkey Vulture	•	•			•	
Goshawk	•	•	•		•	
Sharp-shinned Hawk	•	•			•	
Cooper's Hawk	•	•			•	
Red-tailed Hawk	•	•			•	
Red-shouldered Hawk	•	•			•	
Broad-winged Hawk	•	•			•	
Bald Eagle	•	•		•	•	
Marsh Hawk	•	•		•		•
Osprey	•	•		•		

Species						
Killdeer	•	•	•	•		•
Ruddy Turnstone	•	•	•	•	•	
American Woodcock	•	•		•		
Common Snipe	•	•	•	•	•	•
Upland Sandpiper	•	•	•		•	
Spotted Sandpiper	•	•	•		•	
Solitary Sandpiper	•	•	•		•	
Greater Yellowlegs	•	•	•		•	
Lesser Yellowlegs	•	•	•		•	
Pectoral Sandpiper	•	•	•		•	
Least Sandpiper	•	•	•		•	
Semipalmated Sandpiper	•	•	•		•	
Sanderling	•	•	•		•	
Wilson's Phalarope	•	•	•		•	
Herring Gull	•	•	•		•	
Ring-billed Gull	•	•	•		•	
Bonaparte's Gull	•	•	•		•	
Common Tern	•	•	•		•	
Caspian Tern	•	•	•		•	
Black Tern	•	•	•		•	
Mourning Dove	•	•	•		•	
Yellow-billed Cuckoo	•	•	•		•	

Checklist—Continued

(✓) SPECIES	SPRING	SUMMER	FALL	WINTER	WETLANDS	FIELDS	WOODS
Black-billed Cuckoo	•	•	•				•
Screech Owl	•	•	•	•			•
Great Horned Owl	•	•	•	•			•
Snowy Owl				•		•	•
Barred Owl	•	•	•	•			•
Saw-whet Owl	•	•	•	•			•
Whip-poor-Will	•	•	•			•	•
Common Nighthawk	•	•	•			•	•
Chimney Swift	•	•	•				•
Ruby-throated Hummingbird	•	•	•			•	•
Belted Kingfisher	•	•	•		•		

(✓) SPECIES	SPRING	SUMMER	FALL	WINTER	WETLANDS	FIELDS	WOODS
Purple Martin	•	•	•			•	•
Blue Jay	•	•	•	•			•
Common Crow			•	•			•
Common Raven				•			•
Black-capped Chickadee	•	•	•	•			•
Tufted Titmouse	•	•	•	•			•
White-breasted Nuthatch	•	•	•	•			•
Red-breasted Nuthatch	•	•	•	•			•
Brown Creeper	•	•	•				•
House Wren	•	•	•				•
Winter Wren	•	•	•				•

Species							
Long-billed Marsh Wren	•	•		•			
Short-billed Marsh Wren	•	•		•		•	•
Gray Catbird	•	•	•	•	•		
Brown Thrasher	•	•	•	•	•		
American Robin	•	•	•	•			
Wood Thrush	•	•	•	•			
Hermit Thrush	•	•	•	•			
Swainson's Thrush	•	•	•	•			
Gray-cheeked Thrush	•	•	•	•			
Veery	•	•	•	•			
Eastern Bluebird	•	•	•	•	•		
Blue-gray Gnatcatcher	•	•	•	•			
Golden-crowned Kinglet	•	•	•	•	•		
Ruby-crowned Kinglet	•	•	•	•	•		
Cedar Waxwing	•	•	•	•			
Northern Shrike	•	•	•	•			
Loggerhead Shrike	•	•	•	•	•		
Starling	•	•	•	•			
Yellow-throated Vireo	•	•	•	•			

Species							
Common Flicker	•	•	•				
Pileated Woodpecker	•	•	•	•	•		
Red-headed Woodpecker	•	•	•	•	•		
Yellow-bellied Sapsucker	•	•	•	•	•		
Hairy Woodpecker	•	•	•	•	•		
Downy Woodpecker	•	•	•	•	•		
Eastern Kingbird	•	•	•	•	•		
Great Crested Flycatcher	•	•	•	•	•		
E. Phoebe	•	•	•	•	•		
Yellow-bellied Flycatcher	•	•	•	•	•		
Willow Flycatcher	•	•	•	•	•		
Alder Flycatcher	•	•	•	•	•		
Least Flycatcher	•	•	•	•	•		
E. Wood Pewee	•	•	•	•	•		
Olive-sided Flycatcher	•	•	•	•	•		
Horned Lark	•	•	•				
Tree Swallow	•	•	•	•			
Bank Swallow	•	•	•	•			
Rough-winged Swallow	•	•	•	•			
Barn Swallow	•	•	•	•			
Cliff Swallow	•	•	•	•			

Checklist—Continued

√	SPECIES	SPRING	SUMMER	FALL	WINTER	WETLANDS	FIELDS	WOODS
	Solitary Vireo	•	•	•				•
	Red-eyed Vireo	•	•	•				•
	Warbling Vireo	•	•	•				•
	Black-and-white Warbler	•	•	•				•
	Golden-winged Warbler	•	•					•
	Tennessee Warbler	•	•			•		•
	Nashville Warbler	•	•	•				•
	Northern Parula	•	•	•				•
	Yellow Warbler	•	•	•				•
	Magnolia Warbler	•	•	•				•
	Cape May Warbler	•	•	•			•	•
	Black-throated Blue Warbler	•	•					•
	Yellow-rumped Warbler	•						•
	Black-throated Green Warbler	•	•	•				•
	Blackburnian Warbler	•	•	•				•

√	SPECIES	SPRING	SUMMER	FALL	WINTER	WETLANDS	FIELDS	WOODS
	Northern Oriole	•	•	•				•
	Brewer's Blackbird	•	•	•			•	
	Common Grackle	•	•	•			•	•
	Brown-headed Cowbird	•	•	•		•	•	•
	Scarlet Tanager	•	•	•				•
	Cardinal	•	•	•				•
	Rose-breasted Grosbeak	•	•	•				•
	Indigo Bunting	•	•	•				•
	Dickcissel	•	•	•				•
	Evening Grosbeak	•	•	•				•
	Purple Finch	•	•	•			•	•
	Pine Grosbeak	•	•	•			•	•
	Common Redpoll	•	•	•				•
	Pine Siskin	•	•	•				•

	Col 1	Col 2	Col 3	Col 4	Col 5	Col 6	Col 7
Chestnut-sided Warbler	•				•	•	
Bay-breasted Warbler	•	•			•	•	•
Blackpoll Warbler	•	•			•	•	•
Pine Warbler	•	•		•	•	•	
Prairie Warbler	•	•	•		•	•	
Palm Warbler	•	•			•	•	•
Ovenbird	•	•			•	•	•
Northern Waterthrush	•	•	•		•	•	
Connecticut Warbler	•	•		•	•	•	
Mourning Warbler	•	•	•		•	•	
Common Yellowthroat	•	•	•		•	•	
Canada Warbler	•	•			•	•	•
American Redstart	•	•			•	•	•
House Sparrow	•	•	•		•	•	•
Bobolink	•	•			•	•	
E. Meadowlark	•	•			•	•	
W. Meadowlark	•	•			•	•	
Red-winged Blackbird	•	•		•	•	•	

	Col 1	Col 2	Col 3	Col 4	Col 5
American Goldfinch	•	•		•	
Red Crossbill	•	•		•	
White-winged Crossbill	•	•		•	
Rufous-sided Towhee	•	•		•	
Savannah Sparrow	•	•		•	
Grasshopper Sparrow	•	•		•	
Henslow's Sparrow	•	•		•	
Vesper Sparrow	•	•		•	
Dark-eyed Junco	•	•		•	
Tree Sparrow	•	•		•	
Chipping Sparrow	•	•		•	
Field Sparrow	•	•		•	
White-crowned Sparrow	•	•		•	
White-throated Sparrow	•	•		•	
Fox Sparrow	•	•		•	
Lincoln's Sparrow	•	•		•	
Swamp Sparrow	•	•	•	•	
Snow Bunting	•	•		•	

not sufficient for observing most small bird species. The most important advice about buying a pair of binoculars is to check with several others who have used them for a considerable period of time. Such experienced birders will be able to recommend some good manufacturers.

A spotting scope, a monocularlike instrument, is very helpful, especially for birds of prey, shorebirds, and waterfowl at great distances. Again, check with an experienced birder before investing in such an instrument. In my own work, I have found a 20 power spotting scope to be the most useful and efficient.

Reference Material. Every bird-watcher in the Pigeon River Country should have a good field guide. Two excellent ones are Roger Tory Petersen's *A Field Guide to the Birds,* and Robbins, et al., *Birds of North America.* I have found the latest edition of the Petersen guide to be the most useful because it covers only birds of eastern North America rather than birds of the entire continent.

Learn to quickly find the pictures of bird groups in your field guide. There is nothing quite so frustrating as seeing a bird clearly and not being able to find a plate showing similar species in the book. Become familiar with where the ducks, geese, and swans are shown, as well as what part of the book contains the warblers and sparrows; this will pay off many times over when you are in the field with binoculars focused on a very small bird! In the "Bibliographic Notes," there is a list of other useful bird books.

BIRD CONSERVATION

Birds are part of natural ecosystems, and, like all animals, in order for them to survive as a group they deserve our protection through wise management. Although feeding wild birds brings great enjoyment to humans, a more important consideration must be a concern for disappearing habitats, pollution, and the total impact of human activities on the natural world.

26

Vegetation

EUGENE E. OCHSNER

Eugene Ochsner, a chemist, personnel manager, and plant manager in his 41-year career with the Du Pont Corporation, was a conservationist with an interest in Native American studies, archaeology, camping, and wildflower photography. Two of his sons were in the National Park Service. When he retired in 1965, Eugene and his wife, Priscilla, moved to their home in northern Michigan.

With the final retreat northward of the great ice sheets that covered Michigan, simple mosses, arctic plants, and dwarf willows began to appear. In the still much cooler temperatures than what are found today, vegetation was mostly ground hugging. The terrain was much the same as what can be seen today in the far north of Canada and around the shores of Hudson Bay.

As the climate slowly warmed, other plants, shrubs, and trees moved in from the south. Tundra gradually gave way to shrubs such as the bog laurel, bog rosemary, Labrador tea, sphagnum moss, and black spruce—the first of the stately trees that eventually covered much of Michigan. Dwarf willows were supplanted by larger trees of the same species, and the larch (tamarack) made its appearance.

Frére Marie-Victorin describes what happened: "First came these ever ready pioneers: the Black Spruce, and the Balsam Fir, and the Larch and later the stately Pines. Then followed the Aspens and the Birches, the Alders and the Viburnums. The Sugar Maple took possession of the well drained Glacial Moraines [ridges of sand, gravel, and clay brought down by the ice sheets from Canada] alongside the valleys, and the Hemlock fought its way among the deciduous trees. Meanwhile had come the wiry Grasses and the coarse Sedges, the legions of Goldenrods and the hundreds after hundreds of herbaceous or shrubby plants."

FLORA FOUND IN BOGS

Plants that grew after the ice melted are still to be found, particularly in the cooler bogs. These bogs are found along streams and creeks, as well as in glacial lakes that have filled in or are quite shallow such as Hardwood and Grass lakes. These act as microenvironments to preserve boreal (northern) vegetation. Good examples can be found along the Tin Shanty Bridge Road, just north of the Black River bridge, around the shores of Hardwood Lake, and in the extensive bog that borders Hardwood Creek to the south.

Orchids bloom in June and sometimes as late as August. These include the ragged fringed, rose pogonia, leafy green rein, tall white bog, queen lady's slipper (showy), common ladies' tresses, arethusa, hooded ladies' tresses, and grass pink (or calopogon).

In the entire United States, four main types of insect-trapping plants are found. Three of these types grow in Pigeon River Country bogs; it is too far north for the Venus flytrap. In standing northern water, the flat-leaved bladderwort grows with its distinctive small yellow blossom above the water and the rest of the plant submerged. This insectivorous plant captures tiny aquatic life with small, transparent sacs or bladders attached to the roots. When an aquatic insect passes by, it is sucked into the open sac and the trapdoor closes, providing nourishment to the bladderwort.

In slightly less boggy areas, the pitcher plant grows. It has quite large flowers on tall stems and generally grows in clumps. It has tube-shaped leaves, lined inside with downward-pointing hairs. Insects entering the pitcherlike tube cannot crawl out and drown in a reservoir of water at the bottom of the tube.

The third type of insectivorous plant in the Pigeon River Country is the round-leaved sundew, which is found in drier parts of bogs, sometimes on decaying logs. It has padlike leaves in a flat rosette pattern. Each leaf bears numerous radiating hairs, each of which has a highly visible drop of sticky material. Once an insect makes contact with the sticky material it cannot pull free, dies, and provides nourishment to the plant.

Other flowering plants in and around bogs include gentians of several varieties, cranberries, marsh Saint-John's-wort, tall blue flag, marsh blue-bell (the stems are covered with stiff, short hairs that resemble thorns), and several varieties of thistles. In the level, open, tree-free sections of bogs will be found sedge grass, shrubby Saint-John's-wort, and leatherleaf. On banks sloping up from the bogs, look for polygala (gaywings), which bloom deep pink in early spring. Also found on slopes and in nearby woods are lesser pyrola and round-leaved pyrola (shinleaf). Pyrola leaves contain a drug related to aspirin and have been used on bruises and wounds to relieve pain. Such a leaf dressing is called shinplaster, hence the common name. Look for polygala in early spring; the rest of the plants discussed here bloom in early summer.

FLORA FOUND IN HIGHER, DRIER AREAS

In higher, drier areas, on glacial moraines and in woods and clearings, numerous flowering plants and shrubs exist, including bindweed, a relative of the morning glory and sweet potato. Bindweed is a ground-hugging plant that spreads across the ground. The common white trillium blooms early in spring, generally in partially open beech forests and sometimes in very large patches. Another early bloomer, and a flower few people see, is the partridgeberry. Later in the year bright red berries form, which have a pleasant, aromatic flavor; they were eaten by Indians, and birds relish them still. Early in the growing season large numbers of starflowers, a low-growing plant with a distinctive white blossom, are scattered throughout the woods. Later, in the deep woods, princes' pine (pipsissewa) and wild lily of the valley bloom. Growing in very poor soil, sometimes right in the bare sand roads, are bird-foot violets. One of the earliest spring flowers is trailing arbutus, which blooms white or pale pink or sometimes deep pink. The arbutus has tough, wiry, trailing stems and leathery leaves but a delightful fragrance. Members of the orchid family found away from the bogs in early and midsummer include pink lady's slipper [moccasin flower], which generally grows in patches, and yellow lady's slipper. Purple fringed orchids grow along streams. A very low growing but spectacular variety is the rams head lady's slipper, a quite rare orchid that sometimes has a habit of growing under a concealing bush. The slender ladies' tresses grows a flowering spike with an exaggerated spiral.

During the height of summer, many flowers are visible. A partial list includes daisies, spotted star thistle, and fireweed, which springs up mainly in burned-over land and puts out a tall spike of pink flowers. In open areas, orange hawkweed, one of the many plants introduced from Europe, now grows wild here. At this time of year, one generally sees the intense blue berries of the yellow bead lily (clintonia); the fruiting body is blue, but the blossom is yellow and blooms early in spring. Here and there, in open fields is the harebell, a low-growing, single-stem plant with a single blue bell hanging down. It seems as though the slightest wind will blow this delicate flower away, but it survives quite well in its environment.

Later in summer and early fall other plants bloom, mostly in open areas. These include several members of the aster family, ironweed, rattlesnake weed, and mullein and boneset, both of which were used extensively by Indians and early settlers to make medicinal teas and infusions and other panaceas. A brilliant, cardinal red flower growing on a sometimes tall spike is a cardinal flower. It is often confused with the Indian paintbrush but is a more brilliant color. Wintergreen has bright red berries by late summer, the final stage of waxy, white blossoms that appeared earlier. It is a low-growing plant with tough, perennial leaves, and the berries are delicious. It is also known as teaberry, and an extract made from it is used to flavor teas, candies, medicines, and chewing gum. The ripe berries are good in muffins.

NONFLOWERING PLANTS

Nonflowering plants such as mushrooms, lichens, and mosses are legion! Morels grow in black and white varieties, and many people wander through the Pigeon River Country searching for them, mainly in beech woods. The "Bibliographic Notes" lists a few books on fungi found in the area. It is wise to consult a person thoroughly knowledgeable on the subject. Many mushrooms are poisonous and others inedible.

Among other nonflowering plants growing in the area, certain interesting ones are British soldiers (or red crest lichen) found on dead stumps and logs. Red caps topping the plant are unmistakable. There are various creeping club mosses (ground pine), which send out runners for long distances. Ground pines were once in great demand for floral arrangements and wreaths, but this practice is now forbidden by state law. To spot pixie cups, you must look closely for upright trumpetlike tubes extending from the base. Of various ferns, the common bracken grows almost everywhere and forms a dense cover on the forest floor. Early in spring, fiddleheads (new sprouts) make an acceptable substitute for asparagus but are inedible after the leaf itself starts to form. Lastly, if you see a clump of ghostly white plants growing five to six inches high, chances are they are Indian pipe. They are inedible but interesting to examine.

Look along running streams in spring for cowslip, with its brilliant globe-shaped yellow flowers, and in clear, running streams for watercress. To view water lilies, good locations are near the Round Lake Campground and Grass Lake.

EDIBLE FRUITS AND NUTS

Many edible fruits, nuts, and berries grow in the Pigeon River Country. Outstanding in this regard is the blueberry, both the variety that ripens in midsummer and the highbush blueberry, which ripens slightly later. Many large patches of this delightful and delicious fruit can be found in burned-over and cleared areas. This is also true of the huckleberry, a very dark berry that is often interspersed with the blueberry and is equally delicious. Then there are blackberries, which sometimes grow in dense stands and are a favorite food of birds, bears, and humans. There are two varieties of red raspberry, the common variety, which grows on bushes several feet high, and the dwarf, which is ground hugging and somewhat uncommon. Wild strawberries can be found in open places where there is adequate sunshine. Very common are the large shrubs, almost trees, that bear juneberries. These are also known as shadbushes or serviceberries and make delicious pies, jams, and jellies.

Many beech trees grow in drier areas of the forest. These are notable for their steely-gray bark, large size, dense wood, and the fact they bear a triangular-shaped nut encased in a spiky husk that opens after a frost in late fall. The nuts are delicious if you can beat the squirrels and chipmunks to them. Beaked hazelnuts grow on tall bushes, sometimes in pure stands. These are a small variety of filbert. Witch hazel is sometimes confused with hazelnut, as the bushes look similar. The small, hard, fruiting body is inedible for humans but a favorite of grosbeaks. In late fall or early winter, a spectacular wavy, filamentlike, yellow blossom appears, one of the last flowers to bloom in the year.

A WORD OF CAUTION

A field guide or similar reference is a big help in identifying flowers, mosses, ferns, trees, plants, and mushrooms. Suggested reference material is listed in the "Bibliographic Notes." A word of caution: please leave any flowers and plants you find so that others may enjoy them. And do not mutilate birch trees by stripping off bark. It is illegal in Michigan to disturb or gather any of the following endangered plants.

all orchids
all trilliums
all gentians

The state in 2006 listed 76 natural plants in trouble throughout Michigan.

About 50 species of orchid grow in Michigan in various habitats. In most cases, the seeds are so dustlike as to be almost microscopic. Many species have an extremely long germination period. Some lady's slipper varieties take seven to 14 years to pass from seed to full growth. Some have the ability to remain underground for many years, waiting for just the right conditions of temperature and moisture to grow and blossom.

Trailing arbutus grows in white pine stands, which are much less common than they were in the virgin forest. It is practically impossible to transplant arbutus from the wild to the home garden. Henry Ford spent thousands of dollars years ago trying to do this on his estate in Dearborn, without success.

TREES

North on Fisherman's Trail, near its intersection with Webb Road in the northwest corner of Pigeon River Country, can be found some very tall specimens of red (Norway) pine and eastern white pine of similar size to what the first Europeans saw. In swampy areas are northern white cedar and in the cooler, boggy areas the eastern hemlock. Larch (tamarack), which sometimes grows in large stands in the area, is unique in the United States, together with the southern cypress (which does not grow this far north). The larch bears cones and has needles, but in the fall the needles turn golden yellow and drop off, leaving the branches bare all winter. In the spring, delicate new needles grow again. Where clear-cutting of timber has occurred, dense stands of aspen (popple) spring up.

The tree with the ghostly white, papery bark is the silver, or white, birch. Yellow birch has similar paperlike bark of a yellowish color. Both of these trees were useful to Indians and early explorers in constructing canoes from bark. Cooking vessels were also made from the bark. Hot rocks were dropped into the vessel to bring contents to a boil. Many other containers were made from birchbark.

American elm, found in the area, was likewise a valuable tree to Indians, who used the bark for canoes and wigwam coverings. Spruce, found in damp areas, has a long tapered shape. The fine rootlets were gathered and stripped of the enclosing bark and the tough strands used to bind birch or elm bark for canoes or wigwams. In addition, a gum from the tree was used to waterproof canoe seams.

White ash, a tree with tough wood and small, springy branches, is generally scattered and does not occur in dense stands. Indians used the flexible small branches as a framework on which to construct dome-shaped dwellings. The wood was also used to construct bows. American basswood is present, but, like the white ash, it is not found in clumps. Indians carved the soft wood into containers and made dugout canoes from single logs.

Scattered through the forest is black cherry, a tree sought out by birds when the fruit is ripe. This tree can attain large size, unlike chokecherry and pin cherry, which are large bushes or small trees. Several varieties of maples can be found, sometimes in large stands. Sugar or hard maple produces a sap in early spring that can be boiled down to produce maple syrup. Indians introduced this delicacy to the early settlers. Indians also boiled the sap down further to make sugar. At one time, wood from red maples was extensively used to produce wooden forms (lasts) for the shoe industry, as well as bowling pins.

The Pigeon River Country has a great variety of trees. On the high, well-drained ground, a mixed conifer-hardwood forest exists, while in the wetter areas conifers such as spruce, tamarack, and cedars prevail. In well-drained areas, several varieties of oaks can be seen, notably the bur oak, white oak, and northern red oak. Acorns from these oaks were extensively gathered by the Indians for food. They shelled the acorns, crushed the meat with stones, and washed the pulp in several changes of water to remove the bitter tannin. The meal was dried for further use to be formed into cakes and baked.

An abbreviated guide to some Pigeon River Country plants.

Marsh cinquefoil, *Potentilla palustris,* purple flower, bog edges
Purple fringed orchid, *Habernaria grandiflora,* along streams
Flat-leaved bladderwort, *Utricularia intermedia,* underwater in bogs, with a bright yellow flower above the surface
Round-leaved sundew, *Drosera rotundifolia,* ground hugging, with a rosette of red leaves and a small white or pink flower on a tall stem

Fringed gentian, *Gentiana crinita,* blue flower, sometimes along roads

Marsh Saint-John's-wort, *Hypericum virginicum,* pink blossoms, in bogs

Polygala, *Polygala paucifolia,* (gaywing), resembles an orchid, grows along bog edges and damp spots in woods, blossoms a deep pink

Partridgeberry, *Mitchella repens,* white fuzzy flower in spring, red berry in fall, a low-growing plant in dry areas

Twinflower, *Linnea borealis,* small creeping plant with two bell-shaped pink flowers on a single stem, in dry areas

Hairy honeysuckle, *Lonicera hirsuta,* top leaves united opposite on stem, flowers orange-yellow later turning to bright red berries resting in top leaves as in a nest

Grass-of-Parnassus, *Parnassia asarifolia,* in dry areas, white flower striped with green on stem about eight inches high, not a grass

Nine-bark, *Physocarpus opulifolius,* tall bush growing along streams, bark shreds off older stems, white flowers in a rounded cluster

Staghorn sumac, *Rhus typhina,* in open, in dense stands, large erect shrub with dark red fruiting body at end of stem, fruit separated from woody stem makes a good pink lemonade when soaked in water

Poison ivy, *Rhus toxico dendron,* can grow almost anywhere, poisonous to touch at any time of year, has three leaflets, two joined at base and the third extended slightly on a short stem, dark green shiny leaves

Four-leaved milkweed, *Asclepias quadrifolia,* up to two feet high in woods, erect stem topped with pink, lavender or white flowers arranged in a crown

Cranberry blossoms, *Vaccinium oxycoccus,* grows on sphagnum moss hummocks in bogs with small white blossoms in spring

Humans are capable of widespread destruction. Some plant species could be wiped out quickly. Draining a swamp or bog can eliminate sensitive flora. Forest fires can cause extensive change. Even bogs are not immune to fire. A few years ago in Michigan's Upper Peninsula, crews from all over the United States were brought in to extinguish fire in a large bog. They were kept on the job for months, and it was only with the coming of heavy snowfall that the smoldering fire was finally extinguished.

While it may appear to a hiker that vegetation trampled down soon resurrects itself and towering trees are indestructible, such is not the case. Where people have disregarded established trails, human compaction has obliterated vegetation. Giant sequoias in California have died as the result of compaction of soil around their bases, which chokes off the root system—simply the result of people tramping around their bases.

Let us hope the Pigeon River Country and other areas with wilderness values will be preserved so our children can enjoy the plants, some of which are relics of the Ice Age.

Gene Ochsner proposed three locations in the Pigeon be designated as natural areas under a state law that would allow them to be managed specifically for their special qualities rather than as potential timber resources. His 1987 proposal reached the state level during the Engler administration, when the governor systematically left vacancies on boards unfilled, including the board that recommends natural areas to the legislature. The process remains disabled. Joe Jarecki says no activities are allowed in the areas that might compromise the nomination, but neither can a management plan be implemented to enhance their special qualities. The sites are 220 acres at Pigeon River Pines with nearly half dominated by century-old white pines; 160 acres of large northern hardwoods at Grindstone Creek; and 680 acres of remote wilderness at Dog Lake. They remain formally unprotected from habitat disruptions just outside the forest or access by people inside it.

Gene and Priscilla in the early 1990s pressed through the advisory council for a statewide study of nongame flora and fauna, but game continued to get the major share of attention. Optimists expect a new ecological approach in forest management to give nongame wildlife closer consideration and give more systematic attention to unusual habitats such as orchid sites. The state enacted a law in 1992 expressing the goal "to encourage the lasting conservation of biological diversity," but the legislature never prepared a required strategy for implementation. One outside study concluded Michigan has no coordinated assessment system for biodiversity and "few agencies cooperate to improve land management across ownership boundaries." The DNR finally began biodiversity conservation planning in 2005 through a committee that included Brian Mastenbrook.

Since before history, the Muska koo, or Swampy Cree, an Algonquin Indian people, has inhabited the north-woods subarctic regions, where moist, coniferous forests, swamps and lakes, and cold winters abound. Howard A. Norman gathered and translated some of their poems in a book, *The Wishing Bone Cycle*. They are like voices echoing from the long past.

All the warm nights
sleep in moonlight

keep letting it
go into you

do this
all your life

do this
you will shine outward
in old age

the moon will think
you are
the moon

Presence

Over the years since we first published *The Pigeon River Country,* a fundamental question has persisted: What draws us to places like this forest, where the outdoors itself predominates, extends far beyond an easy walk, contains plants and animals in their natural settings, woodlands, meadows, and streams? The usual answers—that it's pretty, quiet, and restful—seem superficial and are not entirely accurate. Sometimes the outdoors is none of those things: severe storms can bare ugly teeth, putting dirt and debris in our eyes, toppling branches and trees down upon us, crashing bolts of electricity deep into our psyche if not our person. Blizzards can immobilize and kill. Blackflies and crawling insects can drive us to distraction. Can we look at the forest honestly and still find what attracts us?

All of the mammals alive when our first edition was published in 1985 are long dead, with the possible exception of a few black bear. *Ursus americanus,* the only bear species in Michigan, lives five to 30 years in the wild, elk not more than 15 to 20 years in ideal conditions, bobcats 10 to 15, white-tailed deer, coyotes, fox, and muskrat five to 10 years. Some raccoons, badgers, mink, long-tailed weasels, and porcupines get as old as 10; martens, beavers, and bats as old as 15; and northern river otter as old as 20. But most mammals in the Pigeon River Country and elsewhere die much sooner: woodchucks, squirrels, chipmunks, bog lemmings, shrews, voles, moles, and mice all in a year or two.

Some say the basic message of nature is indifference, conflict, hostility, and death. While deer, elk, porcupines, rabbits, hares, muskrat, woodchucks, beaver, and voles are vegetarians, most mammals consume other mammals; the half-ounce least weasel eats mice, small birds, moles, and voles. Yet we know from personal experience that in returning to the forest, or any place outdoors where our own civilization is hardly in evidence, there is something deeply satisfying. In leaving the Pigeon River valley myself nearly a decade ago for life in a cultural mecca, the contrast could not be clearer. Sometimes just stepping outside into a yard surrounded by trees brings a rush reminiscent of those long moments spent in the forest. There's the air, the sound. There's something else, more profound.

In the outdoors, everything is communicating. We're immersed in electromagnetic and chemical fields of information. Life operates in a delicate balance, constantly monitoring temperature, velocity, and all the elements essential to continued existence. Plants continuously interact with their surroundings. All living beings do the same as they try to remain in balance. An imbalance can cascade into a breakdown in organization, death of one form dissolving into others.

This interaction among living things draws us to the outdoors. It operates at all levels from our connection with the sun and stars to activity at the cellular level and below.

When we look closely at something outdoors, its color or shape, we shift from thinking to sensing. Our cardiac cycle slows, our eyes dilate, peripheral vision increases, and pinpoint sharpness decreases. Brain activity is embedded within the heart's wave patterns. Brain alpha waves are reduced. The hippocampus starts sorting the magnetic information coming to the heart, looking for patterns of information, finding meaning from this background of data.

Recent cardiological research is confirming that the human heart is an instrument of unmatched power in both perceiving and communicating with the world beyond the human body. The heart generates electromagnetic energy in a wide range of frequencies. It makes hormones and sends them into a stream of messages throughout the body. The heart physically affects how we feel and how we think. Fluctuating fields of information coming in contact with us are the very source of "the deep feelings that come from our immersion in wild landscapes," according to Stephen Harrod Buhner, who studies the living earth.

The plants we're standing near use the same hormones we do. All organisms with two or more cells produce hormones. They help plants bend and turn, help animals survive through seasons, and no doubt do much more involving emotions, which are the hormones' specialty. We are not divorced from these beings; we are a collection of many of them, sharing packages of codes for burning oxygen, extracting nutrients, sensing, and feeling.

We can get in our cars and drive alone to the forest. But when we get there we have brought all manner of beings with us.

Bacteria are not only our fellow beings, they are the fellows who make up human beings. A recent estimate is that 90 percent of our cells are composed of bacteria. If we bend and pick up a thimbleful of unpolluted soil, we likely hold 99.9 percent of the million known species of bacteria. Our cousins.

And here the author speculates, for I believe there are connections among the life forms that populate us and those outside our skin. Those connections, I believe, account for the deep relationship we feel with the outdoors, where life interacts most freely. A few scientists courageous enough to work outside the mainstream are exploring these connections, and we will surely know more about them from a scientific perspective some day. Genomes are passed around intact among species, meaning that we are similar at many levels. And bacteria are as much a part of the Pigeon River Country as are the elk.

Although they pervade the forest and everywhere else on earth, bacteria have operated with us knowing hardly anything about their activities until the last few years. They gather into bands to hunt prey and into massive numbers to fend off enemies, volunteer to die on behalf of the greater community, and exchange messages among themselves and even among different colonies. In short, bacteria, too small for us to see, carry out social activities previously thought to be solely human. They conduct courtship and mating, using the same pheromones we do. Any two can get together and transfer genes, creating new combinations. According to the new view of symbiosis, that's how larger organisms evolved. It's evolution driven by partnerships rather than the genetic typographical errors we have heard so much about.

It's not all rosy. Members of the bacteria kingdom are still mostly known for those few among them that do not fit well with other life such as the *Mycobacterium tuberculosis*. Tubercle bacillus, or tuberculosis (TB), infects about one in every three people worldwide. It kills some two million people a year, getting into the hollow cavities one-tenth of a millimeter across in the lungs where gas is exchanged with blood. It does its worst damage in the lungs. Tuberculosis is believed to have begun in domesticated cattle.

Bovine TB infected Michigan's deer for apparently brief periods in the early to mid–twentieth century as free-ranging cattle mixed with deer. The bacteria can stay alive for months on hay. In the 1940s on private land, citizens put out truckloads of corn, sugar beets, carrots, apples, and other feed to help increase the deer population and provide hunting opportunities over the bait pile. In the late 1990s, TB was emerging again in deer, and by 2001 it began to appear in a few elk who had died for other reasons. Elk carcasses are routinely tested. Then TB disappeared from the Pigeon River Country in 2005.

There is competition and conflict for habitat, as well as cooperation, among beings attempting to use resources for their own ends. There is also impact from those of us who seek to do no particular harm. The Pigeon River Country has been increasingly pressured by popularity. That gives us even more incentive to recognize features large and small that this forest shares with others closer to where we live and also shares sometimes with the outdoors in our neighborhoods—places we can visit and appreciate, thereby easing those pressures.

In a forest on a warm day, we may think nothing is happening except, perhaps, the flights of a few butterflies. If we lift a rock, small creatures begin to scurry. Entomologist Edward O. Wilson goes no more than a few hundred feet into a forest before taking in the world beneath some log: soil scent, a wolf spider carrying a white silken egg, millipedes coiling in defense, a centipede glistening in brown armor, what he calls the giants. At one-tenth that size are thousands of animals he looks at on a white ground cloth. In microscopic films of water are 10 billion bacteria in every thimbleful of soil and plant matter. It's a world where millions of organisms are dying bloodlessly every second, taken apart by other organisms and assimilated every second into millions of new organisms.

These are characteristics of the forest every bit as much as, say, a Witness Tree. And they are by some measure more engaging. When we stand by the Witness Tree, we surely feel an odd sensation knowing that a surveyor looked at this same live being before we had constructed a single house anywhere nearby, built a road, invented cars or electric lights, or were ourselves even born. A wonder of survival, still alive and growing.

If we think about it, we surely feel even more complex sensations just standing among life forms that are changing around us, reorganizing all those creatures who eventually sink to the forest floor expended. We can see blackbirds from time to time starting to recycle some unfortunate mammal who came to a quick end along a road. The greater share of such activity takes place unobserved by us, conducted by life forms beyond our vision, perhaps beyond our imagination, but not really beyond our natural capacities to absorb information about what's happening simply by standing there in the outdoors.

The outdoors is a presence, a now that never ends.

Arch Reeves says it's not hard to move in remote swamps on snowshoes, ducking under low branches, climbing over logs, if we know what we find will be pleasurable. "The woods is never the same," he says. "A person's system has to feel that today is different—the weather, the wind. I go where other people aren't. Some place may be beautiful, but if I go and there's a crowd it's not special. I'm more of a solitary person."

Books about the outdoors abound but cannot really provide what the forest itself gives us. While books, poetry, the arts, can be part of the journey, being outdoors ourselves is essential, with its myriad paths as varied as the experience of creatures living in it.

We can find solace, frustration, disappointment, or bewilderment in stories about the forest. But they are like maps: the experience itself does not come from the map. And it's good to keep in mind, perhaps while watching clouds roiling through a blue sky beyond spruce tops, that accounts of a Pigeon River controversy can drift away from the forest itself—as surely as philosophical musings might—into stories about society, politics, people, human events.

There seem to be some conclusions about the outdoors: that it is indifferent to outcomes, that it continues amid rapid or slow change, that it ranges from inviting to deadly. But even these are words within a context narrower than the outdoors itself. We tend to see things around us through such constructions. One profound benefit of the outdoors experience is that the constructions can fall away and the experience continues. We can stop thinking about it yet be effected deeply. Literature, particularly poetry, explores such effects. It approaches profound matters slyly, playfully, rhythmically, and can shock, dislodge, and inform us in ways that ordinary communication does not. Modern works, in particular, reflect not so much the harmony of nature as other, troubling things.

Canadian poet and novelist Margaret Atwood says, "You aren't and can't be apart from nature. . . . [I]t's a potential source of power and vision—partly because the alternative is to lock yourself away or become a machine." And this crucial observation: "Perhaps because of my earlier scientific background, I like things that can't ever be quite pinned down."

For Atwood, who spent much of her early life in the bush learning informally from her entomologist father, the "North is . . . the place where you go to find something out. It's the place of the unconscious."

Mary Oliver's "Snowy Night":

> Last night, an owl
> in the blue dark
> tossed
> an indeterminate number

of carefully shaped sounds into
the world, in which,
a quarter of a mile away, I happened
to be standing.

I couldn't tell
which one it was—
the barred or the great-horned
ship of the air—

it was that distant. But, anyway,
aren't there moments
that are better than knowing something,
and sweeter? Snow was falling,

so much like stars
filling the dark trees
that one could easily imagine
its reason for being was nothing more

than prettiness. I suppose
if this were someone else's story
they would have insisted on knowing
whatever is knowable—would have hurried

over the fields
to name it—the owl, I mean.
But it's mine, this poem of the night,
and I just stood there, listening and holding out

my hands to the soft glitter
falling through the air. I love this world,
but not for its answers.
And I wish good luck to the owl,

whatever its name—
and I wish great welcome to the snow,
whatever its severe and comfortless
and beautiful meaning.

Theodore Roethke grew up a little over a hundred miles south of the
Pigeon River Country. His childhood experience in the fields and woods
outside Saginaw, along with his careful observations of his father's large

greenhouse operation there, increasingly became his subjects. Other memories seemed to have no meaning for him. Roethke's uncle and father owned a woods and swamp out Gratiot Avenue, described by the poet as "a wild area of cut-over second-growth timber, which my father and uncle had made into a small game preserve." In his poem "The Premonition," Roethke recalls the image of his father's face disappearing "in a maze of water" as his father rises up after dipping his hand in a stream. The natural image contains an ambiguity, an abstraction, giving the listener a hint of the expansiveness of rivers.

Roethke constructs a poem, "The Lost Son," out of memories of his father's death and the tangibles of the outdoors: snail, rat, rickety bridge, spongy ground, "a slow drip over stones," bog holes, spider, otter, eel, cat, moss. His biographer, Allan Seager, says "merely beautiful scenery did not inspire" Roethke. He found the source of poetry to be his wonder at the life of the natural world. "Poetry is written for the whole man," Roethke said. He found his images in his Michigan childhood, and only in his last book of poetry did he introduce natural images from the West Coast.

"I grew up in Michigan and have fished your country there," he wrote to Ernest Hemingway. On a path to the Black River, bracken and softer ferns mingle with blueberries and raspberry bushes among the grasses. In "I'm Here," Roethke tells of flower crowns brushing against him as he runs through high grass, trailing his finger in a stream, and his body rocking "in and out of itself" as it delighted "in thresholds."

Hemingway wrestled with the deep problem of loss in similarly tangible language about nature. His work continues to generate analysis and reflection even while the popular image of him as a macho man continues to fade. One critic, Susan F. Beegel, drew attention recently to Hemingway's rigorous and extensive study of nature while he was a boy. Beegel says his writing style and content were more heavily influenced by his time spent at the streams and in the woods of Michigan than is commonly recognized. He was taught in school and his father's nature club to describe the natural world "with a scientist's unwavering gaze, respect for truth, interest in detail, and objective language."

His mother said Ernest, when he was 19 months old, could give the names of 40 birds on seeing their pictures, including plover, kingfisher, chickadee, woodpecker, and hawk. At five, he peered for hours through a microscope at rocks and insects. The emphasis of his training was go to nature and observe; don't study texts—study nature itself.

Despite his clarity of language in describing the specifics of nature, the deep issues at the heart of his writing remain as complex and unresolved as nature itself. Beegel reports that popular views of evolution as meaning simply "kill or be killed" influenced Hemingway's understanding of nature's brutality. It was only later that people generally became aware of other principles in the success of species such as interdependence and cooperation. Theodore Roosevelt, president when Hemingway was a boy, introduced the idea of "renewable organic resources" that could be perpetuated through "wise use." But the popular view for many years afterward was that some creatures, such as game animals and songbirds, were "good" while others, especially big predators and scavengers, were "evil." Finally, science itself in Hemingway's day concentrated on examining creatures who were dead, a tradition that is only now beginning to change with the development of high-resolution binoculars, video and audio equipment, sophisticated cameras, mass spectrometers, and the pioneering efforts of a growing number of naturalists who try to observe without disturbing the lives they are studying.

Hemingway envisioned his literary work as an iceberg with one-eighth above water. Beneath the surface, Carlos Baker said, were "symbols operating everywhere." In "Big Two-Hearted River" they included the ritual of moral conduct—in hiking through difficult terrain, making a camp in the face of darkness, and fishing in accordance with standards of fairness. Even deeper, the symbols included two sinister atmospheres, one in the burned soil as the protagonist starts his journey, the other beyond his pine grove destination in a dark swamp where the fishing would have been "tragic." Hemingway's art was to explore the relationship between "what I see and what I feel." What nature made him feel is a rich field to visit in his fiction but too elusive to summarize. In fact, his view was that discourse could break and even falsify the fragile connection with nature. The rituals, the connections, even the silences help convey what he wanted to say.

Written words do not come close to the actual experience of a cumulus cloud rising against a clear, deep sky. Their power is in evoking memory. An advantage words seem to have over experience is that they can provide a context, a vision, a viewpoint in which elements seem related, to have meaning. Although, science is finding that humans, indeed all life forms, have greater capacities than are recognized in our modern world to extract meaning from direct perception.

When we stand on a crisp morning noticing dew sparkling at the tip of pine needles, we are not the only ones aware. When the doe, stock still, stares intently at us before bounding off, she's not alone in her awareness.

This awareness of our surroundings is something we share with all life, down to the cell. What it feels like is another matter.

We have assumed that only complex life forms like ourselves feel the rush of sensation in a forest the way we do. I believe evidence is accumulating that awareness is quite basic and more similar in all other life than we might imagine, surely not identical, but similar. We humans can speculate about the experience in ways not available to other categories of life, but the sensation itself is not so easily dismissed as ours alone. We don't really understand life around us very well. It can be instructive to assume, even if just for the sake of a good argument, that the grasses we're standing on, the insects moving through them, the mammals keeping their distance, all operate with the same basic bacterial machinery we do to provide the sensation of the morning around us, enriched for us by our range of senses and enriched in other ways for others by theirs.

Just this possibility behooves us to give wholehearted support to approaches that consider all life in the forest—ecology—not just economy or convenience or favorites.

Arch Reeves bought one of the first snowmobiles made and found it was destroying the area. He put a bobcat up a tree in an hour and hadn't even gotten his exercise yet. He gave it away and put on snowshoes. He estimates that if he was blindfolded and helicoptered to any remote place in the Pigeon River Country, any swamp, he could orient himself within 15 minutes. "It does not seem big. It is not that big. It is to a lot of people."

Asked if there are any people learning the Pigeon the way he and Doug Mummert learned it, by spending so much time walking around in it, Arch Reeves said, "If there are, they're keeping quiet about it, the way I did."

Bibliographic Notes

A listing of sources used in making this book, further thoughts, and some recommendations for additional study.

PREFACE

http://dalefranz.org will post updates about hydrocarbon pressures on the forest.

Kenneth Glasser, interview with the author, August 21, 2007. Oil and gas details from Peter Gustafson, interview with the author, August 22, 2007.

The Pigeon River Country Association has created a 21 × 22 inch folding map of the area for printing in late 2007 with main roads and forest two-track trails on one side and High Country Pathway text descriptions on the other. It is available for purchase at http://www.pigeonrivercountryforest.org/. The state of Michigan at http://www.dnr .state.mi.us/spatialdatalibrary/PDF_Maps/Management_Areas/Pigeon_River.pdf offers an online map showing wells, mineral rights ownership, political boundaries, and geographic features with zoom tool available.

Joe Jarecki is quoted from the Pigeon River Country Advisory Council minutes of June 23, 1995.

INTRODUCTION

Lower Michigan terrain: In part from Michigan Department of State Highways and Transportation and Michigan DNR, "Milepost Interstate 75, the Michigan Bicentennial Highway."

Transcript of Joseph Sax's talk provided by Sandra M. Franz to the Pigeon River Country Association.

Pathway information in part from Jerry Grieve, "One of Michigan's Best Kept Secrets," *Natural Resources Register* (Lansing: DNR, 1984).

Michigan law requires ORV routes to be posted with orange signs. Cheboygan and Montmorency counties allow ORVs on their county roads under certain circumstances;

Otsego County does not allow ORVs on county roads in the forest. They are permitted on the Michigan Cross Country Cycle Trail, which crosses the northeast corner of the Pigeon River Country.

Snowmobiles are allowed on all county roads in the forest. Various sources, including Joe Jarecki, interview with the author, August 31, 2006.

Chief Pokagon: Article in *The Chatauquan,* November 1895, quoted in W. B. Mershon, *The Passenger Pigeon* (New York, Outing Publishing, 1907), out-of-print copies provided by Edward Caveney Jr. and William Granlund. Also available at the Bentley Historical Library, University of Michigan.

Passenger pigeon history: Based primarily on A. W. Schorger, *The Passenger Pigeon: Its Natural History and Extinction* (Madison: Regents of the University of Wisconsin, 1955; rpt, Norman: University of Oklahoma Press, 1973); and Mershon, *The Passenger Pigeon.*

John James Audubon quotations describing visit to Green River roost abridged from Mershon, as taken from Audubon's *Ornithological Biography.*

One million and one billion seconds calculated by Terence Dickinson, *The Universe and Beyond,* 4th ed.: Revised and Expanded (Buffalo, NY: Firefly Books, 2004).

Alaskan king crab: *New York Times,* October 1983, reprinted in *Detroit Free Press,* 10 October 1983.

Lewis Perry, interview with the author, 1977.

Land added to the forest includes 549 acres of former Black River Rod and Gun Club at the foot of the Tyrolean Hills ski area east of the north end of Sawyer Road, adding 1.1 miles of Black River frontage to the forest; and 226 acres of Kronlund property on Chandler Dam Road, with more than 2,100 feet of the Black River running through it. More than 12,000 acres have been added to the Pigeon River Country with the proceeds of oil and gas royalties since drilling began. The Natural Resources (Land) Trust Fund, created from royalties through the efforts of the Michigan United Conservation Clubs in the midst of the Pigeon oil controversy, by 2006 had spent $600 million to acquire and improve public land in Michigan. It took a revision of the Concept of Management in 2007 to put the additional land, including 5,000 acres northeast of Blue Lakes and 3,000 acres near Johnson's Crossing, under overall management plans for such things as vehicle access and a ban on ORVs.

Forest use: Ned Caveney, Tenth Annual Report, 1983, Pigeon River Country State Forest; Annual Report, 1982, Pigeon River Country Study Committee, Richard J. Moran, editor. Frederick Law Olmsted is quoted in Joseph L. Sax, *Mountains Without Handrails: Reflections on the National Parks* (Ann Arbor: University of Michigan Press, 1980), a discussion of recreation pressure on natural lands.

Black, Pigeon, and Sturgeon Rivers: Some details from Janet D. Mehl, *Trout Streams of Michigan,* vol. 2 (Lansing: Michigan United Conservation Clubs, 1983); "Pigeon River Natural River Plan," June 1982, Division of Land Resources Programs, DNR; and David Smethurst interview with the author.

NORTH WOODS

"Way of Life," chapter 43 of Lao Tsu, *Tao Te Ching,* translated by Gia-fu Feng and Jane English (New York: Vintage, 1972).

Some material on glaciers is from Farley Mowat, *The Snow Walker* (New York: Bantam, 1977); and John McPhee, *In Suspect Terrain* (New York, Farrar Straus Giroux, 1983).

Michael Delp, unpublished poem, courtesy of the author.

Glacial, forest, and weather information is in part from Glenda Daniel and Jerry Sullivan, *A Sierra Club Naturalist's Guide to the North Woods of Michigan, Wisconsin, and Minnesota* (San Francisco, Sierra Club Books, 1981); James E. Fitting, *Archaeology of Michigan* (Bloomfield Hills, MI: Cranbrook Institute of Science, 1975); Vincent J. Schaefer and John A. Day, *A Field Guide to the Atmosphere* (Boston: Houghton Mifflin, 1981); S. Dunlop and F. Wilson, *The Larousse Guide to Weather Forecasting* (New York: Larousse, 1982); Alan Fry, *Wilderness Survival Handbook* (New York: St. Martin's, 1981); Peter Farb, *The Forest* (New York: Time, 1961); *Encyclopaedia Britannica* (Chicago: William Benton, 1966); and Robert S. Wood, *The 2 Oz. Backpacker* (Berkeley: Ten Speed, 1982).

Wetlands nationwide: U.S. Fish and Wildlife Service 2005 report, http://wetlandsfws.er.usgs.gov/status_trends/national_reports/trends_2005_report.pdf.

FORAYS

Chief Blackbird is quoted from Chief Mack-E-Te-Be-Nessy, *History of the Ottawa and Chippewa Indians of Michigan* (Ypsilanti: Ypsilantian Job Printing House, 1887; reprint, Petoskey: Little Traverse Regional Historical Society).

Indian history: G. I. Quimby, *Indian Life in the Upper Great Lakes, 11,000 B.C. to A.D. 1800* (Chicago: University of Chicago Press, 1960); W. B. Hinsdale, "Indian Modes and Paths of Travel," Papers of Michigan Association of Science and Letters, 1926; Dwight Goss, "The Indians of Grand River Valley," in *Michigan Pioneer and Historical Collections* (Hinsdale: MASAL, 1926), 30:172; Fitting, *Archaeology of Michigan;* Ronald J. Mason, *Great Lakes Archaeology* (New York: Academic Press, 1981); G. I. Quimby, *Indian Culture and European Trade Goods,* (Madison: University of Wisconsin Press, 1966); conversation with William Lovis, 1982; conversation with John O'Shea, 1982; Joseph Epes Brown, *The Spiritual Legacy of the American Indian* (New York: Crossroads, 1982); Jamake Highwater, *The Primal Mind: Vision and Reality in Indian America* (New York: New American Library, 1982).

Chamberlain is quoted from *Michigan Pioneer and Historical Collections,* reprinted in *Historic Michigan,* edited by G. N. Fuller, vol. 1 (Lansing: National Historical Association, 1924).

Ward is quoted from *The Autobiography of David Ward* (New York: Privately printed by Frederic Fairchild Sherman, 1912), from the library of William Granlund.

Road survey of 1839 is quoted in Fuller, *Historic Michigan.* Mrs. Jameson's mosquito story is from Anna Jameson, *Winter Studies and Summer Rambles,* quoted in Walter Havighurst, *Great Lakes Reader* (New York: Collier Macmillan, 1966).

History of Otsego County: Many sources, including Lewis Perry, interview with the author, 1977; and various issues of *Our Home Town,* a newsletter published in Vanderbilt, 1966, 1968, 1971.

Mary Mead Smith, in 1934, wrote an early version of her recollections for the *Otsego County Herald Times,* January 14, 1926, and the Study Club, copy in the Granlund files.

Menzies: Details from *Vanderbilt Review,* January 8, 1885, reprinted December 3, 1968 in *Our Home Town,* copy in Yuill family files; Lewis A. Perry, "History of Corwith Township," 1975.

Lila Woodin Widger, "Facts Concerning Berryville as Told by Frank Woodin," copy in Granlund files.

Average loads of 75 pounds carried by settlers: "Elmira History," copy in Granlund files.

Randolph history: Dorothy Kuster article of 1931, reprinted in *Our Home Town,* June 2, 1964, copy in Yuill files.

Yuill holdings reported by Richard Yuill, 1984.

THE LOG HOUSE

Mary Winters Clapp, "The Log House: The Winters Family History," a privately distributed article, copy in Granlund files, used with the permission of the author.

Frank J. Shipp notes, Granlund files.

Pinecone story: Mrs. Elon Sumerix, *Our Yesterdays,* quoted in "Lumberjacks and Cooks," *Bay City Times,* March 9, 1978.

LUMBERING

Charles Blanchard quoted in Laura Marlatt and Beatrice Laux, "History of Otsego Lake Village," copy in Granlund files.

Clarence Cross, "Memories of Salling," copy in Granlund files.

Mrs. Goodrich: material in Granlund files.

Lumbermen details: Otsego County Historical Society, Yuill files.

Reverend Nield: Mrs. Cora Moore, paper prepared for the Women's Club of Elmira, copy in Granlund files.

Hutchins sleigh story: Shirley Glidden, "Tomorrow's Saturday," paper prepared for History 340, Central Michigan University, 1971, copy in Granlund files.

Smoke over Gaylord: *Otsego County Herald,* December 25, 1903, microfilm, Otsego Country Library.

Metz fire: James Smith, letter to Ford Kellum, 1970; R. L. Dodge, *Michigan Ghost Towns,* vol. 2 (Sterling Heights, MI: Glendon, 1971).

Bruce Catton, *Waiting for the Morning Train* (New York: Doubleday, 1972), recounts other details of lumbering in northern lower Michigan.

LOVEJOY

Several bits of Lovejoy prose have been collected by photocopy from the Michigan DNR files, particularly by Jerry Myers, Roger Conner, and M. Rupert Cutler, whose 1976 "Forestry and the Pigeon River Country Controversy," paper prepared for the Society of American Foresters, is a source for this chapter.

Other sources: P. S. Lovejoy, "Free Hunting or—," *Country Gentleman,* October 1930; Aldo Leopold, "Obituary P. S. Lovejoy," *Journal of Wildlife Management,* January 1943; various clippings compiled by Jerry Myers. "Ecological Engineering" was delivered by Lovejoy as an address March 8, 1935, and may be found in Ann Arbor: *Thirty-Sixth and Thirty-Sev-*

enth Annual Reports of The Michigan Academy of Science, Arts, and Letters, 1935, Bentley Historical Library, University of Michigan.

Dave Smethurst, George Burgoyne, and Jim McMillan quoted from advisory council minutes, March 17, 2000.

James Kates, *Planning a Wilderness: Regenerating the Great Lakes Cutover Region* (Minneapolis: University of Minnesota Press, 2001), provides a broader picture of Lovejoy's era, including popular novels and a 1923 film that made foresters heroes.

STATE FOREST

As sources, Jerry Myers lists Dr. William C. Latta, head of research, 1964, Pigeon River Research Station; Dr. Robert C. Ball, MSU professor; Dr. Frank Hooper, Institute for Fisheries Research; Dr. Rupert Cutler, MSU; Lee Eckstrom, forester; Ray Pfeifer, forester; Walter and Ona Babcock; Bertha Horsell, William D. Horsell and Janice Boyd; Ruth Gruitch, daughter of P. S. Lovejoy; Merle Pritchard for CCC history; Division of Michigan History, State Archives, Lansing; Glen Sheppard, *North Woods Call;* Gordon Charles, *Traverse City Record-Eagle;* Ken Peterson, *Flint Daily Journal;* "Best of the Boletes," MSU Cooperative Extension Bulletin E926; "May Is Morel Month in Michigan," Extension Bulletin E614; "Michigan Famous and Historic Trees," Michigan Forest Association; Arthur W. Stace, "What Are We Going to Do with 2,208,975 Acres?" DNR, 1941; "Buy Michigan Lumber, Save a Bundle," *Michigan Natural Resources Magazine,* September–October 1980 [the magazine was "privatized" in 1993 and shut down in 1999].

Kim Lentz and Arnold J. Morse, interviews with the author, September 26, 2005; Joyce Angel-Ling, interview with the author, September 27, 2005; *Gaylord Herald Times,* "Lives at Risk in the Big Wild," February 20, 1991. Laurie Marzolo talked with the author, July 8, 2007.

Ken Mudget: Advisory council minutes, 1993–96. Additional information from Joe Jarecki, 2007, and Lisa Lawrason, "In Love with the Pigeon," *Gaylord Herald Times,* July 2005, PrimeTimes section.

OIL

Ford Kellum, interviews with the author 1977, 1984; Jerry Myers, interview with the author, 1984.

Clipping file of Pigeon River Audubon Club provided by Rosemary Martek.

Editorial, "Oil vs. Wilderness? State Must Declare Wilderness the Winner . . . Now and Forever," *Gaylord Herald Times,* June 2, 1971.

Charlton 1–4 drilling: Log of Oil Well, July 15, 1970, DNR files; Niagaran reef diagram, *Oil and Gas News,* drawn by Curt Lundy, reprinted in *Gaylord Herald Times,* May 21, 1981; Arthur Beiser, *The Earth* (New York: Time, 1962); Daniel and Sullivan, *A Sierra Club Naturalist's Guide to the North Woods; Encyclopaedia Britannica;* conversation with Phil Hendges, Shell Oil Co., 1984; conversation with Andrea Sullivan, Geological Survey Division, DNR, 1984.

Petoskey hearing: *North Woods Call,* May 20, 1970; *Gaylord Herald Times,* May 20, 1970.

Other historic details: In part from *North Woods Call;* author's interviews with district and regional DNR geologists, 1977; various legal papers filed on behalf of the Pigeon River Country Association; Peter Vellenga, interview with author and Sam Titus, 1984; conversation with Linda Darnton, 1984; Dennis Holder, "Pleading for the Land: U-M Law Professor Joseph L. Sax Sees the Forest for the Trees—and Storm Clouds on the Horizon," *Detroit Free Press,* November 9, 1980; official minutes of Pigeon River Country Association and advisory council; conversation with Ned Caveney, 1984; Sax dinner talk transcript; Donald Inman, "Pigeon River: An Odyssey of Oil and Elk," *Natural Resources Register,* July 1983; letters and miscellaneous material from the files of Jerry Myers.

Brine details: In part from "Reserve Pit Capping and Soil Testing," Keck Consulting Services, June 26, 1984; Robert J. Compeau, "Staff Position Paper, Oil Well Drilling Mud Disposal," DNR, April 12, 1984; notes taken at meetings of the Pigeon River Country Advisory Council.

Ken Sikkema became a member of the advisory council in 1979 and later served six terms in the Michigan House of Representatives. He served in the Michigan Senate from 1998 to 2007, including four years as Republican Majority Leader.

Shell's 2004 estimate: Advisory Council minutes, March 4, 1994.

No further drilling by Merit: Pigeon River Country State Forest Successor Unit Operator Agreement between Merit and the DNR, August 17, 2004.

Department of Environmental Quality: After Governor John Engler split the DEQ off from the DNR in 1995, word came down from on high to field workers that the DEQ did not want to see any applicants appealing denials to headquarters in Lansing; what was wanted was some way to satisfy applicants. That meant the resource itself was pretty much taken out of consideration by default (off-the-record interviews with field workers by the author). Scientific and enforcement staff was deeply cut. With this atmosphere prevailing in those years, several retired DNR and DEQ top people, including Caveney, Inman, Tanner, and the state's retired environmental enforcement director, Capt. Bill Murphy, formed the Michigan Resource Stewards to combat official environmental transgressions. Their first president was Virginia Pierce, a former district supervisor of the Waste Management Division, DEQ, who said, "The people who have joined the Resource Stewards feel strongly that tending to Michigan's natural resources cannot be left to people who consider only the effect that a decision will have on political contributions." The stewards have worked on several issues on behalf of the Pigeon, including alerting the DNR director in 1999 that all the advisory council appointments had expired. Inman was quoted in Detroit's *Metro Times* on October 7, 1998: "People in our profession aren't usually whistle-blowers. When you work for an agency, you don't publicly speak out against it. You fight inside for changes. But we cared so much about what was happening to the department, and the significant losses we felt were occurring, we took the early out and started trying to get the information about what was really going on out to voter[s] and elected officials."

Keith Schneider, writing from Manistee County about the environment for the *New York Times,* founded the Michigan Land Use Institute in 1995 after seeing environmental degradation resulting from Antrim drilling activity. Consult http://www.mlui.org/pubs/glb/glbfa98/glb-su.fa9822.html; and Glen Sheppard, "Granholm Challenged in Bids for Pigeon, Au Sable Drilling," *North Woods Call,* July 2003, article provided by Au Sable Anglers, http://www.AuSableanglers.org/North%20Woods%20Call/Granholm%20challenged%20in%20bids%20-%20July%202003.htm. Schneider said in an interview with the author on August 14, 2006 that Engler's successor, Jennifer Granholm, turned things around, using royalty money, for example, to rescue environmentally important lands from destruction.

Rick Henderson, interview with the author, July 13, 2006. Thomas Wellman, chief of the DEQ's Mineral and Land Management Section, provided the estimate of 7,000 Niagaran wells in fall 2006 to update our first edition figure of 450 wells drilled statewide. He also provided a copy of the unit operator agreement between Merit and the DNR.

Charlton 4 contamination: advisory council meeting attended by author, September 15, 2006. Randy Sanders, Merit operations manager, said a cleanup of BTEX can be effected by pumping oxygen into the water, causing the contaminants to rise and dissolve at the surface where, as Bud Slingerlend told fellow council members, bacteria break them down.

Antrim gas: Extensive information, maps, and illustrations, somewhat dated, are available at http://www.geo.msu.edu/geo333/Oil&gas.html. Information regarding PRC: Advisory council minutes, March 16, 2001, and March 12, 2004. No new clearing was needed in 2004 since the flow line was laid in a cleared power line corridor, with the last 266 feet running through an opening north of Sturgeon Valley Road. An application for an Antrim well inside the nondevelopment area was denied the same year. Information is from advisory council minutes, March 18, 2005; and http://www.cis.state.mi.us/mpsc/gas/about1.htm.

Michigan Land Use Institute: The initiative was called the Michigan Energy Reform Coalition (MERC), http://www.mlui.org/pubs/specialreports/riversatrisk/rivrisk19.html.

Chronology provided by MLUI, http://www.mlui.org/landwater/fullarticle.asp?fileid=14076. The 1979 Great Lakes permit was issued to the Aztec Producing Company.

"Pigeon River Drilling Part of Delicate Balancing Act," *Traverse City Record-Eagle,* June 13, 2006, http://www.record-eagle.com/2006/jun/13edit.htm. Peter Gustafson, chairman of the advisory council, interview with the author, August 14, 2006.

The Pigeon River Country Association voted at its annual meeting in 2006 (Ray Hoobler, association president, interview with the author, August 2006; association minutes, June 2006). Petroleum engineers say the maximum of 10 wells is based on one well on every 80 acres in section 19 and part of section 30 in eastern Corwith Township, where the ranch is located. Schmude seemed hardly aware that it had bought into a nearly 40-year controversy. The company kept such a low profile that it did not respond to questions about the ranch proposal.

Gordon Charles, *Pigeon River Country: The Big Wild* (Grand Rapids, MI: Eerdmans, 1985), is a detailed account of the early oil controversy from the perspective of Ford Kellum, who lived in Traverse City where Charles was a reporter at the time.

Keith Schneider, "Case Study of the Pigeon River Hydrocarbon Development Plan," on the Michigan Land Use Institute Web site, http://www.mlui.org/pubs/specialreports/riversatrisk/rivrisk.html, from 1997, provides a history of the oil controversy based in part on the files of Glen Sheppard of the *North Woods Call;* it also reports later details about Antrim development. The recent focus of the MLUI has been improving basic urban infrastructure to reduce environmental impact by persuading traditional opponents to work together for positive change such as public transit and land conservation.

THE DAM

W. B. Willers, *Trout Biology* (Madison: University of Wisconsin Press, 1981).

Gaylord Alexander, interview with the author, 1984.

Cecil E. Heacox, *The Compleat Brown Trout* (New York: Winchester, 1974); *McClane's New Standard Fishing Encyclopedia,* edited by A. J. McClane, enlarged and rev. ed. (New York: Holt, Rinehart and Winston, 1974); *Encyclopaedia Britannica.*

Ned Caveney, interview with the author, 1984; conversations with Richard and Carol Armour, 1984; Steve Swan, interview with the author, 1984.

Some details are from accounts in the *Detroit Free Press* and *Gaylord Herald Times.*

Donald Inman, interview with the author, 1984.

Various annual reports and bibliographies of Pigeon River Station research supplied by W. C. Latta and Jerry Myers.

"Pigeon River Natural River Plan," DNR (undated).

G. E. Hendrickson and C. J. Doonan, "Reconnaissance of the Pigeon River, a Cold-Water River in the Northcentral Part of Michigan's Southern Peninsula," report for the U.S. Geological Survey, Washington, DC, 1970.

Letters to and from various DNR employees are from the files of Steve Swan, district fisheries biologist. Gaylord. Fish kill percentages are measured against 1979–80 averages.

Thomas F. Waters, "The 1957 Pigeon River Flood," Michigan Department of Conservation report, March 14, 1960.

Conversations with Jerry Myers.

Early dams: Darrel Fleming and Peter Murdick, interviews with the author, 1984.

Paramahansa Yogananda, *Autobiography of a Yogi,* 11th ed. (Los Angeles, Self-Realization Fellowship, 1974).

Keith Gornick, interview with author, August 9, 2007.

J. Oliver Black, interview with the author, 1984.

The DNR divisions are listed in the *Natural Resources Register,* January 1984.

T. Ray Cummins and Jack Miller, of the U.S. Geological Survey, interviews with the author, 1984. The average velocity of the Pigeon is 1.85 feet per second. The low reading was 2.07, meaning that the river level was that many feet above datum; datum is 886.25 feet above sea level. From the charts that it had been perfecting for 34 years, the USGS calculated that 40 cubic feet of water were flowing past the gauge every second at 9:00 p.m. on July 2.

DNR hearing conducted on July 9, 1984, in Gaylord.

Brown trout repopulate the Pigeon: Fred Snook, interview with the author, October 30, 2006. Ian Frazier described escaping New York to fish the Pigeon and how Fred Snook, "the first truly gifted angler I ever fished with," showed him how to probe the remote waters of the Pigeon and Sturgeon. Cartoonist Ralph Steadman sketched a bait fisherman using a worm for Frazier's "Personal History: Snook, Finding the Perfect Fish," *New Yorker,* October 30, 2006.

Court records from 46th Circuit Court, Gaylord, concluding with consent judgment of September 28, 1988. Golden Lotus was also ordered to pay $2,000 to the Michigan United Conservation Clubs.

Jim Pawloski, interview with the author, April 22, 2005.

Advisory council minutes, August 25, 1995, and September 22, 2001.

Carol Armour, interview with the author, September 23, 2005. Corporation documentation: http://www.dleg.state.mi.us/bcs_corp/dt_corp.asp?id_nbr=832012&name_entity =GOLDEN%20 LOTUS,%20INC.

The USGS data are available at http://waterdata.usgs.gov/mi/nwis/ and rainfall data at http://www.weatherunderground.com/.

HEMINGWAY

Ernest Hemingway, "Up in Michigan," "Now I Lay Me," and "Big Two-Hearted River," *The Short Stories of Ernest Hemingway* (New York: Charles Scribner's Sons, 1966); letters, *Ernest Hemingway: Selected Letters, 1917–1961* (New York: Charles Scribner's Sons, 1981); Carlos Baker, *Ernest Hemingway: A Life Story* (New York: Charles Scribner's Sons, 1969).

Copy of unpublished July 15, 1919, letter from Hemingway to Jenkins provided by Carlos Baker in a May 16, 1977, letter to the author; Hemingway wrote to Jenkins that the Black River was "all clear—no brush and fast as the deuce[,] good wading all the way. And I believe it is the best trout fishing in the states."

BERDINE YUILL

This and all other interviews in part 3, "Voices," have been abridged by the author.

LIVING AT HEADQUARTERS

Kenny Yuill, who helped Bill Horsell cook for the commissioners, was the son of Berdine Yuill.

REMOTE PLACES

Doug Mummert, interview with the author, 1976; descriptions of sections from statement given at a public hearing in Lansing on proposed well sites, 1977.

ECOLOGY

Craig Holdrege, "Skunk Cabbage (*Symplocarpus foetidus*)," Nature Institute, fall 2000, http://natureinstitute.org/pub/ic/ic4/skunkcabbage.htm.

James Lovelock, *The Revenge of Gaia: Earth's Climate Crisis and the Fate of Humanity* (New York: Basic Books, 2006); *The Ages of Gaia: A Biography of Our Living Earth* (New York: Norton, 1988).

Jonathan Amos, in "Deep Ice Tells Long Climate Story," BBC News, reported in the summer of 2006 that a 3.2 km core sample of Antarctica ice showed carbon dioxide levels substantially higher now than they have been for the last 800,000 years.

World Forestry Congress, 1997, cited in Emin Zeki Baskent and Haci Ahmet Yolasigmaz, "Exploring the Concept of a Forest Landscape Management Paradigm," 1997.

James C. McKinley Jr., "To Save Endangered Butterfly, Become a Butterfly," *New York Times,* November 8, 2005, http://www.nytimes.com/2005/11/08/science/earth/08monarch.html.

Charles Siebert, "Planet of the Retired Apes," *New York Times Magazine,* July 24, 2005.

Researchers studied eagles in northern Kazakhstan for six years by collecting and analyzing feathers that had fallen below their nests. The technique, reported in 2005, was called "a welcome breakthrough" by a Princeton professor of ecology. A coauthor of the study, who teaches genetics at Purdue University, said, "In one day, you can obtain more DNA samples than you could trapping eagles for six months to a year." See Laura Tangley, "Raptors' Fidelity Is Proved Without Ruffling Any Feathers," *New York Times,* July 26, 2005.

The pugnose shiner minnow species has shrunk to the Black River and six other Michigan watersheds from its historic presence in at least 18 and is declining over most of its range across southern Canada and the northern United States. Scientists say they know little about the pugnose shiner. It eats green algae, plant material, and cladocerans (freshwater crustaceans, including water fleas). The Hungerford's beetle, an endangered species nationally as well, was found in the Black River's east branch in 1989. It's about the size of a key on a cell phone. The Michigan Natural Features Inventory has information about threatened species at http://web4.msue.msu.edu/mnfi/pub/abstracts.cfm.

Kirk Johnson, "Sharpshooters to Thin Colorado Elk Herd Draws Critics," *New York Times,* May 28, 2006, http://www.nytimes.com/2006/05/28/us/28elk.html?_r=1&oref=slogin.

David C. Evers, ed., *Endangered and Threatened Wildlife of Michigan* (Ann Arbor: University of Michigan Press, 1994).

Anthony DePalma, "Study of Songbirds Finds High Levels of Mercury," *New York Times,* July 25, 2006, http://www.nytimes.com/2006/07/25/nyregion/25birds.html.

Northern Lake Michigan Coastal Species of Greatest Conservation Need, http://www.dnr.state.wi.us/org/land/er/cwcp/habitats/Northern_Lake_Michigan_Coastal.pdf.

J. L. Metcalfe-Smith and S. K. Staton, "Status of the Rayed Bean, *Villosa fabalis* (Bivalvia: Unionidae), in Ontario and Canada," *Canadian Field-Naturalist* 114, no 2 (2000), http://md1.csa.com/partners/viewrecord.php?requester=gs&collection=ENV&recid=5573856. See also "Rayed Bean," http://www.fws.gov/midwest/endangered/clams/rayed-bean-sa.pdf; and "Species at Risk in the Sydenham River Watershed, Draft, June 2001," http://www.sydenhamriver.on.ca/Publications/Fishes%20at%20Risk%20in%20the%20Sydenham%20River%20Watershed.pdf. Other documents, such as freshwater mussel surveys, show no evidence of the mussel in the Manistee or Au Sable, the two rivers closest to the Pigeon, Sturgeon, and Black.

Ocean floor protection: Nick Jans, "'A Beginning' for Conservation," *USA Today,* July 25,

2006, http://www.usatoday.com/news/opinion/columnist/2006-07-25-forum-conservation_x.htm.

DNR budget: Deputy Director Mike Moore, advisory council minutes, March 5, 1993. Jarecki gave us a peek at the stressful balancing act when he suggested in 1993 that the headquarters be closed to visitors because secretarial and recreational support was unavailable.

Advisory council minutes, May 20, 1994.

Habitat information for northern lower Michigan at various scales and overlays, including data from the original surveys in the 1800s: http://www.mcgi.state.mi.us/forestHabi tatTypes/NLP.asp.

The MSU natural features inventory Web site with drop-down menus, http://web4.msue .msu.edu/mnfi/.

Monica G. Turner, Robert H. Gardner, and Robert V. O'Neill, "Ecological Dynamics at Broad Scales," *BioScience* 45 (1995), supplement: Science and Biodiversity Policy, http://links.jstor.org/sici?sici=0006-3568(1995)45%3CS29%3AEDABS%3 E2.0.CO%3B2-L. A host of additional scholarly references to landscape was consulted.

Timothy L. Burger and John Kotar, *A Guide to Forest Communities and Habitat Types of Michigan* (Madison: University of Wisconsin, Department of Forest Ecology and Management, 2003).

The Red Pine Project: Draft guidelines for red pine management based on ecosystem management principles for state forestland in Michigan, prepared by the northern lower Michigan Ecoteam, Michigan DNR, 2004.

Mesic Northern Forest Community Abstract, Michigan Natural Features Inventory, Lansing, 2004. Less than 0.2 percent of the PRC is hemlock forest (172 acres). Information from the 1988 and 2003 forest cover inventory data tables, provided by Joe Jarecki.

National forests: Ned Caveney, interview with the author, September 29, 2006.

Henry Fountain, "Garlic Mustard Casts a Pall on the Forest," *New York Times,* May 2, 2006, reporting on an article in *Public Library of Science Biology.* See also www.ipm.msu.edu/gar licAbout.htm.

Brian Mastenbrook, interview with the author, September 21, 2005. Jarecki reported eight small burns in 2000 on a total of 250 acres.

Keith Kintigh, interview with author, July 29, 2005.

In mid-2002, 23 people chose early retirement from the Wildlife Division statewide. The state funded seven replacements. Of 44 employees leaving the forest, mineral, and fire management divisions, there was money to replace 12. Advisory council minutes, June 21, 2002.

In 2006, financial officials at the DNR told forest headquarters staff to stop selling the High Country Pathway brochure and poster map on behalf of the Pigeon River Country Association, citing possible "liability" for handling the money. The sales were a chief source of money donated by the association to hire an intern to work in the forest each summer. In any case, Joe Jarecki disclosed that his cancer treatments would prevent him from giving an intern the attention needed and suggested that the association instead donate to other forest work. The association then created a new forest area map with accurate Geographic Information System (GIS) measurements of pathways to replace the booklet but prepared to resume the intern program.

Doug Mummert interview with the author, April 21, 2005. In 2007, the Michigan Resource Stewards essentially agreed with Mummert's assessment, reporting that overuse and misuse have become rampant, citing, for example, large guided horse groups as commercial activities that violate the 1973 Concept of Management: *North Woods Call*, "'Big Wild' gets sidelined," March 28, 2007.

The seven-county baiting ban started in 2002 and was to last five years, designed primarily to reduce TB. Lack of compliance remained a problem. Natural Resources Commission minutes, March 9, 2006.

The ash quarantine area map was posted at http://michigan.gov/documents/ MDA_2004-12-13_forest_township_111785_7.pdf#search=%22cheboygan%20 quarantine%22.

William J. Broad, "With a Push from the U.N., Water Reveals Its Secrets," *New York Times*, July 26, 2005. One scientist suggests isotope hydrology can at least give us rapid information about water moving at depths.

Great Lakes and Midwest Climate Change, Wildlife, and Wildlands Case Study, U.S. Environmental Protection Agency. http://yosemite.epa.gov/oar/globalwarming.nsf/ UniqueKeyLookup/SHSU5BPQ23/$File/CS_glum.pdf.

Bill Rockwell, planning section leader, Forest Management Division, Lansing, reported in Advisory council minutes, December 3, 1993.

Dan Sikarski was hired by the Habitat Initiative to help landowners improve wildlife habitat on their properties through voluntary arrangements. The Pigeon River Habitat Initiative is supported by the DNR and a dozen other groups, including the U.S. Fish and Wildlife Service and the Rocky Mountain Elk Foundation. Information was being handled through Huron Pines Resource Conservation and Development, www.huron pines.org. Lisha Ramsdell, Huron Pines watershed project manager, interview with the author, 2006.

Mammoths: "Timeline Says Climate Is Culprit," *New York Times*, May 16, 2006, http://www.nytimes.com/2006/05/16/science/16observ.html.

Many assist forests through organized groups. Jarecki reported in 2001 that the DNR had appointed a committee to help develop criteria for an old growth plan. Called the Old Growth and Biodiversity Stewardship Public Advisory Team (PAT), it included members from the Ruffed Grouse Society, Michigan Nature Association, Michigan Environmental Council, Huron-Manistee National Forest, Michigan Forest Association, Michigan Association of Timbermen, Sierra Club, Nature Conservancy, and Michigan United Conservation Clubs.

Cornelia Dean, "Scientific Savvy? In U.S., Not Much," *New York Times*, August 30, 2005, http://query.nytimes.com/gst/fullpage.html?res=9403E3DD1631F933A0575BC0A9 639C8B63&n=Top%2FReference%2FTimes%20Topics%2FPeople%2FD%2 FDean%2 C%20Cornelia.

John D. Miller et al., "Public Acceptance of Evolution," *Science*, August 11, 2006, reported in "Did Humans Evolve? Not Us, Say Americans," *New York Times*, August 15, 2006, http://query.nytimes.com/gst/fullpage.html?res=9B06E3DB173EF936A2575BC0A 9609C8B63.

Jim Harrison, *True North: A Novel* (New York, Grove, 2004).

David Allen Sibley, *National Audubon Society, the Sibley Guide to Birds* (New York: Knopf, 2000).

WILDLIFE

Wolves in Lower Peninsula: Todd Hogrefe, DNR wildlife division, to Natural Resources Commission, January 6, 2005.

Grouse study, 1999: Meg Clark, report to advisory council, August 27, 1999.

Tim Cwalinski, fisheries biologist, "Forest Treatment Proposal, Black River Watershed Beaver Dam Removal," Gaylord DNR office (undated, distributed in September 2006).

List of species: *Environmental Impact Statement for Potential Hydrocarbon Development on the Pigeon River Country State Forest* (Lansing: DNR, 1975).

July 2006 listings, http://web4.msue.msu.edu/mnfi/data/specialanimals.cfm and http://web4.msue.msu.edu/mnfi/pub/abstracts.cfm?sort=cname. Additional sources are Allen Kurta, *Mammals of the Great Lakes Region* (Ann Arbor: University of Michigan Press, 1995; and Evers, *Endangered and Threatened Wildlife of Michigan*.

Elk research: Rique Campa, PhD, of MSU, reported by Delia Raymer to advisory council, October 11, 1996.

The Tuscarora snowmobile trail was proposed to connect major communities in northeastern lower Michigan, including Gaylord, Indian River, Onaway, Alpena, Cheboygan, and Mackinaw City. About 4.5 miles of the trail would pass through the Pigeon River Country, with a resource impact described by DNR field personnel as a "nightmare." The trail would be installed with the use of culverts, fill, and cutting of vegetation, then groomed daily.

STREAMS AND LAKES

Information in part is from three publications of Trout Unlimited's Michigan chapter, *A Trout Angler's Guide to the Pigeon River, A Trout Angler's Guide to the Black River,* and *A Trout Angler's Guide to the Sturgeon River.* (Charlevoix, Paul H. Young Chapter Trout Unlimited, 1972).

ANIMALS AND PEOPLE

Temple Grandin and Catherine Johnson, *Animals in Translation: Using the Mysteries of Autism to Decode Animal Behavior* (New York: London: Scribner's, 2005).

Graycalm sand is described at http://www2.ftw.nrcs.usda.gov/osd/dat/G/GRAY CALM.html.

"What the Nose Knows," *New York Times,* January 21, 2006, http://select.nytimes.com/gst/abstract.html?res=F20F17F9395B0C728EDDA80894DE404482.

Kenneth Chang, "All Together Now: Synchrony Explains Swaying," *New York Times,* November 8, 2005, http://www.nytimes.com/2005/11/08/science/08find.html.

Carl Zimmer, "Down for the Count," *New York Times,* November 8, 2005, http://www.nytimes.com/2005/11/08/science/08slee.html?pagewanted=print.

Caddis worms: Helmut Tributsch, *How Life Learned to Live: Adaptation in Nature,* translated by Miriam Varon from *Wie das Leben leben lernte* (Cambridge: MIT Press, 1982).

Insects as builders: J. Henri Fabre, *The Insect World of J. Henri Fabre,* translated by Teixeira de Mattos (Boston: Beacon Press, 1949, 1991).

Gilbert Waldbauer, *Insects through the Seasons* (Cambridge: Harvard University Press, 1996).

Evan Thompson, *Mind in Life: Biology, Phenomenology, and the Sciences of Mind* (Cambridge: Harvard University Press, 2007) makes the case that mind is a complex and fundamental feature of life itself, present at all levels.

Genes in blood is explained at http://www.scientific.org/tutorials/articles/riley/riley.html. Also see Matt Ridley, *Genome: The Autobiography of a Species in 23 Chapters* (New York: HarperCollins, 1998). Some 95 to 99 percent of the gut genome is bacterial. Our gut (colon) is composed of 100 trillion microbes, representing more than 1,000 species, all digesting what we eat. Steven Gill, quoted in "Gut Reaction: Researchers Define the Colon's Genome," a June 2, 2006 press release from the Institute for Genomic Research in Rockville, Maryland, http://www.tigr.org/news/pr_06_02_06.shtml.

Mosquito information is widely available. See, for example, *Encyclopaedia Britannica;* Jane E. Brody, "Mosquitos' Tricks Still Exceed Remedies," *Science Times,* August 1994; and Scott F. Gilbert, *Developmental Biology,* 6th ed. (Sunderland, MA: Sinauer Associates, 2000). The genetic codes of viruses can remain intact. See, for example, Samuel Baron, ed., *Medical Microbiology,* 4th ed. (Galveston: University of Texas Medical Branch, 1996).

Arpad A. Vass, "Beyond the Grave—Understanding Human Decomposition," *Microbiology Today,* November 2001, http://www.socgenmicrobiol.org.uk/pubs/micro_today/pdf/110108.pdf See also Mary Roach, *Stiff: The Curious Lives of Human Cadavers* (New York: Norton, 2003).

Bacteria emerging 250 million years later: http://www.wonderquest.com/CellsLifeSpan.htm.

Gilbert Waldaur, *What Good Are Bugs? Insects in the Web of Life* (Cambridge: Harvard University Press, 2003).

The East African jumping spider (Salticidae), *Evarcha culicivora,* took blood from mosquitoes in experiments described in a National Academy of Science journal in 2005. See http://www.ncbi.nlm.nih.gov/entrez/query.fcgi?cmd=Retrieve&db=pubmed&dopt=Abstract&list_uids=16217015&itool=iconabstr&query_hl=4.

Sandra Blakeslee, "Cells That Read Minds," *New York Times,* January 10, 2006.

Henry Fountain, "Trust You? What's in It for Me?" *New York Times,* June 27, 2006; Susan Milius, "Fishy Reputations: Undersea Watchers Choose Helpers That Do Good Jobs," *Science News,* June 24, 2006, http://www.nytimes.com/2006/06/27/science/27observ.html?pagewanted=print.

"Monkey See, Monkey Think: Grape Thefts Instigate Debate on Primate's Mind," *Science News,* March 12, 2005.

"Crow Tools: Hatched to Putter," *Science News,* January 15, 2005.

John Schwartz, "Deer Tape Their Private Moments," *New York Times,* November 1, 2005. The buck and doe in the University of Missouri study were in a fenced 10 acres of woods.

Elk collar information: Brian Mastenbrook, interview with the author, September 21, 2005.

Louis C. Bender and Jonathan B. Haufler, "Social Group Patterns and Associations of Nonmigratory Elk (*Cervus elaphus*) in Michigan," *American Midland Naturalist* 142, no. 1 (2002), http://www.bioone.org/bioone/?request=get-document&issn=0003-0031&volume=142&issue=01&page=0087.

Louis C. Bender et al., "Production and Survival of Elk (*Cervus elaphus*) Calves in Michigan," *American Midland Naturalist* 148, no. 1 (2002), http://www.bioone.org/bioone /?request=get-document&issn=0003-0031&volume=148&issue=01&page=0163.

Louis C. Bender et al., "Body Mass and Antler Development Patterns of Rocky Mountain Elk (*Cervus elaphus nelsoni*) in Michigan," *American Midland Naturalist* 150, no. 1 (2004), http://www.bioone.org/bioone/?request=get-document&issn=0003-0031&vol ume=150&issue=01&page=0169.

Wisconsin elk information: *Milwaukee Sentinel,* March 17, 1995; Wisconsin Department of Natural Resources, http://www.findarticles.com/p/articles/mi_qn4208/is _19950317/ai_n10189347 and http://www.dnr.state.wi.us/org/land/wildlife/elk/ questions.htm.

Pennsylvania elk: http://www.pennsylvaniaelkherd.com/elk00013.htm.

If we are ever to look closely at how we take advantage of our evolved bacterial, fungal, and animal traits, we will first have to more clearly understand the incredible complexity of the other species as well as our interconnection. We are only now starting to emerge from our antibiotic culture, in which we indiscriminately attack microbial life without regard to the consequences. The three-quarters of the million pounds of triclocarban we put in antimicrobial soap and other personal care products each year in the United States ends up in sewage treatment plants. From there it is applied to our agricultural soils as fertilizer and pollutes 60 percent of our streams. It's known to lower birthrates and cause death in small mammals. See A. Cunningham, "Tainted by Cleanser: Antimicrobial Agent Persists in Sludge," *Science News,* May 6, 2006. The results of a Johns Hopkins University study from 2005 may be found in the American Chemical Society online edition of *Environmental Science and Technology,* a peer-reviewed journal. See also "Anti-bacterial Additive Widespread in U.S. Waterways," Johns Hopkins Bloomberg School of Public Health, January 21, 2005, http://www.jhsph.edu/publichealth news/press_releases/2005/halden_triclocarban_triclosan.html.

David Koenig, "Horses a Big-Bucks Business, Study Finds," *Ann Arbor News,* June 30, 2005.

Michael Clark, interview with the author, September 26, 2005.

Schuyler ("Pete") Clapp, interview with the author, September 24, 2005.

Dave Smethurst, interview with the author, April 13, 2005. The horseback plan included building one extra trail camp with seven sites, increasing the number of Elk Hill sites to 10, restricting camping to designated sites, establishment of a reservations-only group camp near each trail camp, placing certain sensitive areas off-limits to riders, and limiting off-site camping with riding animals to designated locations. It was also ruled that uneaten hay must be scattered or carried out of the forest. Advisory council, December 2, 1994; 200 horses at Elk Hill in 2004 from Draft guidelines, Standards and Limitations Committee, November 2, 2004.

Peter Gustafson, interview with the author, August 14, 2006.

Russell Sherman, *Piano Pieces* (New York: North Point, 1997).

W. A. Mathieu, *The Listening Book* (Boston: Shambhala, 1991).

Meredith J. West and Andrew P. King, "Mozart's Starling," http://www.starlingtalk .com/mozart1.htm.

Bernd Heinrich, *Mind of the Raven: Investigations and Adventures with Wolf-Birds* (New York: HarperCollins, 1999).

Henry Fountain, "And Now, Please Welcome Modest Mouse," *New York Times,* November 1, 2005; Claudia Driefus, "Ode with a Nightingale, and a Thrush, and a Lyrebird," *New York Times,* September 20, 2005, http://www.nytimes.com/2005/09/20/science/20CONV.html.

Wrens: Henry Fountain, "The Great Chorale of the Avian World," *New York Times,* September 20, 2005, http://www.nytimes.com/2005/09/20/science/20obse.html. David Attenborough's film, *Life of Birds,* provides a wealth of information and images of birds in their own habitats. Chickadees, according to an article in *Science,* call "seet" at a high pitch upon seeing a predator in the air, causing other birds to remain motionless or hide. They add more "dees" to their chick-a-dee call as the size of the predator decreases, apparently because small predators are more agile and threatening. That call causes chickadees to gather to harass the predator. Henry Fountain, "You Call It Music. They Call It an Air Raid," *New York Times,* June 28, 2005.

Robert Jourdain, *Music, the Brain, and Ecstasy: How Music Captures Our Imagination* (New York: Avon, 1997). He offers a fascinating discussion of the interaction of anticipation and sensation in everyday experience.

A variety of sources on red-shouldered hawks, including the *Journal of Wildlife Management,* is available, at least in summary, online. The U.S. Department of Agriculture, Forest Service, has a file with excellent photographs and tables at http://www.fs.fed.us/r9/wildlife/tes/ca-overview/docs/red_shouldered_hawk_ca_1202final.pdf.

Natural areas have never received sufficient public or official support to become legally recognized in the Pigeon River Country. The 1976 Concept of Management called for two: one hardwood and one pine area. They were so managed informally. Ned Caveney, as early as 1978, promoted designation under the 1972 law, but it apparently was an idea before its time despite support by the advisory council. The Ochsners made it a cause, also to no avail. In 1989, the advisory council unanimously approved a motion urging "that fishing, hunting, trapping, berrypicking, and camping" be allowed in natural areas, even though the Concept of Management said, "The only management to be applied in these [natural] areas will be to protect them from unnatural alteration (the effects of people) and from major natural disasters such as fire, which could totally destroy them."

Biodiversity Conservation Planning Proposal, April 2005, http://www.midnr.com/publications/pdfs/forestslandwater/Biodiversity/BiodiversityConsPlanningProposalApril2005.pdf; earlier summary of biodiversity in Michigan by the University of New Mexico School of Law, http://ipl.unm.edu/cwl/statbio/michigan.html.

Natalie Angier, *The Beauty of the Beastly: New Views of the Nature of Life* (New York: Houghton Mifflin, 1995), provides other instructive material, including the disclosure that hummingbirds spend 80 percent of their day motionless on a twig and beaver spend most of their days resting for all but about five hours, also that we now know all kinds of animals play even though having fun doesn't seem to fit our view that everything they do is designed for survival.

THE BIRDS

John Bull and John Farrand Jr, *National Audubon Society Field Guide to North American Birds (Eastern Region)* (New York: Knopf, 1994). Additional information from the Peterson

Field Guide Series (Boston: Houghton Mifflin, various years); William Clark and Brian Wheeler, *A Field Guide to Hawks of North America* (Boston: Houghton Mifflin, 2nd ed. 2001); Jon Dunn and Kimball Garrett, *A Field Guide to Warblers of North America* (New York: Houghton Mifflin, 1997); Kenn Kaufman, *Advanced Birding* (Norwalk, CT: Easton Press, 1990); Kenn Kaufman, *Field Guide to Birds of North America* (Boston: Houghton Mifflin, 2000); *Field Guide to the Birds of North America,* 4th ed. (Washington, DC: National Geographic Society, 2002); Roger Peterson, *Birds of Eastern and Central North America,* 5th ed. (Boston: Houghton Mifflin, 2002); and David Sibley, *The Sibley Field Guide to Birds of Eastern North America* (New York: Knopf, 2003).

VEGETATION

Frederick W. Case Jr., *Orchids of the Western Great Lakes Region* (Cranbrook Institute of Science, 1964); Shuttleworth, Zim, and Dillon, *Orchids,* Golden Nature Guides (New York: Golden Press); Helen V. Smith, *Michigan Wildflowers* (Cranbrook Institute of Science, 1966); Zim and Martin, *Flowers,* Golden Nature Guides (New York: Golden Press, 1950); William Niering and Nancy Olmstead, *Audubon Society Field Guide to North American Wildflowers* (New York: Knopf, 1979); Roger Tory Peterson and Margaret McKenny, *Field Guide to Wildflowers of Northeastern and North-Central North America* (Boston: Houghton Mifflin, 1974); Herbert Spencer Zim and Floyd Stephen Shuttleworth, *Non-flowering Plants* (New York: Golden Press, 1967); Lange and Hora, *Collins Guide to Mushrooms and Toadstools* (England); Alexander Smith, *Mushroom Hunters Field Guide* (Ann Arbor: University of Michigan Press); Billington, *Shrubs of Michigan,* 2nd ed., Bulletin no. 20 (Cranbrook Institute of Science, 1968); Lee A. Peterson, *Field Guide to Edible Wild Plants of Eastern and Central North America* (Boston: Houghton Mifflin, 1982); Charles Herbert Otis, *Michigan Trees* (Ann Arbor: University of Michigan Press, 1931); G. Collingwood and W. Brush, *Knowing Your Trees,* rev. ed. by D. Butcher (Washington, DC: American Forestry Association, 1979).

AFTERWORD: PRESENCE

Stephen Harrod Buhner, *The Secret Teachings of Plants in the Direct Perception of Nature* (Rochester, VT: Bear, 2004). He discusses bioelectromagnetics, a new field of science, more advanced in Europe, in which electromagnetic spectrum communications among living beings are being explored. Information is available online to the determined seeker.

Energy spectrum: Steven Weinberg, *The Discovery of Subatomic Particles,* rev. ed. (Cambridge: Cambridge University Press, 2003). See also Mark Ward, *Beyond Chaos* (New York: St. Martin's, 2001) (first published under the title *Universality* by Macmillan in Great Britain) on the precarious balance between organization and chaos in life forms.

"Vertebrates, Insects Share the Stress," *Science News,* May 21, 2005.

Helmut Tributsch, *How Life Learned to Live: Adaptation in Nature,* translated by Miriam Varon (Cambridge: MIT Press, 1982).

Bacteria in soil: http://www.wired.com/news/medtech/1,65252–0.html. Steven Gill, a molecular biologist, provided the 90 percent estimate during a telephone interview cited in Maggie Fox, "Scientists Study the Ecosystem in Our Gut," Reuters, June 1, 2006, http://www.msnbc.msn.com/id/13085825/. Bacteria have been found in earth

1,300 feet below the Pacific seafloor in as much abundance as on the seafloor itself. *Nature*, July 21, 2005, as reported in "Life Way Down Under," *New York Times*, July 26, 2005. An account of the earliest life forms found in the Great Lakes region can be found in J. Alan Holman, *Ancient Life of the Great Lakes Basin* (Ann Arbor: University of Michigan Press, 1995), which also has summaries of geology and biology.

The outdoors provides myriad variations in social conduct. Cardinals and coyotes choose a single mate for life, as do beaver and gray fox. Stan Tekiela, *Mammals of Michigan Field Guide* (Cambridge, MN: Adventure Publications, 2005). Starlings swarm together above a roosting site in flocks of up to a quarter million birds, perform their roost activities in pairs, and operate as independent individuals prior to pairing off during the spring roost. Donald W. Stokes, *A Guide to Bird Behavior*, vol. 1 (Boston: Little, Brown, 1979). Martens are believed to live virtually their whole lives as solitary creatures. White-tailed deer sleep in a different spot every night, as do carnivores, except while raising young. Coyotes rush ground squirrels or larger prey but stalk mice and smaller prey. One was observed cooperating with a badger, who dug while the coyote guarded the ground squirrel burrow. John O. Whitaker Jr. and William J. Hamilton Jr., *Mammals of the Eastern United States*, 3rd ed. (Ithaca, NY: Comstock, 1998).

Lynn Margulis introduced the theory of symbiotic relations, called endosymbiosis, in 1966. It took decades for mainstream science to accept the idea. See Lynn Margulis and Dorion Sagan, *Microcosmos: Four Billion Years of Microbial Evolution* (Berkeley: University of California Press, [1986] 1997). See also Lynn Margulis, *Symbiotic Planet: A New Look at Evolution* (New York: Basic Books, 1988); and Lynn Margulis and Dorion Sagan, *Acquiring Genomes: The Theory of the Origins of the Species* (New York: Basic Books, 2002). For the mainstream science view, see Nick Lane, *Power, Sex, Suicide: Mitochondria and the Meaning of Life* (Oxford: Oxford University Press, 2005).

Michigan reported that 341 deer tested positive for TB between 1995 and the summer of 2001, along with 13 coyotes, 2 raccoon, 4 black bear, 2 red fox, 2 opossums, and 4 bobcats from Alcona, Alpena, Crawford, Emmet, Montmorency, and Presque Isle counties, most likely contracted from eating lymph nodes and lungs of infected deer. Alcona, Alpena, Montmorency, and Presque Isle were the high-risk counties, where one privately owned deer and elk herd and 18 cattle herds had TB present. "Bovine Tuberculosis in Michigan," DNR and other agencies brochure, October 2001. Efforts to prevent the spread of TB concentrated on aggressively hunting free-ranging deer and keeping infected deer away from uninfected cows. In 2005, a hunter contracted TB through a cut in his finger while cleaning a lesioned deer but was successfully treated with antibiotics; hunters are encouraged to use gloves when gutting deer.

Edward O. Wilson, *The Future of Life* (New York: Random House, 2002); *Biophilia* (Cambridge: Harvard University Press, 1984).

Henry David Thoreau writes, "I perceive that we . . . live this mean life that we do because our vision does not penetrate the surface of things. . . . In eternity there is indeed something true and sublime. But all these times and places and occasions are now and here. . . . And we are enabled to apprehend at all what is sublime and noble only by the perpetual instilling and drenching of the reality that surrounds us" *The Portable Thoreau*, edited by Carl Bode (New York: Viking, 1964).

Margaret Atwood, *Margaret Atwood Conversations*, edited by Earl G. Ingersoll (Princeton, NJ: Ontario Review Press, 1990); Judith McCombs, ed., *Critical Essays on Margaret Atwood* (Boston: Hall, 1988); Margaret Atwood, *Selected Poems* (New York: Simon and Schuster,

1976); Margaret Atwood, *Selected Poems II, 1976–1986* (Boston: Houghton Mifflin, 1987); Margaret Atwood, *Survival: A Thematic Guide to Canadian Literature* (Toronto: McClelland and Stewart, [1972] 2004).

Mary Oliver, *What Do We Know, Poems and Prose Poems,* (Cambridge, MA: Da Capo, 2002). Mary Oliver was born in Maple Heights, Ohio, near Lake Erie.

Allan Seager, *The Glass House: The Life of Theodore Roethke* (Ann Arbor: University of Michigan Press, [1968] 1991).

Susan F. Beegel, "Eye and Heart: Hemingway's Education as a Naturalist," in *A Historical Guide to Ernest Hemingway,* edited by Linda Wagner-Martin (New York: Oxford University Press, 2000).

Sharon Levy, "Conservation at a Distance: Atomic Detectives" and Emma Marris, "Written in the Elements," in *Nature,* August 3, 2006, report on noninvasive techniques using mass spectrometers to study isotopes in Kirtland's warbler feathers and stable-isotope analysis used in forensics to determine where plants and microbes have lived on earth.

Ronald Berman, *Fitzgerald, Hemingway, and the Twenties* (Tuscaloosa: University of Alabama Press, 2001).

Arch Reeves, interview with the author, August 8, 2006.

GENERAL GUIDES

North woods references include Donald W. Stokes, *A Guide to Nature in Winter, Northeast and North Central North America* (Boston: Little, Brown, 1976); Joseph Bharat Cornell, *Sharing Nature with Children* (Nevada City, CA: Ananda, 1979); Tom Brown Jr. and Brandt Morgan, *Tom Brown's Field Guide to Wilderness Survival* (New York: Berkley, 1983); Tom Brown Jr. and Brandt Morgan, *Tom Brown's Field Guide to Nature Observation and Tracking* (New York: Berkley, 1983); and Glenda Daniel and Jerry Sullivan, *A Sierra Club Naturalist's Guide to the North Woods of Michigan, Wisconsin, and Minnesota* (San Francisco: Sierra Club, 1981). A. J. Morse, who lives in a cabin on the Pigeon River near Sparr, has published *Walking: the Art of Sauntering* (Gaylord, MI: Society of Saunterers, 1984).

Of more recently published works, *Stikky Trees: Learn to Recognize at a Glance the 15 Most Common Trees in the United States—in Just One Hour, Guaranteed* (New York: Laurence Holt, 2005), delivers what it promises. Burton V. Barnes and Warren H. Wagner Jr., *Michigan Trees: A Guide to the Trees of the Great Lakes Region* (Ann Arbor: University of Michigan Press, 2004), is the revised bible for tree identification first written by Charles Herbert Otis with new material about ecosystems. Other useful works include John Eastman, *The Book of Forest and Thicket: Trees, Shrubs, and Wildflowers of Eastern North America* (Harrisburg, PA: Stackpole, 1992; Stan Tekiela, *Wildflowers of Michigan Field Guide* (Cambridge, MN: Adventure Publications, 2000); Lorus Milne and Margery Milne, *National Audubon Society Field Guide to North American Insects and Spiders* (New York: Knopf, 1980); James H. Harding, *Amphibians and Reptiles of the Great Lakes Region* (Ann Arbor: University of Michigan Press, 1997); Matthew M. Douglas and Jonathan M. Douglas, *Butterflies of the Great Lakes Region* (Ann Arbor: University of Michigan Press, 2005); and Donald W. Stokes and Lillian Q. Stokes, *A Guide to Animal Tracking and Behavior* (Boston: Little, Brown, 1986).